Dojo
The Definitive Guide

Other resources from O'Reilly

Related titles

Adding Ajax

Ajax: The Definitive Guide

CSS Cookbook™

CSS: The Definitive Guide

Dynamic HTML:
   The Definitive Reference

JavaScript: The Definitive
   Guide

JavaScript: The Good Parts

Learning JavaScript

Painting the Web

oreilly.com

oreilly.com is more than a complete catalog of O'Reilly books. You'll also find links to news, events, articles, weblogs, sample chapters, and code examples.

oreillynet.com is the essential portal for developers interested in open and emerging technologies, including new platforms, programming languages, and operating systems.

Conferences

O'Reilly brings diverse innovators together to nurture the ideas that spark revolutionary industries. We specialize in documenting the latest tools and systems, translating the innovator's knowledge into useful skills for those in the trenches. Visit *conferences.oreilly.com* for our upcoming events.

Safari Bookshelf (*safari.oreilly.com*) is the premier online reference library for programmers and IT professionals. Conduct searches across more than 1,000 books. Subscribers can zero in on answers to time-critical questions in a matter of seconds. Read the books on your Bookshelf from cover to cover or simply flip to the page you need. Try it today for free.

Dojo
The Definitive Guide

Matthew A. Russell

O'REILLY®

Beijing · Cambridge · Farnham · Köln · Sebastopol · Taipei · Tokyo

Dojo: The Definitive Guide
by Matthew A. Russell

Copyright © 2008 Matthew A. Russell. All rights reserved.
Printed in the United States of America.

Published by O'Reilly Media, Inc., 1005 Gravenstein Highway North, Sebastopol, CA 95472.

O'Reilly books may be purchased for educational, business, or sales promotional use. Online editions are also available for most titles (*safari.oreilly.com*). For more information, contact our corporate/institutional sales department: (800) 998-9938 or *corporate@oreilly.com*.

Editor: Simon St.Laurent
Production Editor: Sumita Mukherji
Copyeditor: Colleen Gorman
Proofreader: Sumita Mukherji

Indexer: Lucie Haskins
Cover Designer: Karen Montgomery
Interior Designer: David Futato
Illustrator: Robert Romano

Printing History:

June 2008:   First Edition.

 This book uses RepKover™, a durable and flexible lay-flat binding.

ISBN: 978-0-596-51648-2
[M]

*This book is dedicated to every single
web developer who has lost sleep because of
ridiculous browser idiosyncrasies.*

Table of Contents

Part II. Dijit and Util

Foreword

Truth be told, it was DHTML that got me kicked out of college.

I still vividly recall the 3 A.M. moments when endless trolling of MSDN documentation and W3C specifications and hundreds of comp.lang.javascript posts all coalesced into dozens of "what if..." moments. Like hot brands on the hide of my brain, each of these tiny discoveries would not let their mark off of me until I had exhausted all inroads into making the browser do what I wanted it to. Back then, a small community of folks were all doing the same, feverishly one-upping each other and posting to the DHTMLCentral forums with each new component, technique, or hack to make things work on Netscape. Nothing about 7 A.M. Latin conjugations or endless lectures on Java™ held much appeal by comparison to discovering the true beauty of closures, or finally, completely understanding prototypal inheritance. Even my Christmas holidays were engulfed in JavaScript learning and hacking. I'm sure my girlfriend and my parents worried for me greatly, but they never said anything. From the ashes of my truncated academic career came an understanding of open source (*http://opensource.org*), lasting friendships, and, eventually, Dojo.

Over time, the job of the DHTML hacker has changed. We know most of the tricks that we can expect a browser to do, and where there is overlap between browsers, we've probably already exploited it...just look at the depth and diversity of modules in Dijit and DojoX. The work of a DHTML/Ajax developer now is to press the available technology into the service of users and developers in ways that are better for end users and developers alike. The story of Dojo is the story of that transition. A beautiful architecture that fails to deliver better things in the lives of users is a failure. Likewise, beautiful graphics and interfaces that aren't maintainable, can't be coherently understood by developers, and that make designer/developer collaboration harder aren't going to get us where we want to be. All of us involved with Dojo have matured along with the Web, and with the release of Dojo 1.0 and this book, it's safe to say that Dojo has fully arrived. The roadmap documents we started so long ago now have all of the boxes checked, sites that serve billions of page views a month lean on Dojo for their entire user experience, and large teams of designers and developers work together to create better experiences on top of the toolkit.

These kinds of accomplishments aren't the work of one person, or even a small team. The number of people who have contributed to Dojo's evolution, believed in the project, and worked together to deliver a better Web are too numerous to mention. We copied what we thought were the best bits of the structures of other projects, and the result has been a level playing field and rules that are fair to users, contributors, and sponsors alike. Dojo is proof that open source isn't just a handy distribution model for closed systems, but that collaborative, open projects can thrive when they adopt policies that let users trust a project and when those inside the project finds ways to trust each other. For all of the technical achievements embodied in the toolkit, I'm most proud that we've done it in the open, with anyone who will join us, and done it honestly. We set out to build a project that values all kinds of contributions, not just code. A project that would help change the tone of open source development to encourage collegial, civil discourse. A project dedicated to building with the community and not to treat users as "them." "They" are "us" and this book makes plain the open philosophy under which the toolkit was built, and by which we encourage all those reading it to help us evolve it for the future.

By the time I met Matthew Russell face-to-face, this book was nearly "in the can." Open source is funny like that—you can work for years with someone, yet the pieces picked up over mailing lists and IRC don't fall into place until you're talking about the mundane and thrilling over a good local ale (or, in a pinch, Guinness). It wasn't until Matthew and I were comparing notes in an old, small, quiet pub in San Francisco's North Beach district that it clicked: his technical depth, curiosity, and ability to meet you on your level are the hallmarks of a great teacher. As I reviewed the draft chapters in turn, I found myself constantly deleting what I'd just written by way of critique as Matthew laid out the concepts in just the right order. Matthew's illuminations make Dojo approachable, friendly, and productive. The constant delight of discovery that glows so brightly when you talk to Matthew in person are a true gift to this volume.

It has been like this for me for nearly four years now as I've had the chance to put faces to the IRC handles and forum posts. In open source, each person enters your world as a technical problem to be solved, a bug to be fixed, or a feature to be considered. Only later is the full measure of the people you're working with made plain, and it's nearly always a breathtaking revelation. The kindness, selfless effort, and talent that are freely given are humbling particularly in light of the personal sacrifices that each person makes to be a part of the project. Matthew's book is a credit to the amazing team I've had the honor to work with.

I can't say that I recommend dropping out of college to work on things that no one will pay you for, but if that fire starts in your brain, don't ignore it. If it leads you to people only half as wonderful as those I've met and now count among my friends, it will be worth every sleepless night.

—Alex Russell
Cofounder, Dojo Toolkit, and Dojo Foundation
President

Preface

Users now demand web applications that look and feel like those of the desktop. Home computers have long since become ubiquitous, web browsers are the enabling platform, and virtually everyone on the planet is a potential end user. Software developers are spending more time than ever getting their applications into the browser for a potential audience of millions—many of them trying to grab a handful of the multibillion dollar advertising wave, while others are capitalizing on the sheer elegance and convenience of an application that is impressive enough that people will be willing to pay for access to it.

Of course, just because the web browser is the enabling platform does not mean that it is the ideal platform—at least not in its current manifestation. Corporate politics, less than uniform implementations of the various specifications for web browser technologies, and a curious evolution of protocols and standards over almost two decades have made deploying an application in the browser a lot more difficult than anyone might have ever predicted.

But in a world where necessity breeds imagination and innovation, there is always hope.

Fortunately, the rich and powerful functionality JavaScript provides makes it possible to manipulate, customize, and augment a web page on the fly, and in doing so, makes it possible to provide a layer of insulation between the developer and the bare metal of the web browsers—even all of them at the same time.

This book is about Dojo, a JavaScript toolkit that provides that layer of insulation between you and the hard knocks of browser inconsistencies by leveraging JavaScript and other web technologies for all that they're worth—not by attempting to build a brittle, superficial layer to reimplement or work around them. Dojo makes a great addition to a project that's already using YUI!* or even a server side framework that might benefit from offloading some of the work over to the client.

---

* *http://developer.yahoo.com/yui/*

Dojo packs the standard JavaScript library you've always wanted, the collection of drop-in replacements for the customized HTML controls and CSS layout hacks you've implemented again and again, and the build tools and unit tests that would have been so handy when it came time for migrating to production. Dojo isn't just a JavaScript toolkit, Dojo is *the* JavaScript toolkit—and right now is a great time to learn how to use it to make your life easier and the experience of your end users everything that it possibly can be. Dojo is revolutionizing web development, and gaining momentum fast.

Whatever web development project may be on your horizon, rest assured that Dojo can help you realize it quickly and with minimal boilerplate so that you're left with the cleanest, most maintainable implementation possible. My sincere hope is that this book relates Dojo's story so effectively that you'll spend minimal time scrambling around for answers and be able to fully concentrate on engaging the challenging (and far more interesting) problems that you've set out to solve.

Why Dojo?

Undoubtedly, there is a swatch of JavaScript toolkits available today, so you might already be wondering what Dojo provides that you can't get somewhere else. Keeping in mind that the very nature of a toolkit or library being built upon a completely interpreted language makes it theoretically possible for any other toolkit to do the very same things, it's not so much what can Dojo do that other can't do; rather, it's more about the effectiveness of getting work done along with the community, philosophy, and licensing aspects that surround it.

You might think of it like this: it's theoretically possible to build a house using only a hammer, a shovel, a saw, and a lot of nails—but at what expense? Clearly, some heavy machinery and some carpenters to support you along the way would be a tremendous boon. The situation with Dojo is quite similar. The following list attempts to highlight (in no particular order) some of the places where Dojo really shines and differentiates itself:

Community
> Although it could be considered a nontechnical issue, Dojo's open community is one of its top strengths. The Dojo Foundation, a nonprofit organization set up for the purpose of providing a vendor-neutral guardian of intellectual property, backs the toolkit (and other interesting projects such as Cometd,* DWR,† and Open-Record‡), and is sponsored and supported by IBM, AOL, Sun, OpenLaszlo,

---

* See *http://www.cometd.com* or *http://www.cometdaily.com* or a great coverage on Comet.
† See *http://getahead.org/dwr* for more on Direct Web Remoting.
‡ See *http://www.openrecord.org* for more on OpenRecord.

Nexaweb, SitePen, BEA, Renkoo, and a slew of the greatest DHTML hackers in the world. If that doesn't tell you that it has good friends backing it, then what possibly could?

As a liberally licensed open source project with extremely low barriers to entry, your voice will be heard if you want it to be heard. If you pop into the IRC chat room *#dojo* on *freenode.net* and start talking, there's virtually no chance that you won't be heard by a committer or significant contributor to the project. Additionally, weekly IRC meetings are currently held on *#dojo-meeting* each Wednesday from 3 to 6 P.M. (PST), and you're more than welcome to pop in and eavesdrop or participate in the official meetings where both strategic and tactical issues are routinely discussed.

Knowing there's transparency in how Dojo is steered strategically and developed tactically is very compelling. As other JavaScript toolkits and libraries become increasingly commoditized, the Dojo community really stands out as different. The organizations and individuals who make up the team of committers (not to mention the thousands of individual developers out there building real web sites and applications) all give Dojo a particular character and grounding for success.

Liberal (and clean) licensing

Dojo is open source software that is liberally licensed under the terms of either the modified Berkeley Software Distribution (BSD) license or the Academic Free License (AFL) version 2.1. Except as noted in a few per-module license files, you get to choose the license you want to adopt for your specific work. All external contributions are required to be compatible with the BSD or AFL licenses, and all contributors must sign a Contributor License Agreement (CLA) that ensures the Dojo Foundation has clear title to all contributions—thereby protecting all users of the toolkit from intellectual licensing conundrums. The benefit of clean licensing is markedly not the case with several other popular JavaScript toolkits (that shall be left unnamed).

Depth and breadth

While some toolkits tackle specific pieces of a problem space, Dojo provides an end-to-end solution for development in the browser. Everything from standard library utilities to turnkey widgets to build tools and a testing framework—it's all in there, so you seldom have to look elsewhere. But don't let the breadth fool you into thinking that there is code bloat, because the build tools allow you to produce custom versions of the toolkit that can be as streamlined as your application permits.

While it is often the case that breadth hampers depth, it's not what happens with Dojo at all. Even inside of Base, the tiny kernel that provides the foundation for the rest of the toolkit, you have more functionality than you can shake a stick at—facilities for universally querying the DOM via CSS3 selectors, AJAX utilities, event normalization amongst various browsers—and then some. That doesn't even begin to touch of the rich library of application, form, and layout widgets, or the build tools.

Although the breadth and depth of Dojo produces a lot of complexity, the infrastructure is painstakingly reviewed on a continual basis by the some of the best web hackers in the world for high quality coding standards, consistent naming conventions, performance, maintainability, and overall ease of use for the application developer. Rest assured that you *will* be able to create a great user experience with Dojo.

Portability

While the JavaScript language is dynamic, powerful, and extremely expressive, there are still myriad issues that come up routinely that amount to fairly mundane engineering efforts. It's quite instructive to go through the motions that solve a central algorithmic problem or engineering conundrum, but at the end of the day, any code that you develop is code that you have to maintain, update, debug, and document.

As if those aren't enough good reasons, the motivation for having a JavaScript standard library may be especially compelling given the existing state of compatibility amongst browsers for various feature sets. While attempting to develop a feature that works uniformly across a set of modern browsers may not always be rocket science, it can be painfully tedious work that can demoralize even the most seasoned professionals.

The bottom line is that it's almost a certainty that as an application developer, you aren't going to be receiving any return on investment (or having very much fun) by jumping through all of those hoops. Instead, pick up production quality code that a *community* of other developers has developed, debugged, and tested—and then consider contributing back. Hopefully, that "giving back" part will come naturally enough once you've saved enough time and money by way of community-supported, open source software.

Pragmatic philosophy

Dojo embraces JavaScript for what it is instead of treating it like it's something that's broken and thereby trying to create a brittle, artificial layer on top of it that almost redefines it. While Dojo exposes tremendous functionality that protects you from the bare metal of the browser and does many things like normalize browser events behind the scenes so that you don't even have to think twice about them, it never attempts to reinvent JavaScript. For example, you won't find Dojo-specific functions for operations like deleting DOM nodes or walking the DOM tree because operations like childNodes, firstChild, lastChild, and removeChild work just fine across all browsers. However, whenever there are known inconsistencies, Dojo steps in to provide you with the tools you need to write portable code.

For that matter, Dojo doesn't attempt to lockout or constrain your use of other JavaScript libraries; it is not uncommon to see it used side-by-side with another technology like DWR or YUI!. And of course, as a client side technology, you are obviously free to use whatever technologies you'd like on the server since Dojo is server-agnostic.

A comprehensive survey of all of the popular JavaScript toolkits would reveal that they all have considerable overlap by virtue of being popular in the first place. So, when it comes time to make a decision about which toolkit or collection of toolkits is right for you, it is worth the time to really ponder the value of community, transparency, licensing, and the philosophy governing the technology in which you are about to invest time and possibly even money. Namely, you want to have support (community and documentation) when you need it, you don't want to invest in a project that's too brittle to be maintained or about to tank, and you want minimize your time working to plug holes that some other toolkit has already plugged.

What's in This Book

Part I of this book is very much a standard library reference that exposes you to the various nooks and crannies of Base and Core, the parts of the toolkit that comprise a JavaScript standard library. Base comes across the wire* at less than 30KB, and is feverishly optimized for speed, size, and utility. Packing rich functionality as diverse as AJAX calls, DOM querying based on CSS selector syntax, standardized event propagation, and functional programming utilities like map and filter, you'll quickly wonder how you ever got by without it. Core includes lots of additional features for operations like animations and drag-and-drop; while they are incredibly useful, they just aren't as common to all use cases as the machinery in Base.

 One caveat about Part I of this book is that it defers a full-blown discussion of the parser until Chapter 11, when Dijit is introduced, because the most common use case of the parser is for parsing widgets. The parser is briefly mentioned in a Chapter 7 sidebar, though, because it is quite helpful for conveniently setting up drag-and-drop.

Part I includes the following chapters:

Chapter 1, *Toolkit Overview*
   Provides a quick introduction to the toolkit including topics such as Dojo's architecture, how to get and install Dojo, how to get Dojo into a web page, and some sections that provide some examples so that you can see Dojo in action.

---

* As we'll be discussing more in subsequent chapters, "across the wire" refers to the size of content after it has been gzipped, because that's normally the way web servers transfer web pages to clients.

Chapter 2, *Language and Browser Utilities*

Provides an extensive overview of commonly used utility functions that are extremely common and useful for any web application. Most of these functions are designed to smooth out browser incompatibilities, plug holes where JavaScript or DOM implementations came up a bit short, and otherwise reduce the boilerplate you have to write to get some work done.

Chapter 3, *Event Listeners and Pub/Sub Communication*

Introduces constructs for managing communication within the page. The two primary paradigms discussed involve directly attaching to a specific event that happens, whether in the DOM, on an `Object`, or a standalone function and the publish/subscribe idiom that involves broadcasting a topic and allowing any arbitrary subscriber to receive and respond as needed.

Chapter 4, *AJAX and Server Communication*

Provides a quick overview of AJAX and the toolkit's machinery for communicating with the server via the *XMLHttpRequest* Object. Deferreds are also discussed, which provide a uniform layer for handling asynchronous events; you might think of Deferreds as almost providing the illusion of having a thread available even though you cannot program threads in JavaScript. Other core facilities such as cross-domain JSON, Remote Procedure Calls, and `IFRAME` transports are discussed.

Chapter 5, *Node Manipulation*

Introduces the toolkit's mechanism for universally querying the DOM using CSS selector syntax, processing the lists of nodes that are returned using convenient built-in functions that allow arbitrary events chains to be built up, and an idiom for separating the behavior of DOM nodes from specific actions defined in HTML markup.

Chapter 6, *Internationalization (i18n)*

Provides a quick overview and examples for internationalizing a web application using the toolkit's utilities; also includes an overview of the various constructs that are available for manipulating inherently international concepts such as dates, time, currency, and number formatting.

Chapter 7, *Drag-and-Drop*

Includes a fairly standalone tutorial on how Dojo makes adding drag-and-drop to an application a breeze.

Chapter 8, *Animation and Special Effects*

Provides a fairly standalone tutorial on Dojo's built-in machinery for animating arbitrary CSS properties via a variety of effects such as wipes, slides, and fades. Utilities for blending and manipulating colors are also included.

Chapter 9, *Data Abstraction*

Provides a discussion of Dojo's data abstraction infrastructure, which provides a mediating layer between application logic and specific backend data formats, whether they be an open standard or a closed proprietary source.

Chapter 10, *Simulated Classes and Inheritance*

Ramps up for Part II on Dijit by introducing machinery for mimicking class-based object-oriented programming with Dojo, which Dijit uses fairly extensively.

Part II systematically explores the rest of the toolkit, including complete coverage of Dijit, the rich layer of drop-in replacements for all of those customized HTML controls that have been written (and rewritten) so many times. Dijit is designed so that it can be used in the markup with little to no programming required, and you'll find that it's possible to build fantastic-looking web pages with a fraction of the effort since they already look and behave much like user interface controls from desktop applications.

Part II concludes with a discussion of the build system and unit testing framework provided by Util. The build system includes a highly configurable entry point to ShinkSafe, a tool that leverages the Rhino JavaScript engine to compress your code—often by a third or more. DOH stands for the Dojo Objective Harness (and is a pun on Homer Simpson's famous "D'oh!" expletive) and provides a standalone system for unit testing your JavaScript code.

Part II includes the following chapters:

Chapter 11, *Dijit Overview*

Introduces Dijit, discusses various issues such as design philosophy, accessibility, the parser (technically a Core facility, but with the most common use case of parsing a page that contains dijits), and patterns for using dijits. The chapter ends with an overview of each major Dijit subproject.

Chapter 12, *Dijit Anatomy and Lifecycle*

Digs deep into how a dijit is laid out on disk as well as how its lifecycle works once it's been instantiated and in memory. Provides a number of short examples that accentuate the finer points of the lifecycle. Understanding the dijit lifecycle is essential for the chapters that follow.

Chapter 13, *Form Widgets*

Provides a quick review of normal HTML forms and then jumps right into a thorough survey of the form widgets, which are by far the most inheritance-intensive collection available. The form widgets are drop-in replacements for all of the common form elements that are used in virtually any web design; assortments of commonly used buttons, specialized text boxes, and sliders are a few of the topics covered. Additional derived elements such as drop-down combo boxes that have been implemented and reimplemented far too many times by now are also included.

Chapter 14, *Layout Widgets*

Introduces the layout widgets, a collection of widgets that provide the skeleton for complex layouts that often involves tricky and tedious CSS, swapping in and out tiles that go from being hidden to visible based on the application's state, tabbed layouts, and more.

Chapter 15, *Application Widgets*

Covers the remaining widgets in the toolkit, which loosely correspond to common application controls such as tooltips, modal dialogs, menus, trees, and rich text editors.

Chapter 16, *Build Tools, Testing, and Production Considerations*

Wraps up the book with some of the most commonly overlooked yet important topics for deploying an application; includes an extensive discussion of the build tools that trivialize the effort entailed in compressing, minifying, and consolidating JavaScript to minimize file size and HTTP latency incurred, a unit testing framework, and other production considerations that help to give your app that last bit of pizzazz.

There are two supplemental appendixes to the book: a concise survey of DojoX, a collection of specialized and experimental extensions, and a Firebug tutorial. While DojoX is an absolute treasure chest of widgets and modules for anything from charting to cryptography to the much acclaimed and highly flexible grid widget, there are fewer guarantees about stability or API consistency for DojoX subprojects than there are for Base, Core, and Dijit; thorough coverage on DojoX could easily span multiple volumes of its own.

The other appendix provides a handy Firebug tutorial that gets you up to speed with all of its great features that will save you time when it becomes necessary to debug or quickly explore new ideas through its command line style interface. If you haven't heard of Firebug, it's a fantastic Firefox add-on that allows you to literally deconstruct every facet of a page—anything from inspecting and manipulating style of DOM nodes to monitoring the network activity to using a command-line interface for executing JavaScript.

What's Not in This Book

While this book necessarily attempts to provide the same kind of depth and breadth of Dojo itself, there were a few topics that just couldn't quite be squeezed into this edition:

Web development 101

While this book provides in depth coverage of Dojo, it doesn't provide a complete web development tutorial that formally introduces elementary constructs such as HTML, JavaScript, and CSS from scratch.

Redundant API documentation

The vast majority* of Dojo's API is definitively explained in this book and is generally captured into tables that are easy to reference. Because there's so much breadth to Dojo, it seemed especially helpful to make sure you get exposed to as much of it as possible so that you'll know what's available when the need arises. Dojo is a fluid project, however, so you'll always want to double-check the online documentation at *http://api.dojotoolkit.org* for the most comprehensive authority. Unlike programming languages and more rigid application frameworks, Dojo is a fluid project with a thriving community, so it is not unlikely that the API may be enhanced for your benefit as new versions are released. But do know that the project is committed to not breaking the 1.x API until at least version 2.0, so in general, any API covered in this book will be perfectly valid for quite some time. Even then, the parts of the API that do change will be well documented ahead of time.

Nonbrowser host environments

This book also doesn't elaborate or provide examples on how you can use Dojo outside of the typical browser environment (such as in a Rhino or Adobe AIR environment) or include coverage on how you can use Dojo in combination with other client-side frameworks such as DWR, YUI!, or Domino.

Open Source Software Is Fluid

Dojo is open source software with a thriving community, and as such, may add new features at any time. This book is written to be completely up-to-date as of Dojo version 1.1, but clearly, future versions could add more functionality. To be sure that you're as current as possible with the latest Dojo happenings, be sure to read the release notes for versions more recent than 1.1.

Also, be advised that Dojo's API is currently frozen until version 2.0, so all of the examples and information in this book should be correct through the various minor releases along the way. Even if you're reading this book and version 2.0 has already been released, the code examples should still work as the unofficial deprecation policy is that whatever is deprecated in a major release may not be axed until the next major release. In other words, anything that is deprecated in version 1.x will survive through until at least the 2.0 release, and maybe longer.

About You

This book assumes that you've done at least a mild amount of web development with client-side technologies such as HTML, JavaScript, and CSS. You by no means, however, need to be an expert in any of these skills and you really don't need to

---

* From a conservative estimate, over 95% of the API for Base, Core, Dijit, and Util is covered in this book.

know anything at all about what happens on a web server because Dojo is a client-side technology; merely having dabbled with them enough to know what they are and how they are used is more than enough.

If you are an existing web developer or even a hobbyist who is able to construct a very simple web page and apply a dab of JavaScript and CSS to liven it up a bit, then you should definitely keep reading. If you haven't even heard of HTML, JavaScript, or CSS, and have never done so much as written a line of code, then you might want to consider picking up a good introduction on web development as a supplement to this book.

Development Tools

With regard to development tools, although you could use your favorite text editor and any web browser to do some effective development with Dojo, this book makes frequent references to Firefox and the wonderful Firebug add-on that you can use to debug and deconstruct web pages as well as tinker around with JavaScript in its console. Although you could use Firebug Lite with another browser like Internet Explorer, the full version of Firebug is vastly superior and you won't be disappointed by it. (In general, a practice that's commonly accepted is to develop with Firefox using Firebug, but test frequently with IE.) You can get Firefox and Firebug from *http://getfirefox.com* and *http://getfirebug.com*, respectively.

Two other tools you may want to consider for Firefox are Chris Pederick's Web Developer Toolbar, available at *http://chrispederick.com/work/web-developer/*, which provides some additional tools that are useful during development, and the Clear Cache Button Firefox add-on, available at *https://addons.mozilla.org/en-US/firefox/addon/1801*, which is a button for your toolbar that you can use to quickly clear your cache. Occasionally, it can be the case that your browser may "act up" and serve you stale content; clearing the cache sometimes helps.

Essential Working Knowledge

Closures, context, and anonymous functions are some of the most important fundamental concepts in JavaScript, and because mastery of the toolkit involves more than a casual understanding of these topics, this section is worth a careful read. Even though it may sound like advanced material, these concepts are essential to mastering the JavaScript language and really understanding some of the underlying design within the toolkit. You could try and pick up this knowledge as you go along, but if you spend a little bit of time up front, you'll find that many selections from the ensuing chapters are considerably easier to understand.

Closures

A *closure* is essentially the coupling of data elements and the scope that contains (or encloses) that data. Although typical situations involving a single global scope that contains some functions are fairly straightforward, nested functions have the ability to really change things up. To illustrate, consider Example P-1.

Example P-1. Minimalist illustration of closures

```
function foo( ) {
  var x = 10;
  return function bar( ) {
    console.log(x);
  }
}

var x = 5;
var barReference = foo( );
barReference( ); //What gets printed? 10 or 5
```

Depending on your programming background, the previous code snippet might actually surprise you. As it turns out, the value 10 is printed to the screen because, in JavaScript, the entire scope chain is taken into account when evaluating a function. In this case, the scope chain that is returned is associated with bar, which is returned from evaluating foo. Thus, when barReference is evaluated, the value for x is looked up on the fly, and is tracked down in the body of foo. This is directly contrary to many programming languages, which would look up the context in the most immediate scope.

 In JavaScript, functions are "first-class" objects that you can pass around, assign to variables, etc., and many of Dojo's design patterns leverage this characteristic heavily.

Although JavaScript closures are normally considered an advanced topic, the sooner you have a firm grasp on closures, the sooner you'll be on your way toward mastering the language and the better you'll understand many pieces of Dojo's design philosophy. In practical terms, that means you'll be more productive, able to track down tricky bugs a lot faster, and perhaps even become a more interesting person. (Well, two out of three isn't bad.) Consult David Flanagan's legendary *JavaScript: The Definitive Guide* (O'Reilly) for an excellent analysis of closures.

Context

JavaScript's extreme dynamism equips it with tremendous flexibility, and one of the most interesting yet least understood facets of its dynamism involves *context*. You probably already know that the default this context for browser-based JavaScript is the global window object. For example, the following statements should evaluate to true for virtually every browser implementation:

```
//the default context for a document is the window
console.log(window ==this); //true
```

```
//document is a shortcut for window.document
console.log(document == window.document); //true
```

With respect to Function objects, the keyword this is specifically used to refer to its immediate context. For example, you may have seen this used in a JavaScript Function object somewhat like the following:

```
function Dog(sound) {
    this.sound = sound;
}

Dog.prototype.talk = function(name) {
    console.log(this.sound + "," + this.sound + ". My name is", name);
}

dog = new Dog("woof");
dog.talk("fido"); //woof, woof. my name is fido
```

If you come from Java or a similar object-oriented background, the way that sound is looked up relative to the current object probably seems familiar enough. Nothing interesting is happening yet. However, matters can get more complicated if you bring in the built-in call function. Take a moment to study the following contrived example that introduces the call function at work:

```
function Dog(sound) {
    this.sound = sound;
}

Dog.prototype.talk = function(name) {
    console.log(this.sound + "," + this.sound + ". my name is", name);
}

dog = new Dog("woof");
dog.talk("fido"); //woof, woof. my name is fido

function Cat(sound) {
    this.sound = sound;
}

Cat.prototype.talk = function(name) {
    console.log(this.sound + "," + this.sound + ". my name is", name);
}

cat = new Cat("meow");
cat.talk("felix"); //meow, meow. my name is felix
```

cat.talk.call(dog, "felix") //woof, woof. my name is felix

Whoa! That last line did something pretty incredible. Through the cat object instance, it invoked the talk method that is bound to the cat prototype and passed in the name parameter to be used as usual; however, instead of using the sound that is bound to cat's this, it instead used the sound value that is bound to dog's this because dog was substituted in for the context.

It's well worth a few moments to tinker around with the call function to get more comfortable with it if it's new to you. In many less dynamic programming languages, the ability to redefine this would almost be ludicrous. As a potent language feature, however, JavaScript allows it, and toolkits like Dojo leverage this kind of inherent dynamism to do some amazing things. In fact, some of these amazing things are coming up in the next section.

> Although the intent of this book isn't to provide exhaustive JavaScript language coverage that you could read about in *JavaScript: The Definitive Guide*, you may find it instructive to know that apply is a function that works just like call except that instead of accepting an unspecified number of parameters to be passed into the target function, it accepts only two parameters, the latter parameter being an Array, which can contain an unsaid number of values that become the built-in arguments value for the target function. Essentially, you'll choose the one most convenient for you.

Anonymous functions

In JavaScript, Function objects may be passed around just like any other type. Although using anonymous functions inline can definitely provide some syntactic sugar that reduces the clutter and makes code more maintainable, a perhaps more significant feature of anonymous functions is that they provide a closure that protects the immediate context.

For example, what does the following block of code do?

```
//Variable i is undefined.

for (var i=0; i < 10; i++) {
    //do some stuff with i
}
console.log(i); // ???
```

If you thought that the console statement prints out undefined, then you are sorely mistaken. A subtle but important characteristic of JavaScript is that it does not support the concept of blocked scope outside of functions, and for this reason, the values of i and any other "temporary" variables defined during iteration, conditional logic, etc., live on long after the block executes.

If it's ever prudent to explicitly provide blocked scope, you *could* wrap the block inside of a Function object and execute it inline. Consider the following revision:

```
(function( ) {
  for (var i=0; i < 10; i++) {
    //do some stuff with i
  }
})( )
console.log(i); // undefined
```

Although the syntax is somewhat clumsy, keeping it clear of artifacts can sometimes prevent nasty bugs from sneaking up on you. Many Base language functions introduced in the following chapters provide closure (in addition to syntactic sugar and utility) to the code block being executed.

Conventions Used in This Book

The following typographical conventions are used in this book:

Plain text

> Indicates menu titles, menu options, menu buttons, and keyboard accelerators (such as Alt and Ctrl).

Italic

> Indicates new terms, URLs, email addresses, filenames, file extensions, pathnames, directories, and Unix utilities.

`Constant width`

> Indicates commands, options, switches, variables, attributes, keys, functions, types, classes, namespaces, methods, modules, properties, parameters, values, objects, events, event handlers, XML tags, HTML tags, macros, the contents of files, or the output from commands.

`Constant width bold`

> Shows commands or other text that should be typed literally by the user.

`Constant width italic`

> Shows text that should be replaced with user-supplied values.

 This icon signifies a tip, suggestion, or general note.

 This icon indicates a warning or caution.

Style Conventions

Two additional conventions should also be noted as they relate to effectively communicating the meaning of content:

Qualifying references

> Fully qualified namespaces are generally not used when the context is obvious. For example, if a code listing just introduced a `dijit.form.Button` widget, then the following discussion might opt to simply refer to the widget as `Button`.

Some terms such as *constructor* may be used in multiple ways within the same paragraph or context. Whenever this happens, the constant width font is used to differentiate whenever possible. For example, the sentence, "You create a widget by invoking an ordinary JavaScript constructor function, but a widget also has a special lifecycle method called constructor that can be used to perform initialization tasks" attempts to de-conflict the meaning of the term "constructor" by applying the constant width font.

API listings

In general, this book strives to provide standalone API listings by using a convention that relates the types of parameters by standardized constructor function names. For example, consider a function that would be invoked along the lines of loadUpArray("foo", 4) and return back ["foo", "foo", "foo", "foo"]. The API listing would be related as follows:

```
loadUpArray(/*String*/ value, /*Integer*/ length) //returns Array
```

Because JavaScript is a very dynamic, weakly typed language, however, there are some situations in which a parameter or value returned from a function could be any possible value. In these cases, the convention Any will be used to relate this feature. Whenever a parameter is optional, a question mark follows its type, like so: /*Integer?*/.

If you end up browsing Dojo source code, you may notice that some of the parameter names in the source code differ from the names the API listings use in this book. Because JavaScript function parameters are unnamed and positional, their actual names so far as an API listing is inconsequential; this language characteristic was leveraged to relate API listings in the most intuitive manner. As much care as possible was taken to provide API listings in the most uniform way possible, but there are bound to be small deviations occasionally.

Using Code Examples

This book is here to help you get your job done. In general, you may use the code in this book in your programs and documentation. You do not need to contact us for permission unless you're reproducing a significant portion of the code. For example, writing a program that uses several chunks of code from this book does not require permission. Selling or distributing a CD-ROM of examples from O'Reilly books *does* require permission. Answering a question by citing this book and quoting example code does not require permission. Incorporating a significant amount of example code from this book into your product's documentation *does* require permission.

We appreciate, but do not require, attribution. An attribution usually includes the title, author, publisher, and ISBN. For example: "*Dojo: The Definitive Guide*, by Matthew A. Russell. Copyright 2008 Matthew A. Russell, 978-0-596-51648-2."

If you feel your use of code examples falls outside fair use or the permission given above, feel free to contact us at *permissions@oreilly.com*.

Safari® Books Online

When you see a Safari® Books Online icon on the cover of your favorite technology book, that means the book is available online through the O'Reilly Network Safari Bookshelf.

Safari offers a solution that's better than e-books. It's a virtual library that lets you easily search thousands of top tech books, cut and paste code samples, download chapters, and find quick answers when you need the most accurate, current information. Try it for free at *http://safari.oreilly.com*.

We'd Like to Hear from You

Please address comments and questions concerning this book to the publisher:

O'Reilly Media, Inc.
1005 Gravenstein Highway North
Sebastopol, CA 95472
800-998-9938 (in the United States or Canada)
707-829-0515 (international or local)
707-829-0104 (fax)

We have a web page for this book, where we list errata, examples, and any additional information. You can access this page at:

http://www.oreilly.com/catalog/9780596516482

To comment or ask technical questions about this book, send email to:

bookquestions@oreilly.com

For more information about our books, conferences, Resource Centers, and the O'Reilly Network, see our web site at:

http://www.oreilly.com

Acknowledgments

Writing this book has been much more than a brief stint of moonlighting and baptism by fire. Rather, it has been a journey that started long before I'd ever even heard of Dojo, JavaScript, or computers. This book is the logical fruition of life-changing events—all involving incredible people. What follows is an ultra-condensed, semi-chronological storyboard of the key happenings that all played a part in the pages that you're about to read.

This book is the culmination of seemingly disparate events in my life, but the common thread amongst all of these events is the incredible people involved in each step along the way. It is with much delight that I give so many thanks to:

- The LORD, for He is good and His steadfast love endures forever!
- Lucille Tabor, who provided a young child a mother and a home.
- Jerry Russell, who purchased a poor boy his first computer.
- David Kade, who taught a hopeful student how to think in another language.
- Deborah Pennington, who almost single-handedly turned a young punk's life around.
- Kellan Sarles, who taught an aspiring writer how to converse on paper.
- Gary Lamont, who engaged an emerging mind to think like a computer scientist.
- Derrick Story, who gave a want-to-be writer an opportunity.
- Abe Music, who first introduced me to Dojo.
- Simon St.Laurent, Tatiana Apandi, Colleen Gorman, Rachel Monaghan, and Sumita Mukherji, who provided the editorial guidance and insight that smoothed out so many of this book's rough edges.
- So many new friends from #dojo, who so generously reviewed this book's manuscript and provided feedback that made all of the difference in quality; in no particular order: Adam Peller, Sam Foster, Karl Tiedt, Bill Keese, Dustin Machi, Pete Higgins, James Burke, Peter Kristoffersson, Alex Russell, and Dylan Schiemann.
- Baseeret, who is the love of my life.
- The LORD, for He is good and His steadfast love endures forever!

—Matthew A. Russell
June 2008

## PART I

Base and Core

This part of the book provides a guided tour of Base and Core, the elements of the toolkit that comprise a powerful JavaScript standard library. *Base* is the kernel of the toolkit and is optimized to include an awesome amount of functionality that comes across the wire at under 30KB. Every feature included in Base has been scrutinized for utility, speed of execution, and size. You'll quickly find that once you start using Base, you won't want to live without it—nor do you have to: getting Base into your page is as simple as writing a single SCRIPT tag that can even be cross-domain loaded from one of AOL's geographically edge-cached servers. In addition to providing the logical base of the toolkit, everything in Base is included in the base-level dojo namespace, so finding the most commonly used functions and data members is always just a few keystrokes away.

Core supplements Base with additional functionality that you will certainly be using sooner rather than later, but in an effort to keep Base as lean and mean as possible, Core was packaged separately because its features are not quite common enough for all use cases. Still, pulling in resources from Core is just a dojo.require function call away, which is similar to #include from C programming or import from Java; from then on out, it's as though you had it all along. And as you'll see in Chapter 16 on Util, you can actually use the Dojo build system to combine exactly which additional non-Base resources you need into a single script; thus, Core functionality need not be any further away than Base for production settings. The kinds of features you'll find in Core include animation machinery (dojo.fx), drag-and-drop facilities (dojo.dnd), a data management layer (dojo.data), cookie handling (dojo.cookie), and more.

Familiarity with the arsenal of tools in Base and Core is absolutely essential to becoming a productive Dojo developer, and the chances are good that this machinery can supplement your swath of tools and techniques, regardless of their origin or how long you've already been using them. After mastering Base and Core, you'll spend less effort on the common, mundane tasks that many developers squander precious time on, and spend more time on the far more interesting aspects of your project that require creativity and out-of-the-box thinking.

## CHAPTER 1

Toolkit Overview

This chapter provides an overview of Dojo's architecture, takes you through install-ing Dojo, introduces some domain-specific jargon, runs through the bootstrapping process, and then provides some example code that should whet your appetite for the chapters that follow. Like any other introduction, much of this chapter paints in broad strokes and sets the tone for the rest of the book. Hopefully, you'll find it help-ful as you begin your journey with the toolkit.

Overview of Dojo's Architecture

As you're about to see, describing Dojo as a *toolkit* is no mere coincidence. In addi-tion to providing a JavaScript standard library of sorts, Dojo also packs a collection of feature-rich, turnkey widgets that require little to no JavaScript coding at all, build tools, a testing framework, and more. This section provides an overview of Dojo's architecture from a broad point of view, shown in Figure 1-1. As you'll see, the orga-nization for the rest of this book is largely driven by the toolkit's architecture. Even though DojoX is displayed as an independent entity from Dijit, DojoX resources could also be built upon Dijit resources, just as your own custom widgets could leverage any combination of Dijit and DojoX resources.

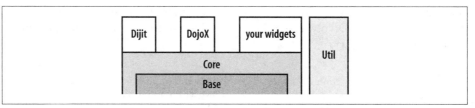

Figure 1-1. One depiction of how the various Dojo components can be thought of as relating to one another

Base

The kernel of Dojo is *Base*, an ultra-compact, highly optimized library that provides the foundation for everything else in the toolkit. Among other things, Base provides convenient language and AJAX utilities, a packaging system that allows you to pull in Dojo resources on-the-fly instead of requiring them to all be slurped in when the page loads. It also supplies you with tools for creating and manipulating inheritance hierarchies, a means of almost universally querying the DOM using CSS3 selectors, and a fabric that standardizes DOM events amongst various browsers. Everything that Base provides is available in the top level of the toolkit's namespace as a `dojo.*` function or attribute. Base comes packaged as a single file, *dojo.js*, which comes across the wire at under 30KB, and when you consider that most Flash-based advertisements that inundate the web are considerably larger than 30KB, such a small number seems quite amazing.

If you look at the actual size of *dojo.js* on disk, you'll see that it is around 80KB, but because web servers generally process content as it comes "across the wire" to the browser, it's the size of the compressed content that drives the amount of time it takes to download. If you manually apply gzip compression to *dojo.js*, you should see that it reduces in size by about one-third of the original size.

One other really interesting thing about Base is that it is designed to *bootstrap* the Dojo essentials automatically by simply including the *dojo.js* file into the page. To oversimplify things a bit, bootstrapping basically entails detecting the environment, smoothing out browser incompatibilities, and loading the `dojo` namespace. Various configuration options can also be specified to automatically parse any widgets in the page and perform other initialization tasks. (All coming up in future chapters.)

Base provides a tremendous wealth of utility for many standard operations you'll commonly need to achieve when doing just about anything in JavaScript. Even if you don't use anything else in the toolkit, Base will probably be a valuable resource that you won't want to live without once you've experienced the productivity boost it provides. There is no Dojo without Base; everything in the toolkit depends or builds on it one way or another.

With the contents of the Base being settled and fairly uniform, the terms "Base" is being used less and less within the project as time goes on, and you may even hear the term "Base" used interchangeably with "dojo.js."

Core

Core builds on Base by offering additional facilities for parsing widgets, advanced animation effects, drag-and-drop facilities, internationalization (i18n), back-button handling, managing cookies, and more. Resources available through Core are often used frequently and provide fundamental support for common operations, but were not deemed universal enough to include in Base. Although the distinction between what did and didn't make it into Core may not be a perfect boundary, Dojo's packaging system trivializes the amount of effort required to pull in additional modules and resources as needed with a simple mechanism that works like a #include from C or an import statement from Java.

In general, distinguishing between Base and Core is simple: any module or resource that you have to explicitly import into the page external to *dojo.js* is a part of Core if it is associated with the dojo namespace. Core facilities usually do not appear in the Base level namespace, and instead appear in a lower-level namespace such as dojo.fx or dojo.data.

Dijit

Describing Dojo as just a JavaScript standard library of sorts would only be telling you a small part of its story; Dojo also packs a fantastic library of widgets called *Dijit* (short for "Dojo widget") that is ready to use out of the box and often doesn't require you to write any JavaScript at all. Dijits conform to commonly accepted accessibility standards such as ARIA* and come with preconfigured internationalization that spans many common locales. Dijit is built directly upon Core (providing a strong testament to Core's integrity), so whenever you need a custom widget of your own devising, you'll be using the very same building blocks that were used to create everything else in Dijit. The widgets that you create with Dojo are ultra-portable and can easily be shared or deployed onto any web server or often even run locally without out a web server at all via the *file://* protocol.

Plugging a dijit into a page is as easy as specifying a special dojoType tag inside of an ordinary HTML tag—a dream come true for layout designers and users who aren't interested in doing a lot (or any) JavaScript programming. In fact, a key benefit of using Dijit for application developers is that it allows you to achieve incredibly rich functionality without having to dig into tedious implementation details. Even if you're more of a library-writing type or a custom widget developer, following Dijit's style and conventions ensures that your widgets will be portable and easy to use—essentials for any reusable software component.

---

* A standard for accomplishing Accessible Rich Internet Applications: *http://www.w3.org/WAI/intro/aria*.

The Dijit battery can be roughly divided into general-purpose application widgets like progress bars and modal dialogs, layout widgets like tab containers and accordion panes, and form widgets that provide super-enhanced versions of old hats like buttons and various input elements.

DojoX

DojoX is a collection of subprojects that officially stands for "Dojo Extensions," although it is often called "Extensions and Experimental." The "extensions" subprojects in DojoX accounts for stable widgets and resources that while extremely valuable just don't fit nicely into Core or Dijit; the "experimental" subprojects account for widgets that are highly volatile and in more of an incubation stage.

Each DojoX subproject is required to come with a *README* file that contains a synopsis of its status. Although DojoX subprojects strive to meet accessibility and internationalization initiatives consistent with Dijit, it is not generally the case that they're always quite that refined. Be that as it may, lots of heavy machinery for real world applications lives in DojoX, including the grid widget, data converters for common web services, etc. DojoX also provides a sandbox and incubator for fresh ideas, while simultaneously ensuring that the high standards and stable APIs for resources in Core and Dijit are not compromised. In that regard, DojoX strikes a sensitive balance for critical issues central to any community-supported OSS project.

Util

Util is a collection of Dojo utilities that includes a JavaScript unit-testing framework and build tools for creating custom versions of Dojo for production settings. The unit-testing framework, DOH,[*] does not have a specific coupling to Dojo and provides a simple set of constructs that can be used to automate quality assurance on any JavaScript code. After all, you do want to implement well-defined, systematic tests for your JavaScript code, don't you?

The essence of the build tools is that they shrink the size of your code and can aggregate into a set of layers, where each layer is nothing more than a collection of other JavaScript files. The compression is accomplished via ShrinkSafe, a patched version of Mozilla's powerful Rhino JavaScript engine that compresses JavaScript code without mangling public APIs, and the aggregation is accomplished with a collection of custom scripts that are also run by Rhino. Other auxiliary components in Util do things like inline HTML template strings (more on this when Dijit is formally introduced in Chapter 11) into JavaScript files—another trick for reducing latency.

---

[*] As you might already have been thinking, DOH is also a pun on Homer Simpson's famous expletive; the test runner can optionally play a "D'oh!" sound effect when a test fails.

While reading this section, you may understand what build tools do for you, but it may not be clear why you'd want them. In short, build tools that consolidate and minify your JavaScript code *significantly* reduce the HTTP latency, which yields a serious performance advantage when it comes time for production.

Like DOH, ShrinkSafe may be used independently of Dojo, and for production settings there is almost never a good reason not to use it, given that it is not uncommon for it to reduce the JavaScript footprint by 50% or more. The performance difference between loading many large JavaScript files via a series of synchronous requests and retrieving one or two compressed JavaScript files can be quite staggering.

Prepping for Development

You don't need any fancy tools nor do you have to be able to configure a beast of a web server like Apache to learn how to develop with Dojo. In fact, very few examples in this entire book require you to interact with a web server at all. Most resources will be resolved via relative paths on your local machine or they will be cross-domain loaded, so for the most part, it's just you, your favorite text editor, and your web browser.

There are three primary ways you can download Dojo and prep for development: downloading an official release, checking out the latest and greatest from Subversion, and using a cross-domain (XDomain) build that's available from AOL's Content Developer Network (CDN). Let's walk through each of these options. Although downloading an official release to your local machine may be the most typical approach, there can be specific value in the other approaches as well.

Getting Dojo

There are three primary ways you can use Dojo: downloading an official release to your local environment, checking out a copy from Subversion to your local environment, and using an XDomain build from AOL's CDN. This section walks you through each of these options.

Downloading an official release

Downloading the latest official Dojo release is by far the most traditional way to prep for development. An "official" release is really nothing more than a tagged, blessed snapshot from the Subversion repository that has been well-tested and that comes with some helpful release notes. You can find official releases of the toolkit at *http:// dojotoolkit.org/downloads*; the only notable caveat when downloading an official release is that it does not come packaged with the build tools. To retrieve the build tools, you either need to use Subversion or download a source release, which you can find at *http://download.dojotoolkit.org/*.

When you uncompress the downloaded archive, you'll find it expands into a folder that has the general form *dojo-release-x.y.z*, where, "x," "y," and "z" correspond to the major, minor, and patch numbers for a particular release. To keep your setup and URLs as generic as possible, you may want to rename the folder in place so that it is simply called *js* (short for JavaScript). Other options include using server directives to alias *dojo-release-x.y.z* to *js*, or using symbolic links on Linux and Unix environments. In any case, this extra effort has the advantage of allowing you to use a relative path such as *www/js* to point to Dojo instead of a more brittle path such as *www/dojo-release-x.y.z*.

Creating a symbolic link is easy. On Linux, Mac OS X, or Unix platforms, simply execute a command of the following form from a terminal: `ln -s dojo-release-x.y.z js`. You can read more about symbolic links by reading the man page via the `man ls` command.

Once you have downloaded Dojo, you might initially be surprised that it's all not in one JavaScript file, but don't worry. A quick look at what unpacks reveals that the code base is broken into the same architectural components that we just talked about in the previous section—Base (*dojo/dojo.js*), Core (*dojo*), Dijit (*dijit*), DojoX (*dojox*), and Util (*util*). While we'll systematically work through all of this, the only action that's required to get Base into your page is to provide the relative path to the *dojo.js* file (located at *dojo/dojo.js* via a SCRIPT tag in your page just like any other JavaScript file). Easy as pie.

Downloading from Subversion

The latest official build is probably what you want to use for development. Still, if you're interested in maintaining a copy of the Subversion repository to stay up to date with the bleeding edge, then read this section closely; it walks you through the steps involved in checking out Dojo from Subversion and getting a convenient development environment set up. Developing against the Subversion trunk might be helpful if you want to keep a close eye on a bug that's being fixed, if you want to try out a new feature that's in the works, or if you're a first-class hacker who just can't rest easy unless you're always in the know with the latest.

For the authoritative reference on Subversion, take a look at *Version Control with Subversion*, which is available at *http://svnbook.red-bean. com/*.

Dojo's Subversion repository is located at *http://svn.dojotoolkit.org/src/*, so start there if you're interested in skimming some code in your web browser. You'll want to check out the code from the externals view that can be accessed at *http://svn.dojotoolkit.org/src/view/anon/all/trunk*, however, which keeps things simple by grabbing the entire toolkit in one fell swoop.

 The Subversion externals property provides a way of constructing a working copy that would normally require multiple separate checkouts. You can read more about it at *http://svnbook.red-bean.com/en/1.0/ch07s03.html*.

In order to check out the code, execute the following command from a terminal. (The remainder of this section assumes you've performed the checkout from inside of a folder named *www*.)

```
svn co http://svn.dojotoolkit.org/src/view/anon/all/trunk ./svn
```

Just as if you had downloaded an official release, you'll have an *svn* folder that contains subfolders corresponding to each major component of the toolkit (*dojo*, *dijit*, *dojox*, and *util*) when your Subversion checkout completes. However, your *util* folder will contain the build scripts (and possibly a few other things auxiliary tools used to support the toolkit). We'll delay elaboration on Subversion details, but do note that it is not difficult to have multiple versions of Dojo around—say, the latest official release, a nightly build, and an actual checkout of the repository—and use a server directive or other means of toggling between them all, depending on which version you'd like to use at any given time.

AOL's CDN

AOL hosts a cross-domain version of Dojo on their Content Delivery Network (AOL CDN) and makes it available for you to use by simply providing a few configuration parameters and including a SCRIPT tag that points to the XDomain build of Dojo on AOL's CDN server. Because it's just that easy, all of the examples in this book use the XDomain build so there is minimal fuss when you are trying things out.

As alluded to in the previous two sections, you normally load Dojo by pointing to your own *dojo.js* file; specify a relative path like this one:

```
<script
    type="text/javascript"
    src="www/js/dojo/dojo.js">
</script>
```

Using AOL's XDomain build is just as easy: simply change the src reference and let Dojo (and AOL) take care of the rest. The following SCRIPT tag illustrates this process for Dojo 1.1:

```
<script
    type="text/javascript"
```

```
    src="http://o.aolcdn.com/dojo/1.1/dojo/dojo.xd.js">
  </script>
```

The *dojo.xd.js* was emphasized in the code because if you accidentally specify *dojo.js*, you'll probably get an error instead of the Dojo goodness you were looking for. It is also noteworthy that the *1.1* in the *src* path references the latest bug release for the said version. You could request a specific bug fix release by asking for, say, *1.1.0* or *1.1.1*. You may want to bookmark *http://dev.aol.com/dojo* because it's the ultimate authority on what versions of Dojo are available via the CDN.

Debugging with Firebug

If you've done even a trivial amount of web development, you already know that debugging can sometimes be quite painful, especially when it involves obscure differences between browsers or deviations from the W3C standards. Unfortunately, throwing in a toolkit that wields a lot of power and complexity of its own can sometimes make debugging even tougher, and this might especially be the case for the JavaScript realm that involves the dynamism of closures, dynamic typing, and inconvenient ways of producing debug messages with alert boxes. And then there was *Firebug*, an amazing Firefox extension that made debugging and web development a lot easier.

As a rule of thumb, you should strongly consider developing in Firefox, because Firebug in and of itself is nothing short of incredible in terms of speeding up the development cycle. You can inspect/manipulate anything in the DOM (including style) in real time, log events to the Firebug console, and get error information that's often specific enough to identify your actual problem. (Compare that to a brilliant alert box that asks, "Would you like to debug?")

Of course, do remember to verify that your design is truly cross-platform by frequently sanity testing in IE and other browsers. Although Dojo itself goes to great lengths to work around browser quirks, it is still possible that anomalies can occur—and the sooner you discover these, the better.

Firebug is an amazing tool that's hard to live without once you've experienced it. You can save yourself a lot of time if you develop in Firefox and use Firebug for all that it's worth. However, it's best to frequently test in IE (say, at least every 30 minutes) to catch any hard-to-find anomalies that might creep into your application. For example, if you leave a trailing comma after the last key/value pair in a JavaScript associative array, Firefox forgives you, but IE does not…and the error message you get back from IE isn't very helpful either.

By far the most common function you'll probably use from Firebug is `console.log`, which allows you to print information to the Firebug console from inside of your JavaScript. (We're all tired of alert boxes by now, right?)

Be advised that Dojo aims to integrate as tightly with Firebug as possible, so it comes packaged with Firebug Lite. Thus, even if you must develop in another browser, functions such as console.log are always available to you if you want them.

You can download Firefox and Firebug from *http://www.getfirefox.com* and *http://www.getfirebug.com*, respectively. Appendix A contains a Firebug tutorial that you may find helpful for development.

Browser Security Settings for Running Dojo Locally

Most of the examples in this book are designed to loaded from a locale *file://* protocol, which generally works fine. However, it appears that users of Firefox 3 *may* need to make one small adjustment to load Dojo locally:

1. In the address bar, type about:config and press the Enter key.
2. Change the value of security.fileuri.origin_policy to 3 or greater.

You can read more about this issue at *http://kb.mozillazine.org/Security.fileuri.origin_policy*.

Lightweight Server Responses

Almost all of the content in this book can be demonstrated without a web server. To adequately demonstrate a *select few* pieces of the toolkit, however, it is helpful to serve up some dynamic content coming from a server. When these times arise, we'll use CherryPy (version 3.1+), an extremely easy-to-use web server that's written in Python. You can download and read all about CherryPy at *http://cherrypy.org*, but don't fret, you won't be derailed on your Dojo learning efforts by getting all bogged down with the details of having to learn about a new web server.

Installing CherryPy is as simple as downloading it and following a few short instructions in the *README* file. CherryPy installs just like any other Python module, so there isn't an exposed installation directory, per se. Unlike other, heftier server-side technologies, CherryPy just becomes readily available for you to use whenever you include it via an import statement like other Python modules. In fact, a CherryPy application is nothing more than a standalone Python application that is running its own multithreaded web server; thus, actually executing a "server-side script" is as simple as running a single command in a terminal.

All of the (very few) examples involving the need to serve up some dynamic content or explicitly get a response for the server require nothing more than a single command in a terminal, so don't be scared away—these server-side examples *are* for the faint of heart! Of course, you are more than welcome to skip any examples involving server-side technologies completely; a thorough discussion of what is happening will always accompany them.

For example, if you were asked to invoke the following simple application stored in a file called *hello.py*, you'd do nothing more than type python hello.py on the command line. That's all that it takes to have CherryPy start up and listen on port 8080 for incoming requests. Having already installed CherryPy, the import cherrypy statement shown in Example 1-1 locates it and makes it available for use.

Example 1-1. A very simple CherryPy application

```
1   import cherrypy
2
3   class Content:
4
5       @cherrypy.expose
6       def index(self):
7           return "Hello"
8
9       @cherrypy.expose
10      def greet(self, name=None):
11          return "Hello "+name
12
13  cherrypy.quickstart(Content())
```

For Example 1-1, if you navigate to *http://localhost:8080/* in your web browser, you would access the index method (lines 6–7) and get back the response "Hello", whereas if you navigate to *http://localhost:8080/greet?name=Dojo*, you'd access the greet method (lines 10–11), which processes the name query string parameter and gives back the response "Hello Dojo". That's the general pattern, and given how inherently readable Python code is, it can't get much easier than that.

While you'll never need to write or understand Python code to this book, the previous walk-through was included just to show you how quick and easy it is to do with CherryPy and Python in case you ever need or want create dynamic content of your own. *Learning Python* by Mark Lutz (O'Reilly) is a great reference on Python if you find yourself ever needing to work up more complex Python code. Python's official web presence at *http://www.python.org* and CherryPy's web site at *http://www.cherrypy.org* have great documentation as well.

Terminology

It will be helpful for us to take just a moment and clarify some of the terms that we'll use in discussions throughout the book. A precise explanation of JavaScript's mechanics packs a lot of lingo that requires precise terminology, and the lines only get blurrier when you start building a powerful toolkit on top of it—not to mention a toolkit that does things like simulate classes for a language in which proper classes from an object-oriented context does not exist.

Hopefully, you'll find the following list of terms helpful as we progress through some of these murky waters:

Toolkit

A *toolkit* is simply a collection of tools. It just so happens that toolkits in the computer programming realm are frequently used within the context of user interface design. Dojo is most accurately defined as a toolkit because it's more than just a library of supporting code that provides a set of related functions and abstractions; it also provides items such as deployment utilities, testing tools, and a packaging system. It's easy to get wrapped around the axle on library versus framework versus toolkit, and so forth, but Dojo has been dubbed a toolkit, so let's go with it.

Module

Physically, a Dojo *module* is nothing more than a JavaScript file or a directory containing a cohesive collection of JavaScript files. As it turns out, this top-level directory also designates a *namespace* for the code it contains. In a logical sense, modules in Dojo are similar to the concept of packages in other programming languages in that they are used to compartmentalize related software components. Do note, however, that while Dojo's *packaging system* refers to the actual mechanism that performs tasks such as determining and fetching dependencies, Dojo modules themselves are not called "packages."

Resource

When it becomes necessary to split a Dojo module into multiple files, or when a module consists of only a single JavaScript file, each JavaScript file is referred to a *resource*. Although a resource could strictly be used to logically organize the various abstractions that are associated with a module, there is also the consideration of minimizing the size of a JavaScript file. The trade-off essentially amounts to minimizing file size so that you don't download superfluous code that isn't needed, while also not downloading too many small files—all of which are synchronous requests and incur the overhead of communicating back to the web server (although using the build tools to create layers can make this overhead somewhat of a moot point).

Namespace

Physically, Dojo *namespaces* map to the same filesystem hierarchy that specifies modules and resources; logically, the concept of a namespace prevents identically named modules and resources from clashing. Note that while namespaces themselves are neither modules nor resources, the semantic idea behind what they represent does directly map to modules and resources. It is also worthwhile to note that Dojo preserves the global namespace of a page, and any modules you create with Dojo do not pollute the global namespace if implemented properly. Recall that everything in Base fits into the top-level dojo namespace.

First-class

In computer programming, something is *first-class* when it can be passed around without restrictions compared to other entities in the same language. For example, in many programming languages, you cannot pass around functions in the same way that you can pass around other data types such as number or string values. In this particular context, functions would not be considered first-class objects. In our discussions, the most common way this term will be used is to highlight the fact that functions are first-class objects in JavaScript. As we'll see, operations such as assigning functions directly to variables and/or placing them in associative arrays are fundamental to many Dojo design patterns.

Function

A *function* is a code snippet that is defined once, but can be executed multiple times. In JavaScript, functions are first-class objects that can be passed around just like any other variable. A *constructor function* is a function that is used specially via the new operator, which creates a new JavaScript *Function object* and performs initialization on it. Note that all JavaScript *objects* inherit from JavaScript's built-in Object type and have a prototype property that conveys the basis for JavaScript's powerful inheritance mechanism that is based on prototype-chaining. In Dojo parlance, the term *constructor* may also refer to the anonymous function that maps to the constructor key in dojo.declare's associative array and that is used primarily for initializing *properties* of a Dojo *class*.

Object

The most generic concept of an object in JavaScript refers to a compound data type that can contain any number of named *properties*. For example, the simple statement var o = {} uses object literal syntax to create a JavaScript *object*. Because the term "object" gets thrown around so much in this document, the term "associative array" is sometimes used to describe contexts of key-value pairs such as {a : 1, b : 2} instead of calling them objects. Technically speaking, JavaScript only has objects and no classes—even though Dojo simulates the notion of a class via the dojo.declare function, a special function that is used for this express purpose.

Property

In OOP, any piece of data stored in a class is commonly called a *property*. In our Dojo-specific discussions, this term may refer to data contained in Function objects or to data contained in Dojo classes that are defined by dojo.declare.

Method

A function that is a member of a class is commonly referred to as a *method* in broad OOP contexts, JavaScript, and Dojo. Furthermore, in Dojo parlance, the anonymous functions that appear in the dojo.declare statement are said to be methods because dojo.declare provides the basis for a class-based inheritance mechanism. In general, you might just do well to think of a method as a function defined on a class that is subsequently used through an object context.

Class

In Dojo, a declaration that represents a logical entity as defined via the `dojo.declare` function (a special function specifically used to simulate classes and inheritance hierarchies) is referred to as a *class*. Again, this term is being used loosely, because JavaScript does not support classes in the same sense that they exist in languages like Java and C++.

Widget

A Dojo widget is a *Function object* that is created via a `dojo.declare` statement that includes `dijit._Widget` (a base class for all widgets) as an ancestor. Usually, a widget has a visible appearance on the screen and logically bundles HTML, CSS, JavaScript, and static resources into a unified entity that can easily be manipulated, maintained, and ported around just like a file.

Bootstrapping

This section discusses some material that you may want to initially skim over and come back to review once you feel well acquainted with Dojo.

Before you can use Dojo at all, you have to somehow get it into the page. Regardless of whether you install Dojo locally or load it via AOL's CDN, you simply provide a SCRIPT tag that points to the file that loads some JavaScript code, and then magic elves inside of your web browser miraculously causes everything to "just work," right? Well, not quite. Like most other things in computing, it all comes back to pure and simple automation, and Dojo's bootstrap process is not different.

The term "bootstrap" refers to the idea of "pulling yourself up by your own bootstraps." In other words, it's the idea of getting up and running without help from anywhere else. The notional idea of Dojo bootstrapping itself is the same concept as your computer "booting up" when you turn it on.

For the record, Example 1-2 is the absolute minimum effort that is generally required to get some XDomain Dojo goodness into your HTML page. What's especially notable about loading Dojo from the CDN is that *less than 30KB of data comes across the wire*. Chances are good that you'll use the previous code block, or some variation of it, quite often. Save yourself some typing by copying it into a template that you can reuse.

Example 1-2. A minimalist application harness example

```html
<html>
  <head>
    <title>Title Goes Here</title>
    <!-- A lightweight style sheet that smoothes out look and feel across browsers -->
    <link rel="stylesheet" type="text/css"
        href="http://o.aolcdn.com/dojo/1.1/dojo/resources/dojo.css" />

    <script
      type="text/javascript"
      src="http://o.aolcdn.com/dojo/1.1/dojo/dojo.xd.js">
    </script>

    <script type="text/javascript">
        /* If needed, Dojo modules may be asynchronously requested into the page here via
        dojo.require statements... */

        dojo.addOnLoad(function( ) {

            /* Any content that depends upon dojo.require statements goes here... */

        });
    </script>

  </head>
  <body>
    <!-- ... -->
  </body>
</html>
```

The dojo.addOnLoad function accepts another function as its parameter. The examples in this book generally supply this parameter with an anonymous function, although you could opt to define a function like var init = function( ) { /*...*/} and pass it in. Anonymous functions and some of the reasons they are important were briefly discussed in the Preface.

Two new constructs in the previous listing include the dojo.require statement and the dojo.addOnLoad block. The dojo.require statement is discussed at length in the section "Managing Source Code with Modules" in Chapter 2, but in a nutshell, it pulls a named resource into the page for you to use the same way that import works in Java or #include works in C programming. One incredibly important aspect of dojo.require is that it performs *synchronous* loading for local installations of the toolkit but acts *asynchronously* if you are doing XDomain loading. That distinction is especially important as it relates to dojo.addOnLoad.

dojo.addOnLoad

Because `dojo.require` statements act asynchronously over XDomain loads, it is not necessarily safe to immediately use resources you have requested via `dojo.require` when the page loads* because latency and other factors may (and usually will) cause some delay. Then, when you try to reference a module requested via `dojo.require` that is not yet loaded, you get a nice error thrown at you and the entire bootstrapping process most likely screeches to a halt. The technical term for the situation in which the outcome is undefined because of unpredictable timing constraints that compete with one another is called a *race condition*.

For the reasons just mentioned, using `dojo.addOnLoad` is a very good habit to get into because it makes your page as portable as possible—whether or not it is XDomain-loaded.

 A common mistake is not using `dojo.addOnLoad` to safely and portably perform logic that should occur after the page loads and all `dojo.require` statements have been satisfied. The issue usually comes up when you have developed locally and then start switching SCRIPT tags to do XDomain loading.

Given that the previous code snippet uses XDomain loading, there aren't any extra steps involving local installation, so it really is a one-step process to bootstrap the entire toolkit from an existing page.

 Although widgets are not introduced for many more chapters, another nuance of addOnLoad that bears mentioning—because we're on the topic—is that addOnLoad does not fire until after widgets have been parsed in the page (assuming Dojo has been configured to parse widgets on page load).

While bootstrapping is synonymous with "loading a script" at a high level, there's a lot more happening with that loading process than meets the eye. From a bird's eye view, at least two basic actions occur, though not necessarily in this exact order:

Platform configuration
　　Takes into account any custom configuration options that may have been specified through `djConfig`, an associative array that must be defined before the SCRIPT tag that loads Dojo is executed or as an attribute of the SCRIPT tag that loads Dojo. More specifics on `djConfig` are coming up later in this chapter.

---

* Generally speaking, the page load occurring consists of either the window's `onload` event or possibly the `DOMContentLoaded` for Mozilla variations completing.

Determines Dojo should be cross-domain loaded or loaded locally. XDomain loading details happen transparently so long as an Internet connection is available and the inclusion of the XDomain loader was configured at build time. By default, configuring for XDomain loading produces a *dojo.xd.js* (and other *.xd.js* build artifacts), which provides a replacement for standard *dojo.js*.

Based on the environment specified for the particular build of Dojo (usually the browser but it could also be another option such as Rhino or a mobile device), sets up any environment-specific features. Even though you won't generally need to perform browser-specific configuration when using the default build of Dojo for the browser, Base still provides data members like dojo.isIE and dojo.isFF to expose the underlying browser for those few times when you do need them.

Performs browser-specific augmentation such as establishing an XMLHttpRequest (XHR) object for asynchronous calls using Dojo's various AJAX utilities. Workarounds for browser incompatibilities such as normalizing DOM events, standardizing a map of key codes, and extra measures to minimize and prevent memory leaks are also handled.

Namespace establishment and loading

Establishes the dojo namespace so that all of the utility provided by the toolkit does not clobber any existing symbols in the page.

Loads the dojo namespace with the various functions and symbols that constitute Base.

Although less frequently used than dojo.addOnLoad, dojo.addOnUnload is the preferred vehicle for performing logic that should take place when the page unloads.

Configuration with djConfig

Much of the content in this section will make a lot more sense once you've spent some time writing code, so don't feel the need to dwell on it. It's here as a reference more than anything.

Upcoming sections introduce djConfig, a configuration switch that you can place in the SCRIPT tag that bootstraps the toolkit (or define anytime before Dojo bootstraps) to customize where it looks for resources, whether debugging tools should be wired in, and so on.

Table 1-1 provides a synopsis of the key/value pairs you can pass into it to configure the bootstrapping process. (Some of the commentary may introduce constructs that have not yet been introduced. For now, just skim over those and come back to them whenever the occasion calls for it.)

Defining `djConfig` anytime after the SCRIPT tag that loads the toolkit executes has no effect.

Table 1-1. djConfig configuration switches

Key	Value type (default value)	Comment
afterOnLoad	Boolean (false)	Used to facilitate injecting Dojo into a page after it has already been loaded. Useful for hacking on a page or developing widgets that are necessarily lazy-loaded, i.e., for social networking apps, etc.
baseUrl	String (undefined)	Technically, this parameter allows you to redefine the root level path of the toolkit for a local or an XDomain load, usually for the purpose of resolving dependencies such as custom modules. In practice, however, it is almost exclusively used to resolve local modules when bootstrapping over XDomain.
cacheBust	String|Date (undefined)	In the case of a `String` value, appends the value provided to requests for modules so that previous version of the page that is cached locally will be overridden. Typically, this value will be a random string of characters that you generate yourself or a unique identifier for your application version that would prevent nasty bugs from surfacing that may be caused by older versions of modules.
		During the development cycle, you might provide a `Date` value such as `(new Date()).getTime()`, which guarantees a new value each time the page loads and prevents annoying caching problems.
debugAtAllCosts	Boolean (false)	Usually provides more specific debugging information at the cost of performance. You might specify this value to better track down the line number where an error occurred if you are told that an error originated in a build file like *bootstrap.js*, *dojo.js*, or *dojo.xd.js*.
dojoBlankHtmlUrl	String ("")	Used to provide the location for a blank HTML document, which is necessary for using the IFRAME transport via `dojo.io.iframe.create` (discussed in Chapter 4). A default is located at *dojo/resources/blank.html*.
dojoIframeHistoryUrl	String ("")	Used to provide the location for a special file that is used in combination with `dojo.back`, a module for managing the back button (discussed in Chapter 2). A default is located at *dojo/resources/iframe_history.html*.
enableMozDomContentLoaded	Boolean (false)	Gecko-based browsers like Firefox may optionally use the `DOMContentLoaded` event as the trigger to signal that the page has loaded because of a technical nuance related to synchronous XHR request involving a document greater than 65536 bytes.[a]

Table 1-1. djConfig configuration switches (continued)

Key	Value type (default value)	Comment
extraLocale	String or Array ("")	Used to specify additional locales so that Dojo can transparently handle the details associated with providing a localized module. Values may be provided as a String value or as an Array of String values.
isDebug	Boolean (false)	Loads Firebug or Firebug Lite machinery for debugging. Note that stubs for debugging functions such as the various console methods are in place by default so that code doesn't bust if you choose to remove diagnostic information from your application.
libraryScriptUri	String ("")	Used to configure nonbrowser environments such as Rhino and SpiderMonkey (JavaScript engines) in a manner similar to the way that baseUrl works for browser environments.
locale	String (browser provided)	Used to override dojo.locale with a local other than the one that is retrieved from the browser.
modulePaths	Object (undefined)	Specifies a collection of key/value pairs that associates modules with their relative paths on disk. While you'll generally place your modules in the toolkit's root directory, this parameter allows for variations if they are needed. When loading Dojo from the CDN or other XDomain, a baseUrl parameter is also required.
parseOnLoad	Boolean (false)	Specifies whether to automatically parse the page for widgets on page load (essentially just a dojo.parser. parse( ) function call at the appropriate time during the bootstrap process).
require	Array ([])	Provides a convenient way of providing modules that should be automatically required once Base loads. When used in conjunction with afterOnLoad, it designates resources that should be loaded when injecting Dojo into a page after the page has already loaded.
usePlainJson	Boolean (true)	Specifies whether to provide warnings via the console if comment filtered JSON is not used. This value is true by default because not using comment filtered JSON is generally considered more of a security risk than not using it.
useXDomain	Boolean (false)	Used to force XDomain loading. This action is taken by default with XDomain builds. (See "Benefits of Using XDomain Builds" for benefits of using XDomain loading locally.)
xdWaitSeconds	Number (15)	Specifies the number of seconds to wait before timing out a request for resources that are cross-domain loaded.

a *http://trac.dojotoolkit.org/ticket/1704*

The djConfig parameter is modulePaths, while the Base function for setting up individual module paths is dojo.registerModulePath (no "s" on the end).

Most of the time, you will define djConfig in the same SCRIPT tag that bootstraps the toolkit using Object-like syntax. The following example illustrates:

```
<script
    type="text/javascript"
    src=" http://o.aolcdn.com/dojo/1.1/dojo/dojo.xd.js "
    djConfig="parseOnLoad:true,isDebug:true">
</script>
```

However, you might opt to define it prior to the SCRIPT tag that loads the toolkit if you have a lot of configuration switches, or if it's just more convenient to do it that way for your particular situation. Here's a translation of the previous example that produces the very same effect:

```
<script type="text/javascript">
    djConfig = {
        parseOnLoad : true,
        isDebug : true
    };
</script>

<script
  type="text/javascript"
  src="http://o.aolcdn.com/dojo/1.1/dojo/dojo.xd.js ">
</script>
```

Exploring Dojo with Firebug

Although the rest of this book systematically works through the entire toolkit, let's take a moment to tinker around with Dojo from the Firebug console. During development, there may be times when it is helpful to try out a few ideas in isolation, and the Firebug console provides an environment that behaves much like an interpreter.

Exploring Base

To illustrate, transcribe the minimalist HTML page in Example 1-3 into a local file to get started. The only Dojo-specific nuance is the script tag that performs the XDomain loading. Although we haven't covered the djConfig parameter that you'll see is included in the SCRIPT tag, it's just a way of passing in configuration information to Dojo as it bootstraps. In this case, we're specifying that debugging facilities such as the Firebug console should be explicitly available to us. Even if you're using another browser such as IE, the djConfig="isDebug:true" option ensures that Firebug Lite is loaded.

Injecting Dojo

If you decide that you ever want to use Dojo to hack on existing pages out on the Net somewhere, you can do it via dynamic script insertion via Firebug or a bookmarklet. As of version 1.1, the configuration switches afterOnLoad and require were added, which ensure that the normal callback sequence that occurs after page load occurs.

Here's some code that inserts Dojo into an existing page that you can paste and execute in the Firebug console. The only nuance is that you must define djConfig as its own object—not inline with the script tag—if you want to *safely* inject Dojo after the page has loaded because of subtleties with how browsers process dynamic script tags:

```
/*Define djConfig w/ afterOnLoad being set to true. You could also pass in
requests for any additional modules if you needed them. Let's assume you need
the dojo.behavior module.*/
djConfig={afterOnLoad:true,require:['dojo.behavior']}

/* Create the same script tag that would normally appear in the page's head */
var e = document.createElement("script");
e.type="text/javascript";
e.src="http://o.aolcdn.com/dojo/1.1/dojo/dojo.xd.js";

/* And insert it. That's it */
document.getElementsByTagName("head")[0].appendChild(e);
```

Or better yet, you could just create a bookmarklet[a] and load Dojo via a keyboard shortcut or by manually clicking on the bookmark: all that's entailed in creating the bookmarklet is wrapping the previous code block into a function and executing it. In your browser, create a bookmark called "Dojo-ify" and use this code (all one line) as the location:

```
(function() {djConfig={afterOnLoad:true,require:['dojo.behavior']};
var e = document.createElement("script"); e.type="text/javascript";
e.src="http://o.aolcdn.com/dojo/1.1/dojo/dojo.xd.js";
document.getElementsByTagName("head")[0].appendChild(e);})()
```

When you execute the bookmark, this script will load Dojo into the page, giving you full access to the CDN's build of Dojo. At that point, you could hack on the page to your heart's contentment. Just be aware that as of Dojo 1.1, there isn't an addOnLoad equivalent to signal when the toolkit (and any required modules) have completed loading. Dojo 1.2, however, will add in an addOnLoad equivalent. See *http://www.oreillynet. com/onlamp/blog/2008/05/dojo_goodness_part_7_injecting.html* for some helpful details. When you execute the bookmark, this script will load Dojo into the page, giving you full access to the CDN's build of Dojo. At that point, you could hack on the page to your heart's contentment. Just be aware that as of Dojo 1.1, there isn't an addOnLoad equivalent to signal when the toolkit (and any required modules) have completed loading. Dojo 1.2, however, will add in an addOnLoad equivalent. See *http://www. oreillynet.com/onlamp/blog/2008/05/dojo_goodness_part_7_injecting.html* for some helpful details.

—continued—

> Another interesting possibility for injecting Dojo into the page after it loads is for lazy-loading widgets into profiles on social networking apps, public profiles, and so on.

a Bookmarklets are nothing more than snippets of JavaScript code that can be stored as a bookmark. Generally, bookmarklets are designed to augment the behavior in a page.

Example 1-3. A really simple HTML page for illustrating a few features from Base

```html
<html>
    <head>
        <title>Fun with Dojo!</title>

            <link rel="stylesheet"  type="text/css"
              href="http://o.aolcdn.com/dojo/1.1/dojo/resources/dojo.css" />

        <script
            type="text/javascript"
            src="http://o.aolcdn.com/dojo/1.1/dojo/dojo.xd.js"
            djConfig="isDebug:true">
        </script>

        <style type="text/css">
            .blue {color: blue;}
            </style>
    </head>
    <body>
        <div id="d1" class="blue">A div with id=d1 and class=blue</div>
        <div id="d2">A div with id=d2</div>
        <div id="d2">Another div with id=d2</div>
        <div id="d4">A div with id=d3.
            <span id="s1">
                This sentence is in a span that's contained in d1.
                The span's id is s1.
            </span>
        </div>
        <form name="foo" action="">
            A form with name="foo"
        </form>
        <div id="foo"
            A div with id=foo
        </div>
    </body>
</html>
```

Once you've saved out the file, open the page in Firefox, and click on the little green circle with the checkmark in it to expand the Firebug console. Then, click on the caret icon just beside Firebug's search box to open up Firebug in a new window, as shown in Figure 1-2. (If you haven't read the primer on Firebug in Appendix A, this would be a good time to divert and do so.) Clicking on the "Net" tab reveals that the XDomain *dojo.xd.js* file consisting of Base has indeed been downloaded from the CDN.

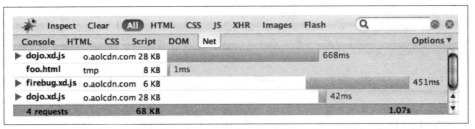

Figure 1-2. Firebug reveals valuable information that you can use to sanity check what is happening with network requests, and more

If you click back on the "Console" tab and type `dojo` on the `>>>` prompt followed by the enter key, you should see a Firebug console message that says something along the lines of `Object global=window isBrowser=true isRhino=false`, which shows you that the global JavaScript object `dojo` is indeed alive and well. Typing in `console.dir(dojo)` would provide an exhaustive tree-view of everything that's contained in Dojo. Although you'll also see a lot of private members that are prefixed with a leading underscore, go ahead try it out for yourself. Skimming the contents of the output will give you a small taste of what's packed up inside of Base.

dojo.byId

Dojo provides `dojo.byId` as a drop-in replacement for `document.getElementById`. Thus, passing in a string value like `dojo.byId("s1")`, for example, shows that it returns a reference that you could store in a variable just like you could with a call to `document.getElementById`. However, in addition to looking up an id value, `dojo.byId` also acts like a no-op if you pass it a DOM node. Internally, the function introspects its argument, so on the application level, you don't have to even think twice. Its complete function signature looks like this:

```
dojo.byId(/*String*/ id | /*DomNode*/ node)  // Returns a DOM Node
```

 Throughout the book, the pipe, |, is used to denote the logical "or" operation in function signatures whenever there is more than one possibility.

Because it appears that `dojo.byId` does almost the very same thing as `document.getElementById`, you may be tempted to just forget about `dojo.byId` all together—but don't! As it turns out, it smooths out some subtle inconsistencies that might just burn you when you least expect it. One well-known bug for `document.getElementById` surfaces IE6 and IE7. To illustrate, type the following into the Firebug Lite console for the sample document we're working on, and you'll see Figure 1-3:

```
document.getElementById("foo") //Isn't the answer *so* obvious?!?
```

Hmm. You probably didn't expect to have the FORM element returned, did you? As it turns out, if it had not appeared first in the document, you should have gotten the

A FORM with name=foo

A DIV with id=foo

```
Clear
>>> document.getElementById("foo")
< FORM id="" />
>>> dojo.byId("foo")
< DIV id="foo" />
```

Figure 1-3. The resulting behavior of document.getElementById versus dojo.byId for the previous document

div element returned. This particular bug arises because the name and id attribute namespaces are merged for IE. So much for cross-browser compatibility on the obvious things in life! Figure 1-4 shows how Dojo protects you from the cold hard metal of the browser, saving you from working around the multitude of inconsistencies that would otherwise prevent your application from being portable.

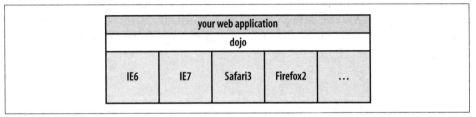

your web application				
dojo				
IE6	IE7	Safari3	Firefox2	...

Figure 1-4. Dojo makes your code more portable by insulating you from browser quirks

But in addition to dojo.byId working around that particular quirk, dojo.byId also returns the first element if more than one element has an id set to the same value, thereby normalizing corner case behavior. For our example document, you can verify that dojo.byId always returns the first element by trying out the following statement:

```
dojo.byId("d2").innerHTML
```

More than anything else, the takeaway from this short lesson is that if you're developing with a JavaScript toolkit, use its API to get work done instead of ways you may have learned with raw JavaScript. Occasionally, you may see an API call that doesn't seem to add any additional value, and the temptation may be to fall back to your own tried-and-true method of getting something accomplished—but resist the temptation! Well-designed APIs do not provide useless functionality.

Viewing an API call as "worthless" may be an indication that you may be confused about the exact utility that the call provides. Whenever this happens, review the documentation to find out what it is you're missing. If the documentation still doesn't convince you, hop on a mailing list or IRC channel and ask someone about it.

dojo.connect

Grabbing a DOM node is admittedly boring, so let's look at something slightly more interesting—like attaching a UI event such as a mouse movement to a node via dojo.connect, the toolkit's machinery for dynamically adding and removing these types of events. Its signature might look complex at first glance, but it's actually quite simple in routine use. Take a look:

```
connect(/*Object|null*/ obj,
        /*String*/ event,
        /*Object|null*/ context,
        /*String|Function*/ method) // Returns a connection handle
```

To try out connect, execute the following code into the Firebug console, and then move your mouse over the content of the sentence contained in the SPAN to see that the mouseover event was set up properly. (You'll probably want to click on the caret icon in the lower-right corner to expand the command prompt to multiline mode.)

```
var handle = dojo.connect(
  dojo.byId("s1"), //context
  "onmouseover", //event
  null, //context
  function(evt) {console.log("mouseover event", evt);} //event
);
```

You should notice that in addition to seeing confirmation in the Firebug console that an event has occurred, you get an actual reference to the event that you can click on and inspect—usually getting vital information relating to where the click occurred on the screen and more.

As it turns out, dojo.connect, like dojo.byId, does a lot of inspecting so that you don't have to think nearly as much about it as you might initially imagine. In fact, any arguments that may be null can be omitted completely. Thus, the previous function call could be reduced to the slightly more readable:

```
var handle = dojo.connect(
  dojo.byId("s1"), //context
  "onmouseover", //event
  function(evt) {console.log("mouseover event",evt);} //event
);
```

Tearing down the connection so that the function that is executed is based on a DOM event is even easier, and is important for preventing memory leaks if you are doing a lot of connecting and disconnecting. Just call dojo.disconnect on the handle you saved, and Dojo takes care of the rest for you:

```
dojo.disconnect(handle);
```

Although it is a simple example, `dojo.connect` demonstrates a key principle behind Dojo's philosophy: make getting from A to B as simple as it should have been all along. Sure—if you're well-versed in your JavaScript, you could go through the motions of setting up, maintaining, and tearing down connections all on your own. However, you'd still incur the cost of boilerplate that would clutter up your design, and let's not forget: every line of code you write is a line you have to maintain. For the aspiring web developers out there and those among us who prefer to keep things simple, calling `dojo.connect` and `dojo.disconnect` is a fine option.

Dojo doesn't do anything that JavaScript can't already do, and for that matter, neither does any other JavaScript toolkit. The tremendous value that Dojo introduces is in smoothing out inconsistencies amongst multiple browsers and making common operations as simple as they should have been all along—protecting you from writing and maintaining all of that boilerplate, which allows you to be as productive as possible.

Another neat feature that demonstrates tremendous power in a tiny package is `dojo.query`, the toolkit's mechanism for quickly querying the page with CSS3 style syntax.

 Chapter 5 covers `dojo.query` in detail and provides a lot more context about CSS3 selectors, if you want to jump ahead and skim over them.

For example, finding all of the DIV elements on the page is as simple as calling:

```
dojo.query("div") //find all of the div elements in the DOM
```

If you try that statement out in the Firebug console, you'll see that you indeed get back a list of DIV elements. Querying the page for the existence of a particular named DIV element is just as easy as it should be as well:

```
dojo.query("div#d2") //check for the existence of a div with id=d2
```

And then there's querying by class:

```
dojo.query(".blue") //returns a list of elements that have the blue class applied.
```

Speaking of classes, you could also filter on particular element types, but because there's only one DIV that has a class applied to it, we'll need to apply the blue class to another element as well. But before you go and start editing the page itself, why not just use another built-in function from Base, `dojo.addClass`, to apply the class like so:

```
dojo.addClass("s1", "blue");  //add the blue class to the SPAN
```

After we apply the blue class to s1, we can illustrate another query with `dojo.query` like so:

```
dojo.query("span.blue") //returns only span elements with the blue class applied
```

Getting the hang of it? Sure, we *could* do all of these things in our own roundabout ways, but isn't it nice to know that the toolkit insulates you from all of that mayhem and provides a single, easy-to-use function instead?

Exploring Dijit

While we could go on and on showcasing Base's easy-to-use API, let's save that for subsequent chapters and instead divert to a quick example of how easy it is to snap some dijits into your page without any additional programming.

Suppose you have the page shown in Example 1-4.

Example 1-4. A very primitive form example

```
<html>
    <head>
        <title>Fun with Dijit!</title>
    <head>
        <body>
        Just Use the form below to sign-up for our great offers:<br /><br />
        <form id="registration_form">
            First Name: <input type="text" maxlength=25 name="first"/><br />
            Last Name: <input type="text" maxlength=25 name="last"/><br />
            Your Email: <input type="text" maxlength=25 name="email"/><br /><br />
            <button onclick="alert('Boo!')">Sign Up!</button>
        </form>
    </body>
</html>
```

Figure 1-5 shows what that page looks like, although it's not very difficult to imagine.

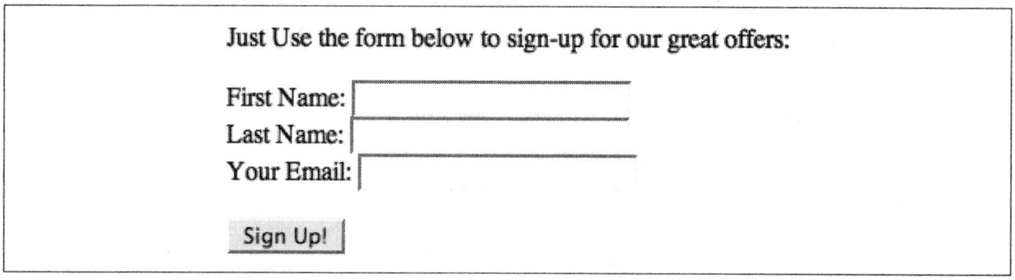

Figure 1-5. A functional but very ugly form

That might have cut it back in '92, but it's wholly unacceptable for this day and age. Take a moment to consider what your normal routine would be at this point: define some classes, apply the classes, write some JavaScript to provide validation routines, etc.

To give you a taste of how the page would look after some Dojoification, take a look at Example 1-5. Don't worry about what every little detail is doing; lots of pages follow on that get into the nooks and crannies of the finer details. For now, just familiarize yourself with the general structure of a page with some dijits snapped into it.

Example 1-5. A form that's not so primitive anymore (thanks to some Dojoification)

```html
<html>
    <head>
        <title>Fun with Dijit!</title>

        <!-- Grab some style sheets for the built-in tundra theme that Dojo offers for
          styling the page, equipping you with a professional style without any additional
          effort required. -->
        <link rel="stylesheet" type="text/css"
          href="http://o.aolcdn.com/dojo/1.1/dijit/themes/tundra/tundra.css" />
        <link rel="stylesheet" type="text/css"
          href="http://o.aolcdn.com/dojo/1.1/dojo/resources/dojo.css" />
        <!-- Add in some plain old CSS to line up the form elements more nicely -->

        <style type="text/css">
            h3 {
                margin : 10px;
            }
            label,input {
                display: block;
                float: left;
                margin-bottom: 5px;
            }
            label {
                text-align: right;
                width: 70px;
                padding-right: 20px;
            }
            br {
                clear: left;
            }
            .grouping {
                width:300px;
                border:solid 1px rgb(230,230,230);
                padding:5px;
                margin:10px;
            }
        </style>

        <!-- Load Base and specify that the page should be parsed for dijits after it
          loads -->
        <script
            type="text/javascript"
            src="http://o.aolcdn.com/dojo/1.1/dojo/dojo.xd.js"
            djConfig="parseOnLoad: true" >
        </script>
```

Example 1-5. A form that's not so primitive anymore (thanks to some Dojoification) (continued)

```
<!-- Load some dijits via dojo.require in the same manner that you would #include
  some files in C programming or perform an import in Java -->
<script type="text/javascript">
    dojo.require("dojo.parser");
    dojo.require("dijit.form.TextBox");
    dojo.require("dijit.form.ValidationTextBox");
    dojo.require("dijit.form.Button");
</script>
<head>

<!-- Specify that the built-in tundra theme should be applied to everything in the
  body of the page. (Dijit relies heavily on CSS so including the appropriate
  theme is crucial.)-->
<body class="tundra">

    <h3>Sign-up for our great offers:</h3>

    <form id="registration_form">

        <!-- Weave some widgets into the page by supplying the tags and including
          a dojoType attribute so the parser can find them and swap them out -->

        <div class="grouping">
            <label>First Name:</label>
            <input type="text"
             maxlength=25
             name="first"
             dojoType="dijit.form.TextBox"
             trim="true"
             propercase="true"/><br>

            <label>Last Name:</label>
            <input type="text"
             maxlength=25
             name="last"
             dojoType="dijit.form.TextBox"
             trim="true"
             propercase="true"/><br>

            <label>Your Email:</label>
            <input type="text"
             maxlength=25
             name="email"
             dojoType="dijit.form.ValidationTextBox"
             trim="true"
             lowercase="true"
             regExp="[a-z0-9._%+-]+@[a-z0-9-]+\.[a-z]{2,4}"
             required="true"
             invalidMessage="Please enter a valid e-mail address"/><br>

            <button dojoType="dijit.form.Button"
             onClick="alert('Boo!')">Sign Up!</button>
```

Example 1-5. A form that's not so primitive anymore (thanks to some Dojoification) (continued)

```
                </div>

            </form>
    </body>
</html>
```

And voilà, Figure 1-6 shows what it looks like, complete simple validation functionality.

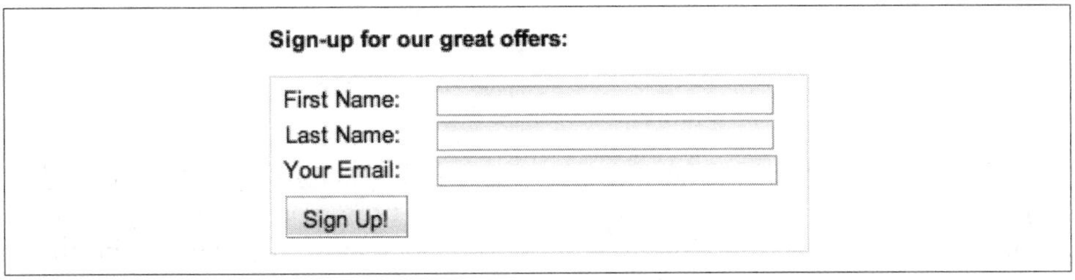

Sign-up for our great offers:

First Name:
Last Name:
Your Email:

Sign Up!

Figure 1-6. A much better looking form, using out-of-the-box dijits

If you're intrigued by the examples in this chapter, and are ready to learn more about Dojo, then you've come to the right place. The following chapters systematically work through the specifics of the toolkit. But first, let's take a quick moment to reflect on what this chapter was all about (as we'll do in every chapter).

Summary

This chapter barely scratched the surface of your journey with Dojo, but it nonetheless covered a lot of ground. After reading this chapter, you should:

- Know where to go to download the toolkit and set up a development environment
- Understand the toolkit's architecture and the key differences between each component
- Understand some of the common parlance used in Dojo development
- Realize some of the benefits of using Firebug during the development cycle
- Understand the basic ideas behind how the toolkit bootstraps itself
- Have an appreciation for how easy it is to use Base and plug out-of-the-box dijits into a page
- Be familiar with the look and feel of Dojo code
- Be excited to read the subsequent chapters and learn more about Dojo

The next chapter will discuss language and browser utilities.

CHAPTER 2

Language and Browser Utilities

This chapter formally introduces the language utilities that you'll find in Base. The language utilities are designed to streamline some of the most commonly worked-around problems in JavaScript programming, and they're designed to be ultra-portable and highly optimized. Regardless of whether you use anything else in the entire toolkit, the constructs presented in this chapter are worth a hard look because they provide augmentation that is difficult to imagine living without once you've gotten used to using them. Manipulating arrays, cloning nodes, adding and removing classes, and calculating margin and content boxes for DOM nodes are among the topics included in this chapter.

Looking Up DOM Nodes

The previous chapter introduced dojo.byId, a toolkit-specific mechanism for looking up DOM nodes in a manner that is more portable and predictable than document. getElementById. Although dojo.byId absolutely pervades Dojo development, there is little value in repeating the previous discussion from Chapter 1; refer back to the previous chapter for a detailed outline involving some of the issues with document. getElementById and how dojo.byId alleviates them. As a reminder, though, here's the full API call for dojo.byId:

```
dojo.byId(/*String*/ id | /*DomNode*/ node, /*DomNode*/doc)  // Returns a DOM Node
```

Example 2-1 lists some other common use patterns.

Example 2-1. Quick reminder about dojo.byId

```
var foo = dojo.byId("foo"); //returns the node with id=foo if one exists
dojo.byId(foo).innerHTML="bar"; //the lookup is a no-op since foo is
                          //a node; then sets innerHTML to "bar"
var bar = dojo.byId("bar", baz); //returns the node with id=bar in document
                          //referenced by baz if one exists
```

Type Checking

In a language with dynamic typing like JavaScript, it's often necessary (and a very good idea) to test the type of variable before performing any operations on it. Although it might not seem like much to test for the type of a variable, it isn't always a freebie, and in practice can simply result in annoyances and bugs because of subtle differences. Base provides a few handy functions to simplify the nuances entailed. Like the other issues we've touched on so far, there are subtleties amongst various browsers involving some of the finer points. The following list summarizes:

isString(/*Any*/ value)
: Returns true if value is a String.

isArray(/*Any*/ value)
: Returns true if value is an Array.

isFunction(/*Any*/ value)
: Returns true if value is a Function.

isObject(/*Any*/ value)
: Returns true if value is an Object (including an Array and Function) or null.

isArrayLike(/*Any*/ value)
: Returns true if value is an Array but also allows for more permissive possibilities. For example, the built-in arguments value that can be accessed from within a Function object is especially an oddball in that it does not support built-in methods such as push; however, it is array-like in that it is a list of values that can be indexed.

isAlien(/*Any*/ value)
: Returns true if value is a built-in function or native function such as an ActiveX component but does not respect the normal checks such as the instanceof Function.

Duck Typing

A concept commonly involved in dynamic programming languages like Python and JavaScript called *duck typing* provides a common thread for many of the functions just introduced. Duck typing is based upon the saying that if it walks like a duck and quacks like a duck, then it's a duck. Basically, what that means is that if a particular data member exhibits the minimal necessary properties to be a particular data type, then that's good enough to assume that it is that particular data type.

For example, the built-in arguments member qualifying as an array via the isArrayLike function hopefully ties this theme together. When you consider the inherent dynamism in a language that does not require you to declare a particular variable to always be a particular data type (dynamic binding), duck typing is a great vehicle to inspect the type of an object when necessary.

For example, invoking the typeof operator on an ordinary array such as [ ] returns object while Base's isArray function performs some duck type checks behind the scenes and returns true for an array such as [ ].

 Duck typing is a fundamental programming concept in JavaScript and much of the toolkit, so this discussion is more practical to your day-to-day programming than you might imagine at first glance.

The bottom line is that Base's type checking functions can save you time and spare you from nonintuitive browser inconsistencies, so use them well, and use them often.

String Utilities

Trimming any existing whitespace from a string is an increasingly common operation. The next time you need to do this, use Base's trim function instead of writing your own.

 There can be subtle performance issues with even the seemingly most trivial utility functions, and using the toolkit provides you with the benefits and collective knowledge of a community that has given careful consideration to such issues.

Here's an example of trim at work:

```
var s = "  this is a value with whitespace padding each side    ";
s = dojo.trim(s); //"this is a value with whitespace padding each side"
```

Core's string module also includes a few other useful string functions. Each of these examples assumes that you have already fetched the dojo.string module via a dojo. require statement.

dojo.string.pad
>   Pads a string value and guarantees that it will exactly fill a particular number of characters. By default, padding fills in on the left. An optional parameter causes padding to fill in from the right:
>
>    ```
>    dojo.string.pad("", 5); // "00000"
>    dojo.string.pad("", 5, " "); // "     "
>    dojo.string.pad("0", 5, "1"); // "11110"
>    dojo.string.pad("0", 5, "1", true); // "01111"
>    ```

dojo.string.substitute
>   Provides parameterized substitution on a string, optionally allowing a transform function and/or another object to supply context:
>
>    ```
>    //Returns "Jack and Jill went up a hill."
>    dojo.string.substitute("${0} and ${1} went up a hill.", ["Jack", "Jill"]);
>    ```

```
//"*Jack* and *Jill* went up a hill."
dojo.string.substitute("${person1} and ${person2} went up a hill.", {person1 :
"Jack", person2: "Jill"});
dojo.string.substitute("${0} and ${1} went up a hill.", ["Jack", "Jill"],
function(x) {
  return "*"+x+"*";
});
```

`dojo.string.trim`

At the cost of a little more size than Base's implementation, Core's `string` module provides a slightly more efficient version of `trim` that can be used when performance really matters:

```
dojo.string.trim( /* your string value */);
```

Array Processing

Arrays are one of the most fundamental data structures in any imperative programming language, including JavaScript. Unfortunately, however, standardized array operations are not supported by all mainstream browsers, and as long as that is the case, it's immensely helpful to have a toolkit that protects you from the bare metal. For that matter, even if the next version of each major browser supported arrays in a completely uniform manner, there would still be way too many people out there using older browsers to begin thinking about going back to the bare metal anytime soon.

 You may find it interesting that the various language tools have been optimized for performance, providing wrapped usage of the native Array implementations wherever possible, but emulating functionality for browsers like IE when it is missing.

Fortunately, Dojo strives to keep up with Mozilla's feature rich implementation of the Array object (*http://developer.mozilla.org/en/docs/Core_JavaScript_1.5_Reference*). As long as you have the toolkit with you, you'll never be caught defenseless again. And in case you have already forgotten from our discussion of `dojo.byId` in Chapter 1 that you really can't take much for granted in the current browser ecosystem, the next section should reinvigorate your enthusiasm and might even surprise you.

Finding Locations of Elements

Two very routine array operations involve finding the index of an element, which is really one and the same as determining if an element exists at all. Base facilitates this process with two self-explanatory operations, `dojo.indexOf` and `dojo.lastIndexOf`. Each of these functions returns an integer that provides the index of the element if it exists; the value -1 is returned if the element was not found at all. These function signatures also include an additional parameter that indicates the value that should be used as an initial location in case you don't want to start from the very beginning or end of the array. The signature is the same for each function:

```
dojo.indexOf(/*Array*/ array, /*Any*/ value, /*Integer?*/ fromIndex)
//returns Integer

dojo.lastIndexOf(/*Array*/ array, /*Any*/ value, /*Integer?*/ fromIndex)
//returns Integer
```

 If you've been primarily developing with Firefox for a while, you may be surprised to learn that native Array objects in IE6 and IE7 do not even support the indexOf method. Unfortunately, this kind of semantic misunderstanding about something that may seem so obvious can be one of the hardest kinds of bugs to track down.

The following code snippet illustrates some basic usage of these methods:

```
var foo = [1,2,3];
var bar = [4,5,6,5,6];
var baz = [1,2,3];

dojo.indexOf([foo, bar], baz); // -1
dojo.indexOf(foo, 3); // 2
dojo.indexOf(bar, 6, 2); // 2
dojo.indexOf(bar, 6, 3); // 4

dojo.lastIndexOf(bar, 6); // 4
```

A more subtle point about these methods is that they perform shallow comparisons, which in the case of complex data types like Array, means that the comparison is by reference. The following snippet clarifies with a concrete example:

```
bop = [4,5,6,5,6, foo]; // bop contains a nested Array
dojo.indexOf(bop, foo); //5, because (a reference to) foo is contained in bop
dojo.indexOf(bop, [1,2,3]); //-1, because foo is not the same object as [1,2,3]
```

Testing Elements for a Condition

It is often the case that you may be interested in knowing if each element of an array meets a particular condition, or if any element of an array meets a particular condition. Base provides the every and some functions for performing this kind of testing. The input parameters are the array, a function that each element of the array is passed into, and an optional parameter that can supply the context (this) for the function:

```
dojo.every([2,4,6], function (x) { return x % 2 == 0 }); //true
dojo.every([2,4,6,7], function (x) { return x % 2 == 0 }); //false
```

```
dojo.some([3,5,7], function f(x) { return x % 2 == 0 }); //false
dojo.some([3,5,7,8], function f(x) { return x % 2 == 0 }); //true
```

Iterating Over Elements

The forEach function passes each element of an array into a function that takes a single parameter and does not return any value at all. It is generally used to iterate over each element of an array as an ordinary for loop. Here's the signature:

```
dojo.forEach(/*Array*/ array, /*Function*/ function) // No return value
```

In its simplest form forEach works like so:

```
dojo.forEach([1,2,3], function(x) {
    console.log(x);
});
```

Some obvious benefits of forEach is that it introduces less clutter than explicitly introducing a for loop and requiring you to manage a counter variable and also allows you to introduce the Array variable inline. However, perhaps the most important thing that it does is leverage the closure provided by the function as the second parameter to protect the immediate context from the counter variable and other variables that may be introduced in the loop's block from persisting. Like other utility functions, forEach provides an optional parameter that can supply the context for the inline functions.

To illustrate how forEach can save you from unexpected consequences, consider the following snippet of code:

```
var nodes = getSomeNodes();

for(var x=0; x<nodes.length; x++){
    nodes[x].onclick = function(){
        console.debug("clicked:", x);
    }
}
```

Which value of "x" would you expect here? Since the enclosure is over the *lexical variable* x and not the value of x, all calls get the *last value*. forEach gets us out of this handily by creating a new lexical scope. This variation illustrates how to iterate over the array and produce the expected value:

```
var nodes = getSomeNodes();
var idx = 0;
dojo.forEach(nodes, function(node, idx){
    node.onclick = function(){
        console.debug("clicked:", idx);
    }
});
```

Transforming Elements

While the map and filter functions have the same function signature as forEach, they're very different in that they apply some custom logic to each element of the array and return another array without modifying the original one.

 While you could technically modify the original array through the custom map and filter functions, it's generally expected that map and filter will be free of side effects. In other words, introduce side effects with a lot of discretion and an explicit comment saying as much.

As programmers from functional programming languages (or even programming languages with functional extensions like Python) know all too well, map and filter grow on you quickly because they provide so much functionality with such concise syntax.

The map function might almost sound mysterious if you haven't encountered it before; it's actually named self-descriptively because it builds a mapping from the array you give it via a transform function. The following example illustrates:

```
var z = dojo.map([2,3,4], function(x) {
  return x + 1
}); //returns [3,4,5]
```

For comparison purposes, consider how you might compute the value for z in the example above without the map function:

```
var a = [2,3,4];
var z = [];
for (var i=0; i < a.length; i++) {
  z.push(a[i] +1);
}
```

Like forEach, one of the benefits of using map directly is that the overall expression is clearer, resulting in more maintainable code. You also get the same kind of anonymous function benefit in that a closure surrounds the code block, whereas variables introduced via intermediate calculations would pollute the context without the closure.

The filter function is also a self-descriptive function in that it filters an array according to a function's criteria. Here it is at work:

```
dojo.filter([2,3,4], function(x) {
  return x % 2 == 0
}); //returns [2,4]
```

Implementing a block of equivalent code is relatively simple but does require more bookkeeping and clutter—and more opportunity for typos and bugs:

```
var a = [2,3,4];
var z = [];
for (var i=0; i < a.length; i++) {
```

```
    if (a[i] % 2 == 0)
        z.push(a[i]);
}
```

Like the other array functions provided by Base, you can also provide additional parameters that supply context for or `map` or `filter` if you need them:

```
function someContext() { this.y = 2; }
var context = new someContext;
dojo.filter([2,3,4], function(x) {return x % this.y==0}, context); //returns [2,4]
```

String-As-Function Style Arguments

Base also provides the ability to create the shorthand "string-as-function" type arguments for the `forEach`, `map`, `filter`, `every`, and `some` functions. In general, this approach is less verbose than writing a function wrapper and is especially handy for really simple cases where you're doing a quick transform. Basically, you just provide a string value with the function body in it versus the entire function. Three special keywords have special context if they appear in the string:

`item`
> Provides a reference to the item that is currently being processed

`array`
> Provides a reference to the entire array that is being processed

`index`
> Provides a reference to the index of the item that is currently being processed

Consider the following example, which demonstrates two equivalent approaches for achieving the same end:

```
var a = new Array(1,2,3,...);

//A lot of extra typing for very little purpose
a.forEach(function(x) {console.log(x);}); //approach one

//A lot less typing so that you can get work done quickly
a.forEach("console.log(item)"); //approach two
```

 Using the shortened string-as-function approach to array-like methods can make your code more concise, but it may make it difficult to track down bugs, so use discretion. For example, consider the following variation of the previous code snippet:

```
var a = new Array(1,2,3,...);
a.forEach("console.log(items)"); //oops...extra "s" on items
```

Because there's an extra "s" on the special term `item`, it won't act as the iterator anymore, effectively rendering the `forEach` method as a no-op. Unless you have an especially good eye for tracking down these types of misspellings, this could cost you debugging time.

Managing Source Code with Modules

If you've programmed for any amount of time, you've been exposed to the concept of grouping related pieces of code into related blocks, whether they be called libraries, packages, or modules, and pulling in these resources when you need them via a mechanism like an `import` statement or a `#include` preprocessor directive. Dojo's official means of accomplishing the same kind of concept is via `dojo.provide` and `dojo.require`, respectively.

In Dojo parlance, reusable chunks of code are called *resources* and collections of related resources are grouped into what are known as *modules*. Base provides two incredibly simple constructs for importing modules and resources: `dojo.require` and `dojo.provide`. In short, you include a `dojo.provide` statement as the first line of a file that you want to make available for a `dojo.require` statement to pull into a page. As it turns out, `dojo.require` is a lot more than just a placeholder like a `SCRIPT` tag; it takes care of mapping a module to a particular location on disk, fetching the code, and caching modules and resources that have previously been `dojo.require`d. Given that each `dojo.require` statement incurs at least one round trip call to the server if the resource is not already loaded, the caching can turn out to be a tremendous optimization; even the caching that you gain from requiring a resource one time and ensuring it is available locally from that point forward is a great optimization.

Motivation for Managing the Mayhem

For anything but the smallest of projects, the benefits of using this approach are irrefutable. The ease of maintenance and simplicity gained in extending or embedding code in multiple places is a key enabler to getting work done quickly and effectively. As obvious as it may sound, importing code in the manner just described hasn't always been obvious to web developers, and many web projects have turned into difficult-to-maintain monstrosities because of improper source code management in the implementation. For example, a typical workflow has been to take a JavaScript file that's in a static directory of a web server and to insert it into the page using a `SCRIPT` tag like so:

```
<script src="/static/someScript.js" type="text/javascript"></script>
```

OK, there's probably nothing wrong with that for one or two script tags—but what about when you have multiple pages that need the same tools provided by the scripts? Well, then you might need to include those `SCRIPT` tags in multiple pages; later on down the road you might end up with a lot of loose scripts, and when you have to start manually keeping track of all of them, the situation can get a little bit unwieldy. Sure, back in the day when a few hundred lines of JavaScript might have been all that was in a page, you wouldn't have needed a more robust mechanism for managing resources, but modern applications might include tens of thousands of lines of JavaScript. How can you possibly manage it all without a good tool for fetching on demand and lazy loading?

In addition to mitigating the configuration management nightmare that might otherwise await you, the dojo.provide and dojo.require abstraction also allows the build tools that are provided in Util to do pretty amazing things like condense multiple files (each requiring a synchronous request) into a single file that can be requested and endure much less latency. Without the right abstractions that explicitly define dependences, build tool features that could be freebies suddenly become impossibilities.

A final benefit of a well-defined system like dojo.provide and dojo.require is the ability to manage related resources by clustering them into namespaces so that overall naming collisions are minimized and code is more easily organized and maintained. Even though dojo *namespaces* are really just hierarchies of nested objects simplified with dot notation, they are nonetheless quite effective for organizing namespaces and accomplish the very same purpose.

In fact, organizing resources by namespace is so common that Dojo provides a Base function called dojo.setObject. This function works by accepting two arguments. The first argument is an object hierarchy that will be automatically created, and the second value is what will be mapped to the hierarchy:

```
dojo.setObject(/* String */ object, /* Any */ value, /* Object */ context)
//returns Any
```

Example 2-2 illustrates.

Example 2-2. Namespace organization with dojo.setObject

```
var foo  = {bar : {baz : {qux : 1}}}; //nest some objects the 'long' way
console.log(foo.bar.baz.qux); //displays 1

//Or you could opt to do it in one crisp statement without matching all of the braces...
dojo.setObject("foo.bar.baz.qux", 1); //crisper syntax
console.log(foo.bar.baz.qux); //displays 1

//If you supply an optional context, the Object is set relative to the context instead of
//the global context, dojo.global
var someContext = {};
dojo.setObject("foo.bar.baz.qux", 23, someContext);
console.log(someContext.foo.bar.baz.qux); //displays 23
```

The use of dojo.setObject is nothing more than syntactic sugar, but it can significantly declutter code and the tediousness of matching braces, etc., whenever you do need it.

 The OpenAjax Alliance (*http://www.openajax.org*), a consortium of vendors banding together to promote openness and standards amongst advanced web technologies, strongly encourages the practice of using dotted object notation to organize namespaces.

Custom Module Example Over XDomain

A short concrete example is in order to put dojo.require and dojo.provide into perspective. First, consider a simple module that provides a trivial function, such as Fibonacci. In Example 2-3, the resource is also associated with a module. Although grouping resources into modules is not strictly necessary, it is almost always good practice. Throughout this book, you'll commonly see dtdg (for *Dojo: The Definitive Guide*) used to denote a generic namespace for modules.

Fibonacci Sequence

The Fibonacci is a sequence named after the 13th-century mathematician Leonardo of Pisa and reveals some intriguing properties of numbers. As it happens, Fibonacci numbers turn up in pseudorandom number generators, optimization techniques, music, nature, and are closely related to the golden ratio.

The Fibonacci sequence is defined as follows:

```
fibonacci(0) = 0
fibonacci(x <= 1) = x
fibonacci(x > 1) = fibonacci(x-1) + fibonacci(x-2)
```

You can read more about it at *http://en.wikipedia.org/wiki/Fibonacci_number*.

Example 2-3. Defining a simple simple module (dtdg.foo)

```
/*
   The dojo.provide statement specifies that this .js source file provides a
   dtdg.foo module. Semantically, the dtdg.foo module also provides a namespace for
   functions that are included in the module On disk, this file
   would be named foo.js and be placed inside of a dtdg directory.
*/
dojo.provide("dtdg.foo");

//Note that the function is relative to the module's namespace
dtdg.foo.fibonacci = function(x) {
  if (x < 0)
    throw Exception("Illegal argument");

  if (x <= 1)
    return x;

  return dtdg.foo.fibonacci(x-1) + dtdg.foo.fibonacci(x-2);
}
```

You will almost always want to group your resources into logical modules and associate them with a namespace. In addition to being a good implementation practice, it also prevents you from inadvertently clobbering symbols in the global namespace as well as preventing anyone else from doing the same to you. After all, that's one of the motivators for using dojo.provide and dojo.require in the first place!

In another page somewhere, you determine that you want to use your dtdg.foo module to amaze the elementary school math junkies. Instead of rewriting your well-tested function from scratch and potentially making a mistake that could lead to embarrassment, you instead decide to reuse it via dojo.require. Example 2-4 shows how you would use a local module in conjunction with the rest of the toolkit being loaded over the CDN. This example assumes that the following HTML file is saved alongside a directory called dtdg that contains the module from Example 2-3.

Example 2-4. Using a local module with XDomain bootstrappping

```
<html>
    <head>
        <title>Fun With Fibonacci!title>

        <script
          type="text/javascript"
          src="http://o.aolcdn.com/dojo/1.1/dojo/dojo.xd.js"
          djConfig="baseUrl:'./'">
        </script>

        <script type="text/javascript">
          dojo.registerModulePath("dtdg", "./dtdg");
          dojo.require("dtdg.foo");
          /* at this point, the dojo.require is being satisfied asynchronously
          because we're using an Xdomain build of Dojo. Better wrap any references
          to dtdg.foo in an addOnLoad block */

          dojo.addOnLoad(function( ) {
              dojo.body( ).innerHTML = "guess what? fibonacci(5) = ", dtdg.foo.fibonacci(5);
          });
        </script>

    </head>
    <body>
    </body>
</html>
```

The key concept to take away from the previous listing is that it's fairly straightforward to dojo.require a resource into the page and then use it. However, there are a few finer points worth highlighting.

For local installations, Dojo looks in the root level directory of the toolkit for modules—but when you're performing XDomain loading, the "real" root directory of the toolkit would be somewhere off on AOL's server. Thus, a special configuration switch, baseUrl is passed into djConfig in order to designate the starting point for looking up local modules—dtdg.foo in this case.

 djConfig is simply a means of providing specific configuration parameters to the toolkit. It is covered in the next section, but for now, just roll with it.

The dojo.registerModulePath function simply associates a top-level namespace, its first parameter, to a physical directory that is relative to baseUrl, its second parameter.

 Don't forget to take extra care when configuring module paths with dojo.registerModulePath. It is not uncommon to be off by one level in the directory structure if you forget that the relative directory is specified to the dojo.js file—not the root level of the toolkit. Additionally, ending a module path with a trailing forward slash has been known to intermittently cause problems, so you should take care to avoid that practice as well.

Everything that is defined in the custom module is made available via the call to dojo.require. For example, if the dtdg.foo module had contained additional functions or symbols, they would be available after the dojo.require("dtdg.foo") statement. As usual, we didn't reference anything provided by dtdg.foo outside of the addOnLoad block.

 There is not necessarily a one-to-one mapping between .js source files and the functions that are dojo.provided in them, but it is generally enforced as a matter of style. Exceptions include cases where some functions might not be exposed because they are considered private as far as an API is concerned.

You may have also noticed a call to dojo.body( ) in the previous code listing. Essentially, this call is just a shortcut for returning the body of the current document—as opposed to document.body, which is considerably less convenient.

Fibonacci Example with Local Toolkit Installation

For comparison purposes, Example 2-5 shows the very same example, but this time it uses a local installation of Dojo with the dtdg module located at the root level of the toolkit alongside the *dojo* directory that contains Core so that no reference to baseUrl or or a call to registerModulePath is necessary. This convenience is available because Dojo automatically searches for modules in the directory alongside Core, which is a logical and convenient location to maintain them.

Example 2-5. Using dtdg.foo with a local toolkit installation

```
<html>
    <head>
      <title>Fun With Fibonacci!title>

      <script
        type="text/javascript"
        src="your/relative/path/from/this/page/to/dojo/dojo.js" >
      </script>

      <script type="text/javascript">
        dojo.require("dtdg.foo");
        /* we use an addOnLoad block even though it's all local as a matter of habit*/
        dojo.addOnLoad(function( ) {
            dojo.body( ).innerHTML = "guess what? fibonacci(5) = ", dtdg.foo.fibonacci(5);
        });
      </script>

    </head>
    <body>
    </body>
</html>
```

Building a Magic Genie Example Module

As an example of some of the concepts from this chapter, let's build a module. Because life can be so hard at times, a magic genie that can give us answers whenever we need it would be a godsend. (Dojo might simply be pure automation that seems like magic, but genies are *real* magic.)

To get started building a module, recall that it's a good idea to namespace it. Example 2-6 sticks with the *dtdg* namespace, which we've been using so far in this book, and associates a *Genie* resource with it. If you don't already have a local directory called *dtdg*, go ahead and create one now. Inside of it, open up a new file called *Genie.js*, where we'll include the magic shown in Example 2-6.

Example 2-6. The implementation for a magic genie module

```
//always include the dojo.provide statement first thing
dojo.provide("dtdg.Genie");

//set up a namespace for the genie
dtdg.Genie = function( ) {}

//wire in some predictions, reminiscent of a magic 8 ball
dtdg.Genie.prototype._predictions = [
        "As I see it, yes",
        "Ask again later",
        "Better not tell you now",
        "Cannot predict now",
```

Example 2-6. The implementation for a magic genie module (continued)

```
            "Concentrate and ask again",
            "Don't count on it",
            "It is certain",
            "It is decidedly so",
            "Most likely",
            "My reply is no",
            "My sources say no",
            "Outlook good",
            "Outlook not so good",
            "Reply hazy, try again",
            "Signs point to yes",
            "Very doubtful",
            "Without a doubt",
            "Yes",
            "Yes - definitely",
            "You may rely on it"
    ];

//wire in an initialization function that constructs the interface
dtdg.Genie.prototype.initialize = function( ) {

    var label = document.createElement("p");
    label.innerHTML = "Ask a question. The genie knows the answer...";

    var question = document.createElement("input");
    question.size = 50;

    var button = document.createElement("button");
    button.innerHTML = "Ask!";
    button.onclick = function( ) {
        alert(dtdg.Genie.prototype._getPrediction( ));
        question.value = "";
    }

    var container = document.createElement("div");
    container.appendChild(label);
    container.appendChild(question);
    container.appendChild(button);

    dojo.body( ).appendChild(container);
}

//wire in the primary function for interaction
dtdg.Genie.prototype._getPrediction = function( ) {
    //get a number betweeen 0 and 19 and index into predictions
    var idx = Math.round(Math.random( )*19)
    return this._predictions[idx];
}
```

Essentially, the listing does nothing more than provide a Function object called
dtdg.Genie that exposes one "public" function, initialize.

In Dojo, the convention of prefixing internal members that should be treated as private with a leading underscore is common and will be used throughout this book. It's important to really respect such conventions because "private" members may be quite volatile.

The listing is laden with comments, and from a web development standpoint, the logic should hopefully be easy enough to follow. (If it's not, this would be a great time to review some HTML and JavaScript fundamentals elsewhere before reading on.)

To actually put the magic genie to use, we'll need to modify the basic template, as shown in Example 2-7.

Example 2-7. A web page utilizing the magic genie

```
<html>
    <head>
        <title>Fun With the Genie!</title>

        <script
          type="text/javascript"
          src="http://o.aolcdn.com/dojo/1.1/dojo/dojo.xd.js">
          djConfig="modulePaths:{dtdg:'./dtdg'},baseUrl:'./'">
        </script>

        <script type="text/javascript">
            // require in the module
            dojo.require("dtdg.Genie");

            // safely reference dtdg.Genie inside of addOnLoad
            dojo.addOnLoad(function( ) {

                //create an instance
                var g = new dtdg.Genie;

                //fire it up, which takes care of the rest
                g.initialize( );
            });
        </script>
    </head>
    <body>
    </body>
</html>
```

This example illustrates the reusability and portability of the dtdg.Genie module. You simply require it into the page and, once it's initialized, it "just works." (And so long as the user doesn't read the source code, it truly remains magical.) A finer point worth clarifying is the use of djConfig to configure Dojo before bootstrapping: the modulePaths is inlined to qualify the location of the module relative to baseUrl, which is defined as the current working directory. Thus, from a physical standpoint, the file structure might look like Figure 2-1.

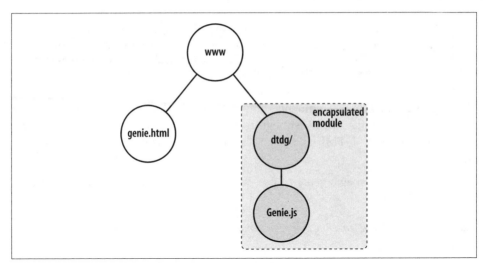

Figure 2-1. The way that your module should be laid out on disk

JavaScript Object Utilities

Three of Base's language utilities facilitate operations you may need to routinely perform on objects: mixin, extend, and clone.

 Dojo uses mixin and extend in its dojo.declare implementation, which is the toolkit's mechanism for simulating class-based inheritance. dojo.declare is covered extensively in Chapter 10.

Mixins

JavaScript allows you to approximate lightweight classes by housing a collection of properties and methods inside a constructor function. You may then create object instances of these classes by invoking the constructor function with the new operator. As you might expect, it can sometimes be quite convenient to add additional properties to an object, whether it be to make something dynamic happen on-the-fly or as part of a well crafted design that maximizes code reuse. Either way, mixin provides a compact way of handling the implementation details for you.

 In terms of object-oriented design with JavaScript, you'll see mixin used extensively throughout the toolkit to reuse blocks of code.

The API for using the toolkit's mixin functions entails providing an indeterminate number of objects, where the first objects gets the other objects *mixed* into it:

```
dojo.mixin(/*Object*/ o, /*Object*/ o, ...) //Returns Object
```

Here's an example of mixin:

```
function Man( ) {
  this.x = 10;
}

function Myth( ) {
  this.y = 20;
}

function Legend( ) {
  this.z = 30;
}

var theMan = new Man;
var theMyth = new Myth;
var theLegend = new Legend;

function ManMythLegend( ) {}
var theManTheMythTheLegend = new ManMythLegend;

//mutate theManTheMythTheLegend by mixing in the three objects
dojo.mixin(theManTheMythTheLegend, theMan, theMyth, theLegend);
```

 Note that all parameters to mixin are actual object instances—not function declarations.

Extending Object Prototypes

Base's extend function works just like mixin except that it adds all properties and methods of the mixins to a *constructor function's prototype* so that all future instances created with the constructor will automatically include these new properties and methods:

```
dojo.extend(/*Function*/constructor, /*Object*/props, ... ) //Returns Function
```

Here's an example:

```
function Man( ) {
  this.x = 10;
}

function Myth( ) {
  this.y = 20;
}

function Legend( ) {
  this.z = 30;
}

var theMan = new Man;
var theMyth = new Myth;
```

```
var theLegend = new Legend;

function ManMythLegend( ) {}

var theManTheMythTheLegend = new ManMythLegend;

dojo.extend(ManMythLegend, theMan, theMyth, theLegend);

var theTheManTheMythTheLegend = new ManMythLegend;
```

Thus, the primary difference to remember is that mixin produces a single object instance that is the result of mixing in additional objects while extend actually modifies a function's prototype.

Another great application for extend is the ability to create classes in a more lightweight fashion than would normally be required when wiring everything up via the prototype property of an Object. Using extend in this way is somewhat a matter of style, although the end result is usually more compact. Here's a retake of our magic genie example from Example 2-6 that illustrates:

```
dojo.provide("dtdg.Genie");

//define the object
dtdg.Genie = function( ) {}

//and now extend it
dojo.extend(dtdg.Genie, {
    _predictions : [
        "As I see it, yet",
        "Ask again later",
        "Better not tell you now",
        "Cannot predict now",
        "Concentrate and ask again",
        "Don't count on it",
        "It is certain",
        "It is decidedly so",
        "Most likely",
        "My reply is no",
        "My sources say no",
        "Outlook good",
        "Outlook not so good",
        "Reply hazy, try again",
        "Signs point to yes",
        "Very doubtful",
        "Without a doubt",
        "Yes",
        "Yes - definitely",
        "You may rely on it"
    ],

    initialize : function( ) {
        var label = document.createElement("p");
        label.innerHTML = "Ask a question. The genie knows the answer...";
```

```
        var question = document.createElement("input");
        question.size = 50;

        var button = document.createElement("button");
        button.innerHTML = "Ask!";
        button.onclick = function( ) {
            alert(dtdg.Genie.prototype._getPrediction( ));
            question.value = "";
        }

        var container = document.createElement("div");
        container.appendChild(label);
        container.appendChild(question);
        container.appendChild(button);

        dojo.body( ).appendChild(container);
    },

getPrediction : function( ) {
    //get a number betweeen 0 and 19 and index into predictions
    var idx = Math.round(Math.random( )*19)
    return this._predictions[idx];
    }
});
```

 Don't accidentally forget and leave a trailing comma after the final element of the Object, which is quite common when refactoring and massive cut/paste operations occur. While Firefox silently forgives you, it may actually do more harm than good because IE will just outright bust.

Cloning Objects

Although JavaScript performs shallow copies in assignments involving JavaScript objects and DOM nodes, you may often find yourself needing to *clone*, or perform deep copies, of object hierarchies. Base's clone function is a highly efficient ticket to achieving just that. Consider the following simple example:

```
function foo( ) {
    this.bar = "baz";
}

var foo1 = new foo;
var foo2 = foo1; //shallow copy

console.log(foo1.bar);
console.log(foo2.bar);

foo1.bar = "qux"; //changing foo1 also changes foo2

console.log(foo1.bar);  // qux
console.log(foo2.bar);  // qux
```

```
foo3 = new foo
foo4 = dojo.clone(foo3); //deep copy

foo3.bar = "qux";

console.log(foo3.bar); // qux
console.log(foo4.bar); // baz
```

Manipulating Object Context

Although the global `window` object provides the outermost layer of context for a web application, there may be times when you need to swap out the default context for another one. For example, you may want to persist the exact state of a session when the user exits an application, or you might have a custom execution environment that's already been preconfigured for a particular circumstance. Instead of having code that manually iterates over sets of conditions to configure the environment each time, you might opt to use Base's window facilities to swap out the existing context for another one.

The following function allows you to change out the `dojo.global` object and `dojo.doc` at will. Note that while `dojo.doc` is simply a reference to the `window.document` by default, it does provide a uniform mechanism for identifying the context's current document, which again can be quite useful for situations in which managed object contexts are involved. `dojo.body()` is a shortcut for obtaining the body of a document.

 The body element is not explicitly defined for a strict XHTML document and some other documents you may encounter.

At a minimum, you should be aware of the following three functions from Base for manipulating context:

```
dojo.doc //Returns Document
dojo.body() //Returns DomNode
dojo.setContext(/*Object*/globalObject, /*Document*/globalDocument)
```

Finally, in the spirit of flexibility, Base also provides two functions that allow you to evaluate a function in the context of either a different `dojo.global` environment or a different `dojo.doc` than the one that currently exists:

```
dojo.withGlobal(/*Object*/globalObject, /*Function*/callback, /*Object*/thisObject,
/*Array*/callbackArgs)
dojo.withDoc(/*Object*/documentObject, /*Function*/callback, /*Object*/thisObject,
/*Array*/callbackArgs)
```

It should be noted that using a Dojo function to operate *extensively* in another document or `window` is not a well-tested usage of the toolkit, so you may encounter support issues if going down that route. Standard usage normally entails loading

Dojo into every document where you plan to use it. For lightweight operations, however, the context functions discussed in this section should work fine.

Partially Applying Parameters

Base's partial function allows you to partially apply parameters to a function as they become available and perform final execution of the function at a later time. Or, you might just need to apply all of the parameters at once and then pass around a function reference that can be executed—which is a little less messy than passing around the function and the parameters all at the same time and a pattern that is commonly used throughout the toolkit. Here's the API for partial:

```
dojo.partial(*/Function|String*/func /*, arg1, ..., argN*/) //Returns Any
```

To illustrate, here's a simple example of partial being used to partially apply parameters to a function that adds a series of numbers:

```
function addThree(x,y,z) { console.log(x+y+z);}

//apply two args now
f = dojo.partial(addThree, 100,10);

//apply the last one later
f = dojo.partial(f, 1);

//now evaluate
f(); //111
```

Curry

Another related concept to partial called *currying* is also worth knowing about. A curry function works like partial in that it returns partial functions that you can pass remaining arguments into; however, these partial functions stand on their own as first-class functions, allowing you to continue filling in missing parameters one at a time. Then, once they have all of their arguments filled, curried functions automatically execute. It may not sound like much, but such behavior is quite sophisticated once you think about it.

To be clear, partial is not synonymous with currying. partial might allow partial arguments to be applied, but it never executes the function automatically once all arguments have been applied. Additionally, the partial function has to explicitly be involved in all instances of applying partial functions and final execution because it does all of the internal bookkeeping for you, i.e., each intermediate partial function can't operate without explicit use of the partial function itself.

If you're interested in a closer look, an implementation of a curry function is available in the module dojox.lang.functional.curry. Appendix B provides survey coverage of DojoX topics.

Hitching an Object to a Specific Context

Base's hitch function is quite similar to partial in that it allows you partially apply parameters to a function, but it also has the interesting twist that it also allows you to permanently bind (or hitch) a function to a specific execution context, regardless of whatever the final execution context becomes. This can be especially handy for situations in which you have callback functions and will never fully know what the final execution context (and thus, this) will be. Here's the API:

```
dojo.hitch(/*Object*/scope, /*Function||String*/method /*, arg1, ... , argN*/)
//Returns Any
```

And to illustrate, here's a simple example that rewires an Object method:

```
var foo = {
    name : "Foo",
    greet : function( ) {
        console.log("Hi, I'm", this.name);
    }
}

var bar = {
    name : "Bar",
    greet : function( ) {
        console.log("Hi, I'm", this.name);
    }
}

foo.greet( ); //Hi, I'm Foo
bar.greet( ); //Hi, I'm Bar

/* Bind bar's greet method to another context */
bar.greet = dojo.hitch(foo, "greet");

/ * Bar is now an impersonator */
bar.greet( ); // Hi, I'm Foo
```

To be clear, because the greet function explicitly references a context with this, the following code would not have successfully rewired the greet method:

```
bar.greet = foo.greet;
bar.greet( );
```

 You might find it interesting to know that with respect to implementation, hitch provides the basis for partial and calling hitch with null as the scope is the functional equivalent of calling partial.

The section "Hitching Up Callbacks" in Chapter 4 provides an example of using hitch to manage the context for data that is used within an asynchronous callback function—one of its most common use cases because the callback function has a different this context than the containing Object.

Delegation and Inheritance

Delegation is a programming pattern that entails one object relying on another object to perform an action, instead of implementing that action itself. Delegation is at the very heart of JavaScript as a prototype-based language because it is the pattern through which object properties are resolved in the *prototype chain*. Although delegation is at the very crux of JavaScript's inheritance implementation, which relies on the prototype chain being resolved at runtime, delegation as a pattern is very different from inheritance in true class-based programming languages like Java and C++, which often (but not always) resolve class hierarchies at compile time instead of runtime. In that regard, it is especially noteworthy that as a runtime feature, delegation necessarily relies on *dynamic binding* as a language feature.

Dojo's delegate function wraps up the details of dispatching delegation of an Object's function through the following API:

```
dojo.delegate(/*Object*/delegate, properties) //Returns Object
```

Building on the previous example, the following blurb demonstrates how you might use delegation to get an Object that dispatches responsibility for a function to its delegate:

```
function Foo( ) {
    this.talk = function( ) {console.log("Hello, my name is", this.name);}
}

// Get a Function object back that has the name property
// but dispatches, or delegates, responsiblity for the talk function
// to the instance of Foo that is passed in.
var bar = dojo.delegate(new Foo, {name : "Bar"});

// The talk method is resolved through the Foo delegate
bar.talk( );
```

Chapter 10 is devoted to the inheritance pattern facilitated by the toolkit's dojo.declare function, which can be used to simulate class hierarchies with JavaScript; the chapter also includes additional discussion on various approaches to accomplishing inheritance patterns.

DOM Utilities

Recall that Dojo intentionally does not attempt to replace core JavaScript functionality; on the contrary, it only augments it where value can be added so that you can write portable code and incur less boilerplate. For this reason, you won't see direct replacements for common DOM operations such as appendChild, removeChild, and so on. Still, there are many utilities that could make DOM manipulation a lot simpler, and this section is all about how Base helps to make that happen.

Ancestry

Base packs several useful functions that augment and supplement common DOM functions. The first of these functions, isDescendant, shown in Table 2-1, is self-descriptive. You provide it two arguments (id values or actual nodes), where the first argument is the node of interest and the second argument is a potential ancestor. If the node of interest is in fact a member of the potential ancestor's DOM tree, the function returns true.

Table 2-1. Base function for manipulating and handling the DOM

Name	Return type	Comment
dojo.isDescendant(/*String | DomNode*/node, /* String | DomNode*/potentialAncestor)	Boolean	Returns a Boolean value indicating if a node has a particular ancestor or not and works in nested hierarchies as would be expected.

Selectability

The need to make a text on the page unselectable via the cursor is not uncommon and sometimes can actually enhance usability. Virtually every browser has a specific way of accomplishing this task, but no need to worry—you have Dojo. Whenever the need arises, just use the dojo.setSelectable function. Here's the self-descriptive API:

```
dojo.setSelectable(/*String | DomNode*/node, /*Boolean*/selectable)
```

 Hopefully, it goes without saying that no client-side operation should ever be relied on to protect sensitive content because if something is being viewed in the browser as a native display, it can and will be reverse-engineered.

Styling Nodes

Base's dojo.style function provides a comprehensive means of getting or setting individual style values for a particular node. Simply provide the node and a style value in DOM-accessor format (e.g., borderWidth, not border-width) to fetch a particular style value. Providing style value in DOM-accessor format as a third argument causes the function to act as a setter method instead of a getter method. For example, dojo.style("foo", "height") would return the height of element with an id of "foo", while dojo.style("foo", "height", "100px") would set its height to 100 pixels. You can also set multiple style properties at the same time by using an Object as the second parameter, like so:

```
dojo.style("foo", {
    height : "100px",
    width : "100px",
    border : "1px green"
});
```

While many applications benefit from dojo.style's ability to manipulate specific style attributes, there is just as common a need for adding, removing, toggling, and checking for the existence of a particular class. Base's suite of functions for manipulating class can do just that, and they all share a common function signature. The first parameter is the DOM node of interest, and the second parameter is a string value indicating the class to manipulate. For example, adding a class to a node is as simple as dojo.addClass("foo", "someClassName"). Note that the class name does not include a leading dot as would define it in the stylesheet.

Table 2-2 summarizes the various facilities for manipulating the appearance of a node.

Table 2-2. Base functions for style handling

Name	Comment
dojo.style(/*DomNode|String*/ node, /*String?|Object?*/style, /*String?*/value)	Provides a means of getting and setting specific style values on a node.
dojo.hasClass(/*DomNode*/node, /*String*/classString)	Returns true only if node has a particular class applied to it.
dojo.addClass(/*DomNode*/node, /*String*/classString)	Adds a particular class to a node.
dojo.removeClass(/*DomNode*/node, /*String*/classString)	Removes a particular class from a node.
dojo.toggleClass(/*DomNode*/node, /*String*/classString)	Adds a class if a node does not have it; removes a class if it does have it.

Manipulating Attributes

Mimicking the same approach as the previous section discussed for styling nodes, Base also provides functions for normalizing the ability to set, get, check for the existence of, and remove attributes. Table 2-3 lists the available functions.

Table 2-3. Base functions for manipulating node attributes

Name	Comment
dojo.attr(/*DOMNode|String*/node, /*String?|Object?*/attrs, /*String?*/value)	Provides a means of getting and setting attributes for a node.
dojo.hasAttr (/*DOMNode|String*/node, /*String*/name)	Returns true only if node has a particular attribute.
dojo.removeAttr (/*DOMNode|String*/node, /*String*/name)	Removes an attribute from a node.

The dojo.attr function works just like dojo.style in that it can set values for individual attributes or multiple attributes depending on whether you use the second and third parameters to specify an attribute and its value, or if you provide an associative array as the second parameter that contains a collection of attributes and values. The `hasAttr` and `removeAttr` functions are self-descriptive and work just as you would expect.

Placing Nodes

The built-in methods for manipulating DOM content such as `appendChild`, `insertBefore`, and so on can get the job done, but sometimes it's a lot more convenient to have a uniform means of placing nodes, and the `dojo.place` function, documented in Table 2-4, provides just that. In a nutshell, you give it three parameters: a node to be placed, a reference node, and a position that defines the relative relationship. The position parameter may take on the values `"before"`, `"after"`, `"first"`, and `"last"`. The values `"before"` and `"after"` may be used to for relative placement in a lateral context, while `"first"` and `"last"` may be used for absolute placement in a context that assumes the reference node is the parent of the node being placed. Position may also be supplied as an `Integer` value, which refers to the absolute position that the node to be placed should have in the reference node's child nodes.

Table 2-4. Placing a node

Name	Comment
`dojo.place(/*String|DomNode*/node,` `/*String|DomNode*/refNode,` `/*String|Number*/position)`	Augments DOM functionality by providing a uniform function for inserting a node relative to another node. Returns a Boolean.

The Box Model

The CSS box model is a fairly simple topic, but because there are so many inconsistent implementations of it that are available on the Web, things get messy pretty quickly. This short section does little more than scratch the surface, because you really do want to turn to an authoritative reference such as Eric Meyer's *CSS: The Definitive Guide* (O'Reilly) to *really* get to the bottom of it all.

> If various inconsistent implementations of the box model aren't enough, there's also the issue of keeping the CSS2 box model and the CSS3 box model straight. You can read about the CSS2 box model in the CSS2 Specification at *http://www.w3.org/TR/REC-CSS2/box.html*, while the CSS3 working draft is at *http://www.w3.org/TR/css3-box/*.

The ultra-condensed version of the story, however, is that the box model was designed as a way of providing flexible visual formatting that controls the height and width of content by arranging a series of nested boxes around a page element. Before any more dialogue, take a look at Figure 2-2, which conveys the basic idea.

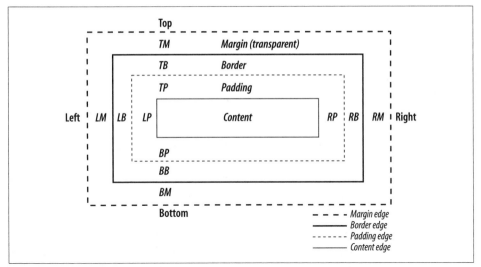

Figure 2-2. The behavior of width and height as defined by CSS 2.1 Box Model

To summarize the differences between content, margin, padding, and border boxes, review the following relevant blurb from the specification:

> The margin, border, and padding can be broken down into left, right, top, and bottom segments (e.g., in the diagram, "LM" for left margin, "RP" for right padding, "TB" for top border, etc.). The perimeter of each of the four areas (content, padding, border, and margin) is called an "edge," so each box has four edges:
>
> 1 - content edge or inner edge
>
> The content edge surrounds the element's rendered content.
>
> 2 - padding edge
>
> The padding edge surrounds the box padding. If the padding has 0 width, the padding edge is the same as the content edge. The padding edge of a box defines the edges of the containing block established by the box.
>
> 3 - border edge
>
> The border edge surrounds the box's border. If the border has 0 width, the border edge is the same as the padding edge.
>
> 4 - margin edge or outer edge
>
> The margin edge surrounds the box margin. If the margin has 0 width, the margin edge is the same as the border edge.

As it turns out, two different means of realizing the box model emerged, which is where the divergence begins: the *content-box* and the *border-box*. The basic difference between the two approaches can be captured by asking what defines how margins and borders are applied to the content area. With the content-box approach, any area incurred by padding and borders is accounted for outside of the explicit width and height of the content, whereas the border-box approach calls for any padding and borders to be accounted for inside the explicit height and width of the content area. In other words, the content-box approach associates a height/width strictly with only the content, whereas the border-box approach associates a height/width with the border inward.

 Many modern browsers support two modes: standards mode and quirks mode. The content-box approach is associated with standards mode while the border-box approach is associated with quirks mode.

If you're not doing anything very fancy and just want to space out some content, the differences may not be apparent, and you can generally get the same net effect in a number of ways. If you need to achieve a very specific look and feel, however, your decisions may already be made for you—and achieving the same look and feel across browsers is exactly where the (lack of) fun begins.

Dojo attempts to normalize the differences in calculating various facets of the box model by exposing the dojo.marginBox attribute, which can take on a value of "content-box" or "margin-box" as well as the dojo.marginBox and dojo.contentBox functions, which can be used to retrieve the coordinates for the boxes. By default, dojo.boxModel is set to "content-box". In all cases, the box parameters provided in the following table refer to an Object containing values for width and height, along with an upper-left coordinate that defines the box's area. A sample margin box would look something like { l: 50, t: 200, w: 300: h: 150 } for a node offset from its parent 50px to the left, 200px from the top with a margin width of 300px, and a margin-height of 150px.

To try it out for yourself, copy the following example into a local file and open it up in Firefox:

```
<body style="margin:3px">
        <div id="foo" style="width:4px; height:4px; border:solid 1px;"></div>
</body>
```

Here's some sample output you'd see in Firebug if you copied over the page and experimented with it, and Figure 2-3 shows what it would look like in the browser:

```
console.log("box model", dojo.boxModel); // content-box
console.log("content box", dojo.contentBox("foo")); // l=0 t=0 w=4 h=4
console.log("margin box", dojo.marginBox("foo")); // l=3 t=3 w=6 h=6
```

Like other functions you've seen in this chapter, calling the functions with only one parameter corresponding to a node returns a value, while calling it with an additional second parameter sets the value for the node. Table 2-5 lists all the properties for working with the box model.

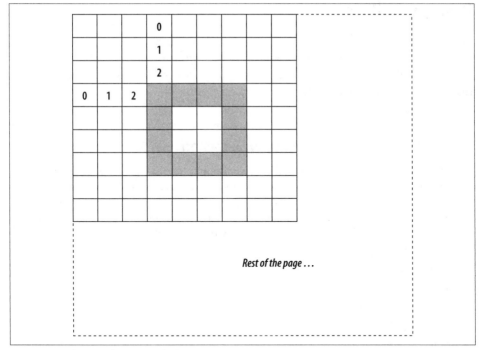

Figure 2-3. The sample page in the browser

Table 2-5. Box model properties

Name	Return type	Comment
dojo.marginBox(/*DomNode|String*/node, /*Object?*/box)	Object	Returns an Object containing the margin box for a node.
dojo.contentBox(/*DomNode|String*/node, /*Object?*/box)	Object	Returns an Object containing the content box for a node.
dojo.coords(/*HTMLElement*/node, /*Boolean*/includeScroll)	Object	Returns margin box data for a node, including absolute positioning data. In addition to the t, l, w, and h values, additional x and y values indicate the absolute position of the element on the page; these values are offset relative to the viewport if includeScroll is set to true. dojo.coords does not act as a setter.

Dijit uses the box model facilities extensively to produce portable widgets across browsers.

Browser Utilities

This section provides an overview of the toolkit's utilities for managing cookies and the browser's Back button—two topics that are quite common in any modern web application. Because both of these topics are provided by Core, you must `dojo.require` them into the page before trying to use them.

Browser Detection

Although Dojo does virtually all of the heavy lifting to standardize browser anomalies, there may be times when you need to do some specific detection yourself—for whatever reason. When the situation arises, you can access the following attributes and treat them as Booleans (any value greater than 1 would imply true) in Base to do a quick check versus cluttering up your design with more boilerplate:

- `dojo.isOpera`
- `dojo.isKhtml`
- `dojo.isSafari`
- `dojo.isMozilla`
- `dojo.isFF`
- `dojo.isIE`
- `dojo.isAIR`
- `dojo.isQuirks`

Note that `isMozilla` will be true if any variation of Mozilla's Gecko rendering engine is used, while `isFF` refers strictly to the Gecko rendering engine as used in the Firefox browser.

The `isQuirks` attribute returns true if the browser is operating in backward-compatibility (quirks) mode. Most browsers default to quirks mode unless the first element of the page is a specific DTD element that signals otherwise.

Cookies

Because HTTP is a stateless protocol, as soon as a web server finishes serving up a page, it knows nothing else about you. While this aspect of the Web is magnificent in many respects, it is less than ideal for situations in which an application could personalize a page based upon preferences you've already defined. For example, it might be nice for a weather-related site to remember your zip code so that you don't have to enter it every single time you visit the page.

Cookies are a concept originally devised by Netscape that mitigate this kind of problem and give browsers a limited form of short-term memory. In short, web page designers can use JavaScript or server-side scripts to create a cookie that contains

---

name-value pairs about your visit to the page. When you visit the page again, scripts can be used to fetch the cookie and dynamically affect your experience. Cookies generally have an expiration date and are always associated with the specific domain from which they originated.

One of the issues with managing cookies from pure JavaScript is that you have to remember the somewhat strict syntax that is expected and build up the string for yourself. For example, to set a cookie for the default domain that consists of a name/value pair of foo=bar with a particular expiration date, you would do this:

```
document.cookie ='foo=bar; expires=Sun, 15 Jun 2008 12:00:00 UTC; path=/'
```

Of course, that's the easy part. When you want to read back out cookie values, you get to parse the String yourself, which might contain lots of name/value pairs.

Dojo provides a basic wrapper around cookie operations that's a lot easier to remember how to use. Table 2-6 outlines the basic API.

Table 2-6. dojo.cookie functions

Name	Comment
dojo.cookie(/*String*/name, /*String*/value, /*Object?*/properties)	Acts as a "getter" for a cookie value (returned as String) when you provide only the first argument, which is the name for a cookie value. Providing the first two values acts as a "setter," which sets the name to the value. The final parameter, properties, may contain the following key/value pairs for specific cookie properties:
	expires (Date|String|Number)
	If this is a number, it indicates the days from today at which the cookie expires; if a date, it provides the date past which the cookie expires (and if expires is in the past, the cookie is deleted); if expires is omitted or is 0, the cookie expires when the browser closes.
	path (String)
	The path to use for the cookie.
	domain (String)
	The domain to use for the cookie.
	secure (Boolean)
	Whether to send the cookie only on secure connections.
dojo.cookie.isSupported( )	Returns a Boolean value indicating if the browser supports cookies.

For example, you might set and retrieve a cookie value like so:

```
dojo.cookie("foo","bar", {expires : 30});
//set a foo/bar key-value pair to expire 30 days from now
dojo.cookie("foo"); //get back the value for foo, which is bar
```

Back Button Handling

For modern web applications, it is pretty much the norm that the entire app lives in a single page that never reloads, and one issue that immediately comes up is managing the Back button so that your application can properly respond to state and potentially even bookmarking. The Core module back provides a simple utility that facilitates the state-tracking portion of the work by allowing you to explicitly define states and respond accordingly when the Back or Forward button is pressed. Table 2-7 describes the API.

Table 2-7. dojo.back functions

Name	Comment
init()	Needs to be called from a SCRIPT tag that exists inside of the page BODY because of a nuance with Internet Explorer. If you know for sure that your application will not need to run on IE, you can optionally ignore calling this function.
setInitialState(/*Object*/args)	Used to define the callback function that should be executed when the page returns to its "first" state. In general, it is recommended that this function be called first thing in addOnLoad.
addToHistory(/*Object*/args)	Provides a way of establishing a particular state via the args that provides callbacks for when the Back and Forward buttons are pressed, as well as an optional identifier in the URL that may be used for convenient bookmarking. Specifically, args has the following form:
	back (Function) The callback function to execute when the state is entered via the Back button being pressed.
	forward (Function) The callback function to execute when the state is entered via the Forward button being pressed.
	changeUrl (Boolean|String) If true, a random identifier is inserted into the URL and used internally for tracking purposes. If a String is provided, the string is inserted into the URL and used for the same purpose with the nicety that it also provides convenient bookmarking. Do not mix and match Boolean and String values; use one or the other.

 Be consistent and use either Boolean values or String identifiers for the changeUrl property for the args Object that is passed to addToHistory.

Example 2-8 illustrates a trivial usage of back to produce callback functions that could provide custom behavior, which hopefully gets the basic idea across. Note that the emphasized lines inside of the body tags are necessary to ensure that IE behaves as expected.

In case you're wondering why the SCRIPT that is included inside of the BODY looks really awkward, it's because of a specific problem with IE that requires a document.write to execute, which cannot happen after the page loads. It's not elegant, but it does work across all browsers and gets you Back button functionality.

Example 2-8. Example of Back button handling

```html
<html>
    <head>
        <title>Fun with Back!</title>


        <link rel="stylesheet" type="text/css"
          href="http://o.aolcdn.com/dojo/1.1/dojo/resources/dojo.css" />


        <script
            type="text/javascript"
            src="http://o.aolcdn.com/dojo/1.1/dojo/dojo.xd.js"
            djConfig="dojoIframeHistoryUrl:'iframe_history.html',isDebug:true"
        ></script>

        <script type="text/javascript">

            dojo.addOnLoad(function() {
                initialState = {
                    back: function() { console.log("Back to initial state"); }
                };
                state1 = {
                    back: function() { console.log("Back to state 1"); },
                    forward: function() { console.log("Forward to state 1"); },
                    changeUrl : true // could also be an id like "state1"
                };
                state2 = {
                    back: function() { console.log("Back to state 2"); },
                    forward: function() { console.log("Forward to state 2"); },
                    changeUrl : true // could also be an id like "state2"
                };

                //set the initial state and move forward two steps in history
                dojo.back.setInitialState(initialState);
                dojo.back.addToHistory(state1);
                dojo.back.addToHistory(state2);
            });
        </script>
    <head>
        <body>
            <script type="text/javascript"
                src="http://o.aolcdn.com/dojo/1.1/dojo/back.js"></script>
            <script type="text/javascript">dojo.back.init();</script>
```

Example 2-8. Example of Back button handling (continued)

```
        Press the back button and have a look at the console.
    </body>
</html>
```

Summary

After reading this chapter, you should:

- Understand Base's general feature set
- Be able to configure djConfig to register module paths and be aware of the various other options you can pass into this structure to configure the bootstrap process
- Understand how to use dojo.addOnLoad and dojo.addOnUnload functions and be aware of how dojo.addOnLoad can protect you from creating race conditions in your code
- Be able to construct and namespace your own modules with dojo.provide and dojo.require
- Understand how (and when) to use the map, filter, and forEach functions
- Know the difference between and be able to effectively use mixin and extend
- Effectively use Dojo's utilities for manipulating style with hasClass, removeClass, addClass, and toggleClass
- Understand the basics of the CSS box model and be able to use functions like coords and marginBox to manipulate the placement of DOM nodes
- Be aware of Base's Array processing utilities
- Be able to wire up arbitrary connections of Object and DOM events
- Be able to manage cookies
- Be able to use Core's facilities for managing the back button for a single page app

Next, we'll take a look at event listeners and pub/sub communication.

## CHAPTER 3

Event Listeners and Pub/Sub Communication

Base provides extremely useful and versatile utilities for communication between JavaScript objects, DOM nodes, and any combination thereof. This chapter introduces these constructs as well as guidelines for when each of them might be most appropriate to employ. As writing portable code that involves DOM events necessarily depends on a standardized event model, you'll also learn a little bit about how Dojo works behind the scenes to smooth out some of the inconsistencies amongst mouse and keyboard events. The chapter concludes with a discussion of publish/subscribe communication, which provides a great vehicle for realizing an architecture with loosely coupled components.

Event and Keyboard Normalization

Some of the oldest code in the toolkit was written to smooth out inconsistencies with the underlying event model amongst different browsers. This section provides a brief overview of the events that you can count on being normalized when you use Dojo to develop an application. The basis of standardization is the W3C model.

Mouse and Keyboard Event Normalization

The dojo.connect machinery that you'll read about in the following section often involves a mouse event on a particular DOM node. Whenever you use Dojo, you can rest assured that the following mouse and keyboard events are supported in accordance with the W3C standard:

```
onclick
onmousedown
onmouseup
onmouseover
onmouseout
onmousemove
```

```
onkeydown
onkeyup
onkeypress
```

 In addition to supporting the standardized W3C events, the nonstandard onmouseenter and onmouseleave events are also supported.

In addition to being able to count on these events firing in a standardized way, you can also rely on the event objects that are passed to event handling functions to also be normalized. In fact, if you ever have a need to normalize events yourself, you can use the following Base function:

```
dojo.fixEvent(/*DOMEvent*/ evt, /*DOMNode*/ sender) //Returns DOMEvent
```

 DOMEvent is the standard convention that'll be used in the rest of the book to refer to the DOM event objects.

In other words, pass in the event and the node that should be treated as the current target, and you'll get back a normalized event that you can count on meeting the W3C specification. Table 3-1 provides a synopsis of some of the most commonly used properties on a DOMEvent.*

Table 3-1. Commonly used properties on DOMEvents

Name	Type	Comment
bubbles	Boolean	Indicates whether the event can bubble up the DOM tree.
cancelable	Boolean	Indicates whether the event can have its default action prevented.
currentTarget	DOMNode	The current node whose event listeners are being processed. (Useful for when an event bubbles.)
target	DOMNode	The node that originally received the event.
type	String	The type of the event, e.g., mouseover.
ctrlKey	Boolean	Indicates if the Ctrl key was depressed when the event fired.
shiftKey	Boolean	Indicates if the Shift key was depressed when the event fired.
metaKey	Boolean	Indicates if the Meta key was depressed when the event fired. (This is the Command key on an Apple computer.)
altKey	Boolean	Indicates if the Alt key was depressed when the event fired.
screenX	Integer	The X coordinate where the event occurred on the screen.

---

* Dojo currently normalizes against the DOM2 specification, which is available at *http://www.w3.org/TR/DOM-Level-2-Events/events.html*. See *http://www.w3.org/TR/DOM-Level-3-Events/events.html* for an overview of the DOM3 Event specification.

Table 3-1. Commonly used properties on DOMEvents (continued)

Name	Type	Comment
screenY	Integer	The Y coordinate where the event occurred on the screen.
clientX	Integer	The X coordinate where the event occurred on the browser window.
clientY	Integer	The Y coordinate where the event occurred on the browser window.

Standardized Key Codes

The toolkit also exposes the following table of named key codes, which are available via dojo.keys. For example, you might detect whether a Shift + Enter key combination was processed via the following code snippet:

```
/* ... snip ... */
  if (evt.keyCode == dojo.keys.ENTER && evt.shiftKey) {
    /* ... */
  }
/* ... snip ... */
```

Table 3-2 provides a list of the constants for accessing keyboard events.

Table 3-2. A listing of the constants Dojo provides for accessing keyboard events via dojo.keys

BACKSPACE	DELETE	NUMPAD_DIVIDE
TAB	HELP	F1
CLEAR	LEFT_WINDOW	F2
ENTER	RIGHT_WINDOW	F3
SHIFT	SELECT	F4
CTRL	NUMPAD_0	F5
ALT	NUMPAD_1	F6
PAUSE	NUMPAD_2	F7
CAPS_LOCK	NUMPAD_3	F8
ESCAPE	NUMPAD_4	F9
SPACE	NUMPAD_5	F10
PAGE_UP	NUMPAD_6	F11
PAGE_DOWN	NUMPAD_7	F12
END	NUMPAD_8	F13
HOME	NUMPAD_9	F14
LEFT_ARROW	NUMPAD_MULTIPLY	F15
UP_ARROW	NUMPAD_PLUS	NUM_LOCK
RIGHT_ARROW	NUMPAD_ENTER	SCROLL_LOCK

Table 3-2. A listing of the constants Dojo provides for accessing keyboard events via dojo.keys (continued)

DOWN_ARROW	NUMPAD_MINUS
INSERT	NUMPAD_PERIOD

Event Listeners

Direct communication channels are constructed by explicitly chaining together functions and/or DOM events so that when one executes, another is automatically invoked afterward. For example, each time an object changes via a "setter" method, you may want to automatically trigger a change in the application's visual interface. Or, perhaps each time one object changes, you might want to automatically update a derived property on another object. The possibilities are endless.

The two primary methods involved in a direct communication scheme are dojo.connect and dojo.disconnect. In short, you use dojo.connect to chain together a series of events. Each call to dojo.connect returns a handle that you should keep and explicitly pass to dojo.disconnect whenever you are ready to dispose of the connection. Conveniently, all handles are disconnected automatically when the page unloads, but manual management of the handles may be necessary for preventing memory leaks in long-running applications that invoke a lot of connections that are used temporarily. (This is particularly the case on IE.) Coming up is the API that was introduced in Chapter 1.

Don't ever connect anything until after the page is loaded. Trying to use dojo.connect before the page is loaded is a very common mistake and can cause you to sink a lot of time into trying to debug something that isn't very easy to track down the first time you run into it. You should always set up your connections within the function that you pass into dojo.addOnLoad to stay safe.

Setting up and tearing down connections is easy. Here's the basic API:

```
/* Set up a connection */
dojo.connect(/*Object|null*/ obj,
        /*String*/ event,
        /*Object|null*/ context,
        /*String|Function*/ method) // Returns a Handle

/* Tear down a connection */
dojo.disconnect(/*Handle*/handle);
```

For all practical purposes, you should treat the handle that is returned from a call to dojo.connect as an opaque object that you don't do anything with except pass to disconnect at a later time. (In case you're wondering, it is nothing special—just a collection of information that is used to manage the connection internally.)

Let's take a look at an example that illustrates a kind of problem that dojo.connect would be suitable for helping us to solve:

```
function Foo() {
    this.greet = function() { console.log("Hi, I'm Foo"); }
}

function Bar() {
    this.greet = function() { console.log("Hi, I'm Bar"); }
}

foo = new Foo;
bar = new Bar;

foo.greet();

//bar should greet foo back without foo
//ever having to know that bar exists.
```

As it turns out, we can solve this little conundrum with one line of code. Modify the previous listing like so, and test this out in Firebug:

```
function Foo() {
    this.greet = function() { console.log("Hi, I'm foo"); }
}

function Bar() {
    this.greet = function() { console.log("Hi, I'm bar"); }
}

foo = new Foo;
bar = new Bar;

//Anytime foo.greet fires, fire bar.greet afterward...
var handle = dojo.connect(foo, "greet", bar, "greet"); //set up the connection

foo.greet(); //bar automatically greets back now!
```

The payout for writing that one line of code was pretty high, don't you think? Notice that the second and fourth parameters to dojo.connect are string literals for their respective contexts and that a handle is returned that can later be used to tear down the connection. In general, you *always* want to tear down the connection at some point, whether it be to accomplish some kind of functional requirement in your design, or when you're performing some final cleanup—such as when an object is destroyed or the page is unloaded. Here's how:

```
var handle = dojo.connect(foo, "greet", bar, "greet");
foo.greet();

dojo.disconnect(handle);

foo.greet(); //silent treatment this time
```

In addition to `dojo.connect` accomplishing so much with so little effort, notice how clean and maintainable the source code remains. No boilerplate, no spaghetti code, no wiring up your own solution, no maintenance nightmare.

Firing methods off in response to happenings in the page is really useful, but sooner or later you'll need to pass around some arguments. As it turns out, one additional feature of connect is that it automatically passes the arguments from the first context's function to the second context's function. Here's an example that shows how:

```
function Foo( ) {
    this.greet = function(greeting) { console.log("Hi, I'm Foo.", greeting); };
}

function Bar( ) {
    this.greet = function(greeting) { console.log("Hi, I'm Bar.", greeting); };
}

foo = new Foo;
bar = new Bar;

var handle= dojo.connect(foo, "greet", bar, "greet");
foo.greet("Nice to meet you");
```

As you might imagine, having the arguments get passed around automatically is quite handy, and this is especially the case when a function is connected to a DOM event such as a mouse click because it gives the function instant access to all of the important particulars of the event such as the target, the mouse coordinates, and so on. Let's investigate with yet another example:

```
//Note that the third argument is skipped altogether since the handler is a
//standalone anonymous function. Using null to placehold the third parameter would
//have produced the very same effect.

dojo.connect(
    dojo.byId("foo"), //Some DOM element
    "onmouseover",
    function(evt) {
      console.log(evt);
    });
```

If you set up a sample page, wire up the connection, and watch the Firebug console, you'll see that the entire event object is available to the event-handling function, empowering you with just about everything you'd ever need to know about what just happened.

"But it's so easy to specify handlers for DOM events. Why would I even bother with learning another fancy library function?" you wonder. Yes, it may not take a brain surgeon to put together some simple event handlers, but what about when you have a complex application that may need to handle lots of sophisticated event handling based on user preferences, custom events, or some other event-driven behavior? Sure, you could handle all of this work manually, but would you be able to connect or disconnect in one line of code with a single consistent interface that's already been written and battle-tested?

Finally, note that while the examples only illustrated one event being chained to another one, there's no reason you couldn't wire up any arbitrary number of ordinary functions, object methods, and DOM events to fire in succession.

Event Propagation

There may be times when you need to suppress the browser's built-in handling of some DOM events and instead provide custom handlers for these tasks yourself via dojo.connect. Two fairly common cases that occur are when you'd like to suppress the browser from automatically navigating when a hyperlink is clicked and when you'd like to prevent the browser from automatically submitting a form when the Enter key is pressed or the Submit button is clicked.

Fortunately, stopping the browser from handling these DOM events once your custom handlers have finished is as easy as using dojo.stopEvent or the DOMEvent's preventDefault method to prevent the event from propagating to the browser. The stopEvent function simply takes a DOMEvent as a parameter:

```
dojo.stopEvent(/*DOMEvent*/evt)
```

 While you can suppress DOM events that participate in a series of dojo.connect functions, there is no way to stop the dojo.connect event chain from within an ordinary function or JavaScript object method.

The following example illustrates stopEvent at work:

```
var foo = dojo.byId("foo"); //some anchor element

dojo.connect(foo, "onclick", function(evt) {
    console.log("anchor clicked");
    dojo.stopEvent(evt); //suppress browser navigation and squash any event bubbling
});
```

Likewise, suppressing automatic submission of a form is just as easy; simply swap out the context of the connection and associate with the submit event. This time, though, we'll use the preventDefault method of a DOMEvent to suppress the event, while allowing bubbling to continue:

```
var bar = dojo.byId("bar"); //some form element

dojo.connect(bar, "onsubmit", function(evt) {
    console.log("form submitted");
    evt.preventDefault(); //suppress browser navigation but allow event bubbling
});
```

Leveraging Closures with dojo.connect

This section covers some semi-advanced content that you may want to skim over but not get bogged down with your first time through this chapter. Do come back to it though, because sooner or later you'll find yourself needing it.

One-time connections

Consider a situation in which you need to establish and soon thereafter tear down a connection that fires only a single time. The following example gets the job done with minimal effort:

```
var handle = dojo.connect(
    dojo.byId("foo"),  //some div element
    "onmouseover",
    function(evt) {
        //some handler goes here...
        dojo.disconnect(handle);
    }
);
```

If you're still getting comfortable with closures, your first reaction might be to object and claim that what we've just done is not possible. After all, the variable `handle` is returned from the call to `dojo.connect`, and yet it is being referenced inside of a function that gets passed to `dojo.connect` as a parameter. To better understand the situation, consider the following analysis of what's going on:

1. The `dojo.connect` function executes, and although an anonymous function is one of its parameters, the anonymous function has not yet been executed.

2. Any variables inside of the anonymous function (such as `handle`) are bound to its scope chain, and although they might exist within the function, they aren't actually referenced until the function actually executes, so there's no possible error that could happen yet.

3. The `dojo.connect` function returns the `handle` variable before the anonymous function ever can ever be executed, so when the anonymous function does execute, it is readily available and passed to the `dojo.disconnect` call.

Setting up connections within a loop

Another situation that frequently occurs during development is that you need to set up connections in the body of a loop. Suppose for now that you simply have a series of elements on the page, foo0, foo1,...foo9, and you want to log a unique number when you move the mouse over each of them. As a first attempt, you might end up with the following code block that will *not* accomplish what you would expect:

```
/* The following code does not work as expected! */
for (var i=0; i < 10; i++) {
    var foo = dojo.byId("foo"+i);
    var handle = dojo.connect(foo, "onmouseover", function(evt) {
```

```
      console.log(i);
      dojo.disconnect(handle);
    });
}
```

If you run the snippet of code in Firebug on a page with a series of named elements, you'll quickly find that there's a problem. Namely, the value 10 is always printed in the console, which means that the final value of i is being referenced across the board and that the same connection is erroneously trying to be torn down in each of the 10 handlers. Taking a moment to ponder the situation, however, it suddenly occurs to you that the behavior that is happening actually makes sense because the closure provided by the anonymous function that is passed into dojo.connect doesn't resolve i until it is actually executed—at which time it is in a final state.

The following modification fixes the problem by trapping the value of i in the scope chain so that when it is referenced later it will actually resolve to whatever value it held at the time the dojo.connect statement executed:

```
for (var i=0; i < 10; i++) {
    (function() {
        var foo = dojo.byId("foo"+i);
        var current_i = i; //trap in closure
        var handle = dojo.connect(foo, "onmouseover",
          function(evt) {
            console.log(current_i);
            dojo.disconnect(handle);
          }
        );
    })(); // execute anonymous function immediately
}
```

The block of code may seem a little bit convoluted at first, but it's actually pretty simple. The entire body of the loop is an anonymous function that is executed inline, and because the anonymous function provides closure for everything that is in it, the value of i is "trapped" as current_i, which can be resolved when the event handler executes. Likewise, the proper handle reference is also resolved because it too exists within the closure provided by the inline anonymous function.

If you've never seen closures in action like this before, you may want to take a few more moments to carefully study the code and make sure you fully understand it. You're probably tired of hearing it by now, but a firm grasp on closures will serve you well in your JavaScript pursuits.

Connecting in Markup

It is worth noting that it is also possible to set up connections for dijits without even the minimal JavaScript writing required by using special dojo/connect SCRIPT tags that appear in markup. You can read more about this topic in Chapter 11 when Dijit is formally introduced.

Publish/Subscribe Communication

While there are plenty of times when the direct "chained" style of communication provided by dojo.connect is exactly what you'll need to solve a problem, there are also a lot of times when you'll want a much more indirect "broadcast" style of communication in which various widgets communicate anonymously. For these circumstances, you might instead use dojo.publish and dojo.subscribe.

A classic example is a JavaScript object that needs to communicate with other objects in a one-to-many type relationship. Instead of setting up and managing multiple dojo.connect connections for what seems like one cohesive action, it's considerably simpler to have one widget publish a notification that an event has transpired (optionally passing along data with it) and other widgets can subscribe to this notification and automatically take action accordingly. The beauty of the approach is that the object performing the broadcast doesn't need to know anything whatsoever about the other objects—or even if they exist, for that matter. Another classic example for this kind of communication involves *portlets*—pluggable interface components (*http://en.wikipedia.org/wiki/Portlet*) that are managed within a web portal, kind of like a dashboard.

> The OpenAjax Hub (*http://www.openajax.org/OpenAjax%20Hub. html*), which you'll read more about in Chapter 4, calls for publish/ subscribe communication to be used as the vehicle for effectively employing multiple JavaScript libraries in the same page.

In many situations, you can achieve exactly the same functionality with pub/sub style communication as you could by establishing connections, so the decision to use pub/sub may often boil down to pragmatism, the specific problem being solved, and overall convenience of one approach over another.

As a starting point for determining which style of communication to use, consider the following issues:

- Do you want to (and can you reliably) expose an API for a widget you're developing? If not, you should strongly prefer pub/sub communication so that you can transparently change the underlying design without constantly wrangling the API.

- Does your design contain multiple widgets of the same type that are all going to be responding to the same kind of event? If so, you should strongly prefer connections because you'd have to write additional logic to disambiguate which widgets should respond to which notifications.

- Are you designing a widget that contains child widgets in a "has-a" relationship? If so, you should prefer setting up and maintaining connections.

- Does your design involve one-to-many or many-to-many relationships? If so, you should strongly prefer pub/sub communication to minimize the overall burden of communication.

- Does your communication need to be completely anonymous and require the loosest coupling possible? If so, you should use pub/sub communication.

Without further delay, here's the pub/sub API. Note that in the case of dojo.subscribe, you may omit the context parameter and the function will internally normalize the arguments on your behalf (just as was the case with dojo.connect):

```
dojo.publish(/*String*/topic, /*Array*/args)
dojo.subscribe(/*String*/topic, *Object|null*/context,
    /*String|Function*/method) //Returns a Handle
dojo.unsubscribe(/*Handle*/handle)
```

Just as the handle that is returned from dojo.connect should be considered opaque, the same applies here for dojo.subscribe.

Let's get to work with a simple example involving dojo.subscribe and dojo.publish:

```
function Foo(topic) {

  this.topic = topic;

  this.greet = function( ) {
    console.log("Hi, I'm Foo");

    /* Foo directly publishes information, but not to a specific destination... */
    dojo.publish(this.topic);
  }

}

function Bar(topic) {

  this.topic = topic;

  this.greet = function( ) {
    console.log("Hi, I'm Bar");
  }

  / * Bar directly subscribes to information, but not from a specific source */
  dojo.subscribe(this.topic, this, "greet");

}

var foo = new Foo("/dtdg/salutation");
var bar = new Bar("/dtdg/salutation");

foo.talk( ); //Hi, I'm Foo...Hi, I'm Bar
```

Although there is no formal standard, the toolkit uses the convention of prefixing and using a forward slash to separate the components of topic names. An advantage of this approach is that the forward slash is uncommon enough in JavaScript code that it is fairly easy to spot (whereas using a dot to separate topic names in source code would be a lot more difficult).

As you can see, whereas connect involves a connection from a specific source to a specific destination, publish/subscribe involves a broadcast that could be sent from any source and could be received by any destination that cares to respond to it in some way. Some amazing power comes built-in with a very loosely coupled architecture because with minimal effort and great simplicity comes the ability to have what amounts to an application that is conceptually a collection of coherent plug-ins.

Let's illustrate how to unsubscribe with an interesting variation on Bar's implementation. Let's have Bar respond to the topic that Foo publishes only a single time:

```
function Bar(topic) {

    this.topic = topic;

    this.greet = function( ) {
        console.log("Hi, I'm bar");
        dojo.unsubscribe(this.handle);

        //yackety yack, don't talk back
    }

    this.handle = dojo.subscribe(this.topic, this, "greet");
}
```

Note that you can also send along an array of arguments by providing an additional second argument to publish that is an Array of values, which gets passed to the subscribe handler as named parameters.

It's a common mistake to forget that the arguments passed from dojo.publish must be contained in an Array and that dojo.subscribe's handler receives these arguments as individual parameters.

For a final rendition of our example, let's say you are not able to reliably change Foo's greet method to include a dojo.publish call because an external constraint exists that prohibits it; perhaps it is code that you do not own or should not be mucking with, for example. Not to worry—we'll use another function, dojo.connectPublisher, to take care of the publishing for us each time a particular event occurs:

```
function Foo( ) {
  this.greet = function( ) {
    console.log("Hi, I'm foo");
  }
}
```

```
function Bar( ) {
  this.greet = function( ) {
    console.log("Hi, I'm bar");
  }

}

var foo = new Foo;
var bar = new Bar;

var topic = "/dtdg/salutation";
dojo.subscribe(topic, bar, "greet");
dojo.connectPublisher(topic, foo, "greet");

foo.greet( );
```

 In case you're interested, behind-the-scenes connectPublisher is basically using dojo.connect to create a connection between a dojo.publish call each time a particular function is called.

In this final example, the primary takeaway is that the dojo.connectPublisher call allowed us to achieve the same result as adding a dojo.publish call to its greet method, but without mangling its source code to achieve that result. In this regard, foo is an indirect sender of the notification and is not even aware that any communication is going on at all. Bar, on the other hand, as a subscriber of the notification, did require explicit knowledge of the communications scheme. This is essentially the opposite of a typical dojo.connect call in which the object that provides the context for a connection has explicit knowledge about some other object or function that provides the "target" of the connection.

Summary

After reading this chapter, you should:

- Be aware that dojo.connect standardizes the event Object that is passed into event-handling functions, providing portability across platforms
- Understand how dojo.connect allows you to arbitrarily chain DOM events, JavaScript Object events, and ordinary functions together to create an event-driven response
- Use publish/subscribe to facilitate connections and achieve a loosely coupled communications backbone in an application
- Be aware of some of the considerations and trade-offs for using dojo.connect versus pub/sub in an application architecture

Next up is AJAX and server communication.

## CHAPTER 4

AJAX and Server Communication

The common thread of this chapter is server-side communications. Performing asynchronous requests, using the IFRAME transport to submit forms behind the scenes, serializing to and from JavaScript Object Notation (JSON), and using JSONP (JSON with Padding) are a few of the topics that are introduced in this chapter. You'll also learn about Deferred, a class that forms the lynchpin in the toolkit's IO subsystem by providing a uniform interface for handling asynchronous activity.

Quick Overview of AJAX

AJAX* (Asynchronous JavaScript and XML) has stirred up considerable buzz and revitalized web design in a refreshing way. Whereas web pages once had to be completely reloaded via a synchronous request to the server to perform a significant update, JavaScript's XMLHttpRequest object allows them to now behave much like traditional desktop applications. XHR is an abbreviation for the XMLHttpRequest object and generally refers to any operation provided the object.

Web pages may now fetch content from the server via an asynchronous request behind the scenes, as shown in Figure 4-1, and a callback function can process it once it arrives. (The image in Figure 4-1 is based on *http://adaptivepath.com/ideas/essays/archives/000385.php.*) Although a simple concept, this approach has revolutionized the user experience and birthed a new era of Rich Internet Applications.

Using JavaScript's XMLHttpRequest object directly isn't exactly rocket science, but like anything else, there are often tricky implementation details involved and boilerplate that must be written in order to cover the common-use cases. For example, asynchronous requests are never guaranteed to return a value (even though they almost always do), so you'll generally need to implement logic that determines when and

---

* Even though the "X" in AJAX specifically stands for XML, the term AJAX now commonly refers to virtually any architecture that employs the XMLHttpRequest object to perform asynchronous requests, regardless of the actual type of data that's returned. Although opting to use the umbrella term XHR would technically be more accurate, we'll follow common parlance and use AJAX in the broader context.

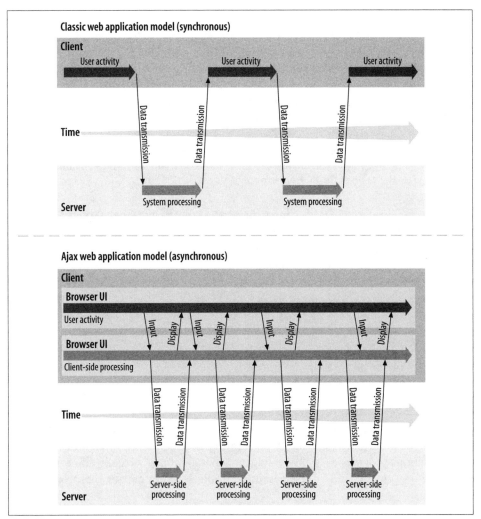

Figure 4-1. The difference between synchronous and asynchronous communication for a web application

how to timeout a request; you may want to have some facilities for automatically vetting and transforming JSON strings into JavaScript objects; you'll probably want to have a concise way of separating the logic that handles a successful request versus a request that produces an error; and so forth.

JSON

JSON bears a brief mention before we move on to a discussion of AJAX because it has all but become the universally accepted norm for lightweight data exchange in AJAX applications. You can read about the formalities of JSON at *http://json.org*, but basically, JSON is nothing more than a string-based representation of JavaScript objects. Base provides two simple functions for converting String values and JavaScript objects back and forth. These functions handle the mundane details of escaping special characters like tabs and new lines, and even allow you to pretty-print if you feel so inclined:

```
dojo.fromJson(/*String*/ json) //Returns Object
dojo.toJson(/*Object*/ json, /*Boolean?*/ prettyPrint) //Returns String
```

 By default, a tab is used to indent the JSON string if it is pretty-printed. You can change the tab to whatever you'd like by switching the value of the built-in attribute dojo.toJsonIndentStr.

Here's a quick example that illustrates the process of converting an Object to a JSON string that is suitable for human consumption:

```
var o = {a:1, b:2, c:3, d:4};
dojo.toJson(o, true); //pretty print
/* produces ...
'{
  "a": 1,
  "b": 2,
  "c":3,
  "d":4
}'
```

AJAX Made Easy

Base provides a small suite of functions suitable for use in a RESTful design that significantly simplifies the process of performing routine AJAX operations. Each of these functions provides explicit mechanisms that eliminate virtually all of the boilerplate you'd normally find yourself writing. Table 4-1 summarizes the property values for args.

Representational State Transfer (REST)

REST stands for "Representational State Transfer" and describes an architectural style that is primarily associated with the web. REST is a very resource-centric style, and in a RESTful architecture, URIs define and address resources. The HTTP methods GET, PUT, POST, and DELETE describe the semantic operations that generally involve the action that is being associated with a resource. For example, a GET request on *http://example.com/foo/id/1* implies that you are trying to fetch the *foo* resource that has an id value of 1, while a DELETE request on the same URI would imply that the same resource should be removed.

An excellent reference on REST is the book entitled *RESTful Web Services* by Leonard Richardson and Sam Ruby (O'Reilly).

Table 4-1. Property values for args

Name	Type (Default)	Comment
url	String ("")	The base URL to direct the request.
content	Object ({})	Contains key/value pairs that are encoded in the most appropriate way for the particular transport being used. For example, they are serialized and appended onto the query string as name1=value2 for a GET request but are included as hidden form fields for the case of an IFRAME transport. Note that even though HTTP allows more than one field with the same name (multivalued fields), this is not possible to achieve via the content property because it is a hash.
timeout	Integer (Infinity)	The number of milliseconds to wait for the response. If this time passes, then the error callback is executed. Only valid when sync is false.
form	DOMNode | String	The DOM node or id for a form that supplies the key/value pairs that are serialized and provide the query string for the request. (Each form value should have a name attribute that identifies it.)
preventCache	Boolean (false)	If true, then a special dojo.preventCache parameter is sent in the request with a value that changes with each request (timestamp). Useful only with GET-type requests.
handleAs	String ("text")	Designates the type of the response data that is passed into the load handler. Acceptable values depend on the type of IO transport: "text", "json", "javascript", and "xml".
load	Function	The load function will be called on a successful response and should have the signature function(response, ioArgs) {/*...*/}.
error	Function	The error function will be called in an error case and should have the signature function(response, ioArgs) {/*...*/}.
handle	Function	A function that stands in for both load and error, and thus should be called regardless of whether the request is successful.
sync	Boolean (false)	Whether to perform a synchronous request.
headers	Object ({})	Additional HTTP headers to include in the request.
postData	String ("")	Raw data to send in the body of a POST request. Only valid for use with rawXhrPost.
putData	String ("")	Raw data to send in the body of a PUT request. Only valid for use with rawXhrPut.

The RESTful XHR functions offered by the toolkit follow; as of Dojo version 1.1, each of these functions sets the X-Requested-With: XMLHttpRequest header to the server automatically. A discussion of the args parameter follows.

All of the XHR functions return a special Object called Deferred, which you'll learn more about in the next section. For now, just concentrate on the discussion at hand.

`dojo.xhrGet(/*Object*/args)`
> Performs an XHR GET request.

`dojo.xhrPost(/*Object*/args)`
> Performs an XHR POST request.

`dojo.rawXhrPost(/*Object*/args)`
> Performs an XHR POST request and allows you to provide the raw data that should be included as the body of the POST.

`dojo.xhrPut(/*Object*/args)`
> Performs an XHR PUT request.

`dojo.rawXhrPut(/*Object*/args)`
> Performs an XHR PUT request and allows you to provide the raw data that should be included as the body of the PUT.

`dojo.xhrDelete(/*Object*/args)`
> Performs an XHR DELETE request.

`dojo.xhr(/*String*/ method, /*Object*/ args, /*Boolean?*/ hasBody)`
> A general purpose XHR function that allows you to define any arbitrary HTTP method to perform asynchronsously.

Although most of the items in the table are pretty straightforward, the arguments that are passed into the load and error functions bear mentioning. The first parameter, response, is what the server returns, and the value for handleAs specifies how the response should be interpreted. Although the default value is "text", specifying "json", for example, results in the response being cast into a JavaScript object so that the response value may be treated as such.

> In the load and error functions, you should always return the response value. As you'll learn later in this chapter, all of the various input/output calls such as the XHR facilities return a type called a Deferred, and returning responses so that callbacks and error handlers can be chained together is an important aspect of interacting with Deferreds.

The second parameter, ioArgs, contains some information about the final arguments that were passed to the server in making the request. Although you may not need to use ioArgs very frequently, you may occasionally find it useful—especially in debugging situations. Table 4-2 describes the values you might see in ioArgs.

Table 4-2. Property values for ioArgs

Name	Type	Comment
args	Object	The original argument to the IO call.
xhr	XMLHttpRequest	The actual XMLHttpRequest object that was used for the request.

Table 4-2. Property values for ioArgs (continued)

Name	Type	Comment
url	String	The final URL used for the call; often different than the one provided because it is fitted with query parameters, etc.
query	String	Defined only for non-GET requests, this value provides the query string parameters that were passed with the request.
handleAs	String	How the response should be interpreted.

XHR Examples

At an absolute minimum, the arguments for an XHR request should include the URL to retrieve along with the load function; however, it's usually a *very* good idea to include an error handler, so don't omit it unless there you're really sure you can't possibly need it. Here's an example:

```
//...snip...
dojo.addOnLoad(function( ) {
    dojo.xhrGet({

        url : "someText.html",  //the relative URL

        // Run this function if the request is successful
        load : function(response, ioArgs) {
            console.log("successful xhrGet", response, ioArgs);

            //Set some element's content...
            dojo.byId("foo").innerHTML= response;

            return response; //always return the response back
        },

        // Run this function if the request is not successful
        error : function(response, ioArgs) {
            console.log("failed xhrGet", response, ioArgs);

            /* handle the error... */

            return response; //always return the response back
        }
    });
});
//...snip...
```

You may not necessarily want plain text back; you may want to time out the request after some duration, and you might want to pass in some additional information a query string. Fortunately, life doesn't get any harder. Just add some parameters, like so:

```
dojo.xhrGet({

    url : "someCommentFilteredJSON.html",
    // Returns something like: /*{'bar':'baz'}*/
```

```
        handleAs : "json",
        // Strip the comments and eval to a JavaScript object

        timeout: 5000, //Call the error handler if nothing after 5 seconds
        content: {foo:'bar'}, //Append foo=bar to the query string

        // Run this function if the request is successful
        load : function(response, ioArgs) {
            console.log("successful xhrGet", request, ioArgs);
            console.log(response);

            //Our handleAs value tells Dojo to strip comments
            //and convert the data to an object

            dojo.byId("foo").innerHTML= response.bar;
            //Display now updated to say 'baz'

            return response; //always return the response back
        },

        // Run this function if the request is not successful
        error : function(response, ioArgs) {
            console.log("failed xhrGet");
            return response; //always return the response back
        }
    });
```

Do note that not specifying a proper value for handleAs can produce frustrating bugs that may not be immediately apparent. For example, if you were to mistakenly omit the handleAs parameter, but try to access the response value as a JavaScript object in your load function, you'd most certainly get a nasty error that might lead you to look in a lot of other places before realizing that you are trying to treat a String as an Object—which may not be immediately obvious because logs may display the values nearly identically.

Although applications tend to perform a lot of GET requests, you are bound to come across a circumstance when you'll need to PUT, POST, or DELETE something. The process is exactly the same with the minor caveats that you'll need to include a putData or postData argument for rawXhrPut and rawXhrPost requests, respectively, as a means of providing the data that should be sent to the server. Here's an example of a rawXhrPost:

```
dojo.rawXhrPost({
    url : "/place/to/post/some/raw/data",
    postData : "{foo : 'bar'}", //a JSON literal
    handleAs : "json",

    load : function(response, ioArgs) {
        /* Something interesting  happens here */
        return response;
    },
```

```
        error : function(response, ioArgs) {
            /* Better handle that error */
            return response;
    }
});
```

General Purpose XMLHttpRequest Calls

Dojo version 1.1 introduced a more general-purpose dojo.xhr function with the following signature:

```
dojo.xhr(/*String*/ method, /*Object*/ args, /*Boolean?*/ hasBody)
```

As it turns out, each of the XHR functions from this chapter are actually wrappers around this function. For example, dojo.xhrGet is really just the following wrapper:

```
dojo.xhrGet  = function(args) {
    return dojo.xhr("GET", args); //Always provide the method name in all caps!
}
```

Although you'll generally want to use the shortcuts presented in this section, the more general-purpose dojo.xhr function can be useful for some situations in which you need to programmatically configure XHR requests or for times when a wrapper isn't available. For example, to perform a HEAD request for which there isn't a wrapper, you could do the following:

```
dojo.xhr("HEAD", {
    url : "/foo/bar/baz",
    load : function(response, ioArgs) { /*...*/},
    error : function(response, ioArgs) { /*...*/}
});
```

Hitching Up Callbacks

Chapter 2 introduced hitch, a function that can be used to guarantee that functions are executed in context. One common place to use hitch is in conjunction with XHR callback functions because the context of the callback function is different from the context of the block that executed the callback function. The following block of code demonstrates the need for hitch by illustrating a common pattern, which aliases this to work around the issue of context in the callback:

```
//Suppose you have the following addOnLoad block, which could actually be any
JavaScript Object
dojo.addOnLoad(function( ) {

        //foo is bound the context of this anonymous function
        this.foo = "bar";

        //alias "this" so that it can be referenced inside of the load callback...
        var self=this;
        dojo.xhrGet({
```

```
        url : "./data",
        load : function(response, ioArgs) {
            //you must have aliased "this" to reference foo inside of here...
            console.log(self.foo, response);
        },
        error : function(response, ioArgs) {
            console.log("error", response, ioArgs);
        }
    });

});
```

While it may not look very confusing for this short example, it can get a bit messy to repeatedly alias this to another value that can be referenced. The next time you encounter the need to alias this, consider the following pattern that makes use of hitch:

```
dojo.addOnLoad(function( ) {

    //foo is in the context of this anonymous function
    this.foo = "bar";

    //hitch a callback function to the current context so that foo
    //can be referenced
    var callback = dojo.hitch(this, function(response, ioArgs) {
        console.log("foo (in context) is", this.foo);
        //and you still have response and ioArgs at your disposal...
    });

    dojo.xhrGet({
        url : "./data",
        load : callback,
        error : function(response, ioArgs) {
            console.log("error", response, ioArgs);
        }
    });

});
```

And don't forget that hitch accepts arguments, so you could just as easily have passed in some parameters that would have been available in the callback, like so:

```
dojo.addOnLoad(function( ) {

    //foo is in the context of this anonymous function
    this.foo = "bar";

    //hitch a callback function to the current context so that foo can be
    //referenced
    var callback = dojo.hitch(
        this,
        function(extraParam1, extraParam2, response, ioArgs) {
```

```
                console.log("foo (in context) is", this.foo);
                //and you still have response and ioArgs at your disposal...
            },
            "extra", "params"
        );

        dojo.xhrGet({
            url : "./data",
            load : callback,
            error : function(response, ioArgs) {
                console.log("error", response, ioArgs);
            }
        });

    });
```

If you may have a variable number of extra parameters, you can instead opt to use arguments, remembering that the final two values will be response and ioArgs.

Deferreds

JavaScript doesn't currently support the concept of threads, but it does offer the ability to perform asynchronous requests via the XMLHttpRequest object and through delays with the setTimeout function. However, it doesn't take too many asynchronous calls running around before matters get awfully confusing. Base provides a class called Deferred to help manage the complexity often associated with the tedious implementation details of asynchronous events. Like other abstractions, Deferreds allow you to hide away tricky logic and/or boilerplate into a nice, consistent interface.

If the value of a Deferred was described in one sentence, however, it would probably be that it enables you to treat all network I/O uniformly regardless of whether it is synchronous or asynchronous. Even if a Deferred is in flight, has failed, or finished successfully, the process for chaining callbacks and errbacks is the exact same. As you can imagine, this behavior significantly simplifies bookkeeping.

> Dojo's implementation of a Deferred is minimally adapted from MochiKit's implementation, which in turn is inspired from Twisted's implementation of the same. Some good background on MochiKit's implementation is available at *http://www.mochikit.com/doc/html/ MochiKit/Async.html#fn-deferred*. Twisted's implementation of Deferreds is available at *http://twistedmatrix.com/projects/core/ documentation/howto/defer.html*.

Some key features of Deferreds are that they allow you to chain together multiple callbacks and *errbacks* (error-handling routines) so they execute in a predictable sequential order, and Deferreds also allow you to provide a canceling routine that you can use to cleanly abort asynchronous requests. You may not have realized it at the time, but all of those XHR functions you were introduced to earlier in the chapter were returning Deferreds, although we didn't have an immediate need to dive into that just then. In fact, all of the network input/output machinery in the toolkit use and return Deferreds because of the flexibility they offer in managing the asynchronous activity that results from network calls.

Before revisiting some of our earlier XHR efforts, take a look at the following abstract example that directly exposes a Deferred, which forms the basis for some of the concepts that are coming up:

```
//Create a Deferred
var d = new dojo.Deferred(/* Optional cancellation function goes here */);

//Add a callback
d.addCallback(function(response) {
    console.log("The answer is", response);
    return response;
});

//Add another callback to be fired after the previous one
d.addCallback(function(response) {
    console.log("Yes, indeed. The answer is", response);
    return response;
});

//Add an errback just in case something goes wrong
d.addErrback(function(response) {
    console.log("An error occurred", response);
    return response;
});

//Could add more callbacks/errbacks as needed...

/* Lots of calculations happen */

//Somewhere along the way, the callback chain gets started
d.callback(46);
```

If you run the example in Firebug, you'd see the following output:

```
The answer is 46
Yes, indeed. The answer is 46
```

Before jumping into some more involved examples, you'll probably want to see the API that a Deferred exposes (Table 4-3).

Table 4-3. Deferred functions and properties

Name	Return type	Comment
addCallback(/*Function*/handler)	Deferred	Adds a callback function to the callback chain for successes.
addErrback(/*Function*/handler)	Deferred	Adds a callback function to the callback chain for errors.
addBoth(/*Function|Object*/ context, /*String?*/name)	Deferred	Adds a callback function that acts as both the callback for successes and errors. Useful for adding code that you want to guarantee will run one way or another.
addCallbacks(/*Function*/callback, /*Function*/errback)	Deferred	Allows you to add a callback and an errback at the same time.
callback(/*Any*/value)	N/A	Executes the callback chain.
errback(/*Any*/value)	N/A	Executes the errback chain.
cancel()	N/A	Cancel the request and execute the cancellation function provided to the constructor, if provided.

Be aware that a Deferred may be in an error state based on one or more combinations of three distinct possibilities:

- A callback or errback is passed a parameter that is an Error object.
- A callback or errback raises an exception.
- A callback or errback returns a value that is an Error object.

Typical use cases normally do not involve the canceller, silentlyCancelled, and fired properties of a Deferred, which provide a reference to the cancellation function, a means of determining if the Deferred was cancelled but there was no canceller method registered, and a means of determining if the Deferred status of the fired, respectively. Values for fired include:

−1: No value yet (initial condition)

0: Successful execution of the callback chain

1: An error occurred

Deferred Examples Via CherryPy

Let's get warmed up with a simple routine on the server that briefly pauses and then serves some content. (The pause is just a way of emphasizing the notion of asynchronous behavior.)

The complete CherryPy file that provides this functionality follows:

```python
import cherrypy
from time import sleep
import os

# a foo.html file will contain our Dojo code performing the XHR request
# and that's all the following config directive is doing

current_dir = os.getcwd()
config = {'/foo.html' :
    {
    'tools.staticfile.on' : True,
    'tools.staticfile.filename' : os.path.join(current_dir, 'foo.html')
    }
}


class Content:

    # this is what actually serves up the content
    @cherrypy.expose
    def index(self):
        sleep(3) # purposefully add a 3 sec delay before responding
        return "Hello"

# start up the web server and have it listen on 8080
cherrypy.quickstart(Content(), '/', config=config)
```

Same Origin Policy

It's instructive to notice that we go through the extra step of setting up CherryPy to serve a static file to us, and from the static file, we perform the XHR request. The reason is because the XMLHttpRequest object that JavaScript provides will not allow you to perform cross-site scripting for security reasons. Hence, we would not be able to open up a local file such as *file:///foo.html* in our browser and use dojo.xhrGet to request a file from *http://127.0.0.1:8080/*. Yes, they're both on your local box, but the domains are still different. As you'll see in the next section, a technique known as JSONP can be used to sidestep the security issue and load content from other domains, which gives way to creating applications like mashups. Other common approaches for loading content from another domain involve opening sockets via Flash-based plug-ins or ActiveX. In any event, be advised that running untrusted code on your domain is a security risk and should never be taken lightly.

Assuming that the CherryPy content is saved in a file called *hello.py*, you'd simply type python hello.py in a terminal to startup the server. You should be able to verify that if you navigate to *http://127.0.0.1:8080/* that "Hello" appears on your screen after a brief delay.

Using Deferreds returned from XHR functions

Once you have CherryPy up and running save the file below as *foo.html* and place it alongside the *foo.py* file you already have running. You should be able to navigate to *http://127.0.0.1:8080/foo.html* and have *foo.html* load up without any issues:

```html
<html>
    <head>
        <title>Fun with Deferreds!</title>

        <script type="text/javascript"
            src="http://o.aolcdn.com/dojo/1.1/dojo/dojo.xd.js">
        </script>

        <script type="text/javascript">
            dojo.addOnLoad(function( ) {

                //Fire off an asynchronous request, which returns a Deferred
                var d = dojo.xhrGet({
                    url: "http://localhost:8080",
                    timeout : 5000,
                    load : function(response, ioArgs) {
                        console.log("Load response is:", response);
                        console.log("Executing the callback chain now...");
                        return response;
                    },
                    error : function(response, ioArgs) {
                        console.log("Error!", response);
                        console.log("Executing the errback chain now...");
                        return response;
                    }
                });

                console.log("xhrGet fired. Waiting on callbacks or errbacks");

                //Add some callbacks
                d.addCallback(
                    function(result) {
                        console.log("Callback 1 says that the result is ", result);
                        return result;
                    }
                );

                d.addCallback(
                    function (result) {
                        console.log("Callback 2 says that the result is ", result);
                        return result;
                    }
                );

                //Add some errbacks
                d.addErrback(
```

```
                    function(result) {
                      console.log("Errback 1 says that the result is ", result);
                      return result;
                    }
                );

                d.addErrback(
                    function(result) {
                      console.log("Errback 2 says that the result is ", result);
                      return result;
                    }
                );
            });
        </script>
    </head>
    <body>
    Check the Firebug console.
    </body>
</html>
```

After running this example, you should see the following output in the Firebug console:

```
xhrGet fired. Waiting on callbacks or errbacks
Load response is: Hello
Executing the callback chain now...
Callback 1 says that the result is Hello
Callback 2 says that the result is Hello
```

The big takeaway from this example is that the Deferred gives you a clean, consistent interface for interacting with whatever happens to come back from the xhrGet, whether it is a successful response or an error that needs to be handled.

You can adjust the timing values in the dojo.xhrGet function to timeout in less than the three seconds the server will take to respond to produce an error if you want to see the errback chain fire. The errback chain fires if something goes wrong in one of the callback functions, so you could introduce an error in a callback function to see the callback chain partially evaluate before kicking off the errback chain.

 Remember to return the value that is passed into callbacks and errbacks so that the chains can execute the whole way through. Inadvertently short-circuiting this behavior causes bizarre results because it inadvertently stops the callback or errback chain from executing—now you know why it is so important to always remember and return a response in your load and error handlers for XHR functions.

Figure 4-2 illustrates the basic flow of events for a Deferred. One of the key points to take away is that Deferreds act like chains.

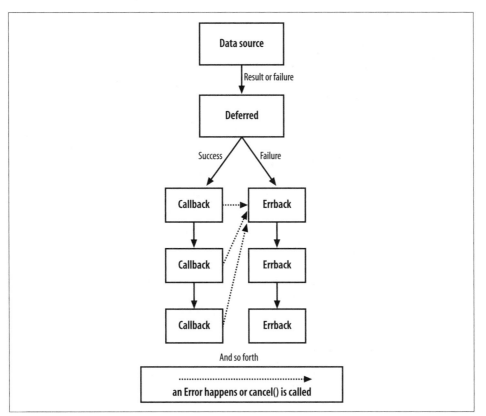

Figure 4-2. The basic flow of events through a Deferred

Injecting Deferreds into XHR functions

Another great feature of a `Deferred` is that you have a clean way of canceling an asynchronous action before it completes. The following refinement to our previous example illustrates both the ability to cancel an in-flight request as well as "injecting" a `Deferred` into the load and error handlers of the request:

```
<html>
    <head>
        <title>Fun with Deferreds!</title>

        <script type="text/javascript"
            src="http://o.aolcdn.com/dojo/1.1/dojo/dojo.xd.js">
        </script>

    <script type="text/javascript">
        dojo.addOnLoad(function() {
```

```
var d = new dojo.Deferred;

  //Add some callbacks
  d.addCallback(
    function(result) {
      console.log("Callback 1 says that the result is ", result);
      return result;
    }
  );

  d.addCallback(
    function (result) {
      console.log("Callback 2 says that the result is ", result);
      return result;
    }
  );

  //Add some errbacks
  d.addErrback(
    function(result) {
      console.log("Errback 1 says that the result is ", result);
      return result;
    }
  );

  d.addErrback(
    function(result) {
      console.log("Errback 2 says that the result is ", result);
      return result;
    }
  );

  //Fire off an asynchronous request, which returns a Deferred
  request = dojo.xhrGet({
    url: "http://localhost:8080",
    timeout : 5000,
    load : function(response, ioArgs) {
        console.log("Load response is:", response);
        console.log("Executing the callback chain now...");

        //inject our Deferred's callback chain
        d.callback(response, ioArgs);

        //allow the xhrGet's Deferred chain to continue..
        return response;
    },
    error : function(response, ioArgs) {
      console.log("Error!", response);
      console.log("Executing the errback chain now...");

      //inject our Deferred's errback chain
      d.errback(response, ioArgs);
```

```
                        //allow the xhrGet's Deferred chain to continue..
                        return response;
                    }
                });
        });
    </script>
    </head>
    <body>
        XHR request in progress. You have about 3 seconds to cancel it.
        <button onclick="javascript:request.cancel()">Cancel</button>
    </body>
</html>
```

If you run the example, you'll see the following output:

```
xhrGet just fired. Waiting on callbacks or errbacks now...
Load response is: Hello
Executing the callback chain now...
Callback 1 says that the result is Hello
Callback 2 says that the result is Hello
```

Whereas pressing the Cancel button yields the following results:

```
xhrGet just fired. Waiting on callbacks or errbacks now...
Press the button to cancel...
Error: xhr cancelled dojoType=cancel message=xhr cancelleddojo.xd.js (line 20)
Error! Error: xhr cancelled dojoType=cancel message=xhr cancelled
Executing the errback chain now...
Errback 1 says that the result is Error: xhr cancelled dojoType=cancel message=xhr
cancelled
Errback 2 says that the result is Error: xhr cancelled dojoType=cancel message=xhr
cancelled
```

Custom canceller

The various XHR functions all have a special cancellation function that is invoked by calling cancel( ), but for custom Deferreds, you can create your own custom canceller, like so:

```
var canceller = function( ) {
    console.log("custom canceller...");
    //If you don't return a custom Error, a default "Deferred Cancelled" Error is
    //returned
}
var d = new dojo.Deferred(canceller); //pass in the canceller to the constructor
/* ....interesting stuff happens...*/
d.cancel( ); // errbacks could be ready to respond to the "Deferred Cancelled" Error
             //in a special way
```

DeferredList

While Deferred is an innate part of Base, Core provides DeferredList, an additional supplement that facilitates some use cases in which you need to manage multiple Deferreds. Common use cases for DeferredList include:

- Firing a specific callback or callback chain when all of callbacks for a collection of Deferreds have fired
- Firing a specific callback or callback chain when at least one of the callbacks for a collection of Deferreds have fired
- Firing a specific errback or errback chain when at least one of the errbacks for a collection of Deferreds have fired

The API for DeferredList follows:

```
dojo.DeferredList(/*Array*/list, /*Boolean?*/fireOnOneCallback, /*Boolean?*/
    fireOnOneErrback,  /*Boolean?*/consumeErrors, /*Function?*/canceller)
```

The signature should be self-descriptive in that calling the constructor with only a single parameter that is an Array of Deferreds produces the default behavior of firing the callback chain when the callback chains for all of the Deferreds have fired; passing in Boolean parameters can control if the callback or errback chain should be fired when at least one callback or errback has fired, respectively.

Setting consumeErrors to true results in errors being consumed by the DeferredList, which is handy if you don't want the errors produced by the individual Deferreds in the list to be directly exposed, and canceller provides a way of passing in custom cancellation function, just like with an ordinary Deferred.

Form and HTTP Utilities

While certain AJAX designs can certainly be breathtaking if implemented properly, let's not forget that certain tried and true elements like plain old HTML forms are far from obsolete and still have prominent roles to play in many modern designs—with or without AJAXification. Three functions that Base provides to transform forms include:

```
dojo.formToObject(/*DOMNode||String*/ formNode) //Returns Object
dojo.formToQuery(/*DOMNode||String*/ formNode) //Returns String
dojo.formToJson(/*DOMNode||String*/ formNode) //Returns String
```

To illustrate the effect of each of these functions, let's suppose we have the following form:

```
<form id="register">

    <input type="text" name="first" value="Foo">
    <input type="button" name="middle" value="Baz" disabled>
    <input type="text" name="last" value="Bar">

    <select type="select" multiple name="favorites" size="5">
        <option value="red">red</option>
        <option value="green" selected>green</option>
        <option value="blue" selected>blue</option>
    </select>

</form>
```

Here's the effect of running each function. Note that the disabled form element was skipped in the transform.

formToObject produces:

```
{
    first: "Foo",
    last : "Bar",
    favorites: [
        "green",
        "blue"
    ]
};
```

formToQuery produces:

```
"first=Foo&last=Bar&favorites=green&favorites=blue"
```

formToJson produces:

```
'{"first": "Foo", "last": "Bar", "favorites": ["green", "blue"]}'
```

Base provides the following additional convenience functions to you for converting a query string to an object and vice versa. They're just as straightforward as you might imagine with the caveat that the *values in query string are converted to strings, even when they are numeric values*:

```
dojo.queryToObject(/*String*/ str) //Returns Object
dojo.objectToQuery(/*Object*/ map) // Returns String
```

Here's a quick snippet to illustrate:

```
//produces {foo : "1", bar : "2", baz : "3"}
var o = dojo.queryToObject("foo=1&bar=2&baz=3");

//converts back to foo=1&bar=2&baz=3
dojo.objectToQuery(o);
```

Cross-Site Scripting with JSONP

While JavaScript's XmlHttpRequest object does not allow you to load data from outside of the page's current domain because of the same origin policy, it turns out that SCRIPT tags are not subject to the "same origin" policy. Consequently, an informal standard known as JSONP has been developed that allows data to be cross-domain loaded. As you might imagine, it is this very capability that empowers web applications[*] to *mash up* data from multiple sources and present it in a single coherent application.

---

[*] Without loading any external plugins, JSONP is your only means of loading cross-domain data. Plug-ins such as Flash and ActiveX, however, have other ways of working around the "same origin" limitation that is placed on the browser itself.

JSONP Primer

Like anything else, JSONP sounds a bit mysterious at first, but it is pretty simple once you understand it. To introduce the concept, imagine that a SCRIPT tag is dynamically created and appended to the HEAD of a page that was originally loaded from *http://oreilly.com*. The interesting twist comes in with the source of the tag: instead of loading from the oreilly.com domain, it's perfectly free to load from any domain, say *http://example.com?id=23*. Using JavaScript, the operation so far is simple:

```
e = document.createElement("SCRIPT");
e.src="http://example.com?id=23";
e.type="text/javascript";
document.getElementsByTagName("HEAD")[0].appendChild(e);
```

Although the SCRIPT tag normally implies that you are loading an actual script, you can actually return any kind of content you'd like, including JSON objects. There's just one problem with that—the objects would just get appended to the HEAD of the page and nothing interesting would happen (except that you might wreck the way your page looks).

For example, you might end up with something like the following blurb, where the emphasized text is the result of the previous JavaScript snippet that dynamically added the SCRIPT tag to the HEAD of the page:

```
<html>
  <head>
    <title>My Page</title>
    <script type="text/javascript" >
      {foo : "bar"}
    </script>
  </head>
  <body>
Some page content.
  </body>
</html>
```

While shoving a JavaScript object literal into the HEAD is of little use, imagine what would happen if you could somehow receive back JSON data that was wrapped in a function call—to be more precise, a function call that is already defined somewhere on your page. In effect, you'd be achieving a truly marvelous thing because you could now asynchronously request external data whenever you want it and immediately pass it into a function for processing. To accomplish this feat, all that it takes is having the result of inserting the SCRIPT tag return the JSON data *padded* with an extra function call such as myCallback({foo : "bar"}) instead of just {foo : "bar"}. Assuming that myCallback is already defined when the SCRIPT tag finishes loading, you're all set because the function will execute, pass in the data as a parameter, and effectively provide you with a callback function. (It's worth taking a moment to let this process sink in if it hasn't quite clicked yet.)

But there's still a small problem: how do you get the JSON object to come wrapped with that extra padding that triggers a callback? Easy—all the kind folks at *example.com* have to do is provide you with an additional query string parameter that allows you to define the name of the function that the result should be wrapped in. Assuming that they've determined that you should pass in your function via the c parameter (a new request that provides c as a query string parameter for you to use), calling http://example.com?id=23&c=myCallback would return myCallback({foo : "bar"}). And that's all there is to it.

Core IO

This section explains the dojo.io facilities that are provided by Core. Injecting dynamic SCRIPT tags to retrieve padded JSON and hacking IFRAMEs into a viable transport layer are the central topics of discussion.

Using JSONP with Dojo

You know enough about Dojo by this point that you won't be surprised to know that it streamlines the work involved in implementing JSONP. To accomplish the same functionality as what was described in the primer, you could use dojo.io.script.get, which takes most of the same parameters as the various XHR methods. Notable caveats are that handleAs really isn't applicable for JSONP, and callbackParamName is needed so that Dojo can set up and manage a callback function to be executed on your behalf.

Here's an example of how it's done:

```
//dojo.io.script is not part of Base, so remember to require it into the page
dojo.require("dojo.io.script");

dojo.io.script.get({
  callbackParamName : "c", //provided by the jsonp service
  url: "http://example.com?id=23",
  load : function(response, ioArgs) {
    console.log(response);
    return response;
  },
  error : function(response, ioArgs) {
    console.log(response);
    return response;
  }
});
```

To clarify, the callbackParamName specifies the name of the query string parameter that is established by *example.com*. *It is not the name of a function you've defined to act as a callback yourself.* Behind the scenes, Dojo manages the callback by creating a temporary function and channeling the response into the load function, following the same conventions as the other XHR functions. So, just allow Dojo to remove that padding for you, and then use the result in the load function and be on your merry way.

 If `callbackParamName` was not specified at all or was incorrectly specified, you'd get a JavaScript error along the lines of `"<some callback function> does not exist"` because the result of the dynamic `SCRIPT` tag would be trying to execute a function that doesn't exist.

Connecting to a Flickr data source

The following example illustrates making a JSONP call to a Flickr data source. Try running it in Firebug to see what happens. It is also worthwhile and highly instructive to examine the error that occurs if you don't provide `callbackParamName` (or misspell it):

```
dojo.require("dojo.io.script");
dojo.io.script.get({
    callbackParamName : "jsoncallback", //provided by Flickr
    url: "http://www.flickr.com/services/feeds/photos_public.gne",
    content : {format : "json"},
    load : function(response, ioArgs) {
     console.log(response);
     return response;
    },
    error : function(response, ioArgs) {
      console.log("error");
      console.log(response);
      return response;
    }
});
```

Getting back JavaScript from a JSONP call

As it turns out, you could also use `dojo.io.script.get` to interact with a server method that returns pure JavaScript. In this case, you'd perform the request in the same manner, except instead of providing a `callbackParamName`, you'd provide a `checkString` value. The "check string" value is a mechanism that allows for checking an in-flight response to see if it has completed. Basically, if running the `typeof` operator on the check string value does not return undefined, the assumption is that the JavaScript has completed loading. (In other words, it's a hack.) Assuming that you had CherryPy set up with the following simple script, you would use a `checkString` value of o to indicate that the script has successfully loaded, as o is the variable that you're expecting to get back via the JSONP call (and when `typeof(o) != undefined`, you can assume your call is complete).

First, the CherryPy script that serves up the JavaScript:

```
import cherrypy

class Content:
    @cherrypy.expose
    def index(self):
        return "var o = {a : 1, b:2}"

cherrypy.quickstart(Content())
```

Assuming you have CherryPy running on port 8080, here's the corresponding Dojo to fetch the JavaScript:

```
dojo.require("dojo.io.script");
dojo.io.script.get({
  checkString : "o",
  timeout : 2000,
  url : "http://localhost:8080",
  load : function(response, ioArgs) {
    console.log(o);
    console.log(response)
  },
  error : function(response, ioArgs) {
    console.log("error", response, ioArgs);
    return response;
  }
});
```

 Note that dojo.io.script.get introspects and determines if you're loading JavaScript or JSON based on the presence of either checkString or callbackParamName.

IFRAME Transports

Core provides an IFRAME transport that is handy for accomplishing tasks behind the scenes that would normally require the page to refresh. While XHR methods allow you to fetch data behind the scenes, they don't lend themselves to some tasks very well; form submissions, uploading files, and initiating file downloads are two common examples of when IFRAME transports come in handy.

Following the same pattern that the rest of the IO system has established, using an IFRAME transport requires passing an object containing keyword arguments, and returns a Deferred. IFRAME transports allow using either GET or POST as your HTTP method and a variety of handleAs parameters. In fact, you can provide any of the arguments with the following caveats/additions from Table 4-4.

Table 4-4. IFRAME transport keyword arguments

Name	Type (default)	Comment
`method`	`String ("POST")`	The HTTP method to use. Valid values include GET and POST.
`handleAs`	`String ("text")`	The format for the response data to be provided to the load or handle callback. Valid values include `"text"`, `"html"`, `"javascript"`, and `"json"`. For any value except `"html"`, the server response should be an HTML file with a `textarea` element that contains the response.
`content`	`Object`	If `form` is another argument, then the content object produce the same result as if they had been hidden form elements. If there is no form property, the `content` object is converted to a query string via `dojo.objectToQuery( )`.

 As of version 1.2, XML is also handled by the IFRAME transport.

File downloads with IFRAMEs

Because triggering a file download via an `IFRAME` is a common operation, let's try it out. Here's a CherryPy file that serves up a local file when you navigate to *http://localhost:8080/*. We'll use this URL in our `dojo.io.frame.send` call to the server:

```
import cherrypy
from cherrypy.lib.static import serve_file
import os

# update this path to an absolute path on your machine
local_file_path="/tmp/foo.html"

class Content:

    #serve up a file...
    @cherrypy.expose
    def download(self):
        return serve_file(local_file_path, "application/x-download", "attachment")

# start up the web server and have it listen on 8080
cherrypy.quickstart(Content(), '/')
```

Here's the HTML file that utilizes the `IFRAME`. You should be able to load it up, and, assuming you've updated the path in the CherryPy script to point to it, you'll get a download dialog when you click on the button.

 The first time a call to `dojo.io.iframe.send` happens, you may momentarily see the IFRAME get created and then disappear. A common way to work around this problem is to create the IFRAME by sending off an empty request when the page loads, which is generally undetectable. Then, when your application needs to do a send, you won't see the side effect.

```
<html>
    <head>
        <title>Fun with IFRAME Transports!</title>

        <script type="text/javascript"
            src="http://o.aolcdn.com/dojo/1.1/dojo/dojo.xd.js">
        </script>

        <script type="text/javascript">
            dojo.require("dojo.io.iframe");

            dojo.addOnLoad(function() {
                download = function() {
                    dojo.io.iframe.send({
                        url : "http://localhost:8080/download/"
                    });
                };
            });
        </script>
    </head>
    <body>
        <button onclick="javascript:download( )">Download!</button>
    </body>
</html>
```

In order to use the "Download!" button multiple times, you may need
to supply a timeout value for the dojo.io.iframe.send function so that
it can eventually time out and make itself available to service another
request.

Form submissions with IFRAMEs

Another common use case for IFRAMEs is submitting a form behind the scenes—
maybe even a form that involves a file upload, which would normally switch out the
page. Here's a CherryPy script that handles a file upload:

```
import cherrypy

# set this to wherever you want to place the uploaded file
local_file_path="/tmp/uploaded_file"

class Content:

    #serve up a file...
    @cherrypy.expose
    def upload(self, inbound):
        outfile = open(local_file_path, 'wb')
        inbound.file.seek(0)
        while True:
            data = inbound.file.read(8192)
            if not data:
                break
```

```
        outfile.write(data)
      outfile.close()

      # return a simple HTML file as the response
      return "<html><head></head><body>Thanks!</body></html>"
# start up the web server and have it listen on 8080
cherrypy.quickstart(Content(), '/')
```

And here's the HTML page that performs the upload. If you run the code, any file you upload gets sent in behind the scenes without the page changing, whereas using the form's own submit button POSTs the data and switches out the page. An important thing to note about the example is that the handleAs parameter calls for an HTML response.

```
<html>
    <head>
        <title>Fun with IFRAME Transports!</title>

        <script type="text/javascript"
          src="http://o.aolcdn.com/dojo/1.1/dojo.dojo.xd.js"
          djConfig="isDebug:true,dojoBlankHtmlUrl:'/path/to/blank.html'">
        </script>

        <script type="text/javascript">
            dojo.require("dojo.io.iframe");

            dojo.addOnLoad(function() {
                upload = function() {
                dojo.io.iframe.send({
                    form : "foo",
                    handleAs : "html", //response type from the server
                    url : "http://localhost:8080/upload/",
                    load : function(response, ioArgs) {
                        console.log(response, ioArgs);
                        return response;
                    },
                    error : function(response, ioArgs) {
                        console.log("error");
                        console.log(response, ioArgs);
                        return response;
                    }
                });
            };
            });
        </script>
    </head>
    <body>
        <form id="foo" action="http://localhost:8080/upload/" method="post"
        enctype="multipart/form-data">
            <label for="file">Filename:</label>
            <input type="file" name="inbound">
            <br />
```

```
                <input type="submit" value="Submit Via The Form">
            </form>

            <button onclick="javascript:upload();">Submit Via the IFRAME Transport
            </button>
        </body>
    </html>
```

The next section illustrates a caveat that involves getting back a response type that's
something other than HTML.

Non-HTML response types

The previous example's server response returned an HTML document that could
have been picked out of the response and manipulated. For non-HTML response
types, however, there's a special condition that you must fulfill, which involves
wrapping the response in a textarea tag. As it turns out, using an HTML document
is the only reliable, cross-browser way that this transport could know when a
response is loaded, and a textarea is a natural vehicle for transporting text-based
content. Internally, of course, Dojo extracts this content and sets it as the response.
The following example illustrates the changes to the previous example that would
allow the response type to be plain text as opposed to HTML.

 Note that while the previous examples for uploading and downloading files did not require the local HTML file to be served up by
CherryPy, the following example does. The difference is that the
IFRAME transport has to access the DOM of the page to extract the
content, which qualifies as cross-site scripting (whereas the previous
examples didn't involve any DOM manipulation at all).

The CherryPy script requires only that a configuration be added to serve up the *foo.html*
file and that the final response be changed to wrap the content inside of a textarea like
so:

```
import cherrypy
import os

# a foo.html file will contain our Dojo code performing the XHR request
# and that's all the following config directive is doing

current_dir = os.getcwd()
config = {'/foo.html' :
    {
    'tools.staticfile.on' : True,
    'tools.staticfile.filename' : os.path.join(current_dir, 'foo.html')
    }
}
```

```
        local_file_path="/tmp/uploaded_file"

    class Content:

        #serve up a file...
        @cherrypy.expose
        def upload(self, inbound):
            outfile = open(local_file_path, 'wb')
            inbound.file.seek(0)
            while True:
                data = inbound.file.read(8192)
                if not data:
                    break
                outfile.write(data)
            outfile.close( )
            return
"<html><head></head><body><textarea>Thanks!</textarea></body></html>"
```

The only notable change to the request itself is that the handleAs type is different:

```
dojo.io.iframe.send({
    form : dojo.byId("foo"),
    handleAs : "text", //response type from the server
    url : "http://localhost:8080/upload/",
    load : function(response, ioArgs) {
        console.log(response, ioArgs); //response is "Thanks!"
        return response;
    },
    error : function(response, ioArgs) {
        console.log("error");
        console.log(response, ioArgs);
        return response;
    }
});
```

Manually creating a hidden IFRAME

As a final consideration, there may be times when you need to create a hidden IFRAME in the page to load in some content and want to be notified when the content finishes loading. Unlike the dojo.io.iframe.send function, which creates an IFRAME and immediately sends some content, the dojo.io.iframe.create function creates an IFRAME and allows you to pass a piece of JavaScript that will be executed when the IFRAME constructs itself. Here's the API:

```
dojo.io.iframe.create(/*String*/frameName, /*String*/onLoadString, /*String?*/url)
//Returns DOMNode
```

Basically, you provide a name for the frame, a String value that gets evaluated as a callback, and an optional URL, which can load the frame. Here's an example that loads a URL into a hidden IFRAME on the page and executes a callback when it's ready:

```
<html>
    <head>
        <title>Fun with IFRAME Transports!</title>

        <script type="text/javascript"
            src="http://o.aolcdn.com/dojo/1./dojo/dojo.xd.js"
            djConfig="isDebug:true,dojoBlankHtmlUrl:'/path/to/blank.html'"
        </script>

        <script type="text/javascript">
            dojo.require("dojo.io.iframe");

            function customCallback() {
                console.log("callback!");

                //could refer to iframe content via dojo.byId("fooFrame")...
            }

            create = function() {
                dojo.io.iframe.create("fooFrame", "customCallback()",
                    "http://www.exmaple.com");
            }
        </script>
    </head>
    <body>
        <button onclick="javascript:create();">Create</button>
    </body>
</html>
```

Be advised that some pages have JavaScript functions in them that break them out of frames—which renders the previous usage of the transport ineffective.

Although you'll often immediately load something into an IFRAME, there may also be times when you need to create an empty frame. If you are using a locally installed toolkit, just omit the third parameter to dojo.io.iframe.create, and you'll get an empty one. If you are XDomain-loading, however, you'll need to point to a local template that supplies its content. There is a template located in your toolkit's directory at *dojo/resources/blank.html* that you can copy over to a convenient location. You also need to add an extra configuration parameter to djConfig before you try to create the IFRAME as shown in examples in this section.

In addition to the IO facilities provided by Core, DojoX also provides IO facilities through the dojox.io module. Among other things, you'll find utilities for XHR multipart requests and helpers for proxying.

JSON Remote Procedure Calls

By now, you may have noticed that even after using Dojo's various XHR methods such as dojo.xhrGet to reduce boilerplate, it is still a somewhat redundant and error-prone operation to repeatedly provide content to the call and write a load callback function. Fortunately, you can use Dojo's RPC (Remote Procedure Call) machinery to mitigate some of the monotony via Core's dojo.rpc module. In short, you provide some configuration information via a Simple Method Description (SMD), create an instance of this service by passing in the configuration, and then use the service instead of the xhrGet et al. If your application has a fairly standard way of interacting with the server and responds in very similar ways for error handling, etc., the benefit of using the rpc module is that you'll generally have a cleaner design that's less error-prone.

Currently, Core provides a JsonService and a JsonpService, which both descend from a base class called RpcService.

 The dojox.rpc module provides additional RPC capabilities, some of which may soon be migrated to Core.

JSON RPC Example

To illustrate some basic usage of the RPC machinery, let's work through an example that uses JsonService to process a list of numbers, providing the sum of the numbers or the sum of the sum of each number squared. The client consists of an SMD that provides two methods, sum and sumOfSquares, which both take a list of numbers:

```
<html>
    <head>
        <title>Fun with JSON RPC!</title>

        <script type="text/javascript"
            src="http://o.aolcdn.com/dojo/1.1/dojo/dojo.xd.js"
            djConfig="isDebug:true">
        </script>
        <script type="text/javascript">
            dojo.require("dojo.rpc.JsonService");
            dojo.addOnLoad(function( ) {

                //construct the smd as an Object literal...
                var o = {
                    "serviceType": "JSON-RPC",
                    "serviceURL": "/",
                    "methods":[
                        {
                            "name": "sum",
                            "parameters":[{name : "list"}]
                        },
```

```
                    {
                        "name": "sumOfSquares",
                        "parameters":[{name : "list"}]
                    }
                ]
            }

            //instantiate the service
            var rpcObject = new dojo.rpc.JsonService(o);

            //call the service and use the Deferred that is returned to add a
    callback
            var sum = rpcObject.sum([4,8,15,16,23,42]);
            sum.addCallback(function(response) {
                console.log("the answer is ", response);
            });
            //add more callbacks, errbacks, etc.

            //call sumOfSquares the very same way...
        });
    </script>
    <body>
  </body>
</html>
```

Hopefully, you see the connection that if there were lots of methods communicating with the server in a very standardized way, the general simplicity of calling an RPC client once you've set it up initially declutters the design significantly. Much of the elegance in using the dojo.rpc.JsonService is that it returns a Deferred so you can add callbacks and errbacks as needed.

In case you'd like to interact with the example, here's an example service script. For simplicity, this script purposely doesn't bring in a JSON processing library, but you'd most certainly want to do that for anything much more complicated than this example:

```python
import cherrypy
import os
# a foo.html file will contain our Dojo code performing the XHR request
# and that's all the following config directive is doing

current_dir = os.getcwd()
config = {'/foo.html' :
    {
    'tools.staticfile.on' : True,
    'tools.staticfile.filename' : os.path.join(current_dir, 'foo.html')
    }
}

class Content:

    @cherrypy.expose
    def index(self):
```

```
###########################################################
# for sheer simplicity, this example does not use a json lib.
# for anything more sophisticated than this example,
# get a good json library from http://json.org
###########################################################

# read the raw POST data
rawPost = cherrypy.request.body.read()

# cast to object
obj = eval(rawPost) #MAJOR security hole! you've been warned...

# process the data
if obj["method"] == "sum":
    result = sum(obj["params"][0])
if obj["method"] == "sumOfSquares":
    result = sum([i*i for i in obj["params"][0]])

# return a json response
return str({"result" : result})

# start up the web server and have it listen on 8080
cherrypy.quickstart(Content(), '/', config=config)
```

Using the JsonpService is very similar to using the JsonService. In your Dojo installation, there is an example SMD file for Yahoo! services located at *dojox/rpc/yahoo.smd* if you want to try it out.

OpenAjax Hub

The OpenAjax Alliance (*http://www.openajax.org/*) is an organization of vendors and organizations that have committed themselves to interoperable AJAX-based web technologies. One of the key issues of the current era of web development is being able to use multiple JavaScript libraries within a single application. While Dojo and some of the other frameworks take precautions to cover the bare minimums for interoperability such as protecting the global namespace, actually using two libraries concurrently so that they are truly interoperable continues to produce challenges in regards to actually passing data back and forth as well as overall programming style and learning curve.

The OpenAjax Alliance has proposed what is known as the OpenAjax Hub, which is a specification for how libraries should interact. You probably won't be surprised to learn that the basic technique for interoperability is the loosely coupled publish/subscribe idiom. To that end, Core provides an OpenAjax module that implements the specification and exposes the following methods via a global OpenAjax object:

- registerLibrary
- unregisterLibrary

- `publish`
- `subscribe`
- `unsubscribe`

As a champion of open standards, you can rest assured that Dojo will strive to stay current with the latest OpenAjax Hub specification, which you can read about at *http://www.openajax.org/member/wiki/OpenAjax_Hub_Specification.*

Summary

After reading this chapter, you should be able to:

- Use Dojo's XHR machinery to perform RESTful operations with a web server
- Understand how `Deferreds` provide the illusion of threads, even though JavaScript does not support threads
- Be aware that the toolkit's entire IO subsystem uses and generally returns `Deferreds` from function calls
- Be able to use Base's functions for converting forms to and from Objects and JSON
- Be able to use Core's IFRAME transport layer for common operations such as uploading and downloading files
- Understand how the RPC machinery can streamline application logic and produce a more maintainable design
- Be aware of the infrastructure Core provides for implementing the OpenAjax Hub

We'll move on to node manipulation in the next chapter.

## CHAPTER 5

Node Manipulation

This chapter provides an overview of query, behavior, and NodeList. These constructs provide concise and highly efficient mechanisms for manipulating DOM nodes. Querying the DOM using query's CSS selector syntax, decoupling events and manipulations from an HTML placeholder with Core's behavior module, and chaining operations together with the syntactic sugar offered by NodeList are among the fun topics coming up.

Much Ado About Querying

As this chapter was being written, a lot of exciting thing were happening with regard to querying the DOM. Some particular points of interest:

- The W3C updated its working draft of the Selectors API in late 2007 (*http://www.w3.org/TR/selectors-api/#documentselector*)
- WebKit has announced a native implementation of querySelector and querySelectorAll, the key constructs in the Selectors API (*http://webkit.org/blog/156/queryselector-and-queryselectorall/*)
- Firefox 3 implemented native support for getElementsByClassName, a mainstay of web developers (*http://ejohn.org/blog/getelementsbyclassname-in-firefox-3/*)

With that said, the facilities you're reading about in this chapter will continue to be a staple of the toolkit and of your own toolbox for years to come. Even with native support for the Selectors API, there will inevitably be quirks that need to be worked around and smoothed out, and some browsers will likely provide only partial implementations initially.

Until the day comes when all browsers implement the Selectors API uniformly, rest assured that the toolkit will keep your code as portable and optimal as it can be by leveraging native implementations where available and simulating implementations where they are lacking.

Query: One Size Fits All

If you've done much JavaScripting, you've no doubt needed to query against the DOM to look up some nodes based on some set of criteria. If you only needed to look them up by tag name, then you probably used document.getElementsByTagName and called it a day. However, if you needed to look up a set of nodes by class, a specific attribute value, or some combination thereof, you may have scratched your head and wondered why there wasn't a built-in getElementsByClass function. Apparently, everyone wondered that very same thing, and then set out to write their own version—some more successful than others.

Although earlier versions of Dojo included specialized implementations of functions like getElementsByClass, the toolkit now includes a function that universally allows you to query the DOM with CSS query syntax. To illustrate the use for a DOM querying Swiss army knife, consider a heroic attempt at implementing a getElementsByClass function (a very common need) yourself:

```
// Lookup elements from a class name, optionally starting at a particular parent node
function getElementsByClassName(/*String*/className, /*DOMNode?*/node) {
  var regex = new RegExp('(^| )' + className + '( |$)');
  var node = node||document.body;
  var elements = node.getElementsByTagName("*");
  var results = [];

  for (var i=0; i < elements.length; i++) {
    if (regex.test(elements[i].className)) {
      results.push(elements[i]);
    }
  }
}
return results;
```

While this function is only 12 lines of code, that's still 12 lines that you have to write, debug, and maintain. If you wanted to query by tags and classes, you'd have to add in an additional parameter to provide the tag name and pass it into the getElementsByTagName function. If you wanted to do anything else, you'd get to write and maintain that logic, too. That's all in addition to the fact that there's probably a corner case or two in which the above function might not work all of the time on all browsers, and that regular expression that may not be intuitively obvious.

Fortunately, dojo.query makes rolling your own query functions a thing of the past. Here's the API that provides universal querying:

```
dojo.query(/*String*/ query, /*String?|DOMNode?*/ root) //Returns NodeList
```

 Although you won't be formally introduced to NodeList for a few more pages, all you really need to know at the moment is that a NodeList is a subclass of Array that has some specialized extensions for manipulating nodes.

To accomplish the previous getElementsByClassName example via query, just pass in a CSS selector for a class name, like so:

```
dojo.query(".someClassName")
```

Querying for a tag type like a DIV and a class name is just as easy; you just update the selector with the additional CSS syntax:

```
dojo.query("div.someClass")
```

Starting to see the beauty in using a quick one liner to query the DOM using a uniform syntax? You'll like it even better as you keep reading. First, however, take a look at Table 5-1 to get a feel for the wide range of common operations you can accomplish with query. See *http://www.w3.org/TR/css3-selectors/* for the definitive reference on CSS selectors.

Table 5-1. Commonly used CSS selectors

Syntax	Meaning	Example
*	Any element	dojo.query("*")
E	Elements of type E	dojo.query("div")
.C	Elements with class C	dojo.query(".baz")
E.C	Elements of type E having class C	dojo.query("div.baz")
#ID	Element with ID ID	dojo.query("#quux")
E#ID	Element of type E with ID ID	dojo.query("div#quux")
[A]	Elements with attribute A	dojo.query("[foo]")
E[A]	Elements of type E with attribute A	dojo.query("div[foo]")
[A="V"]	Elements with attribute A having value "V"	dojo.query("[foo='bar']")
E[A~='V']	Elements of type E having a list of space separated attributes, one of which is exactly equal to "V"	dojo.query("div[foo~='bar']")
E[A^='V']	Elements of type E having an attribute that begins with "V"	dojo.query("div[foo^='bar']")
E[A$='V']	Elements of type E having an attribute that ends with "V"	dojo.query("div[foo$='bar']")
E[A*='V']	Elements of type E having an attribute that contains the substring "V"	dojo.query("div[foo*='bar']")
,	Boolean OR	dojo.query("div,span.baz")
E > F	Element F is a child of element E	dojo.query("div > span")
E F	Element F is an arbitrary descendant of element E	dojo.query("E F")

Warm Up

Let's warm up to dojo.query with a page containing some simple markup as part of a storybook structure. For brevity, only one full scene is included:

```
<div id="introduction" class="intro">
    <p>
        Once upon a time, long ago...
    </p>
</div>

<div id="scene1" class="scene">...</div>

<div id="scene2" class="scene">
    <p>
        At the table in the <span class="place">kitchen</span>, there were three
    bowls of <span class="food">porridge</span>. <span class="person">Goldilocks</span>
    was hungry. She tasted the <span class="food">porridge</span> from the first bowl.
    </p>
    <p>
        "This <span class="food">porridge</span> is too hot!" she exclaimed.
    </p>

    <p>
        So, she tasted the <span class="food">porridge</span> from the second bowl.
    </p>

    <p>
        "This <span class="food">porridge</span> is too cold," she said
    </p>
    <p>
        So, she tasted the last bowl of <span class="food">porridge</span>.
    </p>

    <p>
        "Ahhh, this <span class="food">porridge</span> is just right," she said
    happily and she ate it all up.
    </p>
</div>

<div id="scene3" class="scene">...</div>
```

As was demonstrated in our earlier example, getElementsByTagName returns an array
of DOM nodes for a given type. The dojo.query equivalent is to simply provide the
tag name as the argument string; so, in order to query a page for all of the div elements, you'd simply use dojo.query("div"), like so:

```
dojo.query("div")
//Returns [div#introduction.intro, div#scene1.scene, div#scene2.scene,
//div#scene3.scene]
```

Note that if you want to query against only the children of a particular node instead
of the entire page, you can specify a second argument to query using that second
argument as the root of the tree. For example, to query only scene2 for paragraph
elements instead of the entire page for paragraph elements, provide the second
parameter as a node or the id of a node, like so:

```
dojo.query("p", "scene2")
//Returns [p, p, p, p, p, p]
```

Querying a page for elements of a specific class is just as simple; just indicate the class you're looking for using CSS query syntax, which, according to the specification, means prefixing the class name with a leading dot. For example, you could query all of the elements that currently have the food class applied to them, like so:

```
dojo.query(".food")
//Returns [span.food, span.food, span.food, span.food, span.food,
//span.food, span.food]
```

 Base's addClass and removeClass functions do not expect a leading dot to identify class names and won't return the correct results if you include it. This can be easy to forget when you're just starting out with the toolkit.

Combining the ability to query by tag and class is just as easy: combine the two constructs. Consider the case of wanting to query for span elements that have the place class applied:

```
dojo.query("span.place")
//Returns [span.place]
```

Selecting a class is handy and all, but there are plenty of times when you'll want to select more than one class. Fortunately, you can accomplish this task using the same simple approach that you've already grown to love. For example, you could select all of the elements having food and place applied thusly:

```
dojo.query(".food,.place")
//Returns [span.food, span.food, span.food, span.food, span.food, span.food,
//span.food, span.place]
```

 Parts of a CSS expression that are separated by a comma all stand on their own. They are not left-associative like some mathematical operators or parts of grammar.

As a final example of the versatility of query, consider the case of finding descendants of a particular node. For our story, let's say that you want to find all of the nodes with the food class applied that are a descendant of scene2:

```
dojo.query("#scene2 .food")
//Returns [span.food, span.food, span.food, span.food, span.food, span.food,
//span.food]
```

Note that the child combinator using the > operator would have returned an empty list because there are no nodes reflecting the food class that are direct children of scene2:

```
dojo.query("#scene2 > .food")
//Returns []
```

A common problem is confusing the child combinator (>) with the descendant combinator (a space). The combinator operator returns immediate child nodes while the descendant operator returns descendants that appear anywhere in the DOM hierarchy.

Although this example was necessarily brief, a final word worth mentioning is that reducing the search space as much as possible by providing the most specific query that you can has a significant impact on performance.

State Tracking Example

In addition to the obvious case of finding nodes in the DOM, a powerful facility like dojo.query tends to change the way you solve a lot of common problems because it expands the creative possibilities. As a simple illustration, consider the problem of tracking state in an application, a *very* common piece of any reasonably complex application's design. Perhaps it involves determining whether a particular section of text is highlighted or not, or perhaps it involves knowing whether some action has already been triggered. While you could introduce explicit variables to track every facet of state, using CSS classes to track state often provides a much more elegant solution to the problem.

For example, suppose that you're developing a cutting-edge new search engine for the web that is capable of tagging entities in the document, and that you've indicated that you'd like to explicitly view people in your search results. Let's assume that your search results contained Shakespeare's play *Macbeth*, and that you had requested that "people" be tagged in it. You might get the following results:

```
...
<a rel="person">First Witch</a>
When shall we three meet again
In thunder, lightning, or in rain?

<a rel="person">Second Witch</a>
When the hurlyburly's done,
When the battle's lost and won.

<a rel="person">Third Witch</a>
That will be ere the set of sun.

<a rel="person">First Witch</a>
Where the place?

<a rel="person">Second Witch</a>
Upon the heath.

<a rel="person">Third Witch</a>
There to meet with <a rel="person">Macbeth</a>.

...
```

The long, brittle way

As a developer who has a soft spot for usability, you might want to include a small control panel on the side of the page that toggles highlighting particular entity types in the search results. A low-level JavaScript approach in which you directly manipulate the DOM yourself might look something like the following:

```
function addHighlighting(entityType) {
  var nodes  = document.getElementsByTagName("a");
  for (var i=0; i < nodes.length; i++) {
    if (nodes[i].getAttribute('rel')==entityType) {
      nodes[i].className="highlighted";
    }
  }
}

function removeHighlighting(entityType) {
  var nodes = document.getElementByTagName("a");
  for (var i=0; i < nodes.length; i++) {
    if (nodes[i].getAttribute('rel')==entityType) {
      nodes[i].className="";
    }
  }
}
```

That sort of gets the job done, but it's still a little bit naïve to assume the search results won't ever have any other class associated with them than the highlighted class—because if they did, we'd be directly clobbering it in each of our functions. Thus, we'd also need to engineer some functions for adding and removing classes from nodes that may have multiple classes applied, which would involve a more robust effort requiring us to search over the string value for className and optionally add or remove a class's name. You could use Base's addClass and removeClass functions that you learned about in Chapter 2 to prevent any more cruft from appearing, but that still doesn't minimize the existing cruft.

The short, robust way

Here's the way you could safely attack the problem with query, cruft-free:

```
function addHighlighting(entityType) {
  dojo.query("span[type="+entityType+"]").addClass("highlighted");
}

function removeHighlighting(entityType) {
  dojo.query("span[type="+entityType+"]").removeClass("highlighted");
}
```

For this particular example, you rid yourself of low-level DOM manipulation, writing a for loop, and introducing a conditional logic block in exchange for some elegant CSS syntax—and that's not to overlook the assumption about there not being more than one class applied to the entities in the search results document.

While there isn't anything dojo.query can do for you that you can't do the long way around, hopefully the previous discussion illustrated that dojo.query does provide a single, uniform interface for finding and manipulating elements in the DOM at a very high level and that the additional complexity lies in the query string versus additional conditional logic statements. Not to mention that it's a little less awkward than manipulating the DOM at such a low level in the first place.

If you think there are a lot of cool things you can do with query, just wait until you see the flexibility that NodeList offers. It's the return type from a call to query and is coming up next.

NodeList

A NodeList is a specialized subclass of Array that is expressly designed with some fantastic extensions for manipulating collections of DOM nodes with ease. One of the more seductive features of a NodeList is its ability to provide chaining via the dot operator, although many specialized capabilities such as mapping, filtering, and looking up the index of a node exist as well.

Table 5-2 provides an overview of the NodeList methods available. These methods are named according to the very same convention as Base's Array functions. The only caveats are that they return NodeLists instead of Arrays.

 For a review of the fundamentals involving the following Array manipulations, see the section "Array Processing" in Chapter 2.

Table 5-2. NodeList methods

Name	Comment
indexOf(/*DOMNode*/n)	Returns the first location of an item in the NodeList.
lastIndexOf(/*DOMNode*/n)	Returns the last location of an item in the NodeList.
every(/*Function*/f)	Returns true if the function returns true for every item in the NodeList.
some(/*Function*/f)	Returns true if the function returns true for at least one item in the NodeList.
forEach(/*Function*/f)	Runs each item through a function and returns the original NodeList.
map(/*Function*/f)	Runs each item through a function and returns the results as a NodeList.
filter(/*Function*/f)	Runs each item through a NodeList, returning only the items that meet the function criteria, or applies CSS query filtering to the list of nodes.
concat(/*Any*/item, ...)	Returns a new NodeList with the new items appended, behaving just like the Array.concat method except that it returns a NodeList.
splice(/*Integer*/index, /*Integer*/howManyToDelete, /*Any*/item, ...)	Returns a new NodeList with the new items inserted or deleted, behaving just like the Array.splice method except that it returns a NodeList.

Table 5-2. NodeList methods (continued)

Name	Comment
slice(/*Integer*/begin, /*Integer*/end)	Returns a new NodeList with the new items sliced out, behaving just like the Array.slice method except that it returns a NodeList.
addClass(/*String*/class)	Adds a class to every node.
removeClass(/*String*/class)	Removes a class from every node.
style(/*String|Object*/style)	Gets or sets a particular style to every node when style is a String. Works just like dojo.style to set multiple style values if style is an Object.
addContent(/*String*/ content, /*String?|Integer?*/ position)	Adds a text string or node to the relative position indicated for each node. Valid values for position include first, last, before, and after. Position values first and last are a function of the node's parent, while before and after are relative to the node itself.
place(/*String|Node*/ queryOrNode, /*String*/ position)	Places each item in the list relative to node, or to the first item matched by the query criteria. Valid values for position are the same as with method addContent (see above).
coords( )	Returns the box objects for all elements in the list as an Array—not as a NodeList. Box objects are of the form { l: 50, t: 200, w: 300: h: 150, x: 100, y: 300 }, where l specifies the offset from the left of the screen, t specifies an offset from the top of the screen, w and h correspond to the width and height of the box, and x and y provide the absolute position of the cords.
orphan/*String?*/ filter	Removes DOM nodes from the list according to the filter criteria and returns them as a new NodeList.
adopt(/*String|Array|DomNode*/ queryOrListOrNode, /*String?*/ position)	Inserts DOM nodes relative to the first element of the list.
connect(/*String*/ methodNameOrDomEvent, /*Object*/ context, /*String*/ funcName)	Attaches event handlers to every item in the NodeList, using dojo.connect so event properties are normalized internally. The signature is just like dojo.connect in that you provide a method name or DOM event for connecting along with an optional context and function name. DOM event names should be normalized to all lowercase. For most use cases, you will instead use the shortcuts discussed later in this chapter in "Dom Event Shortcuts."
instantiate(/*String|Object*/ declaredClass, /*Object?*/properties)	Handy for instantiating widgets in bulk.[a] Assuming the NodeList contains a number of arbitrary source nodes, this method tries to parse them into the widget class defined as declaredClass, passing in any widget properties provided in properties.

[a] Widgets are not formally introduced until Chapter 11; consequently, no examples in this chapter demonstrate usage of instantiate.

Array-Like Methods

As you may recall, there are several functions available for manipulating arrays that are included in Base. You'll be pleased to know that many of these same methods are available to NodeList. In particular, indexOf, lastIndexOf, every, some, forEach, map, and filter work just like the corresponding functions for an array—although NodeList's filter function offers some additional features depending on the parameter passed. (More on that shortly.)

To get started, we'll need to create ourselves a NodeList. You can use the same syntax as you would with an array, which explicitly provides some elements to the NodeList, or you can also use a NodeList's built-in concat method to create a NodeList from an existing Array object.

Here are a few of the possible ways to construct a new NodeList:

```
var nl = new dojo.NodeList( ); //create an empty NodeList

var nl = new dojo.NodeList(foo, bar, baz);
//create a NodeList with some existing nodes

var a = [foo, bar, baz];
// suppose there is an existing Array object with some nodes in it

a = nl.concat(a); //turn the  Array into a NodeList
```

 If you create a NodeList with the following approach, you may not end up with what you expect:

```
var nl = new dojo.NodeList([foo, bar, baz]);
```

The previous line of code returns a NodeList that contains an Array object with three numbers in it—this is the exact same result you'd get as a result of new Array([foo,bar,baz]).

Chaining NodeList results

While Dojo's array methods are extremely useful if you don't need to stream in the results of a previous operation into another operation, or if you need to strictly deal with an Array, you may otherwise find NodeLists to be your new data structure of choice because the syntax is quite elegant. The following example illustrates chaining together some operations:

```
var nl = new dojo.NodeList(node1,node2,node3,node4,...);

nl.map(
  /* Map some elements... */
  function(x) {
    /* ... */
  }
)
.filter(
  /* And now filter them... */
  function f(x) {
    /* ... */
  }
)
.forEach(
  function(x) {
    /* Now do something with them... */
  }
);
```

Had we used the standard Dojo functions to accomplish this same workflow, take a look at the clutter that would have been introduced by way of intermediate state variables:

```
var a0 = new Array(node1,node2,node3,node4,...);

/* Map some elements... */
var a1 = dojo.map(a0,
  function(x) {
    /* ... */
  }
);

/* And now filter... */
var a2 = dojo.filter(a1
  function f(x) {
    /* ... */
  }
);

/* Now do something with them... */
dojo.forEach(a2
  function f(x) {
    /* ... */
  }
);
```

Hacking NodeList

Although the very name NodeList implies that the data structure is expressly designed for manipulating DOM nodes, be advised that as a bona fide subclass of Array, it can hold anything you want it to—not just nodes. For example, if you really like the syntactic sugar of chaining together operations with the dot operator, you might end up adopting NodeList as your Array of choice because of the ability to manipulate numbers and other primitives like so:

```
//Suppose you have a NodeList of numbers
var nums = new dojo.NodeList(1,2,3,4,5,6,7,8,9,10)

//You might benefit from this kind of syntactic sugar instead of intermediate
//state variables along the way

nums
.filter(function(x) {/* ... */})
.map(function(x) { /* ... */})
//next operation...
//you get the idea
;
```

Be advised that although chaining together the results of operations via the dot operator can produce really elegant code, the lack of intermediate state variables can also have a significant impact on your ability to debug and maintain an application. As always, use discretion.

String-as-Function style Arguments

Just like Base's methods for manipulating Arrays, you can use the special index, array, and item identifiers if you choose to use String arguments as described in the section "Array Processing" in Chapter 2. To recap, consider the following example:

```
//Suppose you have an existing NodeList called nl...

//Use the item identifier instead of writing out the entire function wrapper
nl.forEach("console.log(item)");
```

Enhanced filtering

In addition to NodeList's filter method, which provides the traditional array-like capabilities like dojo.filter, NodeList also provides CSS query-style filtering when you pass in a String parameter. For example, the previous code block illustrated passing a function into NodeList to operate on each individual piece of data. The following block of code uses CSS query syntax to filter an actual list of DOM nodes by the query string:

```
dojo.query("div")
.forEach(
  /* Print out all divs */
  function f(x) {
    console.log(x);
  })
.filter(".div2") //filter on a specific class and print again.
.forEach(
  /*Now, print only div.div2 divs*/
  function f(x) {
    console.log(x);
  }
});
```

Style

Given that you can use CSS query syntax to fetch a list of nodes, it seems entirely possible that you may want to perform style operations on them. For this very reason, NodeList includes a few methods to help you get the job done. NodeList's style method is especially noteworthy in that it can act as a getter or as a setter depending upon whether you provide a second parameter. This behavior is just like the dojo.style function.

As a reminder of how dojo.style works, recall that dojo.style(someNode, "margin") would return the margin value of a DOM node, while dojo.style(someNode, "margin", "10px") would set the node's margin to a value of 10 pixels.

Manipulating a NodeList is just the same except that there's no need for an explicit first parameter that denotes a particular node anymore. Like any other NodeList function that processed nodes, the method is applied to each node in the list:

```
// dojo.style approach...
var a = [];

/* load the Array with some nodes */

// iterate over the nodes and apply style
dojo.forEach(a, function(x) {
  dojo.style(x, "margin", "10px");
});

//NodeList approach...
dojo.query( /* some query */ )
.style("margin", "10px");
```

NodeList also includes methods for adding and removing classes via addClass and removeClass—again, just like the corresponding dojo.addClass and dojo.removeClass functions. That is, you can manually set style properties for elements via style, or explicitly add or remove classes via addClass and removeClass. Note that the style method is especially useful when you don't actually have an existing class that accomplishes the purpose, whereas the addClass and removeClass methods are useful for those times when you already have classes that you want to toggle on or off. Just like style, the syntax is for these methods is predictable:

```
dojo.query("span.foo", someDomNode).addClass("foo").removeClass("bar");
dojo.query("#bar").style("color","green");
```

Placement

Not surprisingly, a few methods for manipulating the placement of nodes on the page are included as methods of NodeList. You may recognize the coords method, which, like its dojo counterpart, returns an Array containing the coordinate objects for each node in the list. Likewise, NodeList's place method is similar to dojo.place in that it provides a way to insert the entire NodeList into the DOM in a sequential fashion based on a specific position.

The addContent method, however, is a method that doesn't have a corresponding counterpart elsewhere in the toolkit; it provides a way to add a node or text string to a relative position for each item in a NodeList.

Here's an example of using addContent to insert a text string (which gets wrapped as an inline span) after each page container. This particular example might be useful a method for an application in which you have various displays involving tab and stack containers:

```
/* Add a footer message after each container identifed by the pageContainer class*/
var nl = dojo.query("div.pageContainer").addContent("footer goes here!", "after");
```

Recalling that the place method functions by inserting the entire NodeList into the page relative to another node, you might do the following to insert the entire list inside of a container node identified by an id value of debugPane:

```
var nl = dojo.query("div.someDebugNodes").place("#debugPane", "last");
```

dojo.coords, like its counterpart, returns an object of key/value pairs that represent the coordinates for each item in the NodeList. Recall that the coords object includes keys for top and left offsets, length and height, and absolute x and y positions, which can be transformed to be relative to a viewport.

The result of coords is an Array, not a NodeList. Inspect the output of the following blurb in the Firebug console and see for yourself:

```
dojo.forEach(
  dojo.query("div").coords(),
  function(x) { console.log(x); }
);
```

A somewhat unique method provided by NodeList for placement that does not have a dojo counterpart is its orphan method, which applies a simple filter (single CSS selector—no commas allowed) to each of its elements, and each *child element* involved in a relationship that matches the filter criteria is removed from the DOM. These child elements that have been removed—or orphaned—are then returned as a new NodeList. The orphan method is often used to remove nodes from the DOM in a much less kludgy manner than the DOM accessor functions otherwise dictate, which is the following pattern for a node called foo: foo.parentNode.removeChild(foo).

For example, to remove all hyperlink elements that are children of a span from the DOM and return them as a new NodeList, you'd do the following:

```
var nl = dojo.query("span > a").orphan()
```

The > selector is whitespace-sensitive; you must include a whitespace on each side of the selector.

The adopt method is essentially the inverse of the orphan operator in that it allows you to insert elements back into the DOM. The function is quite flexible, allowing you to pass in a particular DOM node, a query string, or a NodeList. The nodes that will be inserted are positioned relative to the *first element* in the NodeList that provides the adopt method. The second parameter providing positional information allows for the usual positional information (first, last, after, and before):

```
var n = document.createElement("div");
n.innerHTML="foo";
dojo.query("#bar").adopt(n, "last");
```

DOM Event Shortcuts

Given that you can do just about everything else with a NodeList, you probably won't be too surprised to find out that you can also batch process nodes to respond to particular DOM events such as blurs, mouse movements, and key presses. Firing custom actions in response to one or more DOM events is such a common occurrence that NodeList provides a built-in method for accomplishing this task with ease.

The following DOM events are offered as events for batch processing with NodeLists:

- onmouseover
- onmouseenter
- onmousedown
- onmouseup
- onmouseleave
- onmouseout
- onmousemove
- onfocus
- onclick
- onkeydown
- onkeyup
- onkeypress
- onblur

As an example, consider the use case of capturing mouse movement events over a particular element. You'd simply fill in the function for the onmouseover function like so:

```
dojo.query("#foobar").onmousemove(
  function(evt) {
    console.log(evt); // you should really do something more interesting!
  }
);
```

The event objects that are available via the DOM Event methods are standardized, because internally dojo.connect is being used. The event model as provided via dojo.connect is standardized in accordance with the W3C specification.

There is no direct way to manage and disconnect the connections you create with NodeList's connect method, although a future 1.x dot release may provide that ability. If it's not enough to have these connections automatically torn down when the page unloads, you can opt to use the normal dojo.connect method inside of a NodeList's forEach method if you have a really good reason to manage the connections yourself.

For example, if you needed to manually manage the connections from the previous example, you might do it like so:

```
var handles =
  dojo.query("a").map(function(x) {
    return dojo.connect(x, "onclick",
      function(evt) { /* ... */ });
  });

/* Sometime later... */
dojo.forEach(handles, function(x) {
  dojo.disconnect(x);
});
```

Animation

You may want to skim this section and then read it again more closely after you've read Chapter 8, which provides complete coverage of animating content.

Producing animations with DHTML has often been perceived as a bit cumbersome—and it certainly can be. NodeList, however, makes this task just as simple as anything else you can do with a NodeList. From an application development standpoint, that means that you can perform fades trivially, and can even perform more complex operations via the _Animation.animateProperty method.

The _Animation that is operated upon has a leading underscore. In this particular context, the leading underscore signifies that the API is not final and, in general, _Animation objects should be treated somewhat opaquely. While the information presented in this section is current as of Dojo 1.1 and the _Animation API is fairly stable, future versions of Dojo could change it.

The methods listed in Table 5-3 involving animation are currently available, but must be explicitly retrieved via a call to dojo.require("dojo.NodeList-fx"). Each of these methods takes an associative array of key/value pairs that provide properties such as the animation duration, position information, colors, etc.

Table 5-3. NodeList extensions for animation

fadeIn	Fades in each node in the list.
fadeout	Fades out each node in the list.
wipeIn	Wipes in each element in the list.
wipeout	Wipes out each element in the list.
slideTo	Slides each element in the list to a particular position.
animateProperties	Animates all elements of the list using the specified properties.
anim	Similar to animateProperties except that it returns an animation that is already playing. See dojo.anim for more details.

As you might already be thinking, animations are fun to toy around with. Dojo makes this so simple to do. Like anything else in the toolkit, you can just open up the Firebug console and start experimenting. You might start out with simple fades, like so:

```
dojo.require("dojo.NodeList-fx");

//Once NodeList-fx has loaded...
dojo.query("p").fadeOut().play()
```

Then, when you're ready to begin trying more advanced animations, add some key/value pairs to the associative array and see what happens:

```
dojo.require("dojo.NodeList-fx");

//Once NodeList-fx has loaded...
dojo.query("div").animateProperty({
  duration: 5000,
  properties: {
    color: {start: "black", end: "green"},
  }
}).play();
```

Note that the actual result of the various effects method is an _Animation object, and that its play method is the standard mechanism for activating it.

Creating NodeList Extensions

While the built-in methods for NodeList are quite useful, it's not going to be long before you'll find that there's this one method that you could really benefit from having on hand. Fortunately, it takes very little effort to inject your own functionality into NodeList. Consider the following use case accomplished via query that returns the innerHTML for each element of a NodeList:

```
dojo.query("p").map(function(x) {return x.innerHTML;});
```

Compared to working up that solution from scratch, you already have a really concise solution, but you could go even further to simplifying matters by using the even more concise String-as-Function syntax with the following improvement:

```
dojo.query("p").map("return item.innerHTML;"); //Used the special item identifier
```

That's definitely an improvement—would you believe that your code could still be even more readable *and concise*? Consider the following extension to NodeList, in which you embed the mapping inside of a more readable and elegant function call that is very intuitively named so that it's completely obvious exactly what is happening:

```
//Extend NodeList's prototype with a new function
dojo.extend(dojo.NodeList, {
    innerHTML : function() {
        return this.map("return item.innerHTML");
    }
});
```

```
//Call the new function
dojo.query("p").innerHTML();
```

What's great about extending NodeList is that for a very little bit of planning up front, you can significantly declutter your design and make it a lot more maintainable at the same time.

The recommended practice for modularizing up this kind of extension is to create a submodule called *ext-dojo* with a resource file called *NodeList.js* inside of it so that you end up with a dojo.require statement that is crystal clear to whoever ends up reading your code. In the end, you have a situation that's a win for everyone. Your final usage of the extension might end up looking like the following example once you're all finished with it:

```
/* ... *
dojo.require("dtdg.ext-dojo.NodeList");

/* ...*/

dojo.query("p").innerHTML();
```

Clearly, you could go as far as to name the resource file *NodeList-innerHTML.js* if you wanted to be pedantic; do whatever makes you most comfortable, so long as you are consistent.

Behavior

Core contains a lightweight extension that builds on top of query to provide a great way for decoupling events and DOM manipulations from an HTML placeholder via the behavior module. It may not be intuitively obvious at first, but the ability to define *behavior* for nodes irrespective of the markup itself can lend an immense of flexibility to a design. For example, it allows you to concisely accomplish tasks such as assigning click handlers to all anchor elements without knowing where or how many anchor elements there will be. You use the same CSS selectors you learned about in Table 5-1 to find the nodes for attaching behavior to, so the possibilities are almost endless.

The behavior module currently provides two API calls; the add method allows you to queue up a collection of behaviors, and the apply method actually triggers those behaviors:

```
dojo.behavior.add(/*Object*/ behaviorObject)
dojo.behavior.apply()
```

Basically, you use add to assign a new behavior to a collection of DOM nodes, but the behavior isn't actually reflected until you call apply. One of the reasons that it's a two-step process is because the pattern of performing multiple add operations before a final apply occurs lends itself to a lot of asynchronous communication patterns, described in Chapter 4.

Chapter 4 introduced a data structure called Deferred that is a staple in Dojo's IO subsystem. Deferreds provide the façade of having a thread available to operate on and lend themselves to successively applying multiple callback and error handling functions. After reading about Deferred patterns, the utility in providing separate functions for add and apply should be apparent.

The Object that you pass into add and apply is quite flexible and can accept a number of variations. In short, the behavior Object contains key/value pairs that map CSS selectors to Objects that supply DOM event handlers. The DOM event handlers themselves come as key/value pairs. Before the example, though, skim over Table 5-4, which provides a summary of the possibilities.

Table 5-4. Behavior Object possibilities

Key	Value	Comment
Selector (String)	Object	The Object should contain key/value pairs that map either DOM event names or the special "found" identifier to event handlers or topic names.
		For example:
		``` { onclick : function(evt) {/*...*/}, onmouseover : "/dtdg/foo/moveover", found : function(node) {/*...*/}, found : "/dtdg/bar/found" } ```
		In the case of a topic being published, the standardized event object is passed along for the subscribe handler to receive.
		In the case of an event handler, the standardized event object is passed into the function.
		In the case of the special "found" identifier, the matching node itself is either passed into the handler or passed along with the topic that is published.
Selector (String)	Function	For each node matching the selector, the handler is executed with each node passed in as the parameter.
Selector (String)	String	For each node matching the selector, the topic name is published. The node itself is passed along for the subscribe handler to receive.

 Remember to provide the keys to the behavior Objects as actual String values whenever the CSS selector requires it. For example, a behavior object of {div : function(evt) {/*...*/} is fine whereas {#foo : "/dtdg/foo/topic"} would not be valid because #foo is not a valid identifier.

Take a moment to read through Example 5-1, which illustrates some of the possibilities as a working example.

Example 5-1. Example of dojo.behavior at work

```html
<html>
    <head>
        <title>Fun with Behavior!</title>

        <link rel="stylesheet" type="text/css"
            href="http://o.aolcdn.com/dojo/1.1/dojo/resources/dojo.css" />
        <script
            type="text/javascript"
            src="http://o.aolcdn.com/dojo/1.1/dojo/dojo.xd.js"
            djConfig="isDebug:true"
        ></script>

        <script type="text/javascript">
            dojo.require("dojo.behavior");

            dojo.addOnLoad(function( ) {
                    /* Pass a behavior Object into dojo.behavior.
                  This object is automatically added once the page loads*/
                  dojo.behavior.add({

                      /* The behavior Object is keyed by any combination of CSS
                      selectors, which can map to a single behavior or a collection of
                      behaviors */

                      /* Mapping a key to a function is equivalent to mapping to {found
                      : function(node) { ... } } */
                      ".container" : function(node) {
                          //apply some generic styling

                          dojo.style(node, {
                              border : "solid 1px",
                              background : "#eee"
                          }
                      },

                      /* Map the key to a collection of behaviors */
                      "#list > li" : {
                          /* DOM events work just like dojo.connect, allowing you to act
                          on the event */
                          onmouseover : function(evt) {dojo.style(evt.target,
                          "background", "yellow");},
                          onmouseout : function(evt) {dojo.style(evt.target,
                          "background", "");},

                          /* String values are published as topics */
                          onclick : "/dtdg/behavior/example/click",

                          /* "found" is a general purpose handler that allows
                           manipulation of the node*/
                          found : function(node) {dojo.style(node, "cursor", "pointer")}
                      }
```

Example 5-1. Example of dojo.behavior at work (continued)

```
            });

            /* Somewhere, out there...a subscription is set up... */
            dojo.subscribe("/dtdg/behavior/example/click", function(evt) {
                console.log(evt.target.innerHTML, "was clicked");
            });
        });
    </script>
<head>

    <body>
        <div class="container" style="width:300px">
            Grocery List:
            <ul id="list">
                <li>Bananas</li>
                <li>Milk</li>
                <li>Eggs</li>
                <li>Orange Juice</li>
                <li>Frozen Pizzas</li>
            </ul>
        </div>
    </body>
</html>
```

As the example demonstrates, any behavior you set up before the page loads is set up automatically. After the page loads, however, you need to first add the behavior and then apply it. The following update adds *another* click handler to list elements:

```
dojo.behavior.add({
  "#list > li" : {
    onclick : "/dtdg/behavior/example/another/click"
  }

});
dojo.behavior.apply();

dojo.subscribe("/dtdg/behavior/example/another/click", function(evt) {
  console.log("an additional event handler...");

});
```

Although one of the key observations you should be making is how decoupled the actual *behavior* of the nodes are from the markup itself, you hopefully just made the connection that behavior's apply function provides you with a great benefit: any behavior you supply on top of existing behavior is added along with the existing behavior. In other words, new behavior doesn't just blow away what was there before; you are able to add behavior in layers and the book keeping is handled without any additional intervention on your behalf.

Summary

After reading this chapter, you should:

- Be able to use dojo.query to universally find nodes in the page
- Have a basic understanding of CSS selector syntax
- Be familiar with NodeLists and recognize the various mappings that hold to other functions such as the Array utilities that the toolkit offers
- Be able to chain together the results from NodeList methods to cleanly and rapidly process DOM elements
- Be aware that it's possible to hack NodeList and instead opt to use other utilities in the toolkit
- Be able to use NodeLists to place DOM nodes, handle animations, set up connections, and manage style
- Understand the value in extending NodeList with custom operations so as to minimize the effort in processing the results from dojo.query
- Be aware of the benefits from decoupling DOM events from an HTML placeholder and how you can achieve this via the behavior module

A discussion of internationalization is coming up next.

CHAPTER 6

Internationalization (i18n)

This chapter provides a brief synopsis of the tools Dojo provides for internationalizing a module. The key topics are defining bundles on a locale basis and using Core's facilities for formatting and parsing dates, currency, and numbers. In case it wasn't quite obvious, internationalization is usually abbreviated as *i18n* simply because it is such a long word to type; thus, the shorthand is the first and last letters, with the number 18 between them to take place of the 18 letters in between.

Introduction

If you have the good fortune of developing an application that becomes even mildly popular, you will certainly want to consider supporting more than one language. Although Dijit, which you'll learn about in Part II of this book, is already internationalized with several common locales, custom modules and widgets of your own devising will require some special attention. Fortunately, the toolkit provides techniques for supporting more than one language in a highly uniform way, saving you the headache of inventing your own system of mapping tokens back and forth; because Dojo manages *how* the loading takes place, you are also freed from thinking of ways to optimize the loading. Additional utilities also support common operations involving numeric formatting, currency, and more.

It's worth pointing out that the i18n facilities are technically part of Core, not Base. XDomain builds; however, include the dojo.i18n module as part of *dojo.xd.js* at the expense of an extra 2KB to workaround some tricky loading issues involving i18n bundles. Regardless, you should still dojo.require("dojo.i18n") into your page to be explicit about your intention to use these facilities as a matter of good form.

Internationalizing a module you've developed is simple because the details of your string table stay compartmentalized inside of a special nls directory that appears in your module directory with your JavaScript source files; nls stands for *native language support*. The nls directory itself breaks down all of the various translations by abbreviations for locales as defined in RFC 3066 (Tags for the Identification of Languages).*

---

* *http://www.ietf.org/rfc/rfc3066.txt.*

For example, the abbreviation for generic English is *en*, the abbreviation for the dialect of English as it is spoken in the United States is *en-us*, and the abbreviation for generic Spanish is *es*. During the bootstrap process, Dojo queries your browser for your particular locale, and stores it internally. You can check it by typing dojo.locale in Firebug. The value of dojo.locale is what Dojo uses to determine the most appropriate translation when loading a module that has been internationalized.

Internationalizing a Module

Let's assume that you've gotten with the times and expanded on your magic genie module from the "Building a Magic Genie Example Module" in Chapter 2 to produce a psychic module. Let's assume that your default language is English, and you've determined that the first additional language you should support is Spanish.

Layout on Disk

Like any other module, your psychic readings module should simply be a source file contained in a typical directory structure:

```
dtdg/
  psychic/
    Psychic.js /* Lots of useful stuff in here */
```

Not surprisingly, an incredible utility provided by your psychic module is the ability to predict the future. As such, users of your module might stick it in a page and use it like so:

```
<script type="text/javascript">
    dojo.require("dtdg.psychic");
    dojo.addOnLoad(function( ) {
      dtdg.psychic.predictFuture( );
    });
</script>
```

Although there's an awful lot of *real* magic that happens in the predictFuture function, the part that we're interested in at the moment is where a String value actually gets written to the screen because that's where the internationalization work happens. As it turns out, the output from your module gets written out with the following logic:

```
dojo.byId("reading").innerHTML = predictFuture( /* magic */ );
```

As a first stab at internationalization, start out with plain old English and plain old Spanish, ignoring any particular dialects. Given this decision, the nls directory might look something like the following:

```
dtdg/
  psychic/
    Psychic.js
    nls/
        readings.js /* The default English translation bundle */
```

```
es/
   readings.js /* The Spanish translation bundle */
en/
   /* The default English translation folder is empty, so
      Dojo looks one level up for it in the nls/ directory */
```

By convention, each of the .js files containing translation information is called a *bundle*. The convention used is that the default translation bundle appears in the top level of the nls directory, but not in a language-specific directory. The basic rationale for this convention is that you always want a default translation to be available in the nls directory, which is the most logical place for it, and there's no value in including an exact copy of the default translation bundle in its own directory, (en in this case) because that would just be one more thing to keep up with.

Defining String Tables

Here's an excerpt from each of the *readings.js* files that shows some of the strings that are translated as part of the final reading.

First, the default *readings.js* file:

```
{
/* ... */
reading101 : "You're a Libra, aren't ya darling?",
reading102: "Can you please tell me your first name only, and your birthday please?",
reading103: "Yep, that's the Daddy."
/* ... */
}
```

And now, the *es/readings.js* file:

```
{
/* ... */
reading101 : "¿Eres un Libra, no, mi corazón?",
reading102: "¿Me puedes dar el nombre y tu cumpleaños por favor?",
reading103: "Sí, el es papá"
/* ... */
}
```

One of the beautiful things about localizing your application with Dojo is the simple manner in which you provide the listing of tokens.

Putting It All Together

It's time to put it all together and show just how easy it is to support multiple languages, but first, have a look at the relevant functions, listed in Table 6-1, that are involved in the process.

Table 6-1. Localization functions

Name	Comment
dojo.i18n.getLocalization(/*String*/moduleName, /*String*/bundleName, /*String?*/locale)	Returns an Object containing the localization for a given resource bundle in a package. By default, locale defaults to dojo.locale; however, providing an explicit value allows you to look up a specific translation.
dojo.i18n.normalizeLocale(/*String?*/locale)	Returns the canonical form of a locale.
dojo.requireLocalization(/*String*/moduleName, /*String*/bundleName, /*String?*/locale)	Loads translated resources in the same manner as dojo.require would load modules. Note that this function is a Base function, not part of Core's i18n module.

Whereas you previously might have looked up reading102 value from a hash value like psychic.reading102, you now do it with help from the toolkit. If you've provided a translation for a particular user's locale, everything "just works." Looking up symbols for your various translations is as simple as the following generic piece of logic:

```
/* Require in Dojo's i18n utilities first... */
dojo.require("dojo.i18n");

/* Then, require in your various translations */
dojo.requireLocalization("psychic", "readings");

function predictFuture( ) {

    /* Deep inside of your predictFuture function somewhere... */
    var future= dojo.i18n.getLocalization("psychic", "readings").reading597;
    return future;
}
```

Note that you can change your value of dojo.locale if you'd like to test out various translations. A good place to change this value is in djConfig block. Here's an example of how you might test out your Spanish translation from a local installation:

```
<head>
    <script type="text/javascript" src="your/path/to/dojo.js"
    djConfig="dojo.locale:'es'">
    </script>
</head>

<!--
    All of your internationalized modules now use the Spanish translation
-->
```

Just like any other module or resource, don't call dojo.i18n.getLocalization as part of an object property definition; instead, call dojo.i18n.getLocalization in a dojo.addOnLoad block:

```
dojo.addOnLoad(function( ) {
    //Returns a localized Object
    var foo = {bar : dojo.i18n.getLocalization( /* ...*/)}
});
```

A nuance you may want to be aware of is that if your default locale is a variant of English and you are testing the Spanish localization, both the *nls/es/readings.js* and the *nls/readings.js* bundles are loaded. In fact, the default bundle that is contained in the *nls/* directory will always be loaded. You can use Firebug's *Net* to verify this behavior for yourself.

Although this particular example didn't involve any dialects of either language, note that dialects are most certainly taken into account when loading localized bundles. For example, if your locale was en-us and there had been an *en-us* bundle provided, Dojo would have attempted to load both the *en-us* bundle and the *en* bundles, flattening them into a single collection for you to query via your various `dojo.i18n.` `getLocalization` calls. The working assumption is that when defining locale specific symbols for English, you want to provide as much general information as possible in the *en* bundle and then override or fill in gaps inside of the dialect specific bundles such as *en-us*.

Use build tools for snappy performance

As a final yet very important observation about internationalization, note that the Dojo build tools provided in Util can automatically take care of the myriad details associated with minimizing the number of synchronous calls and data redundancy when you perform a custom build of your module. It may not seem like much at first, but the build tools combine what could be lots of small resource files together and avoid all of the lookups and the latency that goes along with them. In terms of a snappy page load, it can really make all the difference. Util and the build tools are discussed in Chapter 16.

Dates, Numbers, and Currency

Additional Core facilities provide additional support for manipulating and supporting internationalization of dates, numbers, and currency via the `dojo.date`, `dojo.number`, and `dojo.currency` modules, respectively. In Part II, you'll learn that Dijit makes extensive use of these modules to provide advanced support for commonly used widgets. This section provides a quick inventory of these features.

Dates

Table 6-2 shows a quick overview of the `dojo.date` module. As you'll see, there are some real gems in here if you ever need to perform any routine processing of the built-in `Date` object.

Table 6-2. Summary of the date module

Name	Return type	Comment
dojo.date.getDaysInMonth (/*Date*/date)	Integer	Returns the number of days in date's month.
dojo.date.isLeapYear (/*Date*/date)	Boolean	Returns true if date is a leap year.
dojo.date.getTimezoneName (/*Date*/date)	String	Returns time zone information as defined by the browser. A Date object is needed because the time zone may vary according to issues such as daylight savings time.
dojo.date.compare(/*Date*/ date1, /*Date*/ date2, /*String?*/ portion)	Integer	Returns 0 if the two parameters are equal; returns a positive number if date1 > date 2; returns a negative number if date1 < date2. By default, both date and time are compared, although providing "date" or "time" for a portion produces a comparison strictly by date or time, respectively.
dojo.date.add(/*Date*/date, /*String*/ interval, /*Integer*/ amount)	Date	Provides a convenient way to add an incremental amount to a Date object by providing a numeric amount and the type of units. Units may be "year", "month", "day", "hour", "minute", "second", "millisecond", "quarter", "week", or "weekday".
dojo.date.difference (/*Date*/date1, /*Date*/ date2, /*String*/ interval)	Integer	Provides a convenient way to calculate the difference between two Date objects in terms of a specific type of unit, which may be "year", "month", "day", "hour", "minute", "second", "millisecond", "quarter", "week", or "weekday".

 As of version 1.1 of the toolkit, getTimezoneName is not localized.

Numbers

The dojo.number module provides some handy functions, shown in Tables 6-3 and 6-4, for parsing String values into numbers, formatting a Number in accordance with a specific pattern template, or rounding to a specific number of decimal places.

Table 6-3. Formatting options for the number module that are used in the dojo.number.format and dojo.number.parse functions provided in Table 6-4

dojo.number.format options	Type	Comment
pattern	String	Can be used to override the formatting pattern.
type	String	A format type based on the locale. Valid values include "decimal", "scientific", "percent", "currency", and "decimal". "decimal" is the default.

dojo.number.format options	Type	Comment
places	Number	Provides a fixed number of places to show, which overrides any information provided by pattern.
round	Number	Specifies rounding properties based on a multiple. For example, 5 would round to the nearest 0.5 and 0 would round to the nearest whole number.
currency	String	A currency code that meets the ISO4217 standard. For example, "USD" would signify U.S. Dollars.
symbol	String	A localized currency symbol.
locale	String	Allows a specific locale to be provided which drives formatting rules.

Table 6-4. Summary of the number module

Name	Return type	Comment
dojo.number.format (/*Number*/value, /*Object*/options)	String	Formats a Number as a String using locale-specific settings. Options may take on the values from Table 6-3.
dojo.number.round (/*Number*/value, /*Number*/places)	Number	Rounds a number to a given number of places after the decimal.
dojo.number.parse (/*String*/value, /*Object*/options)	Number	Converts a properly formatted String to a Number using locale-specific settings. Valid options include the following values from Table 6-3: pattern, type, locale, strict, and currency.

Currency

The dojo.currency module, described in Tables 6-5 and 6-6, is similar to dojo.number in that it provides a means of formatting numeric values, only this time it is currency codes as defined in ISO427.[*]

Table 6-5. Formatting options for the currency module as used by the dojo.currency.format and dojo.currency.parse functions

Name	Type	Comment
currency	String	A three-letter currency code as defined in ISO4217 such as "USD".
symbol	String	A value that may be used to override the default currency symbol.
pattern	String	Used to override the default currency pattern.
round	Number	Used to provide rudimentary rounding: -1 means don't round at all, 0 means round to the nearest whole number, and 5 means round to the nearest one-half.

[*] *http://en.wikipedia.org/wiki/ISO_4217.*

Table 6-5. Formatting options for the currency module as used by the dojo.currency.format and dojo.currency.parse functions (continued)

Name	Type	Comment
locale	String	Override the default locale, which determines the formatting rules.
places	Number	The number of decimal places to accept (default is defined by currency.)

Table 6-6. Summary of the currency module

Name	Return type	Comment
dojo.currency.format (/*Number*/value, /*Object?*/options)	String	Formats a Number as a String, using locale-specific settings. Values for options are given in Table 6-5.
dojo.currency.parse (/*String*/ expression, /*Object?*/ options)	Number	Converts a properly formatted String to a Number. Values for options are given in Table 6-5.

 Some of Dojo's build tools can be used to generate support for arbitrary locales and currencies since a lot of this work simply entails building lookup tables of information. See the file located at *util/build-scripts/cldr/README* for more details.

Summary

After reading this chapter, you should be able to:

- Internationalize a module for more than one locale
- Be aware that Core provides utilities for handling currency, numbers, and dates—all of which may be helpful in various internationalization efforts

Next, we'll discuss drag-and-drop.

## CHAPTER 7

Drag-and-Drop

Drag-and-drop (DnD) can give your application incredible desktop-like functionality and usability that can really differentiate it from the others. This chapter systematically works through this topic, providing plenty of visual examples and source code. You might build off these examples to add some visual flare to your existing application, or perhaps even do something as brave as incorporate the concepts and the machinery that Dojo provides into a DHTML game that people can play online. Either way, this is a fun chapter, so let's get started.

Dragging

While drag-and-drop has been an integral part of desktop applications for more than two decades, web applications have been slow to adopt it. At least part of the reason for the slow adoption is because the DOM machinery provided is quite primitive in and of itself, and the event-driven nature of drag-and-drop makes it especially difficult to construct a unified framework that performs consistently across the board. Fortunately, overcoming these tasks is perfect work for a toolkit, and Dojo provides facilities that spare you from the tedious and time-consuming work of manually developing that boilerplate yourself.

Simple Moveables

 This chapter assumes a minimal working knowledge of CSS. The W3C schools provide a CSS tutorial at *http://www.w3schools.com/css/ default.asp*. Eric Meyer's *CSS: The Definitive Guide* (O'Reilly) is also a great desktop reference.

The parser is one of the most commonly used resources in all of Core. As it turns out, however, it is most frequently used to parse widgets in the page and, for this reason, a complete discussion of the parser is delayed until Chapter 11 when Dijit is formally introduced. Although you can feel free to skip ahead and skim that chapter right now, this sidebar provides a quick synopsis that contains all that you need for the moment.

The most common use case for the parser is to find and instantiate widgets before addOnLoad fires as the page is loading. The parser finds widgets by finding all of the tags that contain a special dojoType attribute, which designates the resource name for the widget that should be swapped in. All you need to do to make all of this happen is require the parser via dojo.require like any other resource, supply the parseOnLoad:true directive to djConfig, and include a dojoType tag for each widget placeholder that is in the page. (Actually, you can manually parse widgets as well, but again, we'll defer that discussion until Chapter 11.)

The code listings you'll see in this chapter use the parser in the same way because it is performing a very similar function with respect to drag-and-drop. Namely, it is scanning the page for dojoType tags that identify drag-and-drop resources and taking care of the handiwork behind the scenes that make them interactive.

As a warm up, let's start out with the most basic example possible: moving an object* around on the screen. Example 7-1 shows the basic page structure that gets the work done in markup. Take a look, especially at the emphasized lines that introduce the Moveable class, and then we'll review the specifics.

Example 7-1. Simple Moveable

```
<html>
    <head>
        <title>Fun with Moveables!</title>
        <style type="text/css">
            .moveable {
                background: #FFFFBF;
                border: 1px solid black;
                width: 100px;
                height: 100px;
                cursor: pointer;
            }
        </style>
```

---

* The term *object* is used in this chapter to generically refer to a moveable DOM node. This usage implies nothing whatsoever about objects from object-oriented programming.

Example 7-1. Simple Moveable (continued)

```
          <script
            type="text/javascript"
            djConfig="parseOnLoad:true,isDebug:true"
            src="http://o.aolcdn.com/dojo/1.1/dojo/dojo.xd.js">
          </script>

          <script type="text/javascript">
          dojo.require("dojo.dnd.Moveable");
          dojo.require("dojo.parser");
      </script>
  </head>
  <body>
      <div class="moveable" dojoType="dojo.dnd.Moveable" ></div>
  </body>
</html>
```

As you surely noticed, creating a moveable object on the screen is quite trivial. Once the Moveable resource was required into the page, all that's left is to specify an element on the page as being moveable via a dojoType tag and parsing the page on load via an option to djConfig. There's really nothing left except that a bit of style was provided to make the node look a little bit more fun than an ordinary snippet of text—though a snippet of text would have worked just as well.

In general, anything you can do by parsing the page when it loads, you can do programmatically sometime after the page loads. Here's the very same example, but with a programmatically built Moveable:

```
<!-- ... Snip ... -->

<script type="text/javascript">
    dojo.require("dojo.dnd.Moveable");

    dojo.addOnLoad(function( ) {
        var e = document.createElement("div");
        dojo.addClass(e, "moveable");
        dojo.body( ).appendChild(e);
        var m = new dojo.dnd.Moveable(e);
      });
</script>
</head>
    <body></body>
</html>
```

Table 7-1 lists the methods you need to create and destroy a Moveable.

Table 7-1. Creating and destroying a Moveable

Name	Comment
Moveable(/*DOMNode*/node, /*Object*/params)	The constructor function that identifies the node that should become moveable. `params` may include the following values:
	handle (String | DOMNode) A node or node's `id` that should be used as a mouse handle. By default, the node itself is used.
	skip (Boolean) Whether to skip the normal drag-and-drop action associated with text-based form elements that would normally occur when a mouse-down event happens (`false` by default).
	mover (Object) A constructor for a custom `Mover`.
	delay (Number) The number of pixels to delay the move by (0 by default).
destroy()	Used to disassociate the node with moves, deleting all references so that garbage collection can occur.

 A Mover is even lower-level drag-and-drop machinery that Moveable uses internally. Mover objects are not discussed in this chapter, and are only mentioned for your awareness.

Let's build upon our previous example to demonstrate how to ensure text-based form elements are editable by setting the skip parameter by building a simple sticky note on the screen that you can move around and edit. Example 7-2 provides a working example.

Example 7-2. Using Moveable to create a sticky note

```
<html>
    <head>
        <title>Even More Fun with Moveables! </title>
        <style type="text/css">
            .note {
                background: #FFFFBF;
                border-bottom: 1px solid black;
                border-left: 1px solid black;
                border-right: 1px solid black;
                width: 302px;
                height: 300px;
                margin : 0px;
                padding : 0px;
            }
```

Example 7-2. Using Moveable to create a sticky note (continued)

```
            .noteHandle {
                border-left: 1px solid black;
                border-right: 1px solid black;
                border-top: 1px solid black;
                cursor :pointer;
                background: #FFFF8F;
                width : 300px;
                height: 10px;
                margin : 0px;
                padding : 0px;
            }
        </style>

        <script
            type="text/javascript"
            djConfig="parseOnLoad:true,isDebug:true"
            src="http://o.aolcdn.com/dojo/1.1/dojo/dojo.xd.js">
        </script>

        <script type="text/javascript">
            dojo.require("dojo.dnd.Moveable");
            dojo.require("dojo.parser");
        </script>
    </head>
    <body>
        <div dojoType="dojo.dnd.Moveable" skip=true>
            <div class="noteHandle"></div>
            <textarea class="note">Type some text here</textarea>
        </div>
    </body>
</html>
```

 The effect of skip isn't necessarily intuitive, and it's quite instructive to remove the skip=true from the outermost DIV element to see for yourself what happens if you do not specify that form elements should be skipped.

Although our sticky note didn't *necessarily* need to employ drag handles because the innermost div element was only one draggable part of the note, we could have achieved the same effect by using them: limiting a particular portion of the Moveable object to be capable of providing the drag action (the drag handle) implies that any form elements outside of the drag handle may be editable. Replacing the emphasized code from the previous code listing with the following snippet illustrates:

```
<div id="note" dojoType="dojo.dnd.Moveable"  handle='dragHandle'>
    <div id='dragHandle' class="noteHandle"></div>
    <textarea class="note">This form element can't trigger drag action</textarea>
</div>
```

Drag Events

It's likely that you'll want to detect when the beginning and end of drag action occurs for triggering special effects such as providing a visual cue as to the drag action. Detecting these events is a snap with `dojo.subscribe` and `dojo.connect`. Example 7-3 shows another rendition of Example 7-2.

Example 7-3. Connecting and subscribing to drag Events

```
<html>
    <head>
        <title>Yet More Fun with Moveable!</title>
        <style type="text/css">
            .note {
                background: #FFFFBF;
                border-bottom: 1px solid black;
                border-left: 1px solid black;
                border-right: 1px solid black;
                width: 302px;
                height: 300px;
                margin : 0px;
                padding : 0px;
            }
            .noteHandle {
                border-left: 1px solid black;
                border-right: 1px solid black;
                border-top: 1px solid black;
                cursor :pointer;
                background: #FFFF8F;
                width : 300px;
                height: 10px;
                margin : 0px;
                padding : 0px;
            }
            .movingNote {
                background : #FFFF3F;
            }
        </style>

        <script
            type="text/javascript"
            src="http://o.aolcdn.com/dojo/1.1/dojo/dojo.xd.js">
        </script>

        <script type="text/javascript">
            dojo.require("dojo.dnd.Moveable");

            dojo.addOnLoad(function( ) {
                //create and keep references to Moveables for connecting later.
                var m1 = new dojo.dnd.Moveable("note1", {handle : "dragHandle1"});
                var m2 = new dojo.dnd.Moveable("note2", {handle : "dragHandle2"});
```

Example 7-3. Connecting and subscribing to drag Events (continued)

```
                // system-wide topics for all moveables.
                dojo.subscribe("/dnd/move/start", function(node){
                        console.log("Start moving", node);
                });
                dojo.subscribe("/dnd/move/stop", function(node){
                        console.log("Stop moving", node);
                });

                // highlight note when it moves...
                //connect to the Moveables, not the raw nodes.
                dojo.connect(m1, "onMoveStart", function(mover){
                        console.log("note1 start moving with mover:", mover);
                        dojo.query("#note1 > textarea").addClass("movingNote");

                });
                dojo.connect(m1, "onMoveStop", function(mover){
                        console.log("note1 stop moving with mover:", mover);
                        dojo.query("#note1 > textarea").removeClass("movingNote");
                });
        });

    </script>
  </head>
  <body>
        <div id="note1" dojoType="dojo.dnd.Moveable">
            <div id='dragHandle1' class="noteHandle"></div>
            <textarea class="note">Note1</textarea>
        </div>
        <div id="note2" dojoType="dojo.dnd.Moveable">
            <div id='dragHandle2' class="noteHandle"></div>
            <textarea class="note">Note2</textarea>
        </div>
  </body>
</html>
```

> In the dojo.query function calls, you should recall that the parameter "#note1 > textarea" means to return the textarea nodes that are children of the node with an id of "note1". See Table 5-1 for a summary of common CSS3 selectors that can be passed into dojo.query.
>
> Note from the previous code listing that you do not connect to the actual node of interest. Instead, you connect to the Moveable that is returned via a programmatic call to create a new dojo.dnd.Moveable.

As you can see, it is possible to subscribe to global drag events via pub/sub style communication or zero in on specific events by connecting to the particular Moveable nodes of interest. Table 7-2 summarizes the events that you may connect to via dojo.connect.

For pub/sub style communication, you can use dojo.subscribe to subscribe to the "dnd/move/start" and "dnd/move/stop" topics.

Table 7-2. Moveable events

Event	Summary
onMoveStart(/*dojo.dnd.Mover*/mover)	Called before every move.
onMoveStop(/*dojo.dnd.Mover*/mover)	Called after every move.
onFirstMove(/*dojo.dnd.Mover*/mover)	Called during the very first move; handy for performing initialization routines.
onMove(/*dojo.dnd.Mover*/mover), (/* Object */ leftTop)	Called during every move notification; by default, calls onMoving, moves the Moveable, and then calls onMoved.
onMoving(/*dojo.dnd.Mover*/mover), (/*Object*/leftTop)	Called just before onMove.
onMoved(/*dojo.dnd.Mover*/mover), (/*Object */leftTop)	Called just after onMove.

Z-Indexing

Our working example with sticky notes is growing increasingly sophisticated, but one noticeable characteristic that may become an issue is that the initial z-indexes of the notes do not change: one of them is always on top and the other is always on the bottom. It might seem more natural if the note that was last selected became the note that is on top, with the highest z-index. Fortunately, it is quite simple to adjust z-index values in a function that is fired off via a connection to the onMoveStartEvent.

The solution presented below requires modifying the addOnLoad function's logic and is somewhat elegant in that it uses a closure to trap a state variable instead of explicitly using a module-level or global variable:

```
dojo.addOnLoad(function( ) {
    //create and keep references to Moveables for connecting later.
    var m1 = new dojo.dnd.Moveable("note1", {handle : "dragHandle1"});
    var m2 = new dojo.dnd.Moveable("note2", {handle : "dragHandle2"});

    var zIdx = 1; // trapped in closure of this anonymous function

    dojo.connect(m1, "onMoveStart", function(mover){
        dojo.style(mover.host.node, "zIndex", zIdx++);
    });
    dojo.connect(m2, "onMoveStart", function(mover){
        dojo.style(mover.host.node, "zIndex", zIdx++);
    });
});
```

Recall from Chapter 2 that dojo.style requires the use of DOM accessor formatted properties, not stylesheet formatted properties. For example, trying to set a style property called "z-index" would not work.

Constrained Moveables

Being able to move a totally unconstrained object around on the screen with what amounts to a trivial amount of effort is all fine and good, but sooner than later, you'll probably find yourself writing up logic to define boundaries, restrict overlap, and define other constraints. Fortunately, the drag-and-drop facilities provide additional help for reducing the boilerplate you'd normally have to write for defining drag-and-drop constraints.

There are three primary facilities included in dojo.dnd that allow you to constrain your moveable objects: writing your own custom constraint function that dynamically computes a bounding box (a constrainedMoveable), defining a static boundary box when you create the moveable objects (a boxConstrainedMoveable), and constraining a moveable object within the boundaries defined by another parent node (a parentConstrainedMoveable). The format for each type of boundary box follows the same conventions as are described in Chapter 2 in the section "The Box Model."

Here's a modification of our previous sticky note example to start out with a constrainedMoveable:

```html
<html>
    <head>
        <title>Moving Around</title>
        <style type="text/css">
            .note {
                background: #FFFFBF;
                border-bottom: 1px solid black;
                border-left: 1px solid black;
                border-right: 1px solid black;
                width: 302px;
                height: 300px;
                margin : 0px;
                padding : 0px;
            }
            .noteHandle {
                border-left: 1px solid black;
                border-right: 1px solid black;
                border-top: 1px solid black;
                cursor :pointer;
                background: #FFFF8F;
                width : 300px;
                height: 10px;
                margin : 0px;
                padding : 0px;
            }
            .movingNote {
                background : #FFFF3F;
            }
            #note1, #note2 {
                    width : 302px
            }
        </style>
```

```
<script
    type="text/javascript"
    src="http://o.aolcdn.com/dojo/1.1/dojo/dojo.xd.js">
</script>

<script type="text/javascript">
    dojo.require("dojo.dnd.Moveable");
    dojo.require("dojo.dnd.move");

    dojo.addOnLoad(function( ) {
        var f1 = function( ) {
            //clever calculations to define a bounding box.
            //keep note1 within 50 pixels to the right/bottom of note2
            var mb2 = dojo.marginBox("note2");
            b = {};
            b["t"] = 0;
            b["l"] = 0;
            b["w"] = mb2.l + mb2.w + 50;
            b["h"] = mb2.h + mb2.t + 50;
            return b;
        }

        var m1 = new dojo.dnd.move.constrainedMoveable("note1",
            {handle : "dragHandle1", constraints : f1, within : true});

        var m2 = new dojo.dnd.Moveable("note2", {handle : "dragHandle2"});

        var zIdx = 1;

        dojo.connect(m1, "onMoveStart", function(mover){
            dojo.style(mover.host.node, "zIndex", zIdx++);
        });
        dojo.connect(m2, "onMoveStart", function(mover){
            dojo.style(mover.host.node, "zIndex", zIdx++);
        });
    });

</script>
</head>
<body>
        <div id="note1">
            <div id='dragHandle1' class="noteHandle"></div>
            <textarea class="note">Note1</textarea>
        </div>
        <div id="note2">
            <div id='dragHandle2' class="noteHandle"></div>
            <textarea class="note">Note2</textarea>
        </div>
</body>
</html>
```

When computing bounding boxes for Moveable objects, ensure that you have explicitly defined a height and width for the outermost container of what is being moved around on the screen. For example, leaving the outermost div that is the container for our sticky note unconstrained in width produces erratic results because the moveable div is actually much wider than the yellow box that you see on the screen. Thus, attempting to compute constraints using its margin box does not function as expected.

To summarize, an explicit boundary was defined for the note's outermost div so that its margin box could be computed with an accurate width via dojo.marginBox, and a custom constraint function was written that prevents note1 from ever being more than 50 pixels to the right and to the bottom of note2.

 Attempting to use a constrainedMoveable without specifying a constraint function produces a slew of errors, so if you decide not to use a constraint function, you'll need to revert to using a plain old Moveable.

Defining a static boundary for a Moveable is even simpler. Instead of providing a custom function, you simply pass in an explicit boundary. Modify the previous example to make note2 a boxConstrainedMoveable with the following change and see for yourself:

```
var m2 = new dojo.dnd.move.boxConstrainedMoveable("note2",
{
    handle : "dragHandle2",
    box : {l : 20, t : 20, w : 500, h : 300}
});
```

As you can see, the example works as before, with the exception that note2 cannot move outside of the constraint box defined.

Finally, a parentConstrainedMoveable works in a similar fashion. You simply define the Moveables and ensure that the parent node is of sufficient stature to provide a workspace. No additional work is required to make the parent node a special kind of Dojo class. Here's another revision of our working example to illustrate:

```
<!-- ... snip ... -->
.parent {
    background: #BFECFF;
    border: 10px solid lightblue;
    width: 400px;
    height: 700px;
    padding: 10px;
    margin: 10px;
}
<!-- ... snip ... -->
<script type="text/javascript">
    dojo.require("dojo.dnd.move");

    dojo.addOnLoad(function() {
```

```
        new dojo.dnd.move.parentConstrainedMoveable("note1",
            {
                handle : "dragHandle1", area: "margin", within: true
            });
        new dojo.dnd.move.parentConstrainedMoveable("note2",
            {
                handle : "dragHandle2", area: "padding", within: true
            });
            });

    </script>
</head>
<body>
    <div class="parent" >
        <div id="note1">
            <div id='dragHandle1' class="noteHandle"></div>
            <textarea class="note">Note1</textarea>
        </div>
        <div id="note2">
            <div id='dragHandle2' class="noteHandle"></div>
            <textarea class="note">Note2</textarea>
        </div>
    </div>
</body>
</html>
```

The area parameter for parentConstrainedMoveables is of particular interest. You may provide "margin", "padding", "content", and "border" to confine the Moveables to the parent's area.

 Like ordinary Moveables, you can connect to specific objects or use pub/sub style communication to detect global drag-and-drop events. Because constrainedMoveable and boxConstrainedMoveable inherit from Moveable, the event names for dojo.connect and dojo.subscribe are the same as outlined in Table 7-2 for Moveable.

Dropping

Thus far, this chapter has focused on *dragging* objects around on the screen. This section wraps up the discussion by focusing in on the *dropping* part of it all. To get started, let's first take a look at dojo.dnd.Source, a special container class the toolkit provides a drag-and-drop source. A Source can also act as a target for a drop, but as we'll see in a moment, you can also specify a "pure" target with dojo.dnd.Target. While a Source may act as an origin and a destination, a Target may only act as a destination.

Creating a Source is just like creating a Moveable; you call the constructor function and pass in a node as the first argument and an Object of parameters as the second argument, like so. Table 7-3 lists the relevant methods.

Table 7-3. Creating and destroying a Source

Name	Comment
dojo.dnd.Source(/*DOMNode*/node, /*Object*/params)	Constructor method for creation. Valid values for params are provided in Table 7-1.
destroy()	Prepares the Object to be garbage-collected.

Table 7-4 summarizes key parameters involved in the creation of a Source object.

Table 7-4. Configuration parameters for Source's params in Table 7-3

Parameter	Type	Comment
isSource	boolean	true by default; if false, prevents drag action from being possible.
horizontal	boolean	false by default; if true, constructs a horizontal layout (inline HTML elements required).
copyOnly	boolean	false by default; if true, always copies items instead of moving them (no Ctrl-key required).
skipform	boolean	false by default; like Moveable, controls whether to make text-based form elements editable.
withHandles	boolean	false by default; when true, allows dragging only by handles.
accept	Array	["text"] by default. Specifies the type of object that can be accepted for a drop.

A very common use for a Source is to eliminate some of the bookkeeping that is involved in dragging and dropping items that are arranged in a list-like format. The following code example illustrates:

```html
<html>
    <head>
        <title>Fun with Source!</title>
        <link rel="stylesheet" type="text/css"
          href="http://o.aolcdn.com/dojo/1.1/dijit/themes/tundra/tundra.css" />
        <link rel="stylesheet" type="text/css"
          href="http://o.aolcdn.com/dojo/1.1/dojo/resources/dojo.css" />
        <link rel="stylesheet" type="text/css"
          href="http://o.aolcdn.com/dojo/1.1/dojo/resources/dnd.css" />
        <script
            type="text/javascript"
            djConfig="parseOnLoad:true"
            src="http://o.aolcdn.com/dojo/1.1/dojo/dojo.xd.js">
        </script>

        <script type="text/javascript">
            dojo.require("dojo.dnd.Source");
            dojo.require("dojo.parser");
        </script>
    </head>
```

```
<body>
    <div dojoType="dojo.dnd.Source" class="container">
        <div class="dojoDndItem">foo</div>
        <div class="dojoDndItem">bar</div>
        <div class="dojoDndItem">baz</div>
        <div class="dojoDndItem">quux</div>
    </div>
</body>
</html>
```

Although this initial example may not look like much, there is a tremendous amount of functionality packed into it. For starters, notice that the only Dojo class that is directly involved is Source, and to create a container of items that are drag-and-droppable within that container, you simply provide the token dojoType tag and ensure that the element is parsed; like most other examples, the parseOnLoad parameter passed to djConfig takes care of this task.

Next, take a few moments to tinker around with the example. It might be obvious that you can drag-and-drop single items at a time, but it's important to also note the full gamut of functionality that is offered:

- Clicking selects a single element and results in all other elements becoming unselected.

- Ctrl-clicking toggles the selection state of an item and allows you to build up multiple items at a time; you can also deselect individual items from a multiple selection situation.

- Shift-clicking selects a range of elements from the previous-most selection to the current element being clicked. Any selections before the previous-most selection become unselected.

- Ctrl-Shift-clicking selects a range of elements from the previous-most selection to the current element being clicked, but preserves any selections before the previous-most selection.

- Holding down the Ctrl key while performing a drop results in the selection(s) being copied. Figure 7-1 illustrates some of these actions.

Pure Targets

As mentioned earlier in the chapter, there are bound to be plenty of times when you'll need to employ a Target that can only act as a destination; once items are placed in it, they may not be moved or reordered. Make the following trivial modification to the previous code listing to see a Target in action.

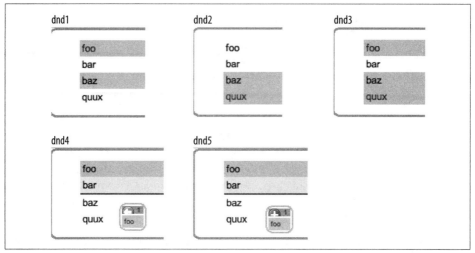

Figure 7-1. dnd1 shows an initial selection using Ctrl-click; dnd2 is the result of performing a Shift-click on quux; dnd3 is the result of performing a Shift-Ctrl-click on quux; dnd4 depicts a move operation by dragging without the Ctrl key; and dnd5 shows a copy operation by dragging with the Ctrl key applied

```
<body>
    <div dojoType="dojo.dnd.Source" class="container">
        <div class="dojoDndItem">foo</div>
        <div class="dojoDndItem">bar</div>
        <div class="dojoDndItem">baz</div>
        <div class="dojoDndItem">quux</div>
    </div>
    <!-- Items added to targets cannot be removed or reordered -->
    <div dojoType="dojo.dnd.Target" class="container"></div>
</body>
```

As you may be able to tell by now, a tremendous amount of functionality is wrapped up into just a few lines of code, and although div elements were used for the example, note that other types of standard HTML elements work equally well. Unordered lists via the ul and li elements are a common choice.

Custom Avatars

The small icon that temporarily appears when an item from a Source is being moved around is called an *avatar*. Although the standard avatar is quite nice, you may want to construct your own at some point. The following code adjustment illustrates how to define custom text for an avatar by overriding the creator method because this method is used to create an avatar representation of one or more nodes. In this particular circumstance, we'll choose to override creator in markup. The layout is also adjusted to a horizontal specification to simultaneously demonstrate how to adjust a layout:

```
<body>
    <div dojoType="dojo.dnd.Source" horizontal=true class="container">
        <span class="dojoDndItem ">foo</span>
        <span class="dojoDndItem ">bar</span>
        <span class="dojoDndItem ">baz</span>
        <span class="dojoDndItem ">quux</span>

        <script type="dojo/method" event="creator" args="item,hint">
            // override the creator function and return the appropriate type
            var node = dojo.doc.createElement("span");
            node.id = dojo.dnd.getUniqueId( );
            node.className = "dojoDndItem";
            node.innerHTML = "<strong style='color: red'>Custom</strong>  "+item;
            return {node: node, data: item, type: ["text"]};
        </script>

    </div>
    <div dojoType="dojo.dnd.Target" horizontal=true class="container"></div>
</body>
```

Note that the arguments passed into creator are item and hint, the actual item being moved and a value specifying a "hint" for the kind of representation of that should be created. Unless you implement your own low-level machinery, hint will always be "avatar". The creator function is expected to return an object representation of item with keys for an actual DOM node, a data representation, and the type of representation. Recall that "text" is the default representation accepted by a Source object.

Drop Events

Subscribing and connecting to events via dojo.subscribe and dojo.connect works just as easy as with Moveable objects. Table 7-5 summarizes public events for pub/sub and connection-style communications, and a code example follows.

Table 7-5. Drop events

Type	Event	Parameters	Summary
subscribe	"/dnd/source/over"	/* Node */ source	Published when the mouse moves over a Source container; the source parameter specifies the container. When the mouse leaves the Source container, another topic is published with null as Source.

Table 7-5. Drop events (continued)

Type	Event	Parameters	Summary
subscribe	"/dnd/start"	/* Node */ source /* Array */ nodes /* Boolean */ copy	Published when a drag beings. Parameter source specifies the Source container that provides the origin of the drop operations. Parameter copy is true for a copy operation and false for a move operation. Parameter nodes is an array of items involved in the drop operation.
subscribe	"/dnd/drop"	/* Node */ source /* Array */ nodes /* Boolean */ copy	Published when a drop occurs (and a drag officially) ends. Parameter source specifies the Source container that provides the origin and destination of the drop operations. Parameter copy is true for a copy operation and false for a move operation. Parameter nodes is an array of items involved in the drop operation.
subscribe	"/dnd/cancel"	N/A	Published when a drop operation is cancelled (for example, when the Esc key is pressed).
connect	onDndSourceOver	/* Node */ source	Called when a mouse moves over a Source container; parameter source specifies the container. When the mouse leaves the Source container, another onDndSourceOver is called again with null as Source.
connect	onDndStart	/* Node */ source /* Array */ nodes /* Boolean */ copy	Called when a drag begins. Parameter source specifies the Source container that provides the origin of the drop operations. Parameter copy is true for a copy operation and false for a move operation. Parameter nodes is an array of items involved in the drop operation.

Table 7-5. Drop events (continued)

Type	Event	Parameters	Summary
connect	onDndDrop	/* Node */ source /* Array */ nodes /* Boolean */ copy	Called when a drop occurs (and a drag officially) ends. Parameter source specifies the Source container that provides the origin and destination of the drop operations. Parameter copy is true if the operation is a copy operation and false for a move operation. Parameter nodes is an array of items involved in the drop operation.
connect	onDndCancel	N/A	Called when a drop operation is cancelled (for example, when the Esc key is pressed).

Go ahead and load up the following full-blown example and use Firebug to inspect the output that occurs from the various topics that we subscribe to and log to the console, and remember that you can drag-and-drop from different Source containers. Figure 7-2 shows the result. Good stuff!

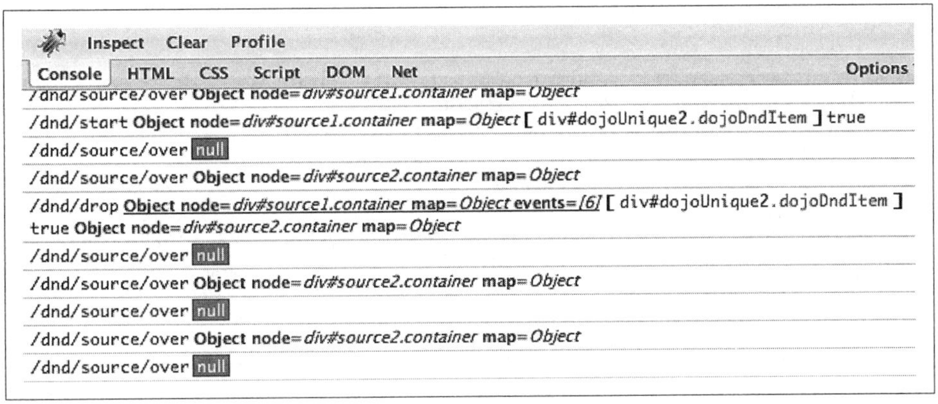

Figure 7-2. Firebug is great for learning the ropes of drag-and-drop

```html
<html>
    <head>
        <title>More Fun with Drop!</title>
        <link rel="stylesheet" type="text/css"
          href="http://o.aolcdn.com/dojo/1.1/dijit/themes/tundra/tundra.css" />
        <link rel="stylesheet" type="text/css"
          href="http://o.aolcdn.com/dojo/1.1/dojo/resources/dojo.css" />
        <link rel="stylesheet" type="text/css"
          href="http://o.aolcdn.com/dojo/1.1/dojo/tests/dnd/dndDefault.css" />
```

```
<script
    type="text/javascript"
    djConfig="parseOnLoad:true"
    src="http://o.aolcdn.com/dojo/1.1/dojo/dojo.xd.js">
</script>

<script type="text/javascript">
    dojo.require("dojo.dnd.Source");
    dojo.require("dojo.parser");

    dojo.addOnLoad(function( ) {
        dojo.subscribe("/dnd/source/over", function(source) {
            console.log("/dnd/source/over", source);
        });
        dojo.subscribe("/dnd/start", function(source, nodes, copy) {
            console.log("/dnd/start", source, nodes, copy);
        });
        dojo.subscribe("/dnd/drop", function(source, nodes, copy) {
            console.log("/dnd/drop", source, nodes, copy);
        });
        dojo.subscribe("/dnd/cancel", function( ) {
            console.log("/dnd/cancel");
        });
    });
</script>
</head>
<body>
    <div id="source1" dojoType="dojo.dnd.Source" class="container">
        <div class="dojoDndItem">foo</div>
        <div class="dojoDndItem">bar</div>
        <div class="dojoDndItem">baz</div>
        <div class="dojoDndItem">quux</div>
    </div>
    <div id="source2" dojoType="dojo.dnd.Source" class="container">
        <div class="dojoDndItem">FOO</div>
        <div class="dojoDndItem">BAR</div>
        <div class="dojoDndItem">BAZ</div>
        <div class="dojoDndItem">QUUX</div>
    </div>
</body>
</html>
```

All it takes to demonstrate some connections is a different addOnLoad function. Note that because we need to have a reference to the Source that is created (not the DOM node), we need to programmatically create the Source instead of relying on the parser to instantiate widgets that are defined in markup. Substitute the following, turn off djConfig's parseOnLoad flag, and take a look at the Firebug console once again:

```
dojo.addOnLoad(function( ) {
    //keep a reference to the Source to use for connecting.
    var s1 = new dojo.dnd.Source("source1");

    dojo.connect(s1, "onDndSourceOver", function(source) {
        console.log("onDndSourceOver for", s1, source);
```

```
    });
    dojo.connect(s1, "onDndStart", function(source, nodes, copy) {
        console.log("onDndStart for ", s1, source, nodes, copy);
    });
    dojo.connect(s1, "onDndStop", function(source, nodes, copy, target) {
        console.log("onDndStop for", s1, source, nodes, copy, target);
    });
    dojo.connect(s1, "onDndCancel", function() {
        console.log("onDndCancel for ", s1);
     });
});
```

Scripting Droppables

While the previous example demonstrated that you could use the Source constructor function to make a node droppable, there is considerably more functionality you can achieve via scripting. Table 7-6 summarizes the functionality that Selector, a lower level class in dojo.dnd, offers. Because Source inherits from Selector, these functions are directly available to you though Source, although you might very well find uses for Selector in and of itself.

Table 7-6. Selector API

Method	Comment
getSelectedNodes()	Returns an Array of the selected nodes.
selectNone()	Deselects all of the nodes.
selectAll()	Selects all of the nodes.
deleteSelectedNodes()	Deletes all selected nodes.
insertNodes(/* Boolean */ addSelected, /* Array */ data, /* Boolean */ before, /* Node */ anchor)	Inserts an Array of nodes, optionally allowing them to be selected via addSelected. If no anchor is supplied, nodes are inserted before the first child of the Selector. Otherwise, they are inserted either before or after the anchor node according to the value of before.
destroy()	Prepares the object for garbage collection.
onMouseDown(/* Object */ event)	Can be connected to via dojo.connect for detecting onmousedown events, although higher-level onDnd methods should first be considered. Parameter event provides standard event info.
onMouseUp(/* Object */ event)	Can be connected to via dojo.connect for detecting onmouseup, although higher-level onDnd methods should first be considered. Parameter event provides standard event info.
onMouseMove(/* Object */ event)	Can be connected to via dojo.connect for detecting mouse motion, although higher-level onDnd methods should first be considered. Parameter event provides standard event info.

Table 7-6. Selector API (continued)

Method	Comment
onOverEvent(/* Object */ event)	Can be connected to via dojo.connect for detecting when the mouse enters the area, although higher-level onDnd methods should first be considered. Parameter event provides standard event info.
onOutEvent(/* Object */ event)	Can be connected to via dojo.connect for detecting when the mouse leaves the area, although higher-level onDnd methods should first be considered. Parameter event provides standard event info.

Summary

 For a really practical example of drag-and-drop at work, be sure to check out ""Drag-and-Drop with the Tree" in Chapter 15, where drag-and-drop is applied to the problem of manipulating the Tree dijit. The Tree is a phenomenal piece of engineering and dnd only makes it better!

After reading this chapter, you should be able to:

- Construct unconstrained Moveable objects and drag them around on the screen
- Define constraints for Moveable objects to control their behavior
- Be able to implement Source and Target containers to create collections of items that can be dragged and dropped to/from/within one another
- Create custom avatars to communicate with the user when a drop operation is about to occur
- Use dojo.connect and dojo.subscribe to receive event notifications for drag-and-drop objects

Next, we'll cover animation and special effects.

## CHAPTER 8

Animation and Special Effects

Animation can add a splash of character to an otherwise bland application. This chapter systematically works through the animation utilities that are built right into Base as well as the dojo.fx (pronounced "effects") module that Core provides. This chapter includes a lot of source code and the bulk of the content builds upon only a few other concepts covered in earlier chapters. As such, this chapter may prove useful as a near-standalone reference.

Animation

The toolkit provides animation facilities in Base and supplements them with additional functionality offered through dojo.fx. The stock functionality offered by Base includes _Animation, a class that acts as a delegate in that it fires callbacks according to its configuration; these callback functions are what manipulate properties of a node so that it animates. Once instantiated, all that has to be done to execute an _Animation is to invoke its play method.

The leading underscore on the _Animation class currently designates at least two things:

- The API isn't definitively final yet, although it is really stable and probably will not change much (if any) between version 1.1 of the toolkit and when it does become final.

- You generally won't be creating an _Animation directly. Instead, you'll rely on auxiliary functions from Base and dojo.fx to create, wrap, and manipulate them on your behalf. You will, however, usually need to run their play methods to start them.

Simple Fades

Before delving into some of the advanced aspects of animations, let's kick things off with one of the simplest examples possible: a simple square on the screen that fades out when you click on it, shown in Figure 8-1. This example uses one of the two fade functions included with Base. The fadeOut function and its sibling fadeIn function accept three keyword arguments, listed in Table 8-1. Figure 8-1 shows an illustration of the default easing function.

Table 8-1. Parameters for Base's fade functions

Parameter	Type	Comment
node	DOM Node	The node that will be faded.
duration	Integer	How many milliseconds the fade should last. Default value is 350.
easing	Function	A function that adjusts the acceleration and/or deceleration of the progress across a curve. Default value is:
		(0.5 + ((Math.sin((n + 1.5) * Math.PI))/2).
		Note that the easing function is only defined from a domain of 0 to 1 for fadeIn and fadeOut.

The node and duration parameters should be familiar enough, but the notion of an easing function might seem a bit foreign. In short, an easing function is simply a function that controls the rate of change for something—in this case an _Animation. An easing function as simple as function(x) { return x; } is linear: for each input value, the same output value is returned. Thus, if you consider the domain for possible *x* values to be decimal numbers between 0 and 1, you notice that the function always returns the same value. When you plot the function, it is simply a straight line of constant slope, as shown in Figure 8-2. The constant slope guarantees that the animation is smooth and occurs at a constant rate of change.

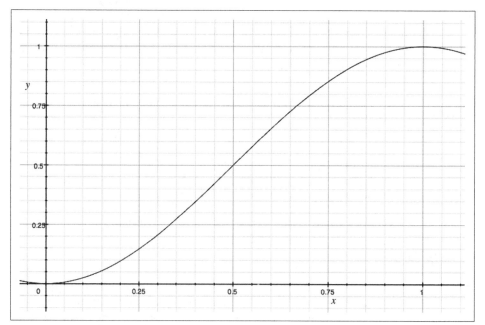

Figure 8-1. A visualization of the default easing function; an easing function is only defined from a scale of 0 to 1 for fadeIn and fadeOut

Example 8-1 demonstrates how to fade out a portion of the screen using the default parameters.

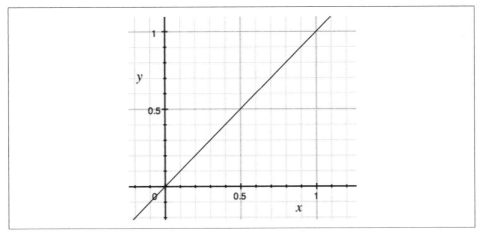

Figure 8-2. An simple easing function that is linear for values between 0 and 1

Example 8-1. Fading out a node

```
<html>
    <head>
        <title>Fun with Animation!</title>
        <style type="text/css">
            @import "http://o.aolcdn.com/dojo/1.1/dojo/resources/dojo.css";
            .box {
                width : 200px;
                height : 200px;
                margin : 5px;
                background : blue;
                text-align : center;
            }
        </style>
        <script
            type="text/javascript"
            src="http://o.aolcdn.com/dojo/1.1/dojo/dojo.xd.js">
        </script>
        <script type="text/javascript">
            dojo.addOnLoad(function( ) {
                var box = dojo.byId("box");
                dojo.connect(box, "onclick", function(evt) {
                    var anim = dojo.fadeOut({node:box});
                    anim.play( );
                });
            });
        </script>
    </head>
    <body>
        <div id="box" class="box">Fade Me Out</div>
    </body>
</html>
```

To contrast the default behavior with a different easing function, shown in Figure 8-3, consider the following revision to the previous addOnLoad block. Note how the default easing function is a relative smooth increase from 0 to 1, while the custom easing function delays almost all of the easing until the very end. This example also uses the dot-operator to run the play method on the _Animation instead of storing an explicit reference, which is cleaner and more customary.

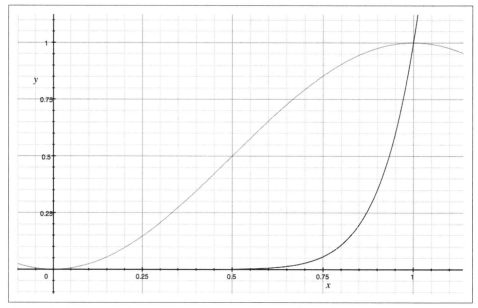

Figure 8-3. An example of a custom easing function juxtaposed with the default easing function

```
dojo.addOnLoad(function( ) {
    var box = dojo.byId("box");
    dojo.connect(box, "onclick", function(evt) {
        var easingFunc = function(x) {
            return Math.pow(x,10);
        }
        dojo.fadeOut({
            node:box,
            easing : easingFunc,
            duration : 3000
        }).play( );
    });});
```

 The dojox.fx.easing module contains a number of excellent easing functions. Check them out if you find yourself in need of some creative possibilities.

Given that simple fades are incredibly common, having them at a distance of one function call away through Base is wonderful. However, it won't be long before you'll start to wonder about what kinds of other slick animations you can create with _Animation.

Animating Arbitrary CSS Properties

Let's build on our current foundation by introducing the rest of the animateProperty function, which accepts one or more of the configuration parameters shown in Table 8-2 in the same manner that fadeIn and fadeOut work.

Table 8-2. The animateProperty function

Parameter	Type	Comment
node	DOM Node | String	The node or a node id that will be animated.
duration	Integer	How many milliseconds the animation should last. Default value is 350.
easing	Function	A function that adjusts the acceleration and/or deceleration of the progress across a curve. Default value is (0.5 + ((Math.sin((n + 1.5) * Math.PI))/2).
repeat	Integer	How many times to repeat the _Animation. By default, this value is 0.
rate	Integer	The duration in milliseconds to wait before advancing to the next "frame". This parameter controls how frequently the _Animation is refreshed on a discrete basis. For example, a rate value of 1000 would imply a relative rate of 1 frame per second. Assuming a duration of 10000, this would result in 10 discrete updates being performed in the _Animation. By default, this value is 10.
delay	Integer	How long to wait before performing the animation after its play method is executed.
properties	Object	Specifies the CSS properties to animate, providing start values, end values, and units. The start and end values may be literal values or functions that can be used to derive computed values: start (String) The starting value for the property end (String) The starting value for the property unit (String) The type of units: px (the default), em, etc.

Replace the existing addOnLoad function with this updated one to test out animateProperty. In this particular case, the width of the node is being animated from 200px to 400px:

```
dojo.addOnLoad(function( ) {
    var box = dojo.byId("box");
    dojo.connect(box, "onclick", function(evt) {
            dojo.animateProperty({
                node : box,
```

```
                  duration : 3000,
                  properties : {
                      width : {start : '200', end : '400'}
                  }
              }).play();
         });
     });
```

It is worthwhile to spend a few moments experimenting with the `animateProperty` function to get a good feel for the kinds of creative things that you can make happen; it is the foundation of most `dojo.fx` animations and chances are that you'll use it *often* to take care of routine matters. It accepts virtually any CSS properties all through the same unified interface. Example 8-2 illustrates that animations adjust other inline screen content accordingly. Clicking on the blue box causes it to expand in the *x* and *y* dimensions, causing the red and green boxes to adjust their position as needed.

Example 8-2. Expanding the dimensions of a node

```html
<html>
    <head>
        <title>More Fun With Animation!</title>
        <style type="text/css">
            @import "http://o.aolcdn.com/dojo/1.1/dojo/resources/dojo.css";
            .box {
                width : 200px;
                height : 200px;
                margin : 5px;
                text-align : center;
            }
            .blueBox {
                background : blue;
                float : left;
            }
            .redBox {
                background : red;
                float : left;
            }
            .greenBox {
                background : green;
                clear : left;
            }
        </style>
        <script
            type="text/javascript"
            src="http://o.aolcdn.com/dojo/1.1/dojo/dojo.xd.js">
        </script>
        <script type="text/javascript">

            dojo.addOnLoad(function() {
                var box = dojo.byId("box1");
                dojo.connect(box, "onclick", function(evt) {
                    dojo.animateProperty({
                        node : box,
```

Example 8-2. Expanding the dimensions of a node (continued)

```
                    duration : 3000,
                    properties : {
                        height : {start : '200', end : '400'},
                        width : {start : '200', end : '400'}
                    }
                }).play();
            });
        });

    </script>
</head>
<body>
    <div id="box1" class="box blueBox">Click Here</div>
    <div id="box2" class="box redBox"></div>
    <div id="box2" class="box greenBox"></div>
</body>
</html>
```

If some of the animateProperty parameters still seem foggy to you, the previous code example is a great place to spend some time getting more familiar with the effect of various parameters. For example, make the following change to the animateProperty function to produce 10 discrete frames of progress instead of a more continuous-looking animation (recall that the duration divided by the rate provides a number of frames):

```
dojo.addOnLoad(function() {
    var box = dojo.byId("box1");
    dojo.connect(box, "onclick", function(evt) {
        dojo.animateProperty({
            node : box,
            duration : 10000,
            rate : 1000,
            properties : {
                height : {start : '200', end : '400'},
                width : {start : '200', end : '400'}
            }
        }).play();
    });
});
```

Given that the default easing function being used is fairly smooth, take a moment to experiment with the effect that various more abrupt functions have on the animation. For example, the following adjustment uses a parabolic easing function, shown in Figure 8-4, in which the values increase in value at much larger intervals as you approach higher domain values, and the discrete effect over the 10 distinct frames should be apparent:

```
dojo.addOnLoad(function() {
    var box = dojo.byId("box1");
    dojo.connect(box, "onclick", function(evt) {
        dojo.animateProperty({
            node : box,
```

```
                duration : 10000,
                rate : 1000,
            easing : function(x) { return x*x; },
                properties : {
                    height : {start : '200', end : '400'},
                    width : {start : '200', end : '400'}
                }
            }).play();
        });
    });
```

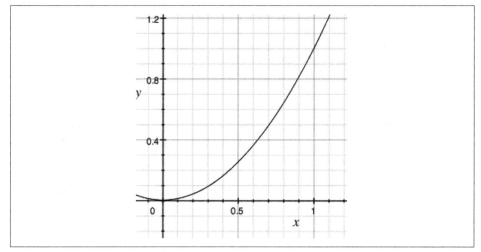

Figure 8-4. An example of a parabolic easing function

Although the examples so far have implied that easing functions are monotonic,* this
need not be the case. For example, try adjusting the working example with an easing
function that is not monotonic, shown in Figure 8-5, to see the effect:

```
dojo.addOnLoad(function() {
    var box = dojo.byId("box1");
    dojo.connect(box, "onclick", function(evt) {
        dojo.animateProperty({
            node : box,
            duration : 10000,
            easing : function(x) {return Math.pow(Math.sin(4*x),2);},
            properties : {
                height : {start : '200', end : '400'},
                width : {start : '200', end : '400'}
            }
        }).play();
    });
});
```

---

* Basically, a function is monotonic if it moves steadily in one direction or the other, i.e., if it always increases
  or if it always decreases.

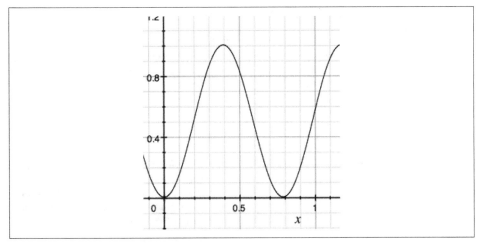

Figure 8-5. An easing function that increases and then decreases in value

Slightly Simplified Syntax

Simplified syntax for properties was added in version 1.1. Previously, you might have animated a node from its existing width to a new width via:

```
dojo.animateProperty({
    node: "foo",
    properties: { width: { end: 500 } } //lots of brackets
}).play();
```

Now, if you provide only an Integer for a properties value, it's assumed to imply end, which means the previous block could be reduced to:

```
dojo.animateProperty({
    node: "foo", properties: { width: 500 } //fewer brackets
}).play();
```

Another new addition that came with version 1.1, dojo.anim, adds a couple of additional enhancements; it works much like animateProperty except that it automatically plays the animation instead of requiring the play function to be called explicitly; thus, when you receive the _Animation back from it, it has already begun. (Calling play() again would result in a no-op.) There are also a couple of common properties that have been moved out of the properties Object as positional arguments.

The full function signature looks like this:

```
dojo.anim(/*DOMNode|String*/node, /*Object*/props, /*Integer?*/duration,
/*Function?*/easing, /*Function?*/onEnd, /*Integer?*/delay)
//Returns _Animation that is playing
```

If these recent enhancements confuses you, don't feel the need to use them right away; they're provided as additional conveniences that are supposed to make your life easier.

Programatically Controlling Animations

Although you generally do not create raw _Animation objects, you still have the ability to control them for most of the common use cases. For example, while an animation is ongoing, you have the ability to pause, restart, and stop it prematurely, inquire about its status, or cue it to a specific point. _Animation provides methods for all of these common tasks, listed in Table 8-3.

Table 8-3. _Animation control functions

Method	Parameters	Comment
stop	/* Boolean */ goToEnd	Stops an animation. If goToEnd is true, then the _Animation advances to the end so that when play is invoked again, it will start from the beginning. goToEnd is false by default.
pause	N/A	Pauses an animation.
play	/* Integer */ delay /* Boolean */ goToStart	Plays an animation, optionally allowing for a delay (in milliseconds) before the play operation. For paused animations, specifying true for goToStart restarts the animation versus continuing where it left off.
status	N/A	Returns the status of an animation. Possible values for status are "paused", "playing", and "stopped".
gotoPercent	/* Decimal */ percent /* Boolean */ andPlay	Stops the animation and then advances its percentage complete between 0.0 and 1.0. Setting andPlay is true (false by default) restarts the animation.

 Notice that *gotoPercent* is not mixedCase, like *goToPercent*. This is one of the few functions in the toolkit that does not use mixedCase, which makes it very easy to mistype.

You may also define any of the methods shown in Table 8-4 as an input to animateProperty. The following table summarizes the functionality provided, and a block of code follows that illustrates a change to animateProperty that you can try to set out the method calls.

Table 8-4. Input methods for animateProperty

Method	Parameters	Comment
beforeBegin	N/A	Fired before the animation begins, providing access to the _Animation and the node for modification immediately before anything happens.
onBegin	/* Object */ value	Fires after the animation has begun cycling, so in effect, this method is somewhat asynchronous. The value parameter is an object containing the current values for the style properties.

Table 8-4. Input methods for animateProperty (continued)

Method	Parameters	Comment
onAnimate	/* Object */ value	Called for each discrete frame of the animation. The parameter is an object containing the current values for the style properties.
onEnd	N/A	Called automatically when the animation ends.
onPlay	/* Object */ value	Called each time play is called (including the first time). The value parameter is an object containing the current values for the style properties.
onPause	/* Object */ value	Called each time pause is called. The value parameter is an object containing the current values for the style properties.
onStop	/* Object */ value	Called each time stop is called. The value parameter is an object containing the current values for the style properties.

Here's a small code snippet you can use to tinker around with these methods firing:

```
dojo.animateProperty({
    node : "box1",
    duration:10000,
    rate : 1000,
    beforeBegin:function(){ console.log("beforeBegin: ", arguments); },
    onBegin:function(){ console.log("onBegin: ", arguments); },
    onAnimate:function(){ console.log("onAnimate: ", arguments); },
    onEnd:function(){ console.log("onEnd: ", arguments); },
    onPlay:function(){ console.log("onPlay: ", arguments); },
    properties : {height : {start : "200", end : "400"} }
}).play();
```

The following adjustments to the working example illustrate some basic methods for controlling an _Animation:

```
<!-- snip -->
<script type="text/javascript">
        dojo.addOnLoad(function() {
            var box = dojo.byId("box1");
            var anim;
            dojo.connect(box, "onclick", function(evt) {
                    anim = dojo.animateProperty({
                    node : box,
                    duration : 10000,
                    rate : 1000,
                    easing : function(x) { console.log(x); return x*x; },
                    properties : {
                        height : {start : '200', end : '400'},
                        width : {start : '200', end : '400'}
                    }
            });
            anim.play();
```

```
                dojo.connect(dojo.byId("stop"), "onclick", function(evt) {
                    anim.stop(true);
                    console.log("status is ", anim.status());
                });
                dojo.connect(dojo.byId("pause"), "onclick", function(evt) {
                    anim.pause();
                    console.log("status is ", anim.status());
                });
                dojo.connect(dojo.byId("play"), "onclick", function(evt) {
                    anim.play();
                    console.log("status is ", anim.status());
                });
                dojo.connect(dojo.byId("goTo50"), "onclick", function(evt) {
                    anim.gotoPercent(0.5, true);
                    console.log("advanced to 50%");
                });
            });
        });

    </script>
  </head>
  <body>
    <div>
        <button id="stop"   style="margin : 5px">stop</button>
        <button id="pause" style="margin : 5px">pause</button>
        <button id="play"   style="margin : 5px">play</button>
        <button id="goTo50"  style="margin : 5px">50 percent</button>
    </div>
    <div id="box1" class="box blueBox">Click Here</div>
    <div id="box2" class="box redBox"></div>
    <div id="box2" class="box greenBox"></div>
  </body>
</html>
```

Core fx

The content of this chapter up to this point has concentrated entirely on the animation facilities that are provided by Base. The existing functionality in Base consisting of fadeIn, fadeOut, and animateProperty covers a tremendous amount of use cases; however, there are a few additional functions provided in Core's fx module that you can get for the cost of one additional dojo.require statement. These facilities for effects include functions for sliding nodes and wiping nodes in and out, as well as chaining, combining, and toggling animations.

Sliding

Sliding nodes is just as easy as fading them. You pass a hash containing configuration parameters to the dojo.fx.slideTo function just like you would with animateProperty. Table 8-5 summarizes.

A Closer Look at _Animation

As previously emphasized, you will generally be using auxiliary functions, especially animateProperty, to perform your animations. Functions like animateProperty act like a wrapper for configuring _Animation objects, although they do return them for you to play, pause, and so on.

In case you are intrigued by _Animation and exactly what it is doing, it is actually pretty simple. With the exception of node and properties, it accepts the same parameters as the animateProperty function from Table 8-2 (not surprising because animateProperty is acting as a wrapper for creating and manipulating and animation) and one additional parameter, curve, which defines the domain for the easing function. The built-in animation functions like animateProperty, fadeIn, and so on have a default domain of 0 to 1, but the curve parameter allows for an arbitrary domain. (And if the term *curve* seems like a misnomer, you probably wouldn't be the first person to think that way. In this context, a curve is a one-dimensional concept, while curves as we are used to seeing them are usually two-dimensional concepts.)

The various parameters, curve, easing, duration, and rate, all fit together and are all worth summarizing once more:

duration

> How long the animation plays.

rate

> How often to refresh the animation; the rate divided by the duration is the total number of discrete frames that appear. The notion of frame rate is important because the progress of the animation is equivalent to relating the current frame number to the final frame number.

curve

> The domain of possible values that get passed to the onAnimate function. Each individual value that is passed into onAnimate is calculated by projecting the result of the easing function on this domain. A curve is represented by an Array accepting two numeric values corresponding to the start and end values for the possible domain.

easing

> A function that accepts input values from 0 to 1, corresponding to the current progress of the animation. The result of the easing function projected onto the "curve" is what gets passed to the onAnimate function. Note that if the easing function returns a value greater than 1.0, the value passed to onAnimate will overextend the endpoint defined by curve, which is fine.

—continued—

To wrap up the various _Animation parameters, let's assume there is an animation that lasts 10 seconds, and the rate is set to 1 second. The input domain defined by curve is set to be 50 through 100, and the easing function is simply function(x) { return 2*x; }.

Based on this configuration, the easing function should be accepting 10 different values 0.1, 0.2, 0.3,..., 1.0 and scaling these values by a factor of 2 such that it outputs outputting the values 0.2, 0.4, 0.6,..., 2.0. The output of the easing function is then projected onto the domain defined by the curve and passed them to the onAnimate function; thus, the onAnimate function accepts the values 50, 60, 70, 80, 90,..., 150.

Here's the code to try it for yourself:

```
new dojo._Animation({
    duration:10000,
    rate : 1000,
    curve: [50,100],
    easing : function(x) {
        console.log("easing: ", 2*x);
        return 2*x;
    },
    onAnimate:function(x){
        console.log("onAnimate: ", x);
    },
    onEnd:function( ){
        console.log('all done.');
    }
}).play( );
```

Table 8-5. Parameters for Core's slide functions

Parameter	Type	Comment
node	DOM Node	The node that will be sliding.
duration	Integer	How many milliseconds the fade should last. Default value is 350.
easing	Function	A function that adjusts the acceleration and/or deceleration of the progress across a curve. Default value is $(0.5 + ((Math.sin((n + 1.5) * Math.PI))/2)$.
		Note that the easing function is only defined from a domain of 0 to 1 for the fadeIn and fadeOut.
left	Integer	Where the node's left corner should be at the end of the slide.
top	Integer	Where the node's top corner should be at the end of the slide.

Example 8-3 illustrates the sliding functions. The only portions of the page that are any different from the previous fade examples are emphasized.

Example 8-3. Sliding a node

```
<html>
    <head>
        <title>Animation Station</title>
```

Example 8-3. Sliding a node (continued)

```
<style type="text/css">
    @import "http://o.aolcdn.com/dojo/1.1/dojo/resources/dojo.css";
    .box {
        width : 200px;
        height : 200px;
        margin : 5px;
        background : blue;
        text-align : center;
    }
</style>
<script
    type="text/javascript"
    src="http://o.aolcdn.com/dojo/1.1/dojo/dojo.xd.js">
</script>
<script type="text/javascript">
    dojo.require("dojo.fx");

    dojo.addOnLoad(function() {
        var box = dojo.byId("box");
        dojo.connect(box, "onclick", function(evt) {
            dojo.fx.slideTo({
                node:box,
                top : "200",
                left : "200"
            }).play();
        });
    });
</script>
</head>
<body>
    <div id="box" class="box">Slide Me</div>
</body>
</html>
```

Wiping

Slides and fades are a lot of fun, but wipes are frequently used and have wonderful utility as well. The basic approach to using them should be no surprise by now. Most of the same arguments apply. Table 8-6 provides a synopsis.

Table 8-6. Parameters for Core's wipe functions

Parameter	Type	Comment
node	DOM Node	The node that will be wiped.
duration	Integer	How many milliseconds the fade should last. Default value is 350.
easing	Function	A function that adjusts the acceleration and/or deceleration of the progress across a curve. Default value is $(0.5 + ((Math.sin((n + 1.5) * Math.PI))/2)$.
		Note that the easing function is only defined from a domain of 0 to 1 for the fadeIn and fadeOut.

Be advised that in some layouts, border, margin, and padding values associated with nodes have been known to affect the layout once wipe animations have completed.

Following suit with the other examples in this chapter, Example 8-4 can get you started.

Example 8-4. Wiping a node

```html
<html>
    <head>
        <title>Animation Station</title>
        <style type="text/css">
            @import "http://o.aolcdn.com/dojo/1.1/dojo/resources/dojo.css";
            .box {
                width : 200px;
                height : 200px;
                text-align : center;
                float : left;
                position : absolute;
                margin : 5px;
            }
        </style>
        <script
            type="text/javascript"
            src="http://o.aolcdn.com/dojo/1.1/dojo/dojo.xd.js">
        </script>
        <script type="text/javascript">
            dojo.require("dojo.fx");

            dojo.addOnLoad(function( ) {
                var box = dojo.byId("box");
                dojo.connect(box, "onclick", function(evt) {
                    dojo.fx.wipeOut({
                        node:box
                    }).play( );
                });
            });
        </script>
    </head>
    <body>
        <div class="box">Now you don't</div>
        <div id="box" style="background : blue" class="box">Now you see me...</div>
    </body>
</html>
```

You may also find it especially interesting to experiment with custom easing functions for wipes. Try our custom, nonmonotonic easing function from earlier and note the interesting bouncy effect with the following addOnLoad change:

```
dojo.addOnLoad(function( ) {
    var box = dojo.byId("box");
    dojo.connect(box, "onclick", function(evt) {
        dojo.fx.wipeOut({
            node:box,
            easing : function(x) { return Math.pow(Math.sin(4*x),2);   },
            duration : 5000
        }).play( );
    });
});
```

Because the easing function increases, decreases, then decreases again, the internal _Animation that wipeOut uses scales the height of the node accordingly.

Chaining and Combining

There's something that's quite remarkable about watching an object slide, fade, and wipe around the screen, but that's not all you can do: you can use another function in Core fx, dojo.fx.chain, to chain together animations. This function is incredibly simple in that its only argument is an Array of _Animation objects and it returns another _Animation for you to play. Let's use it to make the box do something a little more fancy. Table 8-7 lists the functions for combining and chaining.

 As of Dojo version 1.1, the animation functions chain and combine in this section have several known issues relating to how events such as beforeBegin and onEnd are processed when multiple animations are rolled up. The basic gist is that if you are trying to rely on these events for specific hooks in your application's logic, you might be better off using functions like dojo.connect and dojo.subscribe to rig up your own chains and combinations. Of course, for less advanced tasks, chain and combine work fine.

Table 8-7. Animation combination and chaining

Function	Comment
dojo.fx.chain(/* Array */ animations)	Chains together the animations enclosed in the array that is passed in as a parameter and returns a consolidated animation that you can play as usual. The resulting animation is the sequential result of playing each animation back to back.
dojo.fx.combine(/* Array */ animations)	Combines the animations enclosed in the array that is passed in as a parameter and returns a consolidated animation that you can play as usual. The resulting animation provides the effect of playing each of the original animations in parallel.

Example 8-5 demonstrates a box that makes a zigzag pattern across the screen. Note that you define custom easing function and other parameters just as normal.

Example 8-5. Chaining animations together

```
dojo.addOnLoad(function( ) {
    var box = dojo.byId("box");
    dojo.connect(box, "onclick", function(evt) {
        var easing = function(x) { return x; };
        var a1 = dojo.fx.slideTo({
            node:box,
            easing : easing,
            duration : 1000,
            top : "150",
            left : "300"
        });
        var a2 = dojo.fx.slideTo({
            node:box,
            easing : easing,
            duration : 400,
            top : "20",
            left : "350"
        });
        var a3 = dojo.fx.slideTo({
            node:box,
            easing : easing,
            duration : 800,
            top : "350",
            left : "400"
        });
        dojo.fx.chain([a1,a2,a3]).play( );
    });
});
```

But say you want to fade and slide at the same time. No problem. Following the same type API call as dojo.fx.chain, the dojo.fx.combine will do it in a jiffy. Any animations you pass into it through the Array parameter are run in parallel. First, let's look at a simple combination of our slide and fade examples. Example 8-6 shows the relevant change to addOnLoad.

Example 8-6. Combining animations

```
dojo.addOnLoad(function( ) {
    var box = dojo.byId("box");
    dojo.connect(box, "onclick", function(evt) {
        var a1 = dojo.fx.slideTo({
            node:box,
            top : "150",
            left : "300"
        });
        var a2 = dojo.fadeOut({
            node:box
        });
        dojo.fx.combine([a1,a2]).play( );
    });
});
```

It's easy to forget that slideTo is in dojo.fx while fadeIn and fadeOut are in Base, so take a moment to acknowledge that a call like dojo.fx.fadeIn would give you an error. If you do not issue a dojo.require("dojo.fx") before attempting to use anything in dojo.fx, you'll get an error.

Given that chain returns a single _Animation, let's try something more advanced (but still really simple) because it builds on the same fundamentals: in Example 8-7, we'll chain together several fade animations and combine them with several slide animations that we'll also chain together.

Example 8-7. Chaining and combining animations

```
dojo.addOnLoad(function( ) {
    var box = dojo.byId("box");
    dojo.connect(box, "onclick", function(evt) {

        //chain together some slides
        var a1 = dojo.fx.slideTo({
            node:box,
            top : "150",
            left : "300"
        });
        var a2 = dojo.fx.slideTo({
            node:box,
            top : "20",
            left : "350"
        });
        var a3 = dojo.fx.slideTo({
            node:box,
            top : "350",
            left : "400"
        });
        var slides = dojo.fx.chain([a1,a2,a3]);

        //chain together some fades
        var a1 = dojo.fadeIn({
            node:box
        });
        var a2 = dojo.fadeOut({
            node:box
        });
        var a3 = dojo.fadeIn({
            node:box
        });
        var fades = dojo.fx.chain([a1,a2, a3]);

        //now combine the two chains together
        dojo.fx.combine([slides, fades]).play( );

    });
});
```

Toggling

The dojo.fx.Toggler class is essentially a wrapper for configuring the animations for *toggling* (showing and hiding) a node. The class constructor accepts an associative array of parameters that include the show and hide functions as well as the durations for the show and hide functions. Toggler is nice in that there is very little thinking involved about what has to happen. You simply tell it what functions to use, provide the durations, and then manually call its show and hide function accordingly. Both the show and hide function optionally accept a parameter that delays the operation by a said amount of time (Table 8-8).

Table 8-8. Parameters for Core's Toggler function

Parameter	Type	Comment
node	DOM Node	The node to toggle.
showFunc	Function	A function that returns an _Animation for showing the node. Default value is dojo.fadeIn.
hideFunc	Function	A function that returns an _Animation for hiding the node. Default value is dojo.fadeOut.
showDuration	Integer	The duration in milliseconds to run showFunc. Default value is 200 (milliseconds).
hideDuration	Integer	The duration in milliseconds to run hideFunc. Default value is 200 (milliseconds).

Table 8-9 provides the method summary for the class.

Table 8-9. Toggler functions

Method	Comment
show(/*Integer*/delay)	Shows a node over a duration defined by showDuration using showFunc. The optional delay parameter causes the animation to wait by the specified amount before starting.
hide(/*Integer*/delay)	Hides a node over a duration defined by hideDuration using hideFunc. The optional delay parameter causes the animation to wait by the specified amount before starting.

Example 8-8 provides the compulsory source code and another modification to addOnLoad for our working example from Example 8-4.

Example 8-8. Toggling a node

```
dojo.addOnLoad(function( ) {
    var box = dojo.byId("box");
    var t = new dojo.fx.Toggler({
        node : box,
        showDuration : 1000,
        hideDuration : 1000
    });
```

Example 8-8. Toggling a node (continued)

```
    var visible = true;
    dojo.connect(box, "onclick", function(evt) {
        if (visible)
            t.hide( );
        else
            t.show( );

        visible = !visible;
    });
});
```

If you try out the example, you should notice that clicking on the "Now you see me…" box causes it to fade out, while clicking on the "Now you don't" box causes the first box to fade back in.

Animation + Drag-and-Drop = Fun!

Drag-and-drop combined with animations are an incredibly powerful combination. Take a moment to review and experiment with the following block of code, which combines very basic concepts from drag-and-drop in the previous chapter with what you've been learning about in this one; it's illustrated in Figure 8-6.

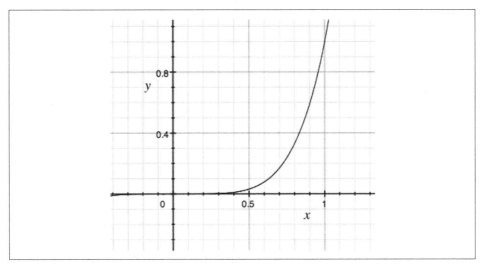

Figure 8-6. A visualization of the x^5 easing function

```
<html>
    <head>
        <title>Animation + Drag and Drop = Fun!</title>

        <script
            type="text/javascript"
            src="http://o.aolcdn.com/dojo/1.1/dojo/dojo.xd.js">
        </script>
```

```
<script type="text/javascript">
    dojo.require("dojo.fx");
    dojo.require("dojo.dnd.move");
    dojo.addOnLoad(function( ){
      var move = new dojo.dnd.Moveable(dojo.byId("ball"));
      var coords;
      dojo.subscribe("/dnd/move/start",function(e){
        // when drag starts, save the coords
        coords = dojo.coords(e.node);
      });

      //now use the coords to control where the image slides back
      dojo.subscribe("/dnd/move/stop",function(e){
        dojo.fx.slideTo({
          node: e.node,
          top: coords.t,
          left: coords.l,
          duration:1200,
          easing : function(x) { return Math.pow(x,5);}
        }).play( );
      });
    });
</script>
</head>
<body>
    <!-- Insert any image into the page here in place of ball.png -->
    <img style="position : absolute; left : 300px; top : 300px;"
            id="ball"
          src="ball.png"/>
</body>
</html>
```

To summarize, the code example detects the start of a global drag event and remembers the coordinates of where that drag began. Then, it waits until the drag event ends, and at that point, moves the image back to its original sport according to the specific easing function. The easing function dictates that the move back will be slow at first, but will rapidly accelerate toward the end in a trendy sort of way.

Colors

Animations and effects in a page may often depend on computing specific color values. Base provides an elementary Color class for encapsulating much of the mundane logic in computing colors, converting them to and from hexadecimal values, and so on. Several auxiliary functions for common operations on colors are also included.

Creating and Blending Colors

The Color class has a flexible constructor that can accept a named string value for a color, a hex string representing a color, or an array of RGB* values. Example 8-9 illustrates the creation of two Color objects and a function Base provides for blending colors.

Example 8-9. Blending Color objects

```html
<html>
    <head>
        <title></title>
        <script
            type="text/javascript"
            src="http://o.aolcdn.com/dojo/1.1/dojo/dojo.xd.js">
        </script>
        <script type="text/javascript">
            dojo.addOnLoad(function( ) {
                var blue = new dojo.Color("#0000ff"); //could also have used "blue"
                var red = new dojo.Color([255, 0, 0]);
                var purple = dojo.blendColors(blue, red, 0.5);
                dojo.style("foo", "background", purple.toCss( ));
            });
        </script>
    </head>
    <body>
        <div id="foo" style="width:200px; height:200px; padding:5px;"></div>
    </body>
</html>
```

The blendColors function accepted the red and blue Color objects and blended them according to a 50/50 mixture to produce the RGB value (128, 0, 128), a neutral shade of purple. The alternative to blending colors is to crunch the numbers yourself—not rocket science, but not very much fun either!

Table 8-10 summarizes the Color class provided by Base.

Table 8-10. Color functionality supported by Base

Method	Comment
Color(/* Array | String */color)	The constructor function, which accepts an array of RGB or RGBA values, or a String, which may be a named color like "blue" or a hex string like "#000ff". If no arguments are passed, the Color object is constructed with the RGBA tuple (255,255,255,1).

* RGB is shorthand for "red green blue," one of the standard ways of representing colors in CSS. RGBA is shorthand for "red green blue alpha" and expresses a fourth color component, which represents the transparency of a color.

Table 8-10. Color functionality supported by Base (continued)

Method	Comment
setColor(/* Array | String | Object */ color)	Works on an existing Color object to configure its value in a manner analogous to its constructor function; the preferred way of reusing an existing Color object.
toRgb()	Returns a String value expressing a Color as an RGB value such as (128, 0, 128).
toRgba()	Returns a String value expressing a Color as an RGBA value such as (128, 0, 128, 0.5).
toHex()	Returns a String value expressing a Color as a hex value such as "#80080".
toCss(/* Boolean */ includeAlpha)	Returns a CSS-compliant String value expressing a Color as an RGB value such as (128, 0, 128). By default, includeAlpha is false. This method is the preferred means of transforming a Color object for use in styling a node.
toString	Returns a standardized String value for a Color as an RGBA value.

Most browsers currently implement a deviation of the CSS2 specification, which does not support RGBA tuples for expressing colors, so Color's toCss() function (with no parameter passed in) is probably your choice method of deriving a value acceptable for passing into a method like dojo.style. If you need to express transparency for nodes that have color, use the style value for opacity to do so.

RGBA Support in CSS3

The RGBA syntax for representing color values as included in the CSS3 specification is quite expressive and convenient. The following code snippet provides an illustration of two overlapping blue and red squares, and Figure 8-7 shows how the overlap blends the two to show a purple square in their intersection:

```
<div style="width:200px; height:200px; padding:5px; background:rgba(0,0,255,
0.5)"></div>

<div style="position:absolute; left:100px; top:100px; width:200px; height:
200px; padding:5px; background:rgba(255,0,0,0.5)"></div>
```

Firefox 3 supports RGBA style values natively. You can read more about the CSS3 support in Firefox at *http://developer.mozilla.org/en/docs/CSS_improvements_in_Firefox_3*.

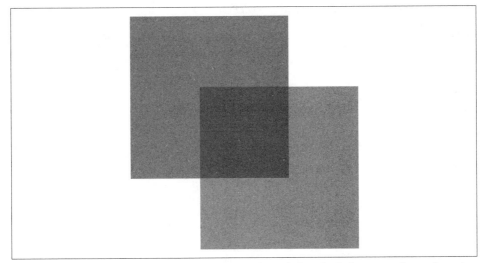

Figure 8-7. An example of how transparency works through the rgba( ) description for a color using Firefox 3

Transparency and opacity are the inverses of one another. If the opacity of something is 1.0, it is fully opaque, and its transparency is therefore 0.0. If its opacity were 0.1, it would be 90% transparent, and you would barely be able to see it.

Named Color Values Available Via Base

One other utility in Base is the configuration of preloaded named colors that is stored in dojo.Color.named, which maps named colors to RGB values. For example, to quickly access the RGB values for maroon, simply use the reference to dojo.Color. named.maroon to get back the RGB array [128,0,0]. Table 8-11 summarizes the named colors that are built into Base. Although you will probably want to use and manipulate Color objects directly, dojo.Color.named may still prove useful during development.

dojo.Color.named is not available from an actual Color object. It is a static collection of color values and no object creation is required to use it. Trying to access a color object instance's .named value will cause an error.

Table 8-11. Named color values available through Base

Name	Red	Green	Blue
black	0	0	0
silver	192	192	192
gray	128	128	128
white	255	255	255
maroon	128	0	0
red	255	0	0
purple	128	0	128
fuchsia	255	0	255
green	0	128	0
lime	0	255	0
olive	128	128	0
yellow	255	255	0
navy	0	0	128
blue	0	0	255
teal	0	128	128
aqua	0	255	255

Additional Color Values Available Via Core

Although not included directly in Base, you can expand dojo.Color.named with more than 100 additional colors including all of the CSS3 named colors complete with SVG 1.0 variant spellings by performing a dojo.require("dojo.colors") statement (see Table 8-12). Note that you can also use the animateProperty function you learned about earlier to to animate the backgroundColor property. For example, you could provide start and end values of "black" and "white", "white" and "#43fab4", etc.

> In addition to expanding dojo.Color.named, dojo.colors provides the additional enhancement of augmenting the Color constructor to accept HSL and HSLA color module formats. The HSL color space attempts to describe perceptual color relationships more accurately then RGB by representing colors in terms of hue, saturation, and lightness. You can read more about the CSS Color module at *http://www.w3.org/TR/ css3-iccprof*.

Table 8-12. Additional named color values available through Core

Name	Red	Green	Blue
aliceblue	240	248	255
antiquewhite	250	235	215
aquamarine	127	255	212

Table 8-12. Additional named color values available through Core (continued)

Name	Red	Green	Blue
azure	240	255	255
beige	245	245	220
bisque	255	228	196
blanchedalmond	255	235	205
blueviolet	138	43	226
brown	165	42	42
burlywood	222	184	135
cadetblue	95	158	160
chartreuse	127	255	0
chocolate	210	105	30
coral	255	127	80
cornflowerblue	100	149	237
cornsilk	255	248	220
crimson	220	20	60
cyan	0	255	255
darkblue	0	0	139
darkcyan	0	139	139
darkgoldenrod	184	134	11
darkgray	169	169	169
darkgreen	0	100	0
darkgrey	169	169	169
darkkhaki	189	183	107
darkmagenta	139	0	139
darkolivegreen	85	107	47
darkorange	255	140	0
darkorchid	153	50	204
darkred	139	0	0
darksalmon	233	150	122
darkseagreen	143	188	143
darkslateblue	72	61	139
darkslategray	47	79	79
darkslategrey	47	79	79
darkturquoise	0	206	209
darkviolet	148	0	211
deeppink	255	20	147
deepskyblue	0	191	255

Table 8-12. Additional named color values available through Core (continued)

Name	Red	Green	Blue
dimgray	105	105	105
dimgrey	105	105	105
dodgerblue	30	144	255
firebrick	178	34	34
floralwhite	255	250	240
forestgreen	34	139	34
gainsboro	220	220	220
ghostwhite	248	248	255
gold	255	215	0
goldenrod	218	165	32
greenyellow	173	255	47
grey	128	128	128
honeydew	240	255	240
hotpink	255	105	180
indianred	205	92	92
indigo	75	0	130
ivory	255	255	240
khaki	240	230	140
lavender	230	230	250
lavenderblush	255	240	245
lawngreen	124	252	0
lemonchiffon	255	250	205
lightblue	173	216	230
lightcoral	240	128	128
lightcyan	224	255	255
lightgoldenrodyellow	250	250	210
lightgray	211	211	211
lightgreen	144	238	144
lightgrey	211	211	211
lightpink	255	182	193
lightsalmon	255	160	122
lightseagreen	32	178	170
lightskyblue	135	206	250
lightslategray	119	136	153
lightslategrey	119	136	153
lightsteelblue	176	196	222

Name	Red	Green	Blue
lightyellow	255	255	224
limegreen	50	205	50
linen	250	240	230
magenta	255	0	255
mediumaquamarine	102	205	170
mediumblue	0	0	205
mediumorchid	186	85	211
mediumpurple	147	112	219
mediumseagreen	60	179	113
mediumslateblue	123	104	238
mediumspringgreen	0	250	154
mediumturquoise	72	209	204
mediumvioletred	199	21	133
midnightblue	25	25	112
mintcream	245	255	250
mistyrose	255	228	225
moccasin	255	228	181
navajowhite	255	222	173
oldlace	253	245	230
olivedrab	107	142	35
orange	255	165	0
orangered	255	69	0
orchid	218	112	214
palegoldenrod	238	232	170
palegreen	152	251	152
paleturquoise	175	238	238
palevioletred	219	112	147
papayawhip	255	239	213
peachpuff	255	218	185
peru	205	133	63
pink	255	192	203
plum	221	160	221
powderblue	176	224	230
rosybrown	188	143	143
royalblue	65	105	225
saddlebrown	139	69	19

Table 8-12. Additional named color values available through Core (continued)

Name	Red	Green	Blue
salmon	250	128	114
sandybrown	244	164	96
seagreen	46	139	87
seashell	255	245	238
sienna	160	82	45
skyblue	135	206	235
slateblue	106	90	205
slategray	112	128	144
slategrey	112	128	144
snow	255	250	250
springgreen	0	255	127
steelblue	70	130	180
tan	210	180	140
thistle	216	191	216
tomato	255	99	71
transparent	0	0	0
turquoise	64	224	208
violet	238	130	238
wheat	245	222	179
whitesmoke	245	245	245
yellowgreen	154	205	50

Summary

This chapter has systematically walked you through Base and Core's tools for animation. A splash of animation, when applied with discretion, can really add that extra bit of *umph* that distinguishes your application from the rest of the crowd. After reading this chapter, you should:

- Be able to use Base's utilities for fading nodes in and out
- Be able to use Base's animateProperty function to animate arbitrary CSS properties
- Understand the effect of easing functions, duration, and rate on an _Animation
- Be aware of Core's facilities that supplement the animation support provided by Base
- Be able to use Core's animation support for additional effects, including wipes and slides

- Be able to chain together animations to run sequentially with `dojo.fx.chain` as well as run multiple animations in parallel with `dojo.fx.combine`
- Be able to use `dojo.fx.Toggler` to hide and show a node via its simple, uniform interface
- Understand how to combine animations with drag-and-drop to create highly interactive page content
- Be able to create and effectively use `Color` objects to eliminate manual computation of color values in your code

 There are amazing graphics and animation tools backed by SVG, VML, and Silverlight backends, provided through the `dojox.gfx` module.

We're going to cover data abstraction in the next chapter.

CHAPTER 9

Data Abstraction

A common bane of web development is writing routines to parse data that is returned from the server into a conveniently accessible format for the core application logic. While many good routines have been developed to parse common response types such as comma-separated values (CSV) and JSON, a lot of boilerplate is still involved in wiring it all up, issuing updates back to the server, potentially maintaining synchronicity between the local store and the server, and so forth. This chapter introduces Dojo's data APIs, which provide a uniform interface for handling data sources—regardless of where they're located, how they're accessed at the transport level, and what their format may be.

Shifting the Data Paradigm

The toolkit's machinery for managing data sources isn't exactly rocket science, but it does require shifting the paradigm ever so slightly, in that it requires that data can be treated as a local resource that is accessed via a uniform API. Traditional approaches have typically entailed treating data as a remote resource, which necessarily entails acquiring boilerplate to retrieve it, writing updates to the server, maintaining synchronicity with the server, and handling variable formats. One of the central issues, historically speaking, is that the wheel was reinvented far too many times and virtually every application used its own brittle approach to managing the burden of handling data.

Dojo gives a set of APIs via the dojo.data module that provide a standardized means for interacting with arbitrary data sources, shown in Figure 9-1. This allows application programmers to escape entanglement with retrieving, parsing, and managing it. The dojo.data API provides a standardized manner for interacting with data whether it's local or remote, which is a tremendous boon when it comes time to deal with larger and larger data sets as an application scales. Best of all, once you've implemented an interface for a specific data format, it becomes an off-the-shelf resource that you can reuse and distribute at will. Generally speaking, these kinds of off-the-shelf resources allow application developers to be more productive by allowing them to focus on far more interesting tasks at hand than I/O management.

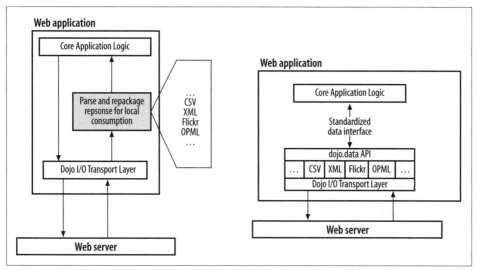

Figure 9-1. Left: a traditional pattern for accessing arbitrary data sources from an application; right: the toolkit's dojo.data abstraction for accessing arbitrary data sources

Data API Overview

The most basic atom of the dojo.data API is called an *item*, which is composed of key/value pairs called *attributes* and *attribute values* in dojo.data parlance; conceptually, you can think of an item as a plain old JavaScript Object. However, although the underlying implementation may very well be a JavaScript Object, be careful to use the provided APIs for accessing it, as the internal representation may be something entirely different. For example, some data abstractions may use a DOM model for storing certain types of data for efficiency reasons, or lazy-load data on the fly even though it seems like it's already local. In cases like these, accessing an item like a plain old JavaScript object would likely cause an unexpected error. We'll come back to specific API calls for accessing an item in the next section.

 Saying that an item has an attribute—but no value for the attribute—is the same as saying that the item doesn't have the attribute at all. In other words, it's nonsensical to think about having an attribute with no value because attributes inherently have a specific state.

Before getting into the capabilities of any one specific API, it's helpful to survey the landscape. Here's an overview of the various dojo.data APIs with a brief summary of what these APIs provide to the application developer. These APIs are interfaces, not implementations; any concrete dojo.data *data store* would define one or more of the upcoming APIs:

dojo.data.api.Read
> Provides a uniform means of reading, searching, sorting, and filtering data items.

dojo.data.api.Write
> Provides a uniform means of creating, deleting, and updating data items.

dojo.data.api.Identity
> Provides a uniform means of accessing an item via a unique identifier.

dojo.data.api.Notification
> Provides a uniform means of notifying a listener of a change, such as create, delete, or update operation, for a data item.

The remainder of this chapter systematically works through each of these APIs and provides plenty of examples so that you can make the most of dojo.data in your own application.

The APIs

This section provides a summary of the data APIs. If you're just getting started, you may want to skim this section to get a feel for the capabilities the APIs and then come back after you've read the rest of the chapter, which has more concrete examples, to explore it further.

The Read API

All data stores will implement the dojo.data.api.Read API because this API provides the means of retrieving, processing, and accessing the data—clearly a prerequisite for any other operation. The complete API specification follows in Table 9-1. The next section discusses a toolkit-provided implementation: ItemFileReadStore.

 The API listings that follow use descriptors like dojo.data.api.Item to convey the notion of a dojo.data item even though an *item* is somewhat of an abstract concept.

Table 9-1. The dojo.data.api.Read API

Name	Comment
getValue(/*dojo.data.api.Item*/item, /*String*/attribute, /*Any?*/default)	Given an item and an attribute name, returns the value for the item. A value of undefined is returned if the attribute does not exist (whereas null is returned only if null is explicitly set as the value for the attribute). An optional parameter of default can be used to return a default value if one does not exist.
getValues(/*dojo.data.api.Item*/item, /*String*/attribute)	Works just like getValue except that it allows for multi-valued attributes. Always returns an array regardless of the number of items returned. You should *always* use getValues for multivalued attributes.
getAttributes(/*dojo.data.api.Item*/item)	Introspects the item to return an Array of String values corresponding to the item's attributes. Returns an empty Array in the event that an item has no attributes.
hasAttribute(/*dojo.data.api.Item*/item, /*String*/attribute)	Returns true if the item has the attribute.
containsValue(/*dojo.data.api.Item*/item, /*String*/attribute, /*Any*/value)	Returns true if the item has the attribute and the attribute has the value, i.e., getValues would return true.
isItem(/*Any*/item)	Returns true if the parameter is an item and came from the specified store. Returns false if item is a literal or if the item came from any other store. (This call is also especially handy for situations when local variable references to items can become stable, which is quite ordinary for stores that implement the Write API.)
isItemLoaded(/*Any*/item)	Returns true if the item is loaded and available locally.
loadItem(/*Object*/args)	Loads an item to the effect that a subsequent call to isItemLoaded would return true. The args object provides the following keys: item An Object providing criteria for the item that is to be loaded (possibly an identifier or subset of identifying data). onItem(/*dojo.data.api.Item*/item) A callback to run when the item is loaded; the loaded item is passed as a parameter. onError(/*Object*/error) A callback to run when an error occurs loading the item; the error Object is passed as a parameter. scope An Object providing the context for callback functions.

Table 9-1. The dojo.data.api.Read API (continued)

Name	Comment
fetch(/*Object*/args)	Executes a given query and provides an assortment of asynchronous callbacks for handling events related to the query execution. Returns a dojo.data.api.Request Object, whose primary purpose is supplying an abort( ) method that may be used for aborting the fetch. The arguments may include the following nine options, which should be honored by all implementations:
	query A String or Object providing the query criteria (similar to SELECT in SQL). Note that the query syntax for each store is implementation-dependent.
	queryOptions An Object containing additional options for the query. All stores should attempt to honor the ignoreCase (Boolean, default false) parameter, which performs a case-insensitive search and the deep (Boolean, default false) parameter can trigger a query of all items and child items instead of only items at the root level in the store.
	onBegin (/*Integer*/size, /*dojo.data.api.Request*/request) Called before the first onItem callback. size indicates the total number of items and request is the original request for the query. If size is unknown, it will be –1. size may not be the total number of items returned since it may have been pared down with start and count.
	onComplete (/*Array*/items, /*dojo.data.api.Request*/request) Called just after the last onItem callback. If no onItem callback is present, items will be an Array of all items that matched the query; otherwise, it will be null. Request, the original request Object.
	onError(/*Object*/error, /*dojo.data.api.Request*/request) Called if there is an error when executing the query. error contains the error information and request contains the original request Object.
	onItem(/*dojo.data.api.Item*/item, /*dojo.data.api.Request*/request) Called for each item that is returned with each item available as item; request contains the original request Object.

Table 9-1. The dojo.data.api.Read API (continued)

Name	Comment
fetch(/*Object*/args) (continued)	scope (Object) If provided, executes all of the callback function in this context; otherwise, executes them in the global context. start (Integer) Provides a starting offset for the returned results (similar to OFFSET in an SQL query). count (Integer) Provides a limit for the items to be returned (similar to LIMIT in a SQL query). sort (Array) An Array of JavaScript Objects providing sort criteria for each attribute. Each Object is applied sequentially and must present an attribute key identifying the attribute name and a descending key identifying the sort order.
getFeatures()	Returns an Object containing key/value pairs that specifies what dojo.data APIs it implements. For example, any API implementing dojo.data.api.Read would necessarily return {'dojo.data.api.Read' : true} for a data store that is read-only.
close(/*dojo.data.api.Request*/request)	Used to close out any information associated with a particular request, which may involve clearing caches, closing connections, etc. The request parameter is expected to be the Object returned from a fetch. For some stores, this may be a no-op.
getLabel(/*dojo.data.api.Item*/item)	Used to return a human-readable label for an item that is generally some kind of identifying description. The label may very well be some combination of attributes.
getLabelAttributes(/*dojo.data.api.Item*/ item)	Used to provide an Array of attributes that will generate an item's label. Useful for assisting UI developers in knowing what attributes are useful for display purposes so that redundant information can be hidden when a display includes an item label.

The Identity API

The Identity API, shown in Table 9-2, builds on the Read API to provide a few additional calls for fetching items based upon their identity. Note that the Read API has no stipulations whatsoever that items be unique, and there are certainly use cases where the notion of an identity may not be pertinent; hence the separation between the two of them. With respect to databases, you might think of the Identity API, loosely, as providing a kind of primary key for each item that records can be identified with. It is often the case that data-enabled widgets require the Identity API, particularly when providing Write functionality. (The Write API is coming up next.)

Table 9-2. The dojo.data.api.Identity API

Name	Comment

getFeatures()	See `dojo.data.api.Read`. Returns:
	
	`{`
	`  'dojo.data.api.Read' : true,`
	`  'dojo.data.api.Identity : true`
	`}`

getIdentity(/*dojo.data.api.Item*/item)	Returns a unique identifier for the item, which will be a `String` or an `Object` that has a `toString` method.
getIdentityAttributes (/*dojo.data.api.Item*/item)	Returns an `Array` of attribute names that are used to generate the identity. Most of the time, this is a single attribute that expressly provides a unique identifier, but it could be more than one depending on the specifics of the actual data source. This function is often used to optionally hide attributes comprising the identity for display purposes.

fetchItemByIdentity(/*Object*/args)	Uses the identity of an item to retrieve it; conforming implementations should return `null` if no such item exists. The keyword `args` may include the following:
	
	`identity`
	    A `String` or `Object` with a `toString` function that is uses to provide the reference for the desired item.
	
	`onError(/*Object*/error)`
	    Called if there is an error when executing the query. `error` contains the error information.
	
	`onItem(/*dojo.data.api.Item*/item)`
	    Called for each item that is returned with each item available as item.
	
	`scope (Object)`
	    If provided, executes all of the callback function in this context; otherwise, executes them in the global context.

The Write API

The Write API, shown in Table 9-3, extends the Read API to include facilities for creating, updating, and deleting items, which necessarily entails managing additional issues such as whether items are *dirty*—out of sync between the in-memory copy and the server—and handling I/O such as save operations.

Table 9-3. The dojo.data.api.Write API

Name	Comment

getFeatures	See `dojo.data.api.Read`. Returns:
	
	`{`
	`  'dojo.data.api.Read' : true,`
	`  'dojo.data.api.Write : true`
	`}`

Table 9-3. The dojo.data.api.Write API (continued)

Name	Comment
newItem(/*Object?*/args, /*Object?*/parentItem)	Returns a newly created item, setting the attributes based on the `args` `Object` provided, where generally the key/value pairs in `args` map directory attributes and attribute values. For stores that support hierarchical item creation, `parentItem` provides information identifying the parent of the new item and the attribute of the parent that the new item should be assigned (which generally implies that the attribute is multivalued and the new item is appended). Returns the newly created item.
deleteItem(/*dojo.data.api.Item*/item)	Deletes and item from the store. Returns a `Boolean` value indicating success.
setValue(/*dojo.data.api.Item*/item, /*String*/attribute, /*Any*/value)	Sets an attribute on an item, replacing any previous values. Returns a `Boolean` value indicating success.
setValues(/*dojo.data.api.Item*/item, /*String*/attribute, /*Array*/values)	Sets values for an attribute, replacing any previous values. Returns a `Boolean` value indicating success.
unsetAttribute(/*dojo.data.api.Item*/item, /*String*/attribute)	Effectively removes an attribute by deleting all values for it. Returns a `Boolean` value indicating success.

save(/*Object*/args)	Saves all local changes in memory, and output is passed to a callback function provided in `args`, which is in the following form:
	
	`onError(/*Object*/error)`
	　　Called if there is an error; `error` contains the error information.
	`onComplete( )`
	　　Called to indicate success, usually with no parameters.
	`scope (Object)`
	　　If provided, executes all of the callback functions in this context; otherwise executes them in the global context.
	　　A `_saveCustom` extension point is available, and if overridden, provides an opportunity to pass the data set back to the server.

revert( )	Discards any local changes. Returns a `Boolean` value indicating success.
isDirty(/*dojo.data.api.Item?*/)	Returns a `Boolean` value indicating if a specific item has been modified since the last `save` operation. If no parameter is provided, returns a `Boolean` value indicating if any item has been modified.

The Notification API

The Notification API, shown in Table 9-4, is built upon the Read and complements the Write API by providing a unified interface for responding to the typical create, update, and delete events. The Notification API is particularly useful for ensuring visuals properly reflect the state of a store, which may be changing or refreshed via Read and Write operations. (The `dijit.Tree` and `dojox.grid.Grid` widgets are great cases in point.)

Table 9-4. The dojo.data.api.Notification API

Name	Comment

getFeatures	See `dojo.data.api.Read`. Returns:
	
	`{`
	`  'dojo.data.api.Read' : true,`
	`  'dojo.data.api.Notification: true`
	`}`

onSet(/*dojo.data.api.Item*/item, /*String*/attribute, /*Object|Array*/old, /*Object|Array*/new)	Called any time an item is modified via `setValue`, `setValues`, or `unsetAttribute`, providing means of monitoring actions on items in the store. The parameters are self-descriptive and provide the item being modified, the attribute being modified, and the old and new value or values, respectively.
onNew(/*dojo.data.api.Item*/item, /*Object?*/parentItem)	Called when a new item is created in the store where `item` is what was just created; `parentItem` is not passed if the created item is placed in the root level. `parentItem`, however, is provided if the item is not a root-level item. (Note that an `onSet` notification is not generated stating that the `parentItem`'s attributes have been modified because it is implied and `parentItem` gives access to that information.)
onDelete(/*dojo.data.api.Item*/item)	Called when an item is deleted from the store where `item` is what was just deleted.

Core Implementations of Data APIs

The previous section provided a summary of the four primary data APIs available at this time. This section works through the two implementations provided by Core—the `ItemFileReadStore` and `ItemFileWriteStore`. As you'll see, the `ItemFileReadStore` implements the Read and Identity APIs, and the `ItemFileWriteStore` implements all four APIs discussed. A good understanding of these two stores equips you with enough familiarity to augment these existing stores to suit your own needs—or to implement your own.

 Although not explicitly discussed in this book, the `dojox.data` sub-project contains a powerful assortment of `dojo.data` implementations for common tasks such as interfacing to CSV stores, Flickr, XML, OPML, Picasa, and other handy stores. Since they all follow the same APIs as you're learning about here, picking them up should be a snap.

ItemFileReadStore

Although it is quite likely that your particular situation may benefit from a custom implementation of dojo.data.api.Read to maximize efficiency and impedance mismatching, the toolkit does include the ItemFileReadStore, which implements the Read and Identity interfaces and consumes a flexible JSON representation. For situations in which you need to quickly get something up and running, you need to do little more than have your application's business logic output data in the format that the ItemFileReadStore expects, and *voilà*, you may use the store as needed.

 One thing to know up front is that the ItemFileReadStore consumes the entire data set that backs it into memory the first time a request is made; thus, operations like isItemLoaded and loadItem are fairly useless.

Hierarchical JSON and JSON with references

Although the ItemFileReadStore does implement the Read API, it packs a number of implementation-specific features of its own, including a specific data format, query syntax, a means of deserializing specific attribute values, specific identifiers for the identity of an item, and so on. Before getting into those specifics, however, have a look at some example data that is compliant for the ItemFileReadStore to consume; there are two basic flavors that relate to how nested data is represented: hierarchical JSON and JSON with references. The hierarchical JSON flavor consists of nested references that are concrete item instances, while the JSON with references flavor consists of data that points to actual data items.

To illustrate the difference between the two, first take a look at a short example of the two variations. First, for the hierarchical JSON:

```
{
    identifier : id,
    items : [
        {
            id : 1, name : "foo", children : [
                {id : 2, name : "bar"},
                {id : 3, name : "baz"}
            ]
        }
        /* more items... */
    ]
}
```

And now, for the JSON with references:

```
{
    identifier : id,
    items : [
```

```
{
    id : 1, name : "foo", children : [
        {_reference: 2},
        {_reference: 3}
    ]
},
{id : 2, name : "bar"},
{id : 3, name : "baz"}
/* more items... */
    ]
k}
```

To recap, the foo item has two child items in both instances, but the hierarchical JSON explicitly nests the items, while the JSON with references uses pointers keying off of the identifier for the item. The primary advantage to JSON with references is its flexibility; it allows items to appear as the child of more than one parent, as well as the possibility for all items to appear as root-level items. Both possibilities are quite common and convenient for many real-world applications.

 The Tree Dijit, introduced in Chapter 15, is a great example that highlights the flexibility and power (as well as some of the shortcomings) of the JSON with references data format.

ItemFileReadStore walkthrough

To get up close and personal with the ItemFileReadStore, consider the data collection represented as hierarchical JSON, shown in Example 9-1, where each item is identified by the name identifier. Note that the identifier, label, and items keys are the only expected values for the outermost level of the store.

Example 9-1. Sample coffee data set
```
{
    identifier : "name",
    label : "name",
    items : [
        {name : "Light Cinnamon", description : "Very light brown, dry , tastes like
toasted grain with distinct sour tones, baked, bready"},
        {name : "Cinnamon", description : "Light brown and dry, still toasted grain with
distinct sour acidy tones"},
        {name : "New England", description : "Moderate light brown , still sour but not
bready, the norm for cheap Eastern U.S. coffee"},
        {name : "American or Light", description : "Medium light brown, the traditional
norm for the Eastern U.S ."},
        {name : "City, or Medium", description : "Medium brown, the norm for most of the
Western US, good to taste varietal character of a bean."},
        {name : "Full City", description : "Medium dark brown may have some slight oily
drops, good for varietal character with a little bittersweet."},
        {name : "Light French", description : "Moderate dark brown with oily drops, light
surface oil, more bittersweet, caramelly flavor, acidity muted."},
```

Example 9-1. Sample coffee data set (continued)

```
        {name : "French", description : "Dark brown oily, shiny with oil, also popular for
espresso; burned undertones, acidity diminished"},
        {name : "Dark French", description : "Very dark brown very shiny, burned tones
become more distinct, acidity almost gone."},
        {name : "Spanish", description : "Very dark brown, nearly black and very shiny,
charcoal tones dominate, flat."}
    ]
}
```

Assuming the file was stored on disk as *coffee.json*, the page shown in Example 9-2 would load the store and make it available via the `coffeeStore` global JavaScript variable.

Example 9-2. Programmatically loading an ItemFileReadStore

```
<html>
    <head>
        <title>Fun with ItemFileReadStore!</title>
        <script
            type="text/javascript"
            src="http://o.aolcdn.com/dojo/1.1/dojo/dojo.xd.js">
        </script>
        <script type="text/javascript">
            dojo.require("dojo.data.ItemFileReadStore");

            dojo.addOnLoad(function( ) {
                coffeeStore = new dojo.data.ItemFileReadStore({url:"coffee.json"});
            });
        </script>
    </head>
    <body>
    </body>
</html>
```

Although the parser isn't formally introduced until Chapter 11, using the parser is so common that it's worthwhile to explicitly mention that the markup variation in Example 9-3 would have achieved the very same effect.

Example 9-3. Loading an ItemFileReadStore in markup

```
<html>
    <head>
        <title>Fun with ItemFileReadStore!</title>
        <script
            type="text/javascript"
            src="http://o.aolcdn.com/dojo/1.1/dojo/dojo.xd.js"
            djConfig="parseOnLoad:true">
        </script>
        <script type="text/javascript">
            dojo.require("dojo.parser");
            dojo.require("dojo.data.ItemFileReadStore");
        </script>
```

Example 9-3. Loading an ItemFileReadStore in markup (continued)

```
    </head>
    <body>
        <div dojoType="dojo.data.ItemFileReadStore" url="./coffee.json"
          jsId="coffeeStore"></div>
    </body>
</html>
```

Regardless of how you declare the store, the API works the same either way. A great exercise is to spend a few minutes in the Firebug console with the existing store. The remainder of this section contains a series of commands and code snippets with the corresponding response values for most of the Read and Identity APIs that you can follow along with and use to accelerate your learning about the ItemFileReadStore.

In addition to using the url parameter to point an ItemFileReadStore at a data set represented as a file, you could also have passed it a variable referencing a JavaScript object that's already in memory via the data parameter.

Fetching an item by identity. Fetching an item from the ItemFileReadStore is generally done in one of two ways, though each way is quite similar. To fetch an item by its identifier, you should use the Identity API's fetchItemByIdentity function, which accepts a collection of named arguments including the identifier, what to do when the item is fetched, and what to do if an error occurs. For example, to query the sample coffeeStore for the Spanish coffee, you could do something like Example 9-4.

Example 9-4. Fetching an item by its identity and then inspecting it

```
var spanishCoffeeItem;
coffeeStore.fetchItemByIdentity({
    identity: "Spanish",
    onItem : function(item, request) {
        //capture the item...or do something with it
        spanishCoffeeItem = item;
    },
    onError : function(item, request) {
        /* Handle the error... */
    }
});

// now do something with the spanishCoffeeItem variable...

//like get its description...
coffeeStore.getValue(spanishCoffeeItem, "description"); //Very dark brown...

//or get its name...
coffeeStore.getValue(spanishCoffeeItem, "name"); // Spanish

//in this case, the name and label are the same...
coffeeStore.getLabel(spanishCoffeeItem); // Spanish
```

Example 9-4. Fetching an item by its identity and then inspecting it (continued)

```
//if you had an item and didn't know what its identity was...
coffeeStore.getIdentity(spanishCoffeeItem); //Spanish
```

A common mistake when you're just starting out is to accidentally confuse the identity of an item with the item itself, which can be a tricky semantic bug to find because the code "looks right." Finding the Spanish coffee item via var item = coffeeStore.fetchItemByIdentity("Spanish") reads as though it makes sense, but when you take a closer look at the API, you realize that it's wrong in at least two ways: the call doesn't return an item back to you, and you have to provide a collection of named arguments to it—not an identity value.

Fetching an item by arbitrary criteria. If you want to fetch an item by an attribute other than the identity, you could use the more generic fetch function instead of fetchItemByIdentity, like so:

```
coffeeStore.fetch({
    query: {name : "Spanish"},
    onItem : function(item, request){console.log(item);}
});
```

However, in addition to accepting fully qualified values for attributes, the fetch function also accepts a small but robust collection of filter criteria that allows for basic regex-style matching. For example, to find any coffee description with the word "dark" in it without regard to case-sensitivity, you follow the process illustrated in Example 9-5.

Example 9-5. Fetching an item by arbitrary criteria

```
coffeeStore.fetch({
    query: {description : "*dark*"},
    queryOptions:{ignoreCase : true},
    onItem : function(item, request) {
        console.log(coffeeStore.getValue(item, "name"));
    }
    /* include other fetch callbacks here... */
});
```

Always use the store to access item attributes via getValue. Don't try to access them directly because the underlying implementation of the store may not allow it. For example, you would not want to access an item in the onItem callback as onItem: function(item, request) { console.log(item.name); }. A tremendous benefit from this abstraction is that it gives way to underlying caching mechanisms and other optimizations that improve the efficiency of the store.

If you're designing your own custom implementation of a store, you may find it helpful to know that dojo.data.util.filter is a short mix-in that can give you the same functionality as the regex-style matching that ItemFileReadStore uses for fetch, and dojo.data.util.simpleFetch provides the logic for its eight arguments: onBegin, onItem, onComplete, onError, start, count, sort, and scope.

Querying child items

The existing coffee store is quite primitive in that it is a flat list of items. Example 9-6 spices it up a bit by adding in a few additional items that contain children to produce a nested structure. The ItemFileReadStore expressly uses the children attribute to maintain a list of child items, and we'll use the JSON with references approach to accommodate the task of grouping coffees into different roasts. Note that the Light French roast has been deliberately placed into the Medium Roasts and the Dark Roasts to illustrate the utility of using references. Because each item needs to maintain a unique identity, it wouldn't be possible to include it as a child of two different parents any other way.

 Although the remainder of this chapter uses a store that consists of only two levels, there is no reason why you couldn't use a data set with any arbitrary number of levels in it.

Example 9-6. Updated sample coffee data set to reflect hierarchy

```
{
    identifier : "name",
    items : [
        {
            name : "Light Roasts",
            description : "A number of delicious light roasts",
            children : [
                {_reference: "Light Cinnamon"},
                {_reference: "Cinnamon"},
                {_reference: "New England"}
            ]
        },

        {
            name : "Medium Roasts",
            description : "A number of delicious medium roasts",
            children : [
                {_reference: "American or Light"},
                {_reference: "City, or Medium"},
                {_reference: "Full City"},
                {_reference: "Light French"}
            ]
        },

        {
```

Example 9-6. Updated sample coffee data set to reflect hierarchy (continued)

```
            name : "Dark Roasts",
            description : "A number of delicious dark roasts",
            children : [
                {_reference: "Light French"},
                {_reference: "French"},
                {_reference: "Dark French"},
                {_reference: "Spanish"}
            ]
        },

        {name : "Light Cinnamon", description : "Very light brown, dry , tastes like
toasted grain with distinct sour tones, baked, bready"},
        ...
    ]
}
```

A common task you might find yourself needing to accomplish is querying the children of an item. In this case, that amounts to finding the individual names associated with any given roast. Let's try it out in Example 9-7 for the Dark Roasts item to illustrate.

Example 9-7. Fetching an item and iterating over its children

```
coffeeStore.fetch({
    query: {name : "Dark Roasts"},
    onItem : function(item, request) {
        dojo.forEach(coffeeStore.getValues(item, "children"), function(childItem) {
            console.log(coffeeStore.getValue(childItem, "name"));
        });
    }
});
```

To recap, we issue a straightforward query for the parent item Dark Roasts, and then once we have the item, we use the getValues function to retrieve the multivalued children attribute and iterate over each with dojo.forEach—all the while remembering to use the getValue function to ultimately access the child item's value.

Note that the whole notion of {_reference: someIdentifier} is simply an implementation detail. There is never a time when you'll want to attempt to query based on the _reference attribute because there really isn't any such thing as a _reference attribute—again, it's just a standardized way of managing the bookkeeping. As far as the dojo.data application programmer is concerned, everything in a dojo.data store should be considered a good old item.

As you hopefully have observed by now, ItemFileReadStore is quite flexible and powerful, which makes it a suitable data format for a variety of situations—especially when you have to prototype an application and get something up and running quickly. As a simple specification, it's not difficult to have a server-side routine spit out data that a web client using dojo.data can digest. At the same time, however, remember that you can always subclass and extend as you see fit—or implement your own.

ItemFileWriteStore

There's no doubt that good abstraction eliminates a lot of cruft when it comes time to serve up data from the server and display it; however, it is quite often the case that you won't have the luxury of not writing data back to the server if it changes—and that's where the ItemFileWriteStore comes in. Just as the ItemFileReadStore provided a nice abstraction for reading a data store, ItemFileWriteStore provides the same kind of abstraction for managing write operations such as creating new items, deleting items, and modifying items. In terms of the dojo.data APIs, the ItemFileWriteStore implements them all—Read, Identity, Write, and Notification.

To get familiar with the ItemFileWriteStore, we'll work through the specifics in much the same way that we did for the ItemFileReadStore using the same *coffee.json* JSON data. As you'll see, there aren't any real surprises; the API pretty much speaks for itself.

Modifying an existing item. You'll frequently use the setValue function, shown in Example 9-8, to change the value of item's attribute by passing in the item, the attribute you'd like to modify, and the new value for the attribute. If the item doesn't have the named attribute, it will automatically be added.

Example 9-8. Setting an item's attribute

```
//Fetch an item like usual...
var spanishCoffeeItem;
coffeeStore.fetchItemByIdentity({
    identity: "Spanish",
    onItem : function(item, request) {
        spanishCoffeeItem = item;
    }
});

//And then add a new attribute foo=bar
coffeeStore.setValue(spanishCoffeeItem, "foo", "bar");

coffeeStore.getValue(spanishCoffeeItem, "foo"); //bar

//Likewise, you could have changed any other attribute except for the identity
coffeeStore.setValue(spanishCoffeeItem, "description", "El Matador...?!?");
```

 Just like in most other data schemes, it doesn't usually make sense to change an item's identity, as the notion of identity is an immutable characteristic; following suit, the ItemFileWriteStore does not support this operation, nor is it recommended in any custom implementation of your own.

One peculiarity to note is that setting an attribute to be an empty string is not the same thing as removing the attribute altogether; this is especially important to internalize if you find yourself needing to use the Write API's hasAttribute function to check for the existence of an attribute. Example 9-9 illustrates the differences.

Example 9-9. Setting and unsetting attributes on items

```
coffeeStore.hasAttribute(spanishCoffeeItem, "foo"); //true

coffeeStore.setValue(spanishCoffeeItem, "foo", ""); //foo=""

coffeeStore.hasAttribute(spanishCoffeeItem, "foo"); //true

coffeeStore.unsetAttribute(spanishCoffeeItem, "foo"); //remove it

coffeeStore.hasAttribute(spanishCoffeeItem, "foo"); //false
```

While the previous examples in this section have demonstrated how to successfully modify an existing item, the changes so far have been incomplete in that an explicit save operation has not occurred. Internally, the ItemFileReadStore keeps track of changes and maintains a collection of *dirty* items—items that have been modified, but not yet saved. For example, after having modified the spanishCoffeeItem, you could use the isDirty function to learn that it has been modified but not saved, as shown in Example 9-10. After the item is saved, however, it is no longer dirty. For now, saving means nothing more than updating the in memory copy; we'll talk about saving back to the server in just a bit.

Example 9-10. Inspecting an item for dirty status

```
/* Having first modified the spanishCoffeeItem... */
coffeeStore.isDirty(spanishCoffeeItem); //true
coffeeStore.save(); //update in-memory copy of the store
coffeeStore.isDirty(spanishCoffeeItem); //false
```

Although it might not be immediately obvious, an advantage of requiring an explicit save operation to commit the changes lends the ability to revert the changes in case a later operation that is part of the same macro-level transaction produces an error or any other deal-breaking circumstance occurs. In relational databases, this is often referred to as a *rollback*. Example 9-11 illustrates reverting a dojo.data store and highlights a very subtle yet quite important point related to local variables that contain item references.

Example 9-11. Reverting changes to an ItemFileWriteStore

```
var spanishCoffeeItem;
coffeeStore.fetchItemByIdentity({
    identity: "Spanish",
    onItem : function(item, request) {
        spanishCoffeeItem = item;
    }
});
```

Example 9-11. Reverting changes to an ItemFileWriteStore (continued)

```
coffeeStore.getValue(spanishCoffeeItem, "description"); //Very dark...

coffeeStore.setValue(spanishCoffeeItem, "description", "El Matador...?!?");

/* Right now, both the spanishCoffeeItemVariable and the store reflect the udpated
description */

coffeeStore.fetchItemByIdentity({
    identity: "Spanish",
    onItem : function(item, request) {
        spanishCoffeeItem = item;
    }
});

coffeeStore.getValue(spanishCoffeeItem, "description"); //El Matador...?!?

coffeeStore.isDirty(spanishCoffeeItem); //true

coffeeStore.revert( ); //revert the store.

// Upon revert( ), the local spanishCoffeeItem variable
// ceased to be an item in the store
coffeeStore.isItem(spanishCoffeeItem); //false

//Fetch out the item again...
coffeeStore.fetchItemByIdentity({
    identity: "Spanish",
    onItem : function(item, request) {
        spanishCoffeeItem = item;
    }
});

coffeeStore.isDirty(spanishCoffeeItem); //false

coffeeStore.getValue(spanishCoffeeItem, "description"); //Very dark...
```

 Although it's theoretically possible to implement a custom store that prevents local item references from becoming stale via slick engineering behind the scenes with dojo.connect or pub/sub communication, the ItemFileWriteStore does not go to such lengths, and you should use the isItem function liberally if you are concerned about whether an item reference has become stale.

Creating and deleting items. Once you have a good grasp on the previous section that worked through the various nuances of modifying existing items, you'll have no problem picking up how to add and delete items from a store. All of the same principles apply with respect to saving and reverting—there's really not much to it. First, as shown in Example 9-12, let's add and delete a top-level item from our existing store. Adding an item involves providing a JSON object just like the server would have included in the original data set.

Example 9-12. Adding and deleting an item from an ItemFileWriteStore

```
var newItem = coffeeStore.newItem({
    name : "Really Dark",
    description : "Left brewing in the pot all day...extra octane to get you through till
5 o'clock."
});

coffeeStore.isItem(newItem); //true
coffeeStore.isDirty(newItem); //true

/* Query the item, save the store, revert the store, etc. */

//Or delete the item...
coffeeStore.deleteItem(newItem);
coffeeStore.isItem(newItem); //false
```

While adding and removing top-level items from a store is trivial, there is just a little bit more effort involved in adding a top-level item that also needs to a be a child item that is referenced elsewhere. Example 9-13 illustrates how it's done. The basic recipe is that you create it as a top-level item, get the children that you want it to join, and then add it to that same collection of children.

Example 9-13. Adding a child item to a JSON with references store

```
//Create a new item
var newItem = coffeeStore.newItem({
    name : "Really Dark",
    description : "Left brewing in the pot all day...extra octane to get you thorugh till
5 o'clock."
});

//Get a reference to the parent with the children
var darkRoasts;
coffeeStore.fetchItemByIdentity({
    identity : "Dark Roasts",
    onItem : function(item, request) {
        darkRoasts = item;
    }
});

//Use getValues to grab the children
var darkRoastChildren = coffeeStore.getValues(darkRoasts, "children");

//And add it to the children using setValues
coffeeStore.setValues(darkRoasts, "children", darkRoastChildren.concat(newItem);

//You could now iterate over those children to see for yourself...
dojo.forEach(darkRoastChildren, function(x) {
    console.log(coffeeStore.getValue(x, "name"));
});
```

Remember to use getValues, not getValue, when fetching multivalued attributes.

Deleting items works in much the way you would expect. Deleting a top-level item removes it from the store but leaves its children, if any, in place, as shown in Example 9-14.

Example 9-14. Deleting a top-level item from an ItemFileWriteStore

```
var darkRoasts;
coffeeStore.fetchItemByIdentity({
    identity : "Dark Roasts",
    onItem : function(item, request) {
        darkRoasts = item;
    }
});

coffeeStore.deleteItem(darkRoasts);

coffeeStore.fetch({
    query : {name : "*"},
    onItem : function(item, request) {
        console.log(coffeeStore.getValue(item, "name"));
    }
});

/* Save the store, or revert the store, or... */
```

Clearly, you could eliminate a top-level item and all of its children by first querying for the children, deleting them, and then deleting the top-level item itself.

Custom saves. You've probably been thinking for a while that saving in memory is great and all—but what about getting data back on the server? As it turns out, the ItemFileWrite store provides a _saveCustom extension point that you can implement to trigger a custom routine that fires anytime you call save; thus, in addition to updating the local copy in memory and clearing any *dirty* flags, you can also sync up to the server—or otherwise do anything else that you'd like. You have the very same API available to you that you've been using all along, but in general, a "full save" would probably consist of iterating over the entire data set, serializing into a custom format—quite likely with the help of dojo.toJson—and shooting it off. Just as the Write API states, you provide keyword arguments consisting of optional callbacks, onComplete and onError, which are fired when success or an error occurs. An optional scope argument can be provided that supplies the execution context for either of those callbacks. Those keyword arguments, however, are passed into the save function—not to your _saveCustom extension.

Example 9-15 shows how to implement a _saveCustom handler to pass data back to the server when save() is called. As you'll see, it's pretty predictable.

Example 9-15. Wiring up a custom save handler for an ItemFileWriteStore

```html
<html>
    <head>
        <title>Fun with ItemFileWriteStore!</title>
        <script
            type="text/javascript"
            src="http://o.aolcdn.com/dojo/1.1/dojo/dojo.xd.js">
        </script>
        <script type="text/javascript">
            dojo.require("dojo.data.ItemFileReadStore");

            dojo.addOnLoad(function( ) {
                coffeeStore = new dojo.data.ItemFileReadStore({url:"coffee.json"}    );
                coffeeStore._saveCustom = function( ) {
                    /* Use whatever logic you need to save data back to the server.
                       This extension point gets called anytime you call an ordinary
                       save( ). */
                }
            });
        </script>
    </head>
    <body>
    </body>
</html>
```

As it turns out, _saveCustom is used less frequently than you might think because it involves passing all of your data back to the server, which is not usually necessary unless you start from a blank slate and need to do that initial batch update. For many use cases—especially ones involving very large data sets—you'll want to use the interface provided by the Notification API that is introduced in the next section to take care of changes when they happen in small bite-size chunks.

Responding to notifications. To round out this section—and the rest of the chapter—we'll briefly review the Notification API that ItemFileWriteStore implements because it is incredibly useful for situations in which you need to respond to specific notifications relating to the creation of a new item, the deletion of an item, or the modification of an item via onNew, onDelete, or onSet, respectively.

As you're probably an expert reading and mapping the APIs back to specific store implementations by now, an example that adds, modifies, and deletes an item from a store is probably self-explanatory. But just in case, Example 9-16 is an adaptation of Example 9-13.

Example 9-16. Using the Notification API to hook events to ItemFileWriteStore

```
/* Begin notification handlers */
coffeeStore.onNew = function(item, parentItem) {
    var itemName = coffeeStore.getValue(item, "name");
    console.log("Just added", itemName, "which had parent", parentItem);
}

coffeeStore.onSet = function(item, attr, oldValue, newValue) {
    var itemName = coffeeStore.getValue(item, "name");
    console.log("Just modified the ", attr, "attribute for", itemName);

    /* Since children is a multi-valued attribute, oldValue and newValue are Arrays that
    you can iterate over and inspect though often times, you'll only send newValue to the
    server to log the update */
}

coffeeStore.onDelete = function(item) {
    // coffeeStore.isItem(item) returns false, so don't try to access the item
    console.log("Just deleted", item);
}
/* End notification handlers */

/* Code that uses the notification handlers */

//Add a top level item - triggers a notification
var newItem = coffeeStore.newItem({
    name : "Really Dark",
    description : "Left brewing in the pot all day...extra octane to get you thorugh till
5 o'clock."
});

var darkRoasts;
coffeeStore.fetchItemByIdentity({
    identity : "Dark Roasts",
    onItem : function(item, request) {
        darkRoasts = item;
    }
});

var darkRoastChildren = coffeeStore.getValues(darkRoasts, "children");

//Modify it - triggers a notification
coffeeStore.setValues(darkRoasts, "children",darkRoastChildren.concat(newItem));

//And now delete it - triggers two notifications
coffeeStore.deleteItem(newItem)
```

The output you see when you run the example should be something like the following:

```
Just added Really Dark, which had parent null
Just modified the children attribute for Dark Roasts
Just modified the children attribute for Dark Roasts
Just deleted Object _0=13 name=[1] _RI=true description=[1]
```

In other words, you get the expected notification when you create the top-level item, a notification for modifying another item's children attribute when you assign the new item as a child, another notification when you remove the child item, and a final notification when you delete the item.

 One subtlety to note about Example 9-16 is that the item reference you receive in the onDelete notification has already been removed from the store, so its utility is likely to be somewhat limited since you cannot legally use it in routine store operations.

Serializing and Deserializing Custom Data Types

Although not mentioned until now, you should be aware of one additional feature provided by ItemFileReadStore and ItemFileWriteStore: the ability to pack and unpack custom data types. The motivation for using a *type map* is that it may often be the case that you need to deal with attributes that aren't primitives, object literals, or arrays. In these circumstances, you're left with manually building up the attributes yourself—introducing cruft in your core logic—or streamlining the situation by tucking away the serialization logic elsewhere.

Implicit type-mapping

Implicit type-mapping for an ItemFileReadStore happens automatically if two special attributes, _type and _value, exist in the data; _type identifies a specific constructor function that should be invoked, which gets passed the _value. JavaScript Date objects are an incredibly common data type that can benefit from being type-mapped; a sample item from our existing data set that has been modified to make use of a date value might look like Example 9-17.

Example 9-17. Using a custom type map to deserialize a value

```
...
{
    name : "Light Cinnamon",
    description : "Very light brown, dry , tastes like toasted grain with distinct sour
tones, baked, bready"
    lastBrewed : {
        '_type' : "Date",
        '_value':"2008-06-15T00:00:00Z"}
    }
}
...
```

It almost looks too easy, but assuming that the Date constructor function is defined, that's it! Once the data is deserialized, any values for lastBrewed are honest to goodness Date objects—not just String representations:

```
var coffeeItem;
coffeeStore.fetchItemByIdentity({
    identity : "Light Cinnamon",
    onItem : function(item, request) {
        coffeeItem = item;
    }
});
coffeeStore.getValue(coffeeItem, "lastBrewed"); //A real Date object
```

Custom type maps

Alternatively, you can define a JavaScript object and provide a named `deserialize`
function and a type parameter that could be used to construct the value. For
`ItemFileWriteStore`, a serialize function is also available. Following along with the
example of managing `Date` objects, a JavaScript object presenting a valid type map
that could be passed in upon construction of the `ItemFileWriteStore` follows in
Example 9-18.

Example 9-18. Passing in a custom type map to an ItemFileReadStore

```
dojo.require('dojo.date');
dojo.addOnLoad(function( ) {
    var map = {
        "Date": {
            type: Date,
            deserialize: function(value){
                return dojo.date.stamp.fromISOString(value);
            },
            serialize: function(object){
                return dojo.date.stamp.toISOString(object);
            }
        }
    };

    coffeeStore = new dojo.data.ItemFileReadStore({
        url:"coffee.json",
        typeMap : map
    });
});
```

 Although we intentionally did not delve into `dojox.data` subprojects in
this chapter, it would have been cheating not to at least provide a good
reference for using the `dojox.data.QueryReadStore`, which is the
canonical means of interfacing to very large server-side data sources.
See *http://www.oreillynet.com/onlamp/blog/2008/04/dojo_goodness_part_
6_a_million.html* for a concise example of using this store along with a
custom server routine. This particular example illustrates how to *effi-
ciently* serve up one million records in the famed DojoX Grid widget.

Summary

After reading this section, you should:

- Be familiar with the dojo.data APIs and understand the basic value provided by each of them
- Understand that the Read, Identity, Write, and Notification APIs are abstract, and that any implementation is possible
- Be aware that the dojox.data subproject provides several really useful custom stores that can save you time accomplishing common tasks such as interfacing to a store of comma-separated values, Flickr, and so on
- Be aware that the toolkit provides ItemFileReadStore and ItemFileWriteStore as generic yet powerful dojo.data implementations that you may customize or otherwise use as a basis for a custom implementation
- Understand the value in using custom type maps to save time manually serializing and deserializing data types

Next, we'll move on to simulated classes and inheritance.

## CHAPTER 10

Simulated Classes and Inheritance

Even though JavaScript loosely approximates classes with Function objects and offers a prototype-based inheritance mechanism that's a little different from what you may be used to if your background is a language like Java or C++, Dojo does a fine job of building upon native JavaScript constructs to simulate classes and class-based inheritance. This chapter dives into `dojo.declare`, the toolkit's vehicle for wiring up classes and inheritance and, in doing so, paves the way for a solid understanding of the Dijit infrastructure, which is coming up in Part II.

JavaScript Is Not Java

Before we get into the core discussion of simulating inheritance hierarchies and classes with Dojo, you must first grok that JavaScript is not Java, nor does Dojo try to fight against JavaScript's style and reimplement portions of the JavaScript language under the hood and force a square peg in a round hole—and this is a very good thing! JavaScript is an incredibly dynamic, weakly typed language, while Java is a more strongly typed language with real classes and class-based inheritance hierarchies that are defined at compile time. JavaScript has prototypal inheritance that can be used to simulate classes and is purely interpreted.

By embracing JavaScript for what it is and leveraging its language features in the most complementary way possible, Dojo benefits from enhancements to the language as it evolves, avoids the maintenance that comes hand-in-hand with massive layers of boilerplate. In the end, this provides you with a streamlined, agile implementation that can keep up with the "release early, release often" philosophy of the modern technological era.

With the notable exception of the form dijits that are introduced in Chapter 13, you won't see a lot of object-oriented design in Dojo because it's not the Dojo way. The Dojo way is to embrace prototypal inheritance and Base constructs like `mixin` and `extend` that take advantage of JavaScript's strengths. At the same time, Dojo does try to be pragmatic, and some topics do lend themselves to object-oriented design and are quite awkward to model without it. Actually, the very reason that this chapter is presented as the last of Part I is because Part II introduces Dijit, which *is* a topic that lends itself quite well to a class-based design.

As you read this chapter, keep this preamble in the back of your mind, because if you come from a strong background in a class-based object-oriented programming language like Java or C++, the temptation will be to superimpose that paradigm onto Dojo and to try to turn everything into an inheritance relationship, which isn't a very natural thing to do for reasons of style or performance. While this chapter does demonstrate the ability to use Dojo for the purpose of simulating deep hierarchies of objects, the assumption is that you'll use discretion when doing so.

Don't Fight the Style!

JavaScript is a dynamically typed interpreted language with many misunderstood features that can take a little getting used to, especially if you're coming from a statically typed, compiled language like C++ or Java. If you find yourself having an awfully hard time solving a problem or fighting too hard to fix a bug, take a moment to back up, make sure you understand the subtleties of what you're trying to accomplish, and ask yourself how you can better leverage built-in features of the language.

If you bend the style enough by translating an algorithm from a language like Java line by line into JavaScript, you may eventually get what you want—but it'll cost you time, code maintainability, efficiency, and a lot of sanity. So, don't fight the style; seek first to understand it, and then use it to your advantage.

One Problem, Many Solutions

In case you're locked into the inheritance paradigm, this section demonstrates multiple approaches to achieving similar results for a simple problem: modeling a circle object. In addition to being a good exercise in demonstrating some out-of-the-box thinking, this section also applies some of the language tools you learned about in Chapter 2.

Typical JavaScript Inheritance

JavaScript programmers have been simulating classes with Function objects for quite a while—sometimes at the expense of abusing the language, other times effectively to solve a particular problem. The inherent nature of a JavaScript Function object is the very mechanism that provides the footing for simulating classes. Namely, it acts as a *constructor function* that is used in conjunction with the new operator to create object instances, and it provides the template for those object instances that are created.

To illustrate, Example 10-1 provides a short code snippet that approximates a simple Shape class in JavaScript. Note that by convention, classes usually begin with a capital letter.

 For just an added touch of simplicity, the examples in this chapter do not use namespaces for qualifying objects. In general, however, you will want to use namespaces, and we'll pick back up using namespaces in Chapter 12.

Example 10-1. A typical JavaScript class

```
// Define a class
function Shape(centerX, centerY, color)
{
  this.centerX = centerX;
  this.centerY = centerY;
  this.color = color;
};

// Create an instance
s = new Shape(10, 20, "blue");
```

Once the JavaScript interpreter executes the function definition, a Shape object exists in memory and acts as the prototypal object for creating object instances whenever its constructor function is invoked with the new operator.

For completeness, note that you could have defined the Shape object using Base's extend function in a slightly more compact fashion:

```
// Create a Function object
function Shape( ) {}

// Extend its prototype with some reasonable defaults
dojo.extend(Shape, {
    centerX : 0,
    centerY : 0,
    color : ""
});
```

Unfortunately, you could only have fun with this class for about three seconds because you'd start to get really bored and want to model something a little more concrete—like a specific kind of shape. While you *could* approximate a new class such as a circle entirely from scratch, a more maintainable approach would be to have a circle class inherit from the shape class that's already defined because all circles are shapes. Besides, you already have a perfectly good Shape class lying around, so why not use it?

Example 10-2 demonstrates one approach to accomplishing this inheritance relationship in JavaScript.

Example 10-2. Typical JavaScript inheritance

```
// Define a subclass
function Circle(centerX, centerY, color, radius)
{
  // Ensure the subclass properties are added to the superclass by first
  //assigning the subclass a reference to the constructor function and then
  //invoking the constructor function inside of the superclass.
  this.base = Shape;
  this.base(centerX, centerY, color);

  // Assign the remaining custom property to the subclass
  this.radius = radius;
};

// Explicitly chain the subclass's prototype to a superclass so that any new properties
//that are dynamically added to the superclass are reflected in subclasses
Circle.prototype = new Shape;

// Create an instance
c = new Circle(10, 20, "blue", 2);

//The circle IS-A shape
```

While you may have found that to be an interesting exercise, it probably wasn't as short and sweet as you might have first thought, and it probably wasn't terribly central to that really cool web application you've been trying to finish up.

Mixin Pattern

For the sake of demonstrating an alternate paradigm to the typical inheritance groupthink, consider Example 10-3's approach of using mixins to model shapes and circles in a different way. It's especially noteworthy to make the connection that mixins heavily leverage duck typing and *has-a* relationships. Recall that the concept of ducktyping is based upon the idea that if something quacks like a duck and acts like a duck, then it may as well be a duck. In our circumstance, the concept translates to the idea that if an object has the properties you'd expect of a shape or circle, that's good enough to call it as much. In other words, it doesn't matter what the object really *is* as long as it has the right properties.

Example 10-3. Mixing in as an alternative to inheritance

```
//Create a plain old Object to model a shape
var shape = {}

//Mix in whatever you need to make it "look like a shape and quack like a shape"
dojo.mixin(shape, {
    centerX : 10,
    centerY : 20,
    color : "blue"
});
```

Example 10-3. Mixing in as an alternative to inheritance (continued)

```
//later on you need something else. No problem, mix it right in
dojo.mixin(shape, {
    radius : 2
});

//Now the shape HAS-A radius
```

For the record, this mixin example is not intended to be an exact drop-in replacement for the previous example that used prototypal inheritance; rather, this mixin example is intended to demonstrate that there are various ways of approaching a problem.

Delegation Pattern

As yet another approach to modeling a relationship between a shape and a circle, consider the pattern of delegation, shown in Example 10-4. Whereas the mixin pattern actually copies properties into a single object instance, the delegation pattern passes on responsibility for some set of properties to another object that already has them.

Example 10-4. Delegation as an alternative to inheritance

```
//Create a plain old Object
var shape = {}

//Mix in what you need for this instance
dojo.mixin(shape, {
    centerX : 10,
    centerY : 20,
    color : "blue"
});

//delegate circle's responsibility for centerX, centerY, and color to shape
//mix in the radius directly
circle = dojo.delegate(shape, {
    radius : 2
});
```

The key takeaways from this revision are that the radius property defined in the object literal is mixed into the circle, but the remaining shape properties are not. Instead, the circle delegates to the shape whenever it is asked for a property that it does not have itself. To sum it all up:

- Requests for radius are provided directly by circle because radius got mixed in.
- Requests for centerX, centerY, and color are delegated to the shape because they don't exist on the circle itself (loosely speaking).
- A request for any other property returns undefined by definition because it doesn't exist in either the circle or the shape.

Although the working example is so simple that the mixin pattern makes more sense to use, the delegation pattern certainly has plenty of uses, especially in situations in which you have large number of objects that all share a particular subset of things that are in common.

Simulating Classes with Dojo

Now that you've had a moment to ponder some of the various inheritance possibilities, it's time to introduce the toolkit's fundamental construct for declaring classes and simulating rich inheritance hierarchies. Dojo keeps it simple by tucking away all of the implementation details involved with class declarations and inheritance behind an elegant little function in Base called dojo.declare. This function is easy to remember because you're loosely *declaring* a class with it. Table 10-1 shows the brief API.

Table 10-1. dojo.declare API

Name	Comment
dojo.declare (/*String*/ className, /*Function|Function[]*/ superclass, /*Object*/ props)	Provides a compact way of declaring a constructor function. The className provides the name of the constructor function that is created, superclass is either a single Function object ancestor or an Array of Function object ancestors that are mixed in, and props provides an object whose properties are copied into the constructor function's prototype.

 As you might suspect, declare builds upon the patterns provided by functions like extend, mixin, and delegate to provide an even richer abstraction than any one of those patterns could offer individually.

Example 10-5 illustrates how you could use dojo.declare to accomplish an inheritance hierarchy between a shape and circle. For now, consider this example as just an isolated bit of motivation. We'll discuss the finer points momentarily.

Example 10-5. Simulating class-based inheritance with dojo.declare

```
// "Declare" a Shape
dojo.declare(
  "Shape", //The class name
  null, //No ancestors, so null placeholds
  {
    centerX : 0, // Attributes
    centerY : 0,
    color : "",

    // The constructor function that gets called via "new Shape"
    constructor(centerX, centerY, color)
    {
```

Example 10-5. Simulating class-based inheritance with dojo.declare (continued)

```
      this.centerX = centerX;
      this.centerY = centerY;
      this.color = color;
    }
  }
);

// At this point, you could create an object instance through:
// var s = new Shape(10, 20, "blue");

// "Declare" a Circle
dojo.declare(
  "Circle", //The class name
  Shape, // The ancestor
  {
    radius : 0,

    // The constructor function that gets called via "new Circle"
    constructor(centerX, centerY, color, radius)
    {
      // Shape's constructor is called automatically
      // with these same params. Note that it simply ignores
      // the radius param since it only used the first 3 named args
      this.radius = radius; //assign the Circle-specific argument
    }
  }
);

// Params to the JavaScript constructor function get passed through
// to dojo.declare's constructor
c = new Circle(10,20,"blue",2);
```

Hopefully you find dojo.declare to be readable, maintainable, and self-explanatory. Depending on how you lay out the whitespace and linebreaks, it even resembles "familiar" class-based programming languages. The only thing that may have caught you off guard is that Shape's constructor is called with the same parameters that are passed into Circle's constructor. Still, this poses no problem because Shape's constructor accepts only three named parameters, silently ignoring any additional ones. (We'll come back to this in a moment.)

Talking about JavaScript constructor functions that are used with the new operator to create JavaScript objects as well as the special constructor function that appears in dojo.declare's third parameter can be confusing. To keep these two concepts straight, the parameter that appears in dojo.declare's third parameter constructor will always be typeset with the code font as constructor, while JavaScript constructor functions will appear in the normal font.

The Basic Class Creation Pattern

The dojo.declare function provides a basic pattern for handling classes that is important to understand because Dijit expands upon it to deliver a flexible creation pattern that effectively automates the various tasks entailed in creating a widget. Chapter 12 focuses on this topic almost exclusively.

Although this chapter focuses on the constructor function because it is by far the most commonly used method, the following pattern shows that there are two other functions that dojo.declare provides: preamble, which is kicked off before constructor, and postscript, which is kicked off after it:

```
preamble(/*Object*/ params, /*DOMNode*/node)
    //precursor to constructor

constructor(/*Object*/ params, /*DOMNode*/node)
    // fire any superclass constructors
    // fire off any mixin constrctors
    // fire off the local class constructor, if provided

postscript(/*Object*/ params, /*DOMNode*/node)
    // predominant use is to kick off the creation of a widget
```

To verify for yourself, you might run the code in Example 10-6.

Example 10-6. Basic dojo.declare creation pattern

```
dojo.addOnLoad(function( ) {
    dojo.declare("Foo", null, {

        preamble: function( ) {
            console.log("preamble", arguments);
        },

        constructor : function( ) {
            console.log("constructor", arguments);
        },

        postscript : function( ) {
            console.log("postscript", arguments);
        }

});

    var foo = new Foo(100); //calls through to preamble, constructor, and postscript
});
```

The constructor is where most of the action happens for most class-based models, but preamble and postscript have their uses as well. preamble is primarily used to manipulate arguments for superclasses. While the arguments that you pass into the JavaScript constructor function—new Foo(100) in this case—get passed into Foo's preamble, constructor, and postscript, this need not necessarily be the case when you have an inheritance hierarchy. We'll revisit this topic again in the "Advanced Argument Mangling" sidebar later in this chapter, after inheritance gets formally introduced in the next section. postscript is primarily used to kick off the creation of a widget. Chapter 12 is devoted almost entirely to the widget lifecycle.

A Single Inheritance Example

Let's dig a bit deeper with more in-depth examples that show some of dojo.declare's power. This first example is heavily commented and kicks things off with a slightly more advanced inheritance example highlighting an important nuance of using dojo.declare's internal constructor method:

```
<html>
    <head>
        <title>Fun with Inheritance!</title>

        <script
            type="text/javascript"
            src="http://o.aolcdn.com/dojo/1.1/dojo/dojo.xd.js">
        </script>

        <script type="text/javascript">
          dojo.addOnLoad(function( )
```

```
//Plain old JavaScript Function object defined here.
function Point(x,y)  {}
dojo.extend(Point, {
    x : 0,
    y : 0,
    toString : function() {return "x=",this.x," y=",this.y;}
});

dojo.declare(
    "Shape",
    null,
    {
        //Clearly define members first thing, but initialize them all in
        //the Dojo constructor. Never initialize a Function object here
        //in this associative array unless you want it to be shared by
        //*all* instances of the class, which is generally not the case.

        //A common convention is to use a leading underscore to denote
        "private" members

        _color: "",
        _owners: null,

        //Dojo provides a specific constructor for classes. This is it.
        //Note that this constructor will be executed with the very same
        //arguments that are passed into Circle's constructor
        //function -- even though we make no direct call to this
        //superclass constructor.

        constructor: function(color)
        {
            this._color = color;
            this._owners = [0]; //See comment below about initializing
            //objects

            console.log("Created a shape with color",
               this._color, "owned by", this._owners);
                        this._owners);
        },

        getColor : function() {return this._color;},
        addOwner : function(oid) {this._owners.push(oid);},
        getOwners : function() {return this._owners;}

        //Don't leave trailing commas after the last element. Not all
        //browsers are forgiving (or provide meaningful error messages).
        //Tattoo this comment on the back of your hand.
    }

);

//Important Convention:
//For single inheritance chains, list the superclass's args first in the
//subclass's constructor, followed by any subclass specific arguments.
```

```
//The subclass's constructor gets called with the full argument chain, so
//it gets set up properly there, and assuming you purposefully do not
//manipulate the superclass's arguments in the subclass's constructor,
//everything works fine.

//Remember that the first argument to dojo.declare is a string and the
//second is a Function object.
dojo.declare(
    "Circle",
    Shape,
    {
        _radius: 0,
        _area: 0,
        _point: null,

        constructor : function(color,x,y,radius)
        {
            this._radius = radius;
            this._point = new Point(x,y);
            this._area = Math.PI*radius*radius;

            //Note that the inherited member _color is already defined
            //and ready to use here!
            console.log("Circle's inherited color is " + this._color);
        },

        getArea: function() {return this._area;},
        getCenter : function() {return this._point;}
    }
);

console.log(Circle.prototype);

console.log("Circle 1, coming up...");
c1 = new Circle("red", 1,1,100);
console.log(c1.getCenter());
console.log(c1.getArea());
console.log(c1.getOwners());
c1.addOwner(23);
console.log(c1.getOwners());

console.log("Circle 2, coming up...");
c2 = new Circle("yellow", 10,10,20);
console.log(c2.getCenter());
console.log(c2.getArea());
console.log(c2.getOwners());
});
</script>
    </head>
    <body>
    </body>
</html>
```

Trailing commas will most likely hose you outside of Firefox, so take extra-special care not to accidentally leave them hanging around. Some programming languages like Python allow trailing commas; if you frequently program in one of those languages, take added caution.

You should notice the output shown in Figure 10-1 in the Firebug console when you run this example.

```
     Inspect   Clear   Profile
  Console   HTML   CSS   Script   DOM   Net
Object declaredClass=dojoshortcut.Circle _radius=0 _area=0
Circle 1, coming up...
Created a shape with color red owned by 0
Circle's inherited color is red
x=1, y=1 x=1 y=1
31415.926535897932
[0]
[0, 23]
Circle 2, coming up...
Created a shape with color yellow owned by 0
Circle's inherited color is yellow
x=10, y=10 x=10 y=10
1256.6370614359173
[0]
```

Figure 10-1. Firebug output from Example 10-6

An important takeaway is that a Function object exists in memory as soon as the dojo.declare statement has finished executing, an honest-to-goodness Function object exists behind the scenes, and its prototype contains everything that was specified in the third parameter of the dojo.declare function. This object serves as the prototypical object for all objects created in the future. This subtlety can be tricky business if you're not fully cognizant of it, and that's the topic of the next section.

A common gotcha with prototype-based inheritance

As you know, a Point has absolutely nothing to do with Dojo. It's a plain old Java-Script Function object. As such, however, you must not initialize it inline with other properties inside of Shape's associative array. If you do initialize it inline, it will behave somewhat like a static member that is shared amongst all future Shape objects that are created—and *this can lead to truly bizarre behavior if you're not looking out for it.*

The issue arises because behind the scenes declare mixes all of the properties into the Object's prototype and prototype properties are shared amongst all instances. For immutable types like numbers or strings, changing the property results in a local change. For mutable types like Object and Array, however, changing the property in one location promulgates it. The issue can be reduced as illustrated in the snippet of code in Example 10-7.

Example 10-7. Prototype properties are shared amongst all instances

```
function Foo( ) {}
Foo.prototype.bar = [100];

//create two Foo instances
foo1 = new Foo;
foo2 = new Foo;

console.log(foo1.bar); // [100]
console.log(foo2.bar); // [100]

// This statement modifies the prototype, which is shared by all object instances...
foo1.bar.push(200);

//...so both instances reflect the change.
console.log(foo1.bar); // [100,200]
console.log(foo2.bar); // [100,200]
```

To guard against ever even *thinking* about making the mistake of inadvertently initializing a nonprimitive data type inline, perform all of your initialization—even initialization for primitive types—inside of the standard Dojo constructor, and maintain a consistent style. To keep your class as readable as possible, it's still a great idea to list all of the class properties inline and provide additional comments where it enhances understanding.

To illustrate the potentially disastrous effect on the working example, make the following changes indicated in bold to your Shape class and take a look at the console output in Firebug:

```
//...snip...

dojo.declare("Shape", null,

{
    _color: null,
    //_owners: null,
    _owners: [0],   //this change makes the _owners member
                    //behave much like a static!

    constructor : function(color) {
    this._color = color;
                    //this._owners = [0];
```

```
                    console.log("Created a shape with color ",this._colora
                        " owned by ", this._owners);
                },

                getColor : function() {return this._color;},
                addOwner : function(oid) {this._owners.push(oid);},
                getOwners : function() {return this._owners;}
            }

    );

//...snip...
```

After you make this change and refresh the page in Firefox, you'll see the output shown in Figure 10-2 in the Firebug Console.

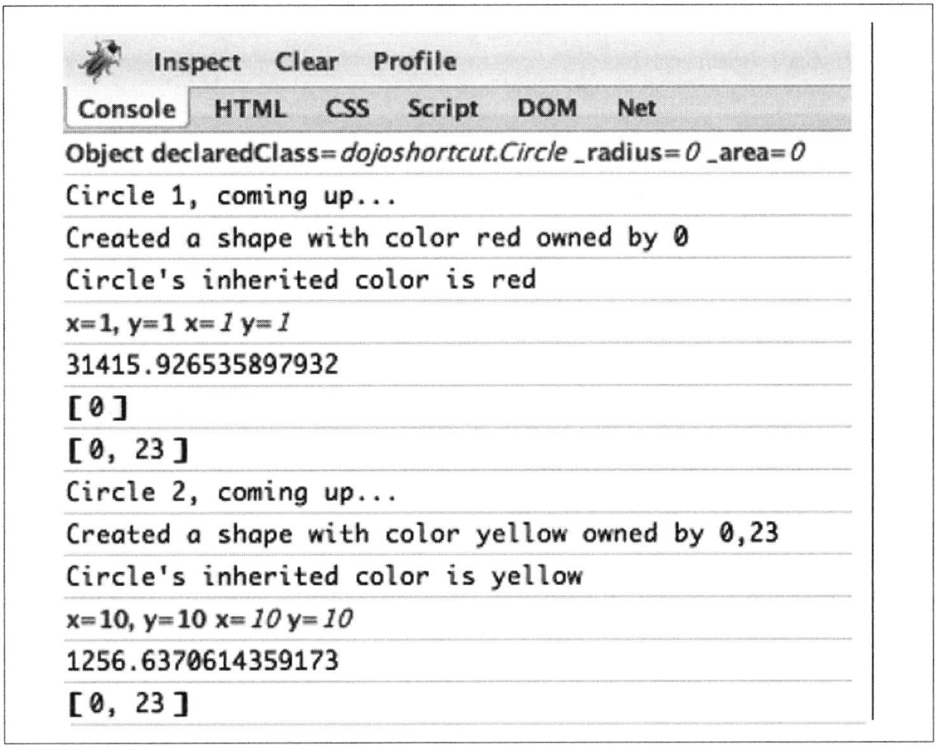

Figure 10-2. Firebug output

Calling an inherited method

In class-based object-oriented programming, a common pattern is to override a superclass method in a subclass and then call the inherited superclass method before performing any custom implementation in the subclass. Though not always the case, it's common that the superclass's baseline implementation still needs to run and that the subclass is offering existing implementation on top of that baseline. Any class created via dojo.declare has access to a special inherited method that, when called, invokes the corresponding superclass method to override. (Note that the constructor chain is called automatically without needing to use inherited.)

Example 10-8 illustrates this pattern.

Example 10-8. Calling overridden superclass methods from a subclass

```
dojo.addOnLoad(function( ) {
    dojo.declare("Foo", null, {

        constructor : function( ) {
            console.log("Foo constructor", arguments);
        },

        custom : function( ) {
            console.log("Foo custom", arguments);
        }

    });

    dojo.declare("Bar", Foo, {

        constructor : function( ) {
            console.log("Bar constructor", arguments);
        },

        custom : function( ) {
            //automatically call Foo's 'custom' method and pass in the same arguments,
            //though you could juggle them if need be
            this.inherited(arguments);
            //without this call, Foo.custom would never get called
            console.log("Bar custom", arguments);
        }

    });

    var bar = new Bar(100);
    bar.custom(4,8,15,16,23,42);
});
```

And here's the corresponding Firebug output on the console:

```
Foo constructor [100]
Bar constructor [100]
Foo custom [4, 8, 15, 16, 23, 42]
Bar custom [4, 8, 15, 16, 23, 42]
```

Multiply Inheriting with Mixins

The previous section introduced how Dojo simulates class-based inheritance and pointed out some critical issues involving JavaScript's finer points that are central to developing with Dojo. Although the primary example demonstrated single inheritance in which a Shape superclass provided the basis for a Circle subclass, Dojo also provides a limited form of multiple inheritance.

The process of defining inheritance relationships by weaving together Function objects in this way is referred to as *prototype chaining* because it's through JavaScript's Object. prototype property that the hierarchy is defined. (Recall that Example 10-2 illustrated this concept within the boilerplate of manually defining an inheritance relationship between a shape and a circle.)

Dojo simulates class-based inheritance by building upon the concept of prototype chaining to establish the hierarchy for single inheritance contexts. However, employing multiple-inheritance relationships is a little bit different because JavaScript limits Function objects to having only one built-in prototype property.

As you might imagine, there are a number of approaches that could be used to circumvent this issue. The approach that Dojo uses is to leverage prototype chaining so that you define a single prototypical ancestor that is the basis for prototype chaining—but at the same time, allowing you to provide other mixins that get injected into the prototypal ancestor. In other words, a class can have only one prototype, but the Function objects that the class creates can get "stamped" with as many constructor functions as you want to throw at it. Granted, the prototypes of those constructor functions won't be taken into account later in the life of the object, but they can be leveraged in very powerful ways nonetheless. Think of these mixins as "interfaces that actually do stuff" or "interface + implementation."

 In multiple-inheritance relationships, the ancestors are provided to dojo.declare inside of a list. The first element of the list is known as the prototypical ancestor, while the latter is commonly a mixin ancestor, or more concisely, a "mixin."

Here's what multiple inheritance looks like with Dojo. The only thing that's different is that the third parameter to dojo.declare is a list instead of a Function object. The first element in that list is the prototypical ancestor, while the other is a mixin:

```
<html>
    <head>
        <title>Fun with Multiple Inheritance!</title>

        <script
            type="text/javascript"
            src="http://o.aolcdn.com/dojo/1.1/dojo/dojo.xd.js">
        </script>
```

```
<script type="text/javascript">
    dojo.addOnLoad(function( ) {
        //A perfectly good Dojo class with a reasonable constructor and no
        //direct ancestors.
        dojo.declare("Tiger", null, {
            _name: null,
            _species: null,

            constructor : function(name)
            {
                this._name = name;
                this._species = "tiger";
                console.log("Created ",this._name +,"the ",this._species);
            }
        });

        //Another perfectly good Dojo class with a reasonable constructor
        //and no direct ancestors.
        dojo.declare("Lion", null, {
            _name: null,
            _species: null,

            constructor: function(name)  {
                this._name = name;
                this._species = "lion";
                console.log("Created ",this._name +," the ",this._species);
            }
        });

        //A Dojo class with more than one ancestor. The first ancestor is the
        //prototypical ancestor, while the second (and any subsequent
        //functions) are mixins. Take special note that each of the
        //superclass constructors execute before this subclass's constructor
        //executes -- and there's really no way to get around that.
        dojo.declare("Liger", [Tiger, Lion], {
            _name: null,
            _species: null,

            constructor : function(name) {
                this._name = name;
                this._species = "liger";
                console.log("Created ",this._name , " the ", this._species);
            }
        });

        lucy = new Liger("Lucy");
        console.log(lucy);
    });
</script>
</head>
<body>
</body>
</html>
```

If you open the previous example and look at the console output in Firebug shown in Figure 10-3, you'll see that both a Tiger and Lion are created before a Liger is created. Just like the previous example with shapes, you do get your subclass, but not until after the necessary superclasses have been created, complete with constructor methods running and all.

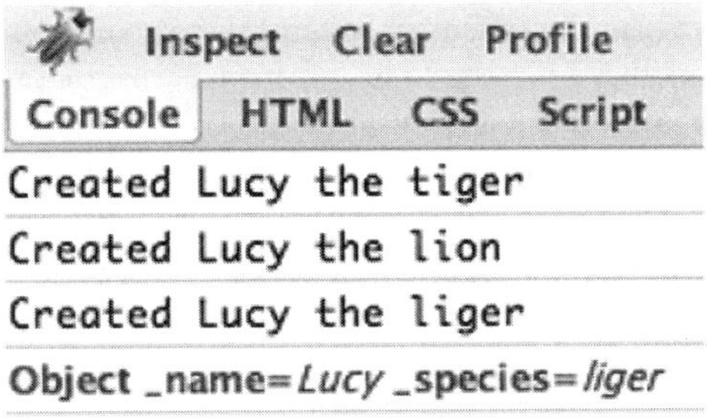

Figure 10-3. Although you do eventually get your Liger, it's not until after the necessary superclasses have been created and properly initialized

Multiple Inheritance Oddities

In the earlier example involving shapes, there was no particular need to be concerned with the argument list from a Circle getting passed up to a Shape because a Circle built directly upon a Shape. Furthermore, it made good sense and was even convenient to include Shape's constructor argument as the first argument of Circle's constructor. In this past example with lions, tigers, and ligers, the constructors are all single argument functions that do the same thing, so there's no real issue there, either.

But wait—what if Tiger and Lion each had custom constructors? For example, Tiger's constructor might specify arguments corresponding to the name and number of stripes, while Lion's constructor might specify the name and mane length. How would you define a Liger's constructor to handle a situation like that? The very same arguments that are passed into Liger's constructor will be passed into Tiger's constructor as well as Lion's constructor, and that just doesn't make any sense.

In this particular instance—when two or more superclasses each require their own custom parameters—your best bet, if you have the option, is to pass in an associative array of named parameters and use these in your constructor instead of relying on the arguments list directly. Passing in custom parameters to superclasses in a multiple-inheritance relationship is not well-supported as of Dojo 1.1, although discussion for this kind of impedance matching is under consideration for a future release.

Advanced Argument Mangling

Dojo 1.0 introduced a new feature, originating in dojo.declare, that approaches the more sophisticated kind of impedance matching that may be used for situations in which you may need to mangle the arguments that are passed into a superclass's constructor.

In short, preamble gets run as a precursor to constructor, and you can use it to change around the arguments that get passed into *superclass* constructors; as of version 1.1, whatever arguments are returned from preamble will be passed into all superclass constructor functions. While this doesn't alleviate the problem illustrated in our earlier Liger example, it may be quite useful for many other situations.

Here's a quick code snippet to illustrate how preamble works:

```
dojo.declare("Foo", null, {
  preamble: function(){
    console.log("Foo preamble: ", arguments);
  },

  constructor: function(){
    console.log("Foo constructor: ", arguments);
  }
});

dojo.declare("Bar", null, {
  preamble: function(){
    console.log("Bar preamble: ", arguments);
  },

  constructor: function(){
    console.log("Bar constructor: ", arguments);
    }
});

dojo.declare("Baz", [Foo, Bar], {
  preamble: function(){
    console.log("Baz preamble: ", arguments);
    return ["overridden", "baz", "arguments"];
  },

constructor: function(){
    console.log("Baz constructor: ", arguments);
  }
});

var obj = new Baz("baz", "arguments", "go", "here");
```

—continued—

The output that you'll see in your Firebug console follows and represents the chrono-logical order of the preamble and constructor calls involved in instantiating Baz. Note how the arguments that are passed into the constructor for the Foo and Bar super-classes are what get returned from preamble. The Baz constructor, however, receives the same arguments that were passed into its own preamble:

```
Baz preamble:    ["baz", "arguments", "go", "here"]
Foo preamble:    ["overridden", "baz", "arguments"]
Foo constructor: ["overridden", "baz", "arguments"]
Bar preamble:    ["overridden", "baz", "arguments"]
Bar constructor: ["overridden", "baz", "arguments"]
Baz constructor: ["baz", "arguments", "go", "here"]
```

In general, a convenient pattern is to design multiple-inheritance relationships such that superclasses don't have constructors that require any arguments. The advantage of this approach is that purposefully defining superclasses without arguments allows the subclass to receive and process as many custom arguments as it needs, while ensuring that any superclasses up the inheritance chain won't be affected by them. After all, because they don't use them in any way, they can't be affected.

Summary

After learning the content in this chapter, you should:

- Understand how to use dojo.declare to simulate classes in Dojo
- Be able to implement single- and multiple-inheritance relationships in Dojo
- Be aware of the dangers involved in initializing JavaScript Objects outside of a Dojo class's constructor
- Know that Function objects are the mechanism used to approximate classes in JavaScript; remember, there aren't "real" classes in JavaScript
- Understand some of the distinctions between prototype-based inheritance and class-based inheritance
- Have a general understanding of how Dojo leverages JavaScript's prototype-based inheritance behind the scenes to simulate class-based inheritance

Part II is next, in which we'll cover Dijit and Util.

Dijit and Util

The first part of this book covered Base and Core, a JavaScript library that can facilitate virtually any web development effort. Part II shifts gears to cover the visual elements of the toolkit, *Dijit*—delivering the much-acclaimed widgets—and *Util*, which provides build tools and a standalone unit-testing framework.

Dijit is a fantastic layer of widgets that provides a complete collection of out-of-the-box form elements, layout containers, and other common controls for achieving a rich user experience on the web. Dijit builds directly on the foundation provided by Base and Core, and is a prime example of the kind of achievement that is possible from using a powerful standard library that insulates you from browser inconsistencies and reduces the boilerplate that you normally write, debug, test, and maintain along the way. In that regard, Dijit is very much the natural outworking of Base and Core.

While Part I of the book presented the fundamental building blocks of the toolkit in a way that empowered you to be a better JavaScript developer, this part of the book focuses on exposing you to all the various dijits (Dojo widgets) that you can simply pull off the shelf, snap into your page, and have it all "just work," with little or no coding required. Designers should especially enjoy this part of the book because it provides a comprehensive survey of the advantages Dijit makes available and how they can be put to work in HTML markup.

Of course, there is tremendous power in having the ability to write your own custom dijits—whether totally from scratch or as a composition of existing stock dijits—so there will be plenty of coverage on that front as well. Digging deep into the anatomy and lifecycle of widgets, mapping out the parallels between declaring widgets in markup versus programmatic creation, and discussing accessibility (a11y, which is an abbreviation for "accessibility" in that the word starts with "a," ends with "y," and has 11 letters in between) are all on the agenda.

After providing complete coverage for Dijit, Part II ends with a discussion of Util, a fantastic collection of build tools including ShrinkSafe, a JavaScript compression system based on the battle-tested Rhino JavaScript engine, and the Dojo Objective Harness (DOH), a standalone unit-testing framework that facilitates testing and quality assurance efforts surrounding your application.

## CHAPTER 11

Dijit Overview

Dijit is the fantastic layer of widgets that the toolkit provides as drop-in replacements for the standard HTML web controls. This chapter paves the way for Part II by starting out with a fairly nontechnical discussion of Dijit's motivation, philosophy, and goals as an off-the-shelf resource, which dovetails into a discussion of how designers and ordinary page creators can use dijits in markup with little to no programming. The chapter concludes with a guided tour that provides a thorough overview of everything included in Dijit.

Motivation for Dijit

Web development is very much an engineering problem, and it has quite an intriguing history, filled with clever hacking and ingenuity. Although the web browser may be the ultimate platform from a conceptual standpoint, the problem from an engineering perspective is that virtually every interesting use case for delivering a rich user experience requires workarounds and augmentation of some form or another. From a *very* conservative estimate, the lack of conformance to standards by major industry players has produced a landscape littered with more than a half-dozen viable configurations, and along the increase of powerful mobile devices with web browsing capabilities, that number is only going to continue growing.

Consequently, developing maintainable applications for the Web has become more difficult than ever; if you don't support as many configurations as possible, you lose market share, popularity, and revenue. Coupling support for various configurations with the already unwieldy yet fairly common practices of mixing HTML, CSS, and JavaScript in fairly ad-hoc ways makes the effort a seemingly impossible effort.

You already know that Base and Core insulate you from browser inconsistencies and minimize the time you spend writing workarounds; Dijit leverages all of the goods from Base and Core to provide an extensible framework for building modular, reusable user interface widgets.

Although technically incorrect, many Dojo users think of "Dijit" as synonymous with "Dojo" because its widgets are in high demand. Still, Dijit is its own subproject in the toolkit and its logical segmentation from the rest of the toolkit makes it easier to manage and improve as time goes by. In addition to providing you with a collection of off-the-shelf widgets, Dijit provides the infrastructure for you to build your own widgets—the same infrastructure that Dijit uses.

Some specific goals of Dijit include:

- Developing a standard set of common widgets for web development in an analogous manner to the way that Swing provides an interface for Java applications or Cocoa provides interface controls for an OS X application
- Leveraging existing machinery from Core and Base to keep the implementation of widgets as simple and portable as possible
- Conforming to accessibility (a11y) standards in accordance with the ARIA (Accessibility for Rich Internet Applications) specification to support the visually impaired and users who need cannot use a mouse
- Requiring that all widgets be globalized, which simplifies internationalization initiatives by ensuring that widgets are localized and supporting cultural formats and bidirectional (bidi) content
- Maintaining a coherent API so that developers can transfer knowledge across multiple widgets and reuse patterns for solving problems
- Supporting a consistent look and feel with stylesheets, yet making widgets easily customizable
- Ensuring that the creation of widgets in markup is just as easy as with JavaScript (or easier)
- Making it simple to augment an existing page with a widget or to scale multiple widgets into a full-blown application
- Providing full support for bidirectional text (realized as of version 1.1)
- Supporting the most common browsers across multiple platforms, including Internet Explorer 6+, Firefox 2+, and Safari 3+[*]

Low Coupling, High Cohesion

Perhaps the most important advantage that Dijit brings to your web development efforts is the ability *encapsulate* user interface components into standalone widgets. If you've done web development for any amount of time, you've no doubt run into the

---

[*] Dijit does not officially support exactly the same array of browsers as Base and Core. The pragmatism behind the decision is that there just isn't a wide enough user base to justify the additional coding, testing, and maintenance for additional browsers like Opera or Konqueror. However, just because "official" support does not exist doesn't mean that it's necessarily difficult to get Dijits working on these platforms—especially when you consider that Konqueror, Firefox, and WebKit (the core of Safari) are all open source projects.

problem of trying to wrap up the HTML, CSS, and JavaScript source files for a user interface into a portable package that is capable of instantiating itself and delivering the intended functionality at the right time with minimal intervention.

 In programming lingo, the problem of developing modular user interface components is well explained by the terms *cohesion* and *coupling*. Cohesion is a measure of how well the source code and resources work together to deliver a piece of functionality, while coupling is a measure of a module's dependency on other modules. When designing things like widgets, your goal is almost always to maximize cohesion and minimize coupling.

Dijit answers the call admirably, and even better, it is a layer of infrastructure that you don't have to write, debug, and maintain. Building off of Base's `dojo.declare` function for simulating classes, as shown in Figure 11-1, Dijit throws in standard lifecycle methods for creation and destruction, a standardized means of responding to events such as key strokes and mouse movements, and the ability to wrap up the visible presentation. It also makes it possible to manage it all via markup or JavaScript—delivering the very same functionality to two distinct audiences.

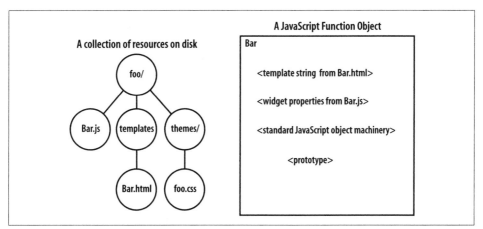

Figure 11-1. Juxtaposing a dijit as a collection of physical resources on disk versus a dijit as a JavaScript Function object

As a designer, snapping a dijit into a page via markup is as simple as including a special `dojoType` tag that the parser recognizes and instantiates into an event-driven DHTML entity. For example, the following snippet, adapted from Chapter 1, illustrates how simple it is to include a customized text box for *approximately* validating an email address as part of a form—all in markup:

```
<input type="text"
    length=25
    name="email"
```

```
dojoType="dijit.form.ValidationTextBox"
trim="true"
lowercase="true"
regExp="[a-z0-9._%+-]+@[a-z0-9-]+\.[a-z]{2,4}"
required="true"
invalidMessage="Please enter a valid e-mail address"/>
```

That's it. Not a single line of JavaScript is required to actually *use* the widget. Sure, many developers may need to develop or extend widgets, which entails writing JavaScript, but the beauty is that once it's written, it becomes a part of your off-the-shelf arsenal. When the page loads, the parser finds the dojoType tag, requests any additional resources that are needed (if any) from back on the server, and transplants a DHTML widget into the page. Laying out a user interface should be that easy!

Of course, anything you can do in markup is also possible with JavaScript. You can dynamically create the very same widget just like any ordinary JavaScript object and insert it into the page with a trivial amount of effort.

As a general pattern, dijit constructor functions have the following signature that accepts a collection of configuration properties and a node reference:

```
dijit.WidgetName(/*Object*/props, /*DOMNode|String*/node)
```

Each dijit has a DOM node reference that is its visible representation, and inserting the DOM node reference into the page is all that is necessary to present it to the user. Once visible, its event handlers are exposed, and it behaves as though they were there all along. Here's how you would programmatically construct the same dijit for validating an email address; the parallel between the two approaches is apparent:

```
<script type="text/javascript">
    var w = new dijit.form.ValidationTextBox({
        length : 25,
        name : "email",
        trim : true,
        lowercase : true,
        regExp : "[a-z0-9._%+-]+@[a-z0-9-]+\.[a-z]{2,4}",
        required : true,
        invalidMessage : "Please enter a valid e-mail address"
    }, n); // n is a node reference somewhere in the page
</script>
```

Accessibility (a11y)

Accessibility is an increasingly important topic in the information age. In addition to a common goal of delivering content to the widest audience possible (with or without disability), political power such as Section 508[*] and other established legislation that sets a minimal standard for technology being accessible to persons with disabilities, and

---

[*] Section 508 refers to a statutory section in the United States' Rehabilitation Act of 1973, requiring federal agencies to make reasonable accommodations to Americans with disabilities.

there are economic incentives as well: the U.S. Department of Labor estimates that the discretionary spending of people with disabilities is in the neighborhood of 175 billion dollars (*http://www.usdoj.gov/crt/ada/busstat.htm*). No matter how you look at it and what your motives might be, a11y is an issue that's hard to ignore.

Common a11y Issues

While this short section cannot even begin to address the myriad details associated with successfully implementing a web application, it should raise your awareness of the issues involved and highlight the ways that Dijit addresses them. Two of the most common accessibility tasks involve supporting users with impaired vision who need screen readers and users who require the ability to completely navigate an application using only the keyboard.

By default, Dijit inherently supports both audiences. Accessibility for users with impaired vision is addressed by detecting if the browser is operating in high-contrast mode and by detecting whether images are disabled for Internet Explorer or Firefox.* If either accessibility-enabling condition is detected, dijits are rendered according to augmented style, images, and templates as necessary.

For example, Figure 11-2 illustrates the rendering for a dijit.ProgressBar in both standard and high-contrast mode.

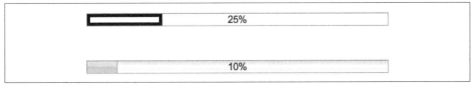

Figure 11-2. Top: the automatic rendering of dijit.ProgressBar when accessibility conditions are detected; bottom: the standard dijit.ProgressBar

Although some of the implementation details can be tedious, here's a basic rule of thumb that goes a long way to achieving accessible widgets for the blind: don't use images (CSS background images or standard images placed with the IMG tag) in such a way that the functionality of a page is impaired if they go missing. A corollary that follows is to ensure alt descriptions are provided; it may seem dirt simple, and it's not always pretty, but it can often get the job done.

The stock widgets provide full keyboard support via standardized use of the tabIndex attribute for controlling the movement of the focus across the application. Additional

---

* The detection of high-contrast mode works quite well on Internet Explorer for Windows, but not so well on the Mac or other browsers. Unfortunately, not all platforms or browsers currently support a11y facets to the same extent (or at all), so your mileage may vary.

machinery explicitly manages the focus of complex controls so that tool tips can be displayed as needed—which might always be the case if a screen reader is in use .[*]

WAI-ARIA

Accessibility initiatives for users with impaired vision and keyboard access are increasing, but in the modern era of Rich Internet Applications, additional support is needed. Common examples of additional support include ensuring users remain aware of changes in state from an XHR call that did not explicitly reload a page, and adequately handling Back button functionality for select actions.

The W3C Web Accessibility Initiative for Accessible Rich Internet Applications (WAI-ARIA) is an effort to ensure that AJAX-powered applications that mimic desktop-like functionality have a set of guidelines for delivering functionality to impaired users. Back in the early 1990s, screen readers could pretty much just read good old HTML. Nowadays, however, widgets are hacked out by lots of nested DIV elements and manipulated with AJAX, which has no meaning to a screen reader. Thus, WAI-ARIA provides the semantics needed to effectively convey information to the blind. For example, these semantics may inform the screen reader that a particular collection of nested DIV elements is a tree, a particular node in the tree currently has the focus, and pressing the Tab key switches focus to the "next" element.

Dijit exposes a collection of functions inspired by WAI-ARIA that are specifically tailored to facilitate adding accessibility to widgets. The W3C working draft "Roadmap for Accessible Rich Internet Applications" (*http://www.w3.org/TR/aria-roadmap/*) is a great starting point to start learning about ARIA and the overall Web Accessibility Initiative. Specific coverage of roles is outlined in "Roles for Accessible Rich Internet Applications" (*http://www.w3.org/TR/aria-role/*), while states are covered in "States and Properties Module for Accessible Rich Internet Applications" (*http://www.w3.org/TR/aria-state/*).

Table 11-1 summarizes the WAI functions.

Table 11-1. WAI functions

Function	Comment
onload( )	Automatically called to detect if the page is in high-contrast mode or has disabled images. You will normally not call this method directly because it is automatically called when the page loads.
hasWaiRole(/* DOMNode */ node)	Returns true if the node has a role attribute.
getWaiRole(/* DOMNode */ node)	Returns the role attribute for a node.

---

[*] A *screen reader* is an assistive device that audibly manages the focus and valid actions that can be performed on active controls.

Table 11-1. WAI functions (continued)

Function	Comment
setWaiRole(/* DOMNode */ node, /* String */ role)	Sets a role attribute for a node.
removeWaiRole(/* DOMNode */ node)	Removes the role attribute from an element.
hasWaiState(/* DOMNode */ node, /* String */ state)	Returns true if a node has a particular state.
getWaiState(/* DOMNode */ node, /* String */ state)	Returns the state value attribute for a node.
setWaiState(/* DOMNode */ node, /* String */ state, * String */ value)	Sets a state value for a node.
removeWaiState(/* DOMNode */ node, /* String */ state)	Removes a state from an element.

In terms of WAI-ARIA, role describes the purpose of a control, and examples of role values might be link, checkbox, toolbar, or slider. state describes the status of a control and is not necessarily a binary function. For example, a control with checkbox role may have a "checked" state that is set to mixed for a partial selection. Other examples of state include checked and disabled, which are both binary (true/false) values.

Dijit for Designers

The fundamentals for using an existing dijit in markup are quite simple: a dojoType tag specifies the type of dijit that should be placed in the page, attributes pass data into the widget upon creation, and *extension points* allow you to override existing widget behavior. While the dojoType tag is required, attributes usually are set to reasonable default values, and extension points always fall back to a reasonable implementation.

> The difference between "methods" and "extension points" is purely a semantic one: *methods* are operations that the application programmer call directly to control a dijit. *Extension points* are methods that the application programmer does not call directly; the dijits calls them itself when an appropriate condition arises. For example, a widget might have an explicit method like setValue that could be called to programmatically adjust it, while a method like onKeyUp would be an extension point in that it gets called automatically each time a key is pressed.

There are several attributes, listed in Table 11-2, that are especially important to be aware of for out-of-the-box usage because these attributes are set directly on a widget's DOM Node. These attributes ultimately ensure that the dijit's underlying HTML markup is as customizable and "proper" as possible.

A Word on DOCTYPE Validation

Technically speaking, it is possible to include dijits on pages and meet HTML 4.01 Strict DOCTYPE validation, but only if the dijits are programmatically created, and their templates meet the specification. When defined in markup, the dojoType tag and any nonstandard attributes single-handedly bust the validity rules for most validators, even though it is certainly possible to write a custom Document Type Definition (DTD) that includes nonstandard attributes like dojoType. For this reason, none of the examples in this book include DOCTYPE tags at the top of the page.

Although standards are important, it's equally important to weigh the cost of not meeting them in some circumstances. For example, using nonstandard attributes in Dojo—a robust, open source, community-supported effort that is about as transparent as any project could possibly get—is a little bit different than incorporating nonstandard attributes as a result of carelessness or ignorance. Dojo pushes the cutting edge, and careful consideration by some of the greatest DHTML hackers in the world goes into decisions that will so obviously cause a few ripples here and there.

In that regard, Dojo has never claimed to be a project that is fully standards-compliant or always loyal to any one metric (and 4.01 Strict DOCTYPE validation is a metric just like any other). It does, however, guarantee specific functionality on a specific subset of browsers, which is—you guessed it—just another metric.

Table 11-2. Common dijit attributes

Attribute	Type	Comment
id	String	A unique identifier for the widget. By default, this value is automatically generated and guaranteed to be unique. If an explicit value is provided that is known already to be in use, the value is ignored, and a unique value is generated.
lang	String	The language to use for displaying the widget. The browser's locale settings are used by default. If an additional locale is desired, specify it via djConfig.extraLocale so the bundle will be available. (In general, this attribute is not used unless it's necessary to display multiple languages on a single page.)
dir	String	Bidirectional support as defined by the HTML DIR attribute. By default, this value is set to ltr (left to right) unless rtl is provided. No other values are valid.
style	String	HTML style attributes that should be passed into the widget's outermost DOM node. By default, no additional style attributes are passed.
title	String	The standard HTML title attribute that can be used for displaying tooltips when hovering over a dijit's DOM node.
class	String	CSS class information to apply to the outermost DOM node. This attribute is particularly useful for overriding all or part of a default theme.

Themes

A Dijit theme is a fully consistent collection of CSS rules that span across the entire set of widgets. To say that another way, you might think of Dijit as being *skinnable*, where a theme is a kind skin that you apply. If you need to pull some widgets off the shelf and put together something quickly, themes are especially good because CSS becomes one less thing that you have to worry about implementing. As of version 1.1, Dojo includes three great-looking, prepackaged themes:

Tundra
> Predominantly light grey and light blue hues named after the Arctic landscape.

Soria
> Predominantly blue on blue, both of which are fairly light hues. Controls have a noticeably glossy "Web 2.0 sheen" look to them. The inspiration for this theme was the beautiful blue sky from a set of photos from Soria, Spain.

Nihilo
> Predominantly white with soft grey outlines with some greyish blue text. Some controls use a yellow shade to denote color. It is rumored that the inspiration for this theme is inspired from the *ex nihilo* concept (to create something out of nothing), with the goal of minimalist elegance—you barely notice it's there.

In your toolkit checkout, you can find a theme tester at *dijit/themes/themeTester.html* that demos the various dijits with a theme of your choice. Actually looking at the themes on your own screen is the best way to feel them out, as a black and white page can't really do them justice.

The structure of the themes directory has the following pattern, although each primary CSS file generally includes @import statements that pull in various other CSS files as part of a maintainable design (the build tools consolidate CSS files, so official builds only deliver the final file, which minimizes HTTP latency in fetching resources):

```
themes/
    tundra/
        tundra.css
        images/
            lots of static images
    soria/
        soria.css
        images/
            lots of static images
    nihilo/
        nihilo.css
            images/
                lots of static images
    <your custom theme could go here; just follow the pattern...>
```

Example 11-1 explicitly emphasizes the parts of the page that are pertinent to the theme.

Example 11-1. Using a theme

```
<html>
    <head>
        <title>Fun With the Themes!</title>

        <!-- pull in the tundra theme -->
        <link rel="stylesheet" type="text/css"
          href="http://o.aolcdn.com/dojo/1.1/dojo/resources/dojo.css" />
        <link rel="stylesheet" type="text/css"
          href="http://o.aolcdn.com/dojo/1.1/dijit/themes/tundra/tundra.css" />

        <script
            type="text/javascript"
            src="http://o.aolcdn.com/dojo/1.1/dojo/dojo.xd.js"
        ></script>

        <script type="text/javascript">
            //require your dijits here
        </script>
    <head>

    <body class="tundra">
        <!-- use your dijits here -->
    </body>
</html>
```

You'll notice that actually using a theme is as simple as pulling in a stylesheet and applying the appropriate class name to the BODY tag, although you could have applied the class name to a different tag on the page if you had a good reason not to style the entire page with a single theme. Themes are designed to be applied to any arbitrary page element, whether it is the entire page, a specific DIV section, or a particular widget. This listing also shows that the *dojo.css* file is also retrieved, which is generally assumed to be the case because it contains some baseline style.

Switching out the theme would be as simple as replacing all of the *tundra* references with either *soria* or *nihilo*. That's it. And that's also as easy as it should be to reskin the page.

We won't belabor the topic of themes because it's really just a system of well-engineered CSS rules, and while it absolutely and positively makes all of the difference to the credibility and desirability of Dijit, it just isn't a topic that lends itself well to the current discussion. If you're interested in themes, however, be sure to pick up a good reference on CSS and start reading through the various CSS files. You'll see definitions like .tundra .dojoButton { /* style goes here */ }, which are usually self-descriptive and easy to locate in Dijit template files or in the page if you are inspecting with Firebug.

Nodes Versus Dijits, DOM Events Versus Dijit Methods

Important distinctions must be made between a dijit versus a DOM node: a dijit is a JavaScript Function object that is instantiated from a collection of resources that may include HTML markup, CSS, JavaScript, and static resources like images; the dijit's visible manifestation is inserted into the page by assigning its domNode attribute (the outermost node in its template) into the page.

The distinction between a dijit and DOM node can be further highlighted by juxtaposing the dojo.byId function, which returns a DOM node given a string value, and Dijit's own dijit.byId, which returns the dijit that is associated with a particular DOM node. The differences are listed in Table 11-3. Using Firebug to execute the two commands on the following Button accentuates the differences:

```
<button id="foo" dojoType="dijit.form.Button">click me</button>
```

Table 11-3. Difference between dojo.byId and dijit.byId

Command	Firebug console result

dojo.byId("foo")	`<button`
	`    id="foo"`
	`    class="dijitStretch`
	`    dijitButtonNode`
	`    dijitButtonContents"`
	`    waistate="labelledby-foo_label"`
	`    wairole="button"`
	`    type="button"`
	`    dojoattachpoint="focusNode,titleNode"`
	`    role="wairole:button"`
	`    labelledby="foo_label"`
	`    tabindex="0"`
	`    valuenow=""`
	`    disabled="false">`

dijit.byId("foo")	`[Widget dijit.form.Button, foo] _connects=[4] _attaches=[0]` `id=foo`

The dojo.byId command returns the DOM node that provides the visible manifestation of an instantiated dijit.form.Button, while the dijit.byId returns a JavaScript Function object that can be examined for all of the standard dijit machinery.

 An incredibly common mistake is to try and run a method on the result of a dojo.byId command. Remember that DOM nodes do not have dijit-related methods.

The corollary to the distinction between a dijit and a DOM node is the analogous distinction between a Dijit event and a DOM event. While many dijits have an onClick event, this event is quite different from a DOM node's onclick event in spite of the obvious similarity in naming convention. Take a moment to load and run the following page in the Firebug console; the output highlights the crux of the matter:

```
<html>
    <head>
        <title>Fun with Button Clicking!</title>


        <link rel="stylesheet" type="text/css"
          href="http://o.aolcdn.com/dojo/1.1/dojo/resources/dojo.css" />
        <link rel="stylesheet" type="text/css"
          href="http://o.aolcdn.com/dojo/1.1/dijit/themes/tundra/tundra.css" />

        <script
            djConfig="parseOnLoad:true"
            type="text/javascript"
            src="http://o.aolcdn.com/dojo/1.1/dojo/dojo.xd.js"
        ></script>

        <script type="text/javascript">
            dojo.require("dojo.parser");
            dojo.require("dijit.form.Button");
            dojo.addOnLoad(function( ) {
                dojo.connect(dojo.byId("foo"), "onclick", function(evt) {
                    console.log("connect fired for DOM Node onclick");
                });

                dojo.connect(dijit.byId("foo"), "onclick", function(evt) {
                    console.log("connect fired for dijit onclick");    //never!
                });

                dojo.connect(dijit.byId("foo"), "onClick", function(evt) {
                    console.log("connect fired for dijit onClick");
                });
            });
        </script>
    <head>
    <body class="tundra">
        <button id="foo" dojoType="dijit.form.Button" onclick="foo">click me
            <script type="dojo/method" event="onClick" args="evt">
                console.log("Button fired onClick");
            </script>
        </button>
    </body>
</html>
```

To summarize, this page defines a simple method in markup for a simple Button,
provides an implementation for its onClick method, and defines three connections:
one for the DOM node's onclick event, and connections for the dijit's onclick and
onClick events. However, dijits do not have an onclick event, so the example demonstrates that the common mistake of trying to connect to it is a pitfall that can produce bugs that are quite hard to track down and fix.

The Parser

The Dojo parser is a Core resource that is the standard means of instantiating a widget defined in markup and ensuring that its visible representation, linked via its domNode, gets inserted into the page. Once the domNode is assigned into the page, the browser renders it on the page. So, while a widget's DOM node is the vital part of the dijit that makes it visible, the totality of the dijit is considerably more. This section provides an introduction to the parser, as well as play-by-play coverage on exactly how it works.

Parsing a Widget When the Page Loads

Aside from seeing some references in the introductory material in Chapter 1 and some exposure in the drag-and-drop examples from Chapter 7, the parser hasn't been formally introduced because its most common use case is instantiating widgets in a page. Without further ado, here's an official example of the parser instantiating a widget from markup. Note the emphasized lines in Example 11-2, which highlight where the parser-related action is happening.

Example 11-2. Automatically parsing a widget

```
<html>
    <head>
        <title>Fun With the Parser!</title>

        <!-- pull in the standard CSS that styles the stock dijits -->

        <link rel="stylesheet" type="text/css"
          href="http://o.aolcdn.com/dojo/1.1/dojo/resources/dojo.css" />
        <link rel="stylesheet" type="text/css"
          href="http://o.aolcdn.com/dojo/1.1/dijit/themes/tundra/tundra.css" />

        <script
            type="text/javascript"
            src="http://o.aolcdn.com/dojo/1.1/dojo/dojo.xd.js"
            djConfig="parseOnLoad:true"
        ></script>

        <script type="text/javascript">
            dojo.require("dojo.parser");
            dojo.require("dijit.form.Button");
        </script>
    <head>

    <body class="tundra">
      <button dojoType="dijit.form.Button" >Sign Up!</button>
    </body>
</html>
```

To summarize what's happening, there's just a simple page that includes an off-the-shelf button from Dijit that does absolutely nothing except look pretty—but for the purposes of introducing the parser without diving into Dijit specifics, this is just fine. The only thing you need to know about the Button dijit at this time is that it is fetched via a call to dojo.require and inserted into the page via the dojoType tag.

 Any custom addOnLoad logic you could include is executed after the widgets are parsed—making it safe for you to reference them.

You won't see any direct invocations of the parser in Example 11-2; that's by design. The vast majority of the time, you simply dojo.require dijits into your page, set the parseOnLoad flag in djConfig, and let the rest happen behind the scenes. In fact, that's all that occurs in this example. It's worth taking a moment to ponder just how absolutely elegant it is that you can take a dijit off the shelf and, in just a few keystrokes, insert it into the page. No additional headache, hassle, or fuss is required.

Manually Parsing a Widget

There are bound to be times when you will need to manually parse a page or some node in the DOM. Fortunately, it's just one function call away. Consider Example 11-3, a variation that manually parses the widget in the page.

Example 11-3. Manually parsing a page

```
<html>
    <head>
        <title>Hello Parser</title>

        <!-- pull in the standard CSS that styles the stock dijits -->

        <link rel="stylesheet" type="text/css"
          href="http://o.aolcdn.com/dojo/1.1/dojo/resources/dojo.css" />
        <link rel="stylesheet" type="text/css"
          href="http://o.aolcdn.com/dojo/1.1/dijit/themes/tundra/tundra.css" />

        <script
            type="text/javascript"
            src="http://o.aolcdn.com/dojo/1.1/dojo/dojo.xd.js"
            djConfig="parseOnLoad: false"
        ></script>

        <script type="text/javascript">
            dojo.require("dojo.parser");
            dojo.require("dijit.form.Button");
            dojo.addOnLoad(function() {
              dojo.parser.parse(); //manually parse after the page loads
            });
        </script>
```

Example 11-3. Manually parsing a page (continued)

```
      <head/>
      <body class="tundra" >
        <button dojoType="dijit.form.Button" >Sign Up!</button>
      </body>
</html>
```

Although manually parsing the entire page is useful, you'll more often need to manually parse a DOM node. The parser accepts an optional argument that provides the root of a node in the DOM tree that it scans for dojoType tags and instantiates. Thus, you provide the parent of the node you wish to parse to the parse function. Here's one possible modification of the previous code block that illustrates:

```
<script type="text/javascript">
    dojo.require("dojo.parser");
    dojo.require("dijit.form.Button");
    dojo.addOnLoad(function( ) {
        //The parser traverses the DOM tree passed in and instantiates widgets.
        //In this case, the button is the only leaf in the tree, so it is all that
        //gets parsed
        dojo.parser.parse(document.getElementsByTagName("button")[0].parentNode);
    });
</script>
```

Trying to manually parse a widget on the page by passing the widget's DOM node into the parse method will fail, and you may not receive any visible indication that parsing failed. Fortunately, if you can locate a reference to a node, referencing its parent through the parentNode is just a few keystrokes away.

Demystifying the Parser

Although what the parser accomplishes really does seem like magic, it really just boils down to rigorous, well-designed automation. As you now know, the parser has two primary use cases: parsing the page on load via djConfig="parseOnLoad:true" or manually parsing a widget. This section elaborates on the details that go into making those two things happen.

Parsing a widget when the page loads entails three basic requirements:

- Include parseOnLoad:true as a key/value pair to djConfig, which the parser will detect when it is loaded and use to trigger automatic parsing.

- Require the parser via dojo.require("dojo.parser") so that the parser is available and can register an automatic call to dojo.parser.parse( ) when the page loads. Because no arguments are passed to the call, the entire body of the page provides the basis for parsing.

- Provide dojoType tags as needed in the markup for widgets that should be parsed.

Manually parsing a widget that has already been defined in markup after the page loads is similar:

- Require the parser via `dojo.require("dojo.parser")`. Because `parseOnLoad` is not detected to be true, no automatic call to `dojo.parser.parse()` occurs.

- Provide the corresponding dojoType tag in the markup for a widget—maybe even dynamically after the page has already loaded.

- Manually call `dojo.parser.parse()`, optionally providing a specific DOM node as an argument as the starting point for the parsing operation.

But what about the actual parsing process? You know—the part about finding all of the dojoType tags and instantiating them into widgets? Again, it's all simple automation when you get right down to it. Here's exactly what happens:

- `dojo.query("[dojoType]")` is called to deterministically fetch the nodes in the page that need to be parsed.

- Class information (as in `dojo.declare` type classes) is distilled from each node; attributes are iterated over and lightweight type conversion is performed. Recall that attributes may provide information to a class's `constructor`.

- Any dojo/method or dojo/connect script tags internal to the node are detected and scheduled for processing. (More on these in the upcoming section "Defining Methods in Markup.")

- An instance of the class is created by using its `constructor` unless a `markupFactory` method is defined, in which case it is used. `markupFactory` is a special method that allows you to define a custom constructor function for widgets that need different initialization in markup than they do via programmatic creation. All dijits inherit from a base class, `_Widget`, which fires off a standard series of lifecycle methods. One of these lifecycle methods inserts the dijit's `domNode` into the page, which makes it visible. Lifecycle methods are discussed in detail in the next chapter.

- If a `jsId` attribute is present, then the class instance is mapped to the global JavaScript namespace. (Common for data stores and widgets that you have a reason to make global.)

- Any connections provided via dojo/connect or dojo/method SCRIPT tags in markup are processed (more on this later in the chapter) and each widget's `startup` lifecycle method is called. `startup` is another standard lifecycle method inherited from `_Widget` (coming up in the next chapter) which allows you to manipulate any widgets that are contained in the one being instantiated.

Hopefully, that didn't make you feel the same way that you did when you learned that Santa Claus wasn't real, but you had to learn sometime. The next chapter focuses exclusively on dijit lifecycle methods where dedicated coverage of these concepts is provided.

Hands-on Dijit with NumberSpinner

This section provides some hands-on usage for a pretty intuitive dijit—the `dijit.form.NumberSpinner`—to warm you up for the chapters that follow. First, we'll work through creating the dijit in markup, and then we'll follow up with programmatic creation.

Creating from Markup

As you learned from an earlier section on the parser, it's pretty trivial to stick a dijit into the page. You require in the resources, provide the `dojoType` attribute in a tag, and have the parser go to work. For completeness, Example 11-4 shows how we'd follow that very same pattern to instantiate a `NumberSpinner` dijit.

Example 11-4. Creating the NumberSpinner widget in markup

```
<html>
    <head>
        <title>Number Spinner Fun!</title>

        <link rel="stylesheet" type="text/css"
          href="http://o.aolcdn.com/dojo/1.1/dojo/resources/dojo.css" />
        <link rel="stylesheet" type="text/css"
          href="http://o.aolcdn.com/dojo/1.1/dijit/themes/tundra/tundra.css" />

        <script
            type="text/javascript"
            src="http://o.aolcdn.com/dojo/1.1/dojo/dojo.xd.js"
            djConfig="parseOnLoad: true"
        ></script>

        <script type="text/javascript">
            dojo.require("dojo.parser");
            dojo.require("dijit.form.NumberSpinner");
        </script>
    <head>
    <body class="tundra">
        <form> <!-- some really awesome form -->
            <input dojoType="dijit.form.NumberSpinner"
                constraints="{min:0,max:10000}" value=1000>
            </input>
            </form>
    </body>
</html>
```

Programmatic Creation

While you'll often create dijits in markup, programmatic creation is no less common and the process is the very same as creating any other Function Object because that's exactly what a dijit is—a Function Object. In general, the constructor for a dijit accepts two parameters. The first is an Object that provides properties that should be passed in, and these are the same properties that you would be including in the tag if you were creating in markup. The second parameter is a source node or the id for a source node that identifies the placeholder that the dijit should replace:

```
var d = new module.DijitName(/*Object*/props, /*DOMNode|String*/node)
```

Example 11-5 programmatically creates the NumberSpinner and produces the very same effect as Example 11-4.

Example 11-5. Programmatically creating the NumberSpinner widget

```html
<html>
    <head>
        <title>Number Spinner Fun!</title>

        <link rel="stylesheet" type="text/css"
          href="http://o.aolcdn.com/dojo/1.1/dojo/resources/dojo.css" />
        <link rel="stylesheet" type="text/css"
          href="http://o.aolcdn.com/dojo/1.1/dijit/themes/tundra/tundra.css" />
        <script
            type="text/javascript"
            src="http://o.aolcdn.com/dojo/1.1/dojo/dojo.xd.js"
        ></script>

        <script type="text/javascript">
            dojo.require("dijit.form.NumberSpinner");
            dojo.addOnLoad(function( ) {
                var ns = new dijit.form.NumberSpinner(
                    //props
                    {
                        constraints : {min:0,max:10000},
                        value : 1000
                    },
                    "foo" //node id
                );

                // do other stuff with ns here...

            });
        </script>
    <head>
    <body class="tundra">
        <form>
            <input id="foo"></input>
        </form>
    </body>
</html>
```

Lots of Niceties

This particular example displays a nice little text box with a control that allows you to adjust the value from either the arrow keys on the keyboard, by clicking the arrow controls on the dijit itself, or though manual keyboard entry. In any case, the min and max and key/value pairs are part of the constraints *attribute* that can be customized to form the upper and lower values for the spinner with the arrow keys or when clicking on the controls; the value attribute provides the default value just like in ordinary HTML. Manually changing the value via manual keyboard entry, however, still changes the value, which may trigger a tooltip-style error message. Figure 11-3 illustrates what happens.

 Recall that Dojo attempts to supplement the existing fabric for developing web applications—not override it. Thus, common attributes for form elements such as the value attribute in the previous code listing's input element still work just like normal.

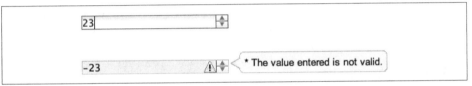

Figure 11-3. Left: a NumberSpinner dijit changing its value via keyboard or mouse control; right: the default display when manual keyboard entry enters a value that is out of bounds

 While techniques from djConfig showed key/value pairs expressing objects constructed in markup without the surrounding curly brackets like djConfig="parseOnLoad:true,isDebug:true", it is more the exception than the rule. Dijit requires that Object attributes in markup be expressed using braces like constraints="{min:0, max:100}".

You've probably already made the connection about the NumberSpinner's keyboard entry and a11y, but there are some other niceties that are worth trying out right away. You've no doubt noticed the numeric formatting that is automatically applied to separate every three digits of numbers greater than 999. Note that if you were rendering the page for a supported locale that used a different separator for the digits, it would have happened automatically: locales like *en-us* use commas to separate values, like 1,000, while Spain, the *es-es* locale, for example, uses dots to separate the digits, like 1.000. Figure 11-4 demonstrates. Try it for yourself by modifying your default locale in djConfig. For example, to set a default locale of Spain, you could do the following:

```
djConfig="locale:'es-es'"
```

Remember that any values in djConfig that are strings need to contain additional quotes around them. The syntax for declaring an associative array inline makes this easy to forget, and unfortunately, the error messages that can result from forgetting it are not always helpful to point you in the right direction. Any djConfig settings need to be loading prior to Base bootstrapping.

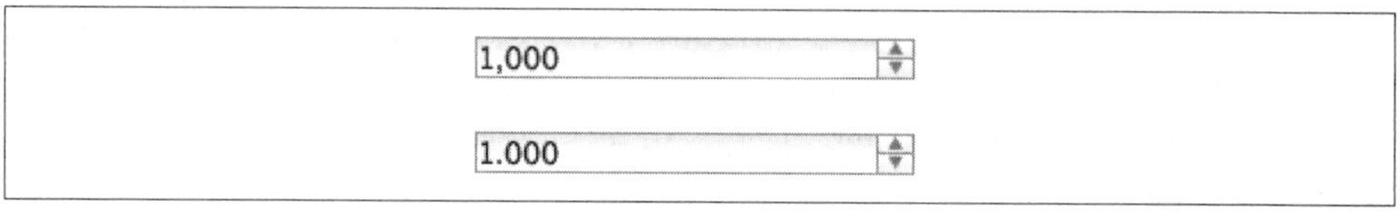

| 1,000 | |
| 1.000 | |

Figure 11-4. Dijits handle special formatting for the supported locales right out of the box with no additional configuration required; the top NumberSpinner was configured with en-us while the bottom NumberSpinner was configured with es-es; the dijit internally took care of the formatting details

Another great out-of-the-box feature that Dijit supports is the notion of controls being *typematic*—that is, they respond in special ways to holding down a mouse button or keyboard key. If you try holding down the mouse button on one of the controls for the NumberSpinner, you should notice that it gradually increases for the first 10 or so numbers and then eventually speeds up and moves rapidly. Not surprisingly, keyboard navigation works the very same way. The Page Up and Page Down buttons also work and adjust the values by multiples of 10 by default.

Defining Methods in Markup

In addition to being able to programmatically write ordinary JavaScript to control and extend widgets, Dojo also provides the ability to define the JavaScript directly in markup by including a special type="dojo/method" attribute in SCRIPT tags. This can be very convenient for designers as well as anyone who needs to rapidly prototype a new idea. What's especially notable about defining methods in markup is that the keyword this refers to the containing widget, so you have instant access to the context you'd expect.

Consider the following update to the example code listing that defines methods in markup:

```
<!-- snip -->

    <script type="text/javascript">
            dojo.require("dojo.parser");
            dojo.require("dijit.form.NumberSpinner");
            dojo.require("dijit.form.Button");
    </script>
    </head>
    <body class="tundra">
        <form>
            <div dojoType="dijit.form.NumberSpinner" jsId="mySpinner"
```

```
            constraints="{min:0,max:10000}" value=1000>
            <script type="dojo/method">
                dojo.mixin(this, {
                    reset : function() { this.setValue(1000); }
                });
            </script>
        </div>
    </form>
    <button dojoType="dijit.form.Button" onClick="mySpinner.reset()">reset</
button>
    </body>
</html>
```

To sum up the effect of the changes, the `jsId` attribute gave the `NumberSpinner` a global variable name `mySpinner`, which was referenced in a Button's `onClick` method. The actual body of the `reset` method was established by the special `script` tag included inside of the dijit. The `script` tag providing anonymous `dojo/method` is executed after its `constructor` runs, so that any values passed in via attributes included in markup would be available.

Also, note that whereas the previous listing used an `input` element to create the spinner, the new listing uses a `div` tag. The reason why an `input` tag will not work with the updated listing is that it does not allow `innerHTML`. The tag had to be switched to a type that does allow `innerHTML` in order for it to work. If you're wondering why a `div` tag wasn't used all along, it really comes back to one primary issue: the ability to have a semantically correct page that works without any JavaScript involved. In other words, the previous form using an `input` element is a semantically correct `input` control even if JavaScript were disabled (for whatever reason), whereas the `div`-based spinner is not. Most of the time, this isn't an problem, but when designing a degradable page, it is very important to know your basic HTML and be aware of these issues.

 The `dojo/method` and `dojo/connect` script tags do not work inside of marked up elements that do not allow `innerHTML`. This isn't a Dojo thing; it's in accordance with the HTML specification. Although not demonstrated with this example, SCRIPT tags containing a `type="dojo/connect"` attribute allow you to set up connections in markup using the same pattern.

While the additional reset button may make a great addition for a mouse-based control, note that pressing the Escape key on the keyboard would have reset the spinner to its original value without any additional work at all.

As an improvement that produces the very same effect but with less code, consider the following change to the `dojo/method` script tag:

```
<script type="dojo/method" event="reset">
    this.setValue(1000);
</script>
```

Instead of being executed automatically a single time after the constructor, which is the case for anonymous dojo/method script tags, this approach performs the work of actually creating the reset method and attaching it to the widget on your behalf. If there had been arguments involved, an additional args attribute could have been specified. For example, args="foo,bar,baz" would have allowed for passing in three named arguments to a method defined in markup.

Overview of Stock Dijits

Because Dojo's widget collection is incredibly extensive, it can be easy to get lost. This section presents a concise inventory of dijits so that you may be familiarized with what's available.

Form Dijits

The very naming convention for a category of "form dijits" implies that the dijits are designed to be used inside of a form. While this is certainly true, form dijits may also be used outside of forms or in a special dijit.form.Form dijit that provides some extra methods and extension points. Here's a very brief overview of what is included in each of those chapters. Recall that all dijits are a11y compatible and easily internationalized, where applicable.

 Go to *http://archive.dojotoolkit.org/nightly/* to view the Dijit test harnesses that contain all of these widgets. It's a great way to get a feel for just how much breadth and depth there really is.

Form

A special container for form widgets that provides handy methods and extension points for serializing to JSON, validating the entire form's contents, setting values for the form all at once, and event handling when the form is submitted.

Button *variations*

Drop-in replacements for ordinary buttons based on BUTTON elements as well as other button-like controls based on INPUT elements like checkboxes and radio elements. Additional button variations include menu-style buttons that have drop-down values (sort of like combo boxes) that are commonly shown in toolbars, and toggle buttons that commonly appear in toolbars such as bold and italic buttons.

ComboBox

A combination of the functionality provided by an ordinary SELECT combo box and a text field defined with an INPUT element, allowing users to choose from pre-filled selections or typing in their own values.

FilteringSelect

A drop-in replacement for an ordinary SELECT element. It may be populated dynamically, making it great for situations in which a very large number of selections may be possible.

NumberSpinner

Similar to a text box based on an INPUT element except that controls allow for making incremental adjustments to the value.

Slider

A draggable handle attached to a scale that may be laid out vertically or horizontally. This widget provides a more interactive way of adjusting a value and is commonly used in conjunction with a display that involves resizing two-dimensional objects in real time.

Textarea

A drop-in replacement for an ordinary TEXTAREA element, but resizes as necessary to fit its enclosed content so that valuable screen real estate isn't lost when the potential size of content may not be predictable or always annotated.

SimpleTextarea

A drop-in replacement for an ordinary TEXTAREA element with some additional machinery to interact with the Form dijit container and layout dijits.

MultiSelect

A drop-in replacement for an ordinary SELECT element that has the multiple=true attribute set. Like SimpleTextarea, it contains some extra machinery for interaction with the Form dijit.

TextBox *variations*

An entire family of feature-rich widgets based upon the INPUT element with a special emphasis for custom validation of values and formatting for common fields like date, time, currency, numbers, etc. An incredible amount of functionality is packed into this family of widgets.

Layout Dijits

Traditional techniques for complex layouts used to involve extensive CSS work. While CSS may not be rocket science, writing, maintaining, and testing it on multiple browsers requires nontrivial effort—especially if you're not a CSS guru. Layout dijits allow the layout to be constructed in markup—without resorting to nested tables—which seems to have made laying out a page a lot simpler. Layout dijits, in general, may be arbitrarily nested, which allows for extremely sophisticated designs at a fraction of the time involved with more traditional CSS-based techniques. Here's a synopsis of what Dijit provides:

ContentPane

> The most basic building block for a layout and provides the actual wrapper for layout tile. Although they could be used as standalones, one or more ContentPane dijits generally exist as part of a container widget.

TabContainer

> A means of providing a familiar, tabbed layout with the tabs appearing horizontally or vertically. Simple layouts with TabContainers generally involve a TabContainer combined with a ContentPane, although arbitrary nesting is always a possibility. Content for tabs that are not initially displayed may be lazy loaded.

StackContainer

> Provides a means of displaying multiple containers of information, but with only one container shown at a time. For example, multiple ContentPanes might contain individual slides for a presentation, and a StackContainer could be used to combine them all into a presentation. StackContainers are also very handy for applications that have multiple "screens" that need to be displayed without the page ever reloading.

AccordionContainer

> Displays one tile at a time, and when another tile is selected, the previously displayed tile folds up with a smooth animation. Content for tiles that are not initially displayed may be lazy-loaded.

BorderContainer

> Provides a convenient way to easily achieve a typical "headline" style or "sidebar" style layout where there are multiple tiles on the screen and some of them span the entire height and width while others do not. Achieving a more complex layout "border-style" layout with up to five tiles on the screen (four tiles around the edges and a center tile that fills in the remainder) is trivial to achieve.

Application Dijits

Application dijits are the "other" category; they are all very common elements for any application that even begins to approach RIA functionality. Menus, toolbars, dialog overlays, and rich text editors are all part of the mix, and these dijits are so easy to use that you can't avoid wanting to:

Menu

> Provides a contextual popup menu similar to what is commonly seen from right-clicking in a desktop application. Menu is also used to build complex buttons like ComboButton and DropDownButton to offer advanced functionality.

Toolbar

> Provides a container for complex buttons such as ToggleButton that supply the controls for a toolbar, although any button dijit may be included in a toolbar.

Dialog

Simulates an ordinary desktop dialog box, complete with a translucent overlay that prevents interaction with content "below" the dialog. Dialog dijits are a fantastic, easily maintainable alternative to pop-up windows for many use cases, especially when any kind of communication or DOM manipulation would be necessary between multiple windows.*

TooltipDialog

A combination of Tooltip and Dialog, which allows for delivering a dialog-style input in a tooltip. A key difference between Dialog and TooltipDialog is that the TooltipDialog may be dismissed by clicking anywhere not on the TooltipDialog, whereas a Dialog provides a translucent underlay that prevents interaction with the rest of the page until the Dialog is explicitly closed.

ProgressBar

Models ordinary progress bars as commonly seen in virtually every desktop application. ProgressBar dijits are the standard way of providing feedback on a long-running operation or an asynchronous call back to the server that takes longer than a few seconds. ProgressBar dijits may be determinate, providing a percentage complete as the indicator, or indeterminate, providing an arbitrary animation that indicates something is happening.

TitlePane

Offers functionality for displaying a pane of information with a title area on top. While the content of the pane may be closed or opened by clicking on an icon in the title area, the title area is always visible.

Tooltip

A much more flexible alternative to the ordinary title attribute for ordinary HTML controls. Timing and arbitrary HTML may be included in the tooltip text.

InlineEditBox

A sort of widget wrapper that displays the widget's value, which appears like a label; however, the widget transforms into its editable form when the text is clicked. (Very rich functionality.)

ColorPalette

By default, displays a 3×4 or 7×10 matrix of commonly used colors for users to select in a highly useful way. ColorPalette may be extended to display arbitrary color configurations.

Editor

Provides the equivalent of a minimally function rich-text editor, complete with a toolbar that is pre-configured for cut/copy/paste, undo/redo, text-alignment, basic markup such as bold/italic/strikethrough, and the ability to create bulleted lists.

---

* For some browsers, manipulating DOM nodes that are in another window isn't even possible because of security restrictions.

The toolbar may be customized as needed. A ridiculous amount of functionality is packed into this dijit, and it's much more lightweight than you might think, as Editor builds off of specific native controls such as Firefox's Midas rich text editor.

Tree

Delivers a tree with nodes that may be arbitrarily nested and closed/expanded as needed. This interface control is commonly used to deliver long, hierarchical lists of information. Content for nodes that are not expanded by default may be lazy-loaded; this dijit uses the terrific dojo.data API to deliver its content.

Dijit API Drive-By

The functions listed in Table 11-4 are too commonly used not to especially call out. They're available as part of Dijit Base and get pulled in whenever you require Dijit resources into the page. You can also fetch them by issuing a dojo.require("dijit. dijit") statement, as they are included in the standard build profile, which you'll read more about in Chapter 16.

 For comprehensive API documentation, visit Dojo's online documentation at *http://api.dojotoolkit.org*.

Table 11-4. Commonly used Dijit functions

Function/Member	Comment
dijit.registry()	The registry contains a complete record of all dijits that are on the page and may be used to explicitly iterate through them, to check for the existence of a particular dijit, etc. For example, you could uniformly manipulate every dijit on a page via the dijit.registry. forEach function or you could query the page for a particular type of widget via dijit.registry. byClass (where "class" is in the OOP sense).
dijit.byNode(/* DOM Node */ node)	Given a node, returns the dijit that represents this node.
dijit.getEnclosingWidget(/* DOM Node */ node)	Given a node, returns the dijit whose DOM tree contains this node. This method is especially handy for situations in which you need a quick reference to a dijit via a DOM event. For example, you might use this method to easily find a dijit via the target property of the event object that is associated with a mouse click when a user clicks the mouse on some part of a dijit.

Table 11-4. Commonly used Dijit functions (continued)

Function/Member	Comment
`dijit.getViewport( )`	Returns the dimensions and scroll position of the viewable area of a browser window—extremely useful for programmatically placing objects on the screen when the exact screen resolution or window size cannot be assumed. Often used in animations.
`dijit.byId(/* String */ id)`	Looks up a dijit on the page by the `id` value included in its original `dojoType` tag or passed in through programmatic creation. This function differs from `dojo.byId` in that `dojo.byId` returns a DOM node, whereas this function returns an actual dijit (a Function object).

While these aren't the only API methods you'll want to be aware of, they're some of the most common ones, and they will save you a lot of time if you can remember that they exist.

Summary

After reading this chapter, you should understand:

- The basic philosophy behind the design of Dijit
- The importance of low coupling and high cohesion in developing a complex application and the way that Dijit leverages these concepts to encapsulate functionality in dijits
- The importance of accessibility (a11y) in an application, as well as W3C Web Accessibility Initiative for Accessible Rich Internet Applications, and the basic a11y approach taken by Dijit
- That dijits can be implemented in markup such that they provide the same functionality as they would had they been created programmatically, and how to apply `dojo/method` and `dojo/connect` SCRIPT tags to a dijit in markup
- The difference between a DOM node and a dijit; the difference between `dojo.byId` and `dijit.byId`; the difference between DOM events and dijit events
- The basic steps the parser takes to instantiate a dijit that is defined in markup
- The basic architectural breakdown of Dijit into form dijits, layout dijits, and general purpose application dijits, as well as where to start looking for a particular kind of dijit

Next we're going to take a look at Dijit's anatomy and lifecycle.

CHAPTER 12

Dijit Anatomy and Lifecycle

Like object-oriented concepts from any other programming paradigm, Dojo widgets—dijits—follow particular patterns for lifecycle events such as creation and destruction, are composed according to a particular an anatomical style, and are described by a somewhat specialized vocabulary. This chapter provides a summary of these topics with an extended discussion on the fundamentals of custom dijit design.

Dijit Anatomy

Although you already know that dijit is short for "Dojo widget," it's helpful to elaborate just a bit before we proceed any further. To be precise, a dijit is any Dojo class that inherits from a foundational class from Dijit called _Widget. This class is part of the toolkit's foundational dijit module, so the fully qualified name of the class is dijit._Widget. There are several other foundational classes from Dijit that you'll learn about, but _Widget is the one that provides the primary ancestor for any dijit.

As you learned in Chapter 10, dojo.declare saves you from writing a lot of mundane boilerplate; dijits follow suit by tucking away a lot of complexity in classes like _Widget. As you're about to see, there are a number of method stubs that you can override to achieve custom behavior, as opposed to engineering your own boilerplate.

 You may be wondering why the _Widget class is prefixed with a leading underscore. When used in relation to dijits, the leading underscore almost always means that it should not be instantiated on its own. Rather, it is usually used as a superclass for an inheritance relationship.

Let's start out our discussion on dijits with the familiar constructs that define a dijit on a physical level—the HTML, CSS, JavaScript, and other static resources that you've been developing with all along. Then, with both feet firmly planted, we'll dig deeper into the dijit lifecycle model by building upon your knowledge of dojo.declare and work through a number of increasingly complex code examples that involve the design of a custom dijit.

Web Development Review

As anyone who's ever touched a computer knows, HTML is the de facto standard for displaying information in a web browser. You can standardize headings, paragraph division, form fields, and generally provide just about any kind of markup that's useful for displaying textual information and images. Still, HTML alone isn't very pleasing to the eye: there's no nice formatting involved, and the content is static. The overall structure of a page is quite simple, and it doesn't change in response to user interaction. Given what we've come to expect over the years, the web would be intolerably boring with HTML alone.

Bring in a dash of CSS, however, and the scene changes significantly. Suddenly, the aesthetic nature of the page improves. Whereas HTML alone provides content with very little visual appeal, CSS adds value by improving a page's layout and typesetting. But style alone still results in a static page that leaves the inherent dynamism of human interaction longing for something with a little more life. You could create some nicely typeset pages with HTML and CSS, but that's about it.

JavaScript provided the dynamism that styled HTML so sorely lacked and gave rise to DHTML, which fueled the increasingly interactive online experience that blossomed into this modern era of rich Internet applications. JavaScript brings a web page to life and enables that sheer contentment we enjoy when a simple mouse click, selection in a combo box, or casual keystroke makes you wonder if the computer is reading your mind.

Although we've all come to know a well-designed, interactive web page when we see one, the experience itself can still be quite difficult to achieve; the JavaScript that controls the HTML and CSS can often be quite complex, and even the cleverest of implementations may not be maintainable or especially noteworthy. The central issue at stake is that the HTML, CSS, and JavaScript can be difficult to integrate into a single, cohesive framework. With little cohesion amongst them in ad-hoc designs, synergy is difficult to achieve, and massive amounts of energy is lost in implementing the not-so-interesting boilerplate. Unfortunately, this laborious process can quickly drain motivation and creativity from the parts of the application that really matter.

Dijits to the Rescue

Fortunately, dijits make matters much easier by providing the foundation upon which you can build a more complex design. They unite the HTML, CSS, and Java-Script into a unified medium, and although not perfect, dijits allow you to think in an object-oriented context much more quickly than you would without them: the end result is that you can quickly get to the heart of your own application before so much of the energy and creativity dries up. Whereas you previously had to provide your own means of uniting the HTML, CSS, and JavaScript, Dojo now does that tiresome work for you, and leaves you to get to the good stuff more quickly.

Just like standalone classes, dijits are self-contained inside of a single directory that corresponds to a namespace. In addition to a single JavaScript file, however, the directory also contains dependencies such as image file and stylesheets. The inherent familiarity of a directory structure provides an innate portability that makes it trivial to share, deploy, and upgrade dijits. Maintenance is also eased because there are no binary formats to unravel, and each component of a dijit can be checked into a version control system like Subversion as a separate file.

While all of the resources that compose a dijit could just be thrown into a single directory in the one-big-pair-of-clown-pants approach, Figure 12-1 displays a common convention for laying out a dijit on disk. Basically, the convention is to just compartmentalize the various facets into subdirectories to make things more manageable.

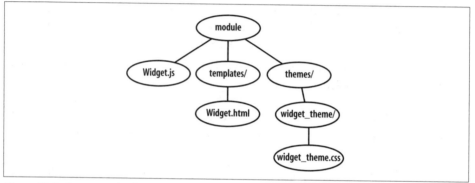

Figure 12-1. Anatomy of a dijit on disk

Dijits unite the HTML, CSS, and JavaScript that are so very central to any web development effort and provide you with a single, unified means of structuring the creativity required of your own application. In the end, you'll save time, effort, and likely obtain a more efficient design. Note that the layout for a minimal dijit that doesn't include a template or CSS is simply a directory with a JavaScript file.

The layout shown in Figure 12-1 shows the template contained in its own separate HTML file, and this setup is typical during the development cycle because it allows members of the development team to work on the template, CSS, and JavaScript files separately.

Fetching the template requires the JavaScript engine to issue a synchronous call back to the server; however, Dojo provides a wonderful way to optimize that synchronous call out the picture entirely: you can include the template as an inline string that's inside of the JavaScript file. Plenty of examples are coming up that illustrate how simple it is to make this happen.

Dijit Lifecycle Methods

Let's now turn our attention to the central dijit lifecycle methods that _Widget provides. As you're about to see, _Widget packs a lot of power with only minimal effort required on your part. By simply including it as the primary superclass ancestor in the inheritance hierarchy, your subclass has immediate access to the standard dijit lifecycle methods it provides, and you may override any of these method stubs to produce custom behavior during the construction and destruction of the dijit.

For example, _Widget provides stubs to override before a dijit appears on screen, immediately after a dijit becomes visible, and when a dijit is just about to be destroyed. Each of these choke points can be immensely valuable times to synchronize with the server-side model, explicitly destroy objects (so as to avoid well-known memory leaks), or do some tactical DOM manipulation. Regardless of the particulars for each and every situation, this is boilerplate that you don't have to write; it's already in place, and you can use it if and when you need it.

To introduce what _Widget offers, Example 12-1 shows a simple class that defines a class inheriting from _Widget and overriding the key methods involved in construction and destruction to produce debugging messages in the Firebug console. As you know from the last chapter, this file would be named *Foo.js*, and would be located in a directory named after the module—nothing more than a class mapped to a namespace.

The key point to observe in this example is that you override the inherited methods from _Widget just like you would expect. Take a look, and then we'll review each of these methods in more detail.

Example 12-1. Subclassing from _Widget

```
dojo.require("dijit._Widget");
dojo.addOnLoad(function() {
    dojo.declare(
      "dtdg.Foo", // the subclass
      dijit._Widget, // the superclass
      {
        /* Common construction methods in chronological order */
        constructor : function() {console.log("constructor");},
        postMixInProperties : function() {console.log("postMixInProperties") ;},
        postCreate : function() {console.log("postCreate");},

        /* Your clever logic goes here */
        talk : function() {console.log("I'm alive!");},

        /* Canonical destructor, implicitly called via destoryRecursive() */
        uninitialize : function() {console.log("uninitialize");}
      }
    );
});
```

Example 12-1. Subclassing from _Widget (continued)

```
foo = new dtdg.Foo( );
foo.talk( );
foo.destroyRecursive( ); /* Calls uninitialize, among other things */
```

When you run that example, you should notice the following output in the Firebug console:

```
constructor
postMixInProperties
postCreate
I'm alive!
uninitialize
```

The _Widget Lifecycle

To come full circle to the discussion about the creation pattern dojo.declare provides from back in Chapter 10, here's how the _Widget lifecycle plugs in:

```
preamble(/*Object*/ params, /*DOMNode*/node)
    //precursor to constructor; can manipulate superclass constructor args

constructor(/*Object*/ params, /*DOMNode*/node)
    // fire any superclass constructors
    // fire off any mixin constrctors
    // fire off the local class constructor, if provided

postscript(/*Object*/ params, /*DOMNode*/node)
    //_Widget implements postscript to kick off the create method...
    _Widget.create(/*Object*/params, /*DOMNode*/node)
    _Widget.postMixInProperties( )
    _Widget.buildRendering( )
    _Widget.postCreate( )
```

The take away is two-fold:

- _Widget builds right on top of what dojo.declare already provides and hooks into the postscript method in order to fire off the create method that systematically calls _Widget specific lifecycle methods.

- A widget, as an ancestor of _Widget, is a bona fide JavaScript Function object. Sure, there's a lot of flare and pizzazz involved, but in the end, it comes right back to the basics.

Lifecycle methods

A flattened version of the lifecycle follows along with a short synopsis of what each _Widget lifecycle method accomplishes. It's flattened out and starts with preamble because it's quite uncommon to override postscript or the create method yourself (although you *could* if you wanted to devise your own widget lifecycle methods instead of using the standard ones). Expanded examples that more thoroughly cover each method appear later in this chapter.

preamble (originating from `dojo.declare`*)*

Preamble provides an opportunity to manipulate arguments before `constructor` receives them. If you override `preamble`, know that the same arguments that would normally be passed to `constructor` are passed to `preamble` and whatever preamble returns is what gets passed into `constructor`. This method is somewhat of an advanced feature and used infrequently compared to other lifecycle methods such as, for example, `postCreate`.

constructor (originating from `dojo.declare`*)*

This is the first method that you can override to perform custom behavior during dijit construction. There are two particularly common operations that are performed in `constructor`. One is including the initialization of dijit properties that are not primitive types. (Recall from Chapter 10 that declaring a complex type like an object or list inline as an object property causes it to be shared by all object instances.) Another common operation is adding any additional properties that are relied upon by other lifecycle methods downstream.

postMixInProperties (originating from `dijit._Widget`*)*

This method is called just after Dojo has walked the inheritance hierarchy and mixed all of the ancestors into the class. Thus, the name *postMixInProperties* literally refers to the time at which all a widget's properties have been mixed into the particular object instance. Therefore, by the time this method executes, your class has full access to those inherited properties and can manipulate them before the dijit visibly appears on the screen. As we'll soon see in an example that illustrates dijits that derive from a template, this method is typically the place where you'll modify or derive placeholders (indicated by `${someWidgetProperty}` style notation) that appear in the template's markup.

buildRendering (originating from `dijit._Widget`*)*

In `_Widget`'s implementation, this method simply sets the internal `_Widget.domNode` property to an actual DOM element so that the dijit physically becomes a part of the page. Given that this method fires directly after `postMixInProperties`, it should now be all the more apparent why `postMixInProperties` is the canonical location for modifying a widget's template.

As you'll soon learn, another foundational Dijit class, `_Templated`, overrides this method to perform all of the myriad details that are involved in fetching and instantiating a dijit's template. Finally, note that just after `buildRendering` is called, the dijit itself is added to Dojo's dijit manager object so that the dijit can be properly destroyed during explicit destructor methods and/or when the page is unloaded. Some browsers do have well-known memory leaks that become relevant for long-running applications, and tracking widgets through a centralized registry is Dojo's way of helping to alleviate that problem. It is quite uncommon to override this method; you'll normally use the default implementation from `_Widget` or `_Templated`.

postCreate (originating from `dijit._Widget`*)*

This method executes once the dijit has been created and visibly placed in the page, so you can use it to perform any actions that might not otherwise be possible or prudent until that time. Take special care to perform actions that affect things such as a dijit's style or placement on the screen in `postMixInProperties` so that they occur before the dijit becomes visible. Performing those actions in `postCreate` may sometimes cause intermittent display "jerks" because you're manipulating the already visible dijit in this method; these issues can be difficult to locate and fix if you've forgotten the fundamental differences between `postMixInProperties` and `postCreate`. Additionally, note that if your dijit contains any child dijits, these children are not safely accessible here. To safely access child dijits, use the lifecycle method `startup` instead. To safely access other nonchild widgets, wait until the page has loaded via using `dojo.addOnLoad`.

startup (originating from `dijit._Widget`*)*

For child widgets declared in markup, this method automatically fires once the widget and *all* child widgets have been created. As such, this is the first safe place that a child widget could safely reference a child. As simple as it sounds, this task is often attempted in `postCreate`, which can lead to inconsistent behavior that can is difficult to detect and repair. For programmatically created widgets that contain other child widgets as part of a *has-a* relationship, you'll need to manually call `startup` yourself when you're sure that all child widgets have been created. The reason that you need to call it yourself for programmatically created widgets containing children is because it wouldn't make sense to proceed with sizing and rendering unless all child widgets have been added. (Otherwise, there could very well be lots of false starts.) This method is the final method stub that you can override for custom behavior to occur during dijit construction.

destroyRecursive (originating from `dijit._Widget`*)*

This method is the generic destructor to call in order to cleanly do away with a dijit and any of its child dijits. In the processing of destructing a dijit, this method calls `uninitialize`, which is the primary stub method that you can override to perform custom tear down operations. *Do not override* `destroyRecursive`. Provide custom tear-down operations in `uninitialize` and call this method (it does not get automatically called), which takes care of the rest for you.

uninitialize (originating from `dijit._Widget`*)*

Override this method to implement custom tear-down behavior when a dijit is destroyed. For example, you might initiate a callback to the server to save a session, or you might explicitly clean up DOM references. This is the canonical location that all dijits should use for these destruction operations.

Knowing the intricacies that distinguish the various lifecycle methods from one another is absolutely essential. Take special care to remember what type of behavior should be occurring in each method.

Especially common mistakes include:

- Trying to manipulate a template after `postMixInProperties` has been called
- Modifying a widget's initial appearance after `postMixInProperties` has been called
- Trying to access child widgets in `postMixInProperties` instead of `startup`
- Forgetting to perform any necessary destruction in `uninitialize`
- Calling `uninitialize` instead of `destroyRecursive`

Essential properties

In addition to the `_Widget` methods just described, there are also some especially notable properties. Just like dijit methods, you can reference these properties with dot notation. You'll generally treat these properties as read-only:

id

> This value provides a unique identifier that is assigned to the dijit. If none is provided, Dojo automatically assigns one. You should never manipulate this value, and in most circumstances, you won't want to use it at all.

lang

> Dojo supports features for internationalization, and this value can be used to customize features such as the language used to display the dijit. By default, this value is defined to match the browser's setting, which usually matches that of the operating system.

domNode

> This property provides a reference to the dijit's most top-level node. This property is the canonical node that is the visible representation of the dijit on the screen, and although you'll probably want to avoid direct manipulation of this property, it is helpful for some debugging scenarios. As previously mentioned, `_Widget`'s default implementation of `buildRendering` sets this property, and any methods that override `buildRendering` should assume this responsibility or else strange, mysterious things may happen. If a dijit doesn't appear on screen, this value resolves to `undefined`.

Just in case you're wondering, here's a simple code snippet with the corresponding Firebug console output that illustrates dijit properties. Again, all of the properties are inherited from `_Widget` and are available via this, when this refers to the context of the associative array that is the third argument to `dojo.declare`:

```
dojo.require("dijit._Widget");
dojo.addOnLoad(function() {
    dojo.declare(
        "dtdg.Foo",
        dijit._Widget,
        {
            talk() : function() {
                console.log("id:", this.id);
                console.log("lang:", this.lang);
                console.log("dir:", this.dir);
                console.log("domNode:", this.domNode);
            }
        }
    );
});
foo = new dtdg.Foo();
foo.talk();
```

Mixing in _Templated

While _Widget provides the foundational stub methods that you can override for creation and destruction events that occur during the lifecycle, _Templated is the previously alluded-to ancestor that actually provides the basis for defining a widget's template in markup and using substitutions and attach points to add functionality to it. Overall, it's a nice separation that lends itself to tooling and separates designer tasks from coding.

The vast majority of _Templated's work involves parsing and substituting into a template file. An important part of this work entails overriding _Widget's buildRendering method, which is where all of the template mangling takes place. Three very important concepts for templates include:

Substitution
> Dijit uses the dojo.string module to perform substitutions into templates using the ${xxx} style dojo.string syntax. This is handy for taking widgets attributes that are passed in on construction and using them to customize templates.

Attach points
> When the special dojoAttachPoint attribute is used in a template node, it provides the ability to directly reference the node via the attribute value. For example, if a node such as <span dojoAttachPoint="foo">...</span> appears in a template, you could directly reference the node as this.foo (in postCreate or later).

Event points
> Similar to attach points, you can use the special dojoAttachEvent attribute to create a relationship between a DOM event for a node in a template and a widget method that should be called when in response to the DOM event. For example, if a node were defined, such as <span dojoAttachEvent="onclick:foo">...</span>, the widget's foo method would be called each time a click occurred on the node. You can define multiple events by separating them with commas.

Like _Widget, _Templated is given more thorough coverage with some isolated examples in just a moment. You're being exposed to it now so that you have a general idea of its overall purpose.

Lifecycle methods

The most notable effect of mixing in _Templated is that it results in overriding _Widget's buildRendering method. Here's a synopsis of buildRendering:

buildRendering
> While _Widget provides this method, _Templated overrides it to handle the messy details associated with fetching and instantiating a dijit's template file for on screen display. Generally speaking, you probably won't implement your own buildRendering method. If you ever do override this method, however, ensure that you fully understand _Templated's implementation first.

Essential properties

Here are _Templated's essential properties:

templatePath
> Provides the relative path to the template file for the dijit, which is simply some HTML. Note that fetching the template for a dijit requires a synchronous network call, although Dojo will cache the template string after it is initially fetched. A discussion of producing a custom build of your dijits with tools from Util so that all template strings are interned is included in Chapter 16.

templateString
> For dijits that have been designed or built to have their template strings interned inside of the JavaScript file, this value represents the template. If both templatePath and templateString are defined, templateString takes precedence.

widgetsInTemplate
> If dijits are defined inside of the template (either path or string), this value should be explicitly set to true so that the Dojo parser will know to search for and instantiate those dijits. This value is false by default. Including dijits inside of other dijit templates can be quite useful. A common mechanism for passing values into child widgets that appear in a parent widget's template is via the ${someWidgetProperty} notation that is used for substitution.

containerNode
> This value refers to the DOM element that maps to the dojoAttachPoint tag in the web page that contains your dijit. It also specifies the element where new children will be added to the dijit if your dijit is acting as a container for a list of child dijits. (Dijits that act as containers multiply inherit from the Dijit _Container class, and the dijits that are contained inherit from the Dijit class _Contained.)

Your First Dijit: HelloWorld

After all of that narrative, you're no doubt ready to see some code in action. This section provides a series of increasingly complex "HelloWorld" examples that demonstrate fundamental concepts involved in custom dijit design.

Let's build a canonical HelloWorld dijit and take a closer look at some of the issues we've discussed. Although this section focuses exclusively on what seems like such a simple dijit, you'll find that there are several intricacies that we'll highlight that are common to developing any dijit.

Figure 12-2 illustrates the basic layout of the HelloWorld dijit as it appears on disk. There are no tricks involved; this is a direct instantiation of the generic layout presented earlier.

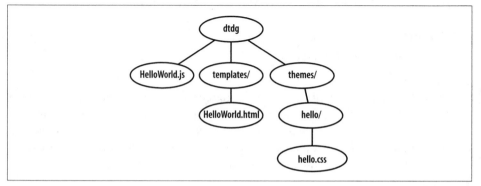

Figure 12-2. Basic layout of a minimalist HelloWorld dijit

HelloWorld Dijit (Take 1: Bare Bones)

The first take on the HelloWorld dijit provides the full body of each component. For brevity and clarity, subsequent iterations provide only relevant portions of components that are directly affected from changes. As far as on disk layout, these examples assume that the main HTML file that includes the widgets is located alongside a *dtdg* module directory that contains the widget code.

HTML page

First, let's take a look at the HTML page that will contain the dijit, shown in Example 12-2. Verbose commenting is inline and should be fairly self-explanatory.

Example 12-2. HelloWorld (Take 1)

```
<html>
  <head>
    <title>Hello World, Take 1</title>

<!--
    Because Dojo is being served from AOL's server, we have to provide a
    couple of extra configuration options in djConfig as the XDomain
    build (dojo.xd.js) gets loaded.

    Thus, we associate the "dtdg" namespace w/ a particular relative path
    on disk by specifying a baseUrl along with a collection of namespace mappings.
    If we were using a local copy of Dojo, we could simply stick the
    dtdg directory beside the dojo directory and it would have been
    found automatically.

    Specifying that dijits on the page should be parsed on page load
    is normally standard for any situation in which you have dojoType tags in the page.

-->
  <script
    type="text/javascript"
    src="http://o.aolcdn.com/dojo/1.1/dojo/dojo.xd.js"
    djConfig=isDebug:true,parseOnLoad:true,baseUrl:'./',modulePaths:{dtdg:'dtdg'}">
  </script>

<!--
    You'll normally include the dojo.css file, followed by
    any of your own specific style sheets. Remember that if you're not using
    AOL's XDomain build, you'll want to point to your own local dojo.css file.
-->
<link
    rel="stylesheet"
    type="text/css"
    href="http://o.aolcdn.com/dojo/1.1/dojo/resources/dojo.css">
</link>

<link
    rel="stylesheet"
    type="text/css"
    href="dtdg/themes/hello/hello.css">
</link>

<script type="text/javascript">

    dojo.require("dojo.parser");

    //Tell Dojo to fetch a dijit called HelloWorld that's associated
    //with the dtdg namespace so that we can use it in the body.
    //Dojo will use the values in djConfig.modulePaths to look up the location.
    dojo.require("dtdg.HelloWorld");
</script>
```

Example 12-2. HelloWorld (Take 1) (continued)

```
</head>
<body>
    <!--
    This is where the Dojo parser swaps in the dijit from the
    dojo.require statement based on our parseOnLoad:true option.
    Any styles applied to the dijit are provided by the style sheets imported.
    -->
    <div dojoType="dtdg.HelloWorld"></div>
</body>
</html>
```

What you just saw is almost the bare minimum that would appear in any page that contains a dijit. There is a token reference to any relevant style sheets that are spiffing up the dijits, the customary reference to Base that bootstraps Dojo, and then we explicitly dojo.require in the parser and HelloWorld dijit we're using in the body of the page. The only remotely tricky thing about any of these things is properly mapping the dtdg module to its path on disk in djConfig.modulePaths.

CSS

A widget's style consists of ordinary CSS and any static support that may be necessary, such as images. The neat thing, however, is that the actual style for the dijit is reflected in the dijit template—not in the DOM element where the dojoType tag is specified. This is particularly elegant because it essentially makes your dijits skinnable, or in Dojo parlance, you can define *themes* for your dijits and change these themes by swapping out stylesheets.

In our example dijit, the style for an individual DIV element is purely pedagogical but does illustrate how you could style your own dijits. Our HelloWorld theme consists of a single CSS file with nothing more than the following style in it:

```
div.hello_class {
    color: #009900;
}
```

Template

Just like the style, our HTML template for the HelloWorld is minimal. We're simply telling Dojo to take the DIV tag that was specified in our HTML page and swap it out with whatever our template supplies—in this case, our template just happens to supply another DIV element with some style and inner text that says "Hello World".

Our actual template file contains nothing more than the following line of HTML:

```
<div class="hello_class">Hello World</div>
```

JavaScript

Although it looks like there's an awful lot going on in the JavaScript, most of the substance is simply extra-verbose commenting. We're still dealing with the basic constructs that have already been reviewed, and you'll see that it's actually pretty simple. Go ahead and have a look, and then we'll recap on the other end. As you'll notice, the JavaScript file is just a standard module:

```
//Summary: An example HelloWorld dijit that illustrates Dojo's basic dijit
//design pattern

//The first line of any module file should have exactly one dojo.provide
//specifying the resource and any membership in parent modules. The name
//of the resource should be the same as the .js file.
dojo.provide("dtdg.HelloWorld");

//Always require resources before you try to use them. We're requiring these
//two resources because they're part of our dijit's inheritance hierarchy.
dojo.require("dijit._Widget");
dojo.require("dijit._Templated");

//The feature rich constructor that allows us to declare Dojo "classes".
dojo.declare(
    "dtdg.HelloWorld",

    //dijit._Widget is the prototypical ancestor that provides important method
    //stubs like the ones below.
    //dijit._Templated is then mixed in and overrides dijit._Widget's
    //buildRendering method, which constructs the UI for the dijit from
    //a template.
    [dijit._Widget, dijit._Templated],
    {
        //Path to the template of this dijit. dijit._Templated uses this to
        //snatch the template from the named file via a synchronous call.
        templatePath: dojo.moduleUrl("dtdg", "templates/HelloWorld.html")
    }
);
```

In the inheritance chain, _Widget provides the prototypical ancestor that our dijit inherits from to become a dijit. Because this first example is minimalist, we didn't need to override any of _Widget's lifecycle methods, but examples that override these methods are coming up. The mixin ancestor, _Templated, provides functionality that pulls in the template by overriding _Widget.buildRendering. The actual template was located via the templatePath property. Although using templatePath instead of templateString incurred the overhead of a synchronous call back to the server, the template gets cached after it has been retrieved. Therefore, another synchronous call would not be necessary if another HelloWorld dijit came to exist in the same page.

The first time Dojo fetches a template file for a dijit, the overhead of a synchronous call back to the server is incurred. Afterward, the template gets cached.

Although this example entails your screen simply displaying a message to the screen, there's a lot more than a print statement behind the scenes that makes this happen. Moreover, the effort involved in HelloWorld is pretty much the minimal amount of effort that would ever be required of any dijit.

Let's solidify your understanding a bit more by filling in some of the method stubs to enhance the dijit. Only instead of taking the direct route, we'll take a few detours. After all, what better way to learn?

HelloWorld Dijit (Take 2: Modifying The Template)

Suppose you want your dijit to be a little less generic. Instead of displaying the same static message every time the page is loaded, a good first step might be to make the custom message that is displayed dynamic. One of the wonderful mechanisms that Dojo employs for keeping the logical concept of a dijit cohesive is that you can reference dijit properties that are defined in your JavaScript source file inside the template. Although referencing dijit properties from inside the template is only useful prior to _Templated's buildRendering method executing, you'll find that initializing some portion of a dijit's display before it appears on the screen is a very common operation.

Referencing a dijit property from inside of the template file is simple. Consider the following revision to the HelloWorld template file:

```
<div class="hello_class">${greeting}</div>
```

In short, you can refer to any property of the dijit that exists from inside of the template file and use it to manipulate the initial display, style, etc. However, there is a small but incredibly important catch: you have to do it at the right time. In particular, dijit properties that are referenced in templates are almost always most appropriately manipulated in the postMixInProperties method. Recall that postMixInProperties is called before buildRendering, which is the point at which your dijit gets inserted into the DOM and becomes visible.

 Recall that the canonical location to manipulate template strings is within the dijit lifecycle method postMixInProperties, which is inherited from _Widget. Manipulating template strings after this point may produce undesirable intermittent display twitches.

Without further ado, Example 12-3 shows how the dijit's JavaScript file should appear if we want to manipulate the properties in the template to display a custom greeting.

Example 12-3. HelloWorld (Take 2: postMixInProperties)

```
//An example of properly manipulating a dijit property referenced
//in a template string via postMixInProperties
dojo.provide("dtdg.HelloWorld");

dojo.require("dijit._Widget");
dojo.require("dijit._Templated");

dojo.declare(
        "dtdg.HelloWorld",
        [dijit._Widget, dijit._Templated],
    {
        greeting : "",

        templatePath: dojo.moduleUrl(
            "dtdg",
            "templates/HelloWorld.html"
        ),

        postMixInProperties: function() {
            //Proper manipulation of properties referenced in templates.
            this.greeting = "Hello World"; //supply as static greeting.
        }
    }
);
```

HelloWorld Dijit (Take 3: Interning the Template)

As alluded to earlier, you can save a synchronous call back to the server by specifying the template string directly inside of your JavaScript file. The next variation on the HelloWorld in Example 12-4 demonstrates just how easy this is to do manually, but keep in mind that the Dojo build scripts found in Util can automate this process for all of your dijits as part of a deployment routine.

Example 12-4. HelloWorld (Take 3: templateString)

```
dojo.provide("dtdg.HelloWorld");
dojo.require("dijit._Widget");
dojo.require("dijit._Templated");

dojo.declare(
```

Example 12-4. HelloWorld (Take 3: templateString) (continued)

```
    "dtdg.HelloWorld",
    [dijit._Widget, dijit._Templated],
    {
        greeting : "",

        //Provide the template string inline like so...
        templateString : "<div class='hello_class'>${greeting}</div>",

        postMixInProperties: function() {
            console.log ("postMixInProperties");

            //We can still manipulate the template string like usual
            this.greeting = "Hello World";
        }
    }
);
```

In this example, templateString provides the template inline, so there's no need for a separate template file. This, in turn, saves a synchronous call to the server. If you can imagine lots of dijits with lots of template strings, it's pretty obvious that baking the template strings into the dijit's JavaScript files can significantly reduce the time it takes to load a page. For production situations, you won't want to do without the Util's build system (Chapter 16) to automate these kinds of performance optimizations for you.

HelloWord Dijit (Take 4: Passing in Parameters)

As yet another improvement to our HelloWorld dijit, let's learn how to pass in custom parameters to dijits through the template. Given the previous example, let's suppose that we want to supply the custom greeting that is to appear in our widget from its markup that appears alongside the dojoType tag. Easy; just pass it in like so:

```
    <div dojoType="dtdg.HelloWorld" greeting="Hello World"></div>
```

Passing in the parameter for a widget that is programmatically created is just as simple:

```
    var hw = new dtdg.HelloWorld({greeting :  "Hello World"}, theWidgetsDomNode);
```

Of course, you are not limited to passing in values that are reflected in the template. You can pass in other parameters that are used in other ways as well. Consider the following DIV element containing a reference to your HelloWorld dijit that specifies two extra key/value pairs:

```
    <div foo="bar" baz="quux" dojoType="dtdg.HelloWorld"></div>
```

Wouldn't it be handy to be able to pass in custom data to dijits like that so that they can use it for initialization purposes—allowing application-level developers to not even have to so much as even peek at the source code and only hack on the template a bit? Well, ladies and gentlemen, you can, and the JavaScript file in Example 12-5 illustrates just how to do it.

Example 12-5. HelloWorld (Take 4: custom parameters)

```
dojo.provide("dtdg.HelloWorld");

dojo.require("dijit._Widget");
dojo.require("dijit._Templated");

dojo.declare(
        "dtdg.HelloWorld",
        [dijit._Widget, dijit._Templated],
    {
        templateString : "<div class='hello_class'>Hello World</div>",

        foo : "",

        //you can't set dijit properties that don't exist
        //baz : "",

        //tags specified in the element that supplies the dojoType tag
        //are passed into the constructor only if they're defined as
        //a dijit property a priori. Thus, the baz="quux" has no effect
        //in this example because the dijit has no property named baz
        constructor: function( ) {

            console.log("constructor: foo=" , this.foo);
            console.log("constructor: baz=" , this.baz);
        }

    }
);
```

As you might have noticed, there's an emphasis on making the point that *you can only pass in values for dijit properties that exist*; you cannot create new dijit properties by tossing in whatever you feel like into the element that contains the dojoType placeholder tag. If you run the previous code example and examine the Firebug console, you'll see the following console output:

```
constructor: foo=bar
constructor: baz=undefined
```

While passing in string values to dijits is useful, string values alone are of limited utility because life is usually just not that simple—but not to worry: Dojo allows you to pass in lists and associative arrays to dijits as well. All that is required is that you define dijit properties as the appropriate type in the JavaScript file, and Dojo takes care of the rest.

The following example illustrates how to pass lists and associative arrays into the dijit through the template.

Including the parameters in the element containing the dojoType tag is straightforward:

```
<div
    foo="[0,20,40]"
    bar="[60,80,100]"
    baz="{'a':'b', 'c':'d'}"
    dojoType="dtdg.HelloWorld"
></div>
```

And the JavaScript file is just as predictable:

```
dojo.provide("dtdg.HelloWorld");

dojo.require("dijit._Widget");
dojo.require("dijit._Templated");

dojo.declare(

        "dtdg.HelloWorld",

        [dijit._Widget, dijit._Templated],

    {
        templateString : "<div class='hello_class'>Hello World</div>",

        foo : [], //cast the value as an array
        bar : "", //cast the value as a String
        baz : {}, //cast the value as an object

        postMixInProperties: function() {
            console.log("postMixInProperties: foo[1]=" , this.foo[1]);
            console.log("postMixInProperties: bar[1]=" , this.bar[1]);
            console.log("postMixInProperties: baz['a']=",  this.baz['a']);
        }

    }
);
```

Here's the output in the Firebug console:

```
postMixInProperties: foo[1]=20
postMixInProperties: bar[1]=6
postMixInProperties: baz['a']=b
```

Note that even though the value associated with the dijit's property bar *appears* to be a list in the page that includes the template, it is defined as a string value in the JavaScript file. Thus, Dojo treats it as a string, and it gets sliced as a string. In general, the parser tries to interpret values into the corresponding types by introspecting them via duck typing.

Take extra-special care not to incorrectly define parameter types in the JavaScript file or it may cost you some debugging time!

HelloWorld Dijit (Take 5: Associating Events with Dijits)

As yet another variation on our HelloWorld dijit, consider the utility in associating a DOM event such as a mouse click or mouse hover with the dijit. Dojo makes associating events with dijits easy. You simply specify key/value pairs of the form DOMEvent: dijitMethod inside of a dojoAttachEvent tag that appears as a part of your template. You may specify multiple key/value pairs or more than one kind of native DOM event by separating them with a comma.

Let's illustrate how to use dojoAttachEvent by applying a particular style that's defined as a class in a stylesheet whenever a mouseover event occurs and remove the style whenever a mouseout event occurs. Because DIV elements span the width of the frame, we'll modify it to be an inline SPAN, so that the mouse event is triggered only when the cursor is directly over the text. Let's apply the pointer style to the cursor.

The changes to the style are simple. We change the reference to an inline SPAN instead of a DIV and change the mouse cursor to a pointer:

```
span.hello_class {
    cursor: pointer;
    color: #009900;
}
```

The JavaScript file in Example 12-6 includes the updated template string, illustrating that the use of dojoAttachEvent is fairly straightforward as well.

Example 12-6. HelloWorld (Take 5: dojoAttachEvent)

```
dojo.provide("dtdg.HelloWorld");

dojo.require("dijit._Widget");
dojo.require("dijit._Templated");

dojo.declare(
        "dtdg.HelloWorld",
        [dijit._Widget, dijit._Templated],
    {
        templateString :
        "<span class='hello_class' dojoAttachEvent='onmouseover:onMouseOver, onmouseout:
        onMouseOut'>Hello World</span>",

        onMouseOver : function(evt) {
            dojo.addClass(this.domNode, 'hello_class');
            console.log("applied hello_class...");
```

Example 12-6. HelloWorld (Take 5: dojoAttachEvent) (continued)

```
        console.log(evt);
    },

    onMouseOut : function(evt) {
        dojo.removeClass(this.domNode, 'hello_class');
        console.log("removed hello_class...");
        console.log(evt);
    }

  }
);
```

See how easy that was? When you trigger an `onmouseover` event over the text in the SPAN element, style is applied with the `dojo.addClass` function, which is defined in Base. Then, when you trigger an `onmouseout` event, the style is removed. Neat stuff!

Did you also notice that the event handling methods included an evt parameter that passes in highly relevant event information? As you might have guessed, internally, `dojo.connect` is at work standardizing the event object for you. Here's the Firebug output that appears when you run the code, which also illustrates the event information that gets passed into your dijit's event handlers:

```
applied hello_class...
mouseover  clientX=64, clientY=11
removed hello_class clientX=65, clientY=16
mouseover  clientX=65, clientY=16
```

 Take care not to misspell the names of native DOM events, and ensure that native DOM event names stay in all lowercase. For example, using ONMOUSEOVER or onMouseOver won't work for the onmouseover DOM event, and unfortunately, Firebug can't give you any indication that anything is wrong. Because you can name your dijit event handling methods whatever you want (with whatever capitalization you want), this can sometimes be easy to forget.

To be perfectly clear, note that the previous example's mapping of onmouseover to onMouseOver and onmouseout to onMouseOut is purely a simple convention, although it does make good sense and results in highly readable code. Also, it is important to note that events such as onmouseover and onmouseout are *DOM events*, while onMouseOver and onMouseOut are *methods associated with a particular dijit*. The distinction may not immediately be clear because the naming reads the same, but it is an important concept that you'll need to internalize during your quest for Dijit mastery. The semantics between the two are similar and different in various respects.

Parent-Child Relationships with _Container and _Contained

After you've been rolling with _Widget and _Templated for a while, it won't be long before you find that it's convenient to have a widget that contains some children widgets. The "has-a relationship" pattern is quite common in programming and it is no different with Dojo. The _Container and _Contained mixins are designed to facilitate the referencing back and forth between parents and children that often needs to happen. Table 12-1 summarizes the API.

Table 12-1. _Container and _Contained mixins

Name	Comment
removeChild(/*Object*/ dijit)	Removes the child widget from the parent. (Silently fails if the widget is not a child or if the container does not have any children.)
addChild(/*Object*/ dijit, /*Integer?*/ insertIndex)	Adds a child widget to the parent, optionally using the insertIndex to place it.
getParent()	Allows a child to reference its parent. Returns a dijit instance.
getChildren()	Allows a parent to conveniently enumerate each of its children dijits. Returns an Array of dijit instances.
getPreviousSibling()	Allows a child widget to reference its previous sibling, i.e., the one "to the left." Returns a dijit instance.
getNextSibling()	Allows a child widget to reference its next sibling, i.e., the one "to the right." Returns a dijit instance.

You'll see these mixins used extensively when you learn about the layout dijits. Next, we'll look at an example.

Rapidly Prototyping Widgets in Markup

Now that you have a feel for exactly how the widget lifecycle works and have seen plenty of examples, it's time to demonstrate a tool that you can use for quick, lightweight prototyping. Declaration is a Dijit resource that allows you to declare a widget in markup without resorting to a separate JavaScript file; this approach can be a tremendous boon during a development cycle when you need to rapidly capture or test out an idea.

Example 12-7 shows our very first HelloWorld widget using Declaration to create a widget in a completely self-contained page.

Example 12-7. HelloWorld (Take 6: Declaration)

```html
<html>
    <head>
        <title>Hello World, Take 6</title>

        <script
            type="text/javascript"
            src="http://o.aolcdn.com/dojo/1.1/dojo/dojo.xd.js"
            djConfig="isDebug:true,parseOnLoad:true">
        </script>

        <link
            rel="stylesheet"
            type="text/css"
            href="http://o.aolcdn.com/dojo/1.1/dojo/resources/dojo.css">
        </link>

        <!-- define your CSS inline -->
        <style type="text/css">
            span.hello_class {
                color: #009900;
                cursor: pointer;
            }
        </style>

        <script type="text/javascript">
            dojo.require("dijit.Declaration");
            dojo.require("dojo.parser");
        </script>
    </head>
    <body>

        <!-- delcare the widget completely in markup -->
        <div
            dojoType="dijit.Declaration"
            widgetClass="dtdg.HelloWorld"
            defaults="{greeting:'Hello World'}">
                <span class="hello_class"
                dojoAttachEvent='onmouseover:onMouseOver, onmouseout:onMouseOut'>
                    ${greeting}
                </span>

                <script type="dojo/method" event="onMouseOver" args="evt">
                    dojo.addClass(this.domNode, 'hello_class');
                    console.log("applied hello_class...");
                    console.log(evt);
                </script>

                <script type="dojo/method" event="onMouseOut" args="evt">
                    dojo.removeClass(this.domNode, 'hello_class');
                    console.log("removed hello_class...");
                    console.log(evt);
```

Example 12-7. HelloWorld (Take 6: Declaration) (continued)

```
            </script>
    </div>

    <!-- now include it into the page like usual -->
    <div dojoType="dtdg.HelloWorld"></div>
    </body>
</html>
```

Hopefully you made the immediate connection that Declaration is *terrific* for quickly working up an example with no hassle. There's no switching between and keeping track of multiple files, declaring module paths, and otherwise spending time on anything except the core task—so you can stay focused on the task at hand and get your work done as effectively as possible. Table 12-2 shows the Declaration API.

Table 12-2. Attributes of Declaration

Attribute	Comment
widgetClass	The widget's class
defaults	Attribute values that you'd normally pass in as parameters for construction
mixins	An Array that defines any mixin ancestors

 The mixins attribute for a Declaration declared in markup must be an Array. This is different from dojo.declare, which allows for the possibility of either an Object ancestor or an Array of Object ancestors.

You'll generally want to refactor the work you do with Declaration after your idea settles, but there's really no faster way to mock-up a good idea in a hurry.

Summary

After reading this chapter, you should:

• Be able to explain how dijits encapsulate the HTML, CSS, and JavaScript into a standalone, portable unit of code

• Understand the key lifecycle events that _Widget provides with stub methods, including the order they execute and the stubs they provide

• Understand how _Templated acts as a mixin ancestor for _Widget and provides supplemental functionality for adding template support to dijits

• Understand the differences and trade-offs between using templatePath and templateString in templated dijits

• Be able to successfully manipulate a dijit's template before it is displayed on screen

• Be able to pass in parameters to dijits through their templates

- Be able to programmatically create a widget and place it into the page
- Know how to add support for DOM events such as onmouseover in your dijits
- Be able to use Declaration to rapidly prototype in markup

A discussion of form widgets is next.

## CHAPTER 13

Form Widgets

This chapter provides systematic coverage of the various dijits that enable you to create fantastic-looking forms with minimal effort. Like everything in Dijit, the controls you'll learn about in this chapter can be defined entirely in markup, require very little JavaScript, and were designed with accessibility considerations in mind. With that said, realize that you're about to embark upon reading a very hefty chapter. The functionality offered by `dijit.form` is quite intense, packing tons of breadth and depth; the form dijits are by far the most object-oriented widgets in the toolkit, so you'll see deeper inheritance hierarchies via `dojo.declare` in this chapter than anywhere else in the book.

Drive-By Form Review

While the HTML 4.01 specification (*http://www.w3.org/TR/html401/*) provides the authoritative specification on forms and is quite worthy of careful reading on its own, this section attempts to summarize some of the most useful content about forms that will help you to get the most out of this chapter. If you're reading this book, a working assumption is that you've designed a form or two, so it is not necessary to belabor fact that a *form* is a collection of one or more controls that capture information and send it back to a server for processing.

However, it is noteworthy to highlight that the AJAX revolution has really skewed the paradigm of passing data to a server for processing. Previously, data would be submitted to a server handler that broke it into convenient key/value pairs, used these hashes as part of a processing routine, and then returned a new page that somehow reflected these form choices. To make the whole process more elegant, the form might have even been included in an `iframe` so that the effect of the page reload would be minimized. Now, however, the `XMLHttpRequest` (XHR) object makes it easy to asynchronously send small chunks of data to a server without an explicit form submission or a page reload of any kind.

Of course, the XHR object, AJAX, and slicker ways of interacting with the user certainly don't make forms obsolete. Forms are still a battle-tested standard; they work even when JavaScript is disabled, and they are important for accessible implementations. In general, it's almost always a good idea to make sure that any fancy way of passing information back to the server is degradable and accessible. In other words, it isn't a matter of "either forms or AJAX"; it's a matter of "both forms and AJAX."

For example, consider Example 13-1, an enhanced version of the plain vanilla form from Chapter 1.

Example 13-1. Simple form

```html
<html>
    <head>
        <title>Register for Spam</title>
        <script type="text/javascript">
            function help() {
                var msg="Basically, we want to sell your info to a 3rd party.";
                alert(msg);
                return false;
            }

            //simple validation
            function validate() {
                var f = document.getElementById("registration_form");

                if (f.first.value == "" || f.last.value == "" || f.email.value == "") {
                    alert("All fields are required.");
                    return false;
                }

                return true;
            }
        </script>
    <head>
    <body>
        <p>Just Use the form below to sign-up for our great offers:</p>
        <form id="registration_form"
            method="POST"
            onsubmit="javascript:return validate()"
            action="http://localhost:8080/register/">

            First Name: <input type="text"  name="first"/><br>
            Last Name: <input type="text" name="last"/><br>
            Your Email: <input type="text" name="email"/><br>
            <button type="submit">Sign Up!</button>
            <button type="reset">Reset</button>
            <button type="button" onclick="javascript:help()">Help</button>

        </form>
    </body>
</html>
```

While as bland as it can possibly get, this form is quite functional, and would behave properly on virtually any browser; the incorporation of a nice CSS stylesheet could make it look quite nice. There's even a Help button to tell the user why the form *really* exists. On the server side, a simple script would process the form, probably after a web server has already distilled the named fields in the form out of their raw format. A functional CherryPy script might process the form, as in Example 13-2.

Example 13-2. CherryPy script to process a form

```
import cherrypy
class Content:
    """
    A routine for processing a form submission.
    Named form fields are easily accessible.
    """

    @cherrypy.expose
    def register(self, first=None, last=None, email=None):

        #add user information to evil database here...

        #send back this customized html page
        return """
        <html>
            <head><title>You're now on our spam list!</title></head>
            <body>
                <p>Congratulations %s %s, you're gonna get spammed!</p>
            </body>
        </html>
        """ % (first, last) #substitute in variables

cherrypy.quickstart(Content( ))
```

While extremely simple, the previous example did touch on several fundamentals regarding forms:

- Forms controls should be enclosed in a FORM tag.
- The FORM tag almost always includes name, method, onsubmit, enctype, and action attributes that provide pertinent information about how the form should be processed.
- The onsubmit attribute is the standard way of performing client-side validation. Returning false from a validation routine prevents the form from being submitted to the server.
- The action attribute provides the URL for submitting the form.
- Form fields that represent meaningful state should include a name attribute, which is what most server-side frameworks will collect into key/value pairs and pass to the specific routine that handles the form submission.

- Forms are innately accessible with the keyboard; tabs move between fields* and the Enter key submits the form. Although not demonstrated, the tabindex attribute can change the default tab order.

- In general, there are multiple kinds of controls, as specified by the type attribute. This particular example illustrated three different kinds of buttons: one for triggering the onsubmit event, one for resetting the form, and one for handling a custom action.

- Submitting a form necessarily reloads the page with whatever the server returns if an action attribute is provided in the form. If no action attribute is provided, custom JavaScript or DHTML actions could be taken by attaching scripts to DOM events such as onlick.

 Throughout this chapter, the term "attribute" is frequently used to describe both form attributes and object attributes. The intended usage should be apparent from context and is not anything to get hung up over.

While nowhere near exhaustive, hopefully this brief review sets the stage for a discussion of the various form dijits. For a great desktop reference on HTML forms, consider picking up *HTML & XHTML: The Definitive Guide* by Chuck Musciano and Bill Kennedy (O'Reilly).

Form Dijits

Form dijits that are explicitly declared suitable for use in bona fide HTML forms, as defined with the FORM tag, are a part of the dijit.form namespace. This section walks through all of the dijits included in this namespace, providing example code and sample screenshots that use Dijit's built-in *tundra* theme. But first, it's worth reiterating that all form dijits are designed to be fully degradable and accessible; in other words, they remain fully functional even if JavaScript, CSS, and images aren't available, and if a keyboard is the only input device available. Accessibility attributes on Windows environments also support high-contrast mode and screen readers.

Figure 13-1 shows the general inheritance structure of the dijit.form module. The diagram does not show every single mixin class along the way, but does convey the general relationships amongst the widgets. The hope is that you'll be able to use it to get a better idea of how the source code is laid out when it comes time to cut your teeth on it.

---

* Mac OS X Firefox 2.0+ users may need to download the Configuration Mania add-on at *https://addons. mozilla.org/en-US/firefox/addon/4420* to enable tabbing into buttons.

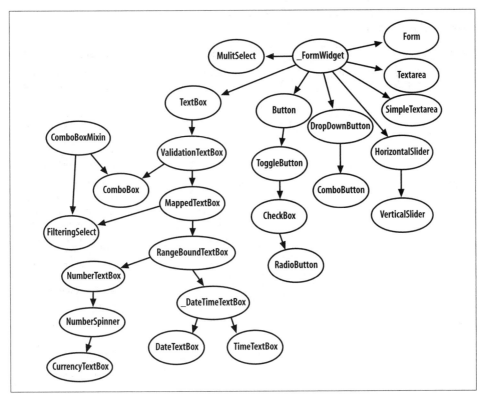

Figure 13-1. The inheritance-rich dijit.form module

In addition to the standard dijit attributes inherited from _Widget, such as domNode, et al., and ordinary HTML attributes included in the HTML 4.01 spec, such as disabled and tabIndex, form dijits all inherit from a base class that explicitly supports the attributes, methods, and extension points listed in Table 13-1.

Table 13-1. Supported attributes, methods, and extension points for form dijits via _FormWidget

Name	Data type	Category	Comment
value	String	Attribute	The current value of the dijit; works just like its pure-HTML equivalent.
name	String	Attribute	The named value for the dijit; works just like its pure-HTML equivalent; useful for form submissions to a server handler.

*Table 13-1. Supported attributes, methods, and extension points for form dijits via
_FormWidget (continued)*

Name	Data type	Category	Comment
alt	String	Attribute	Alternate text that should appear should the browser not be able to display—a somewhat uncommon event for forms, although still common enough for images; works just like its pure-HTML equivalent.
type	String	Attribute	Specifies the type of the element when more than one kind is possible. For example, a button might have type="submit" to trigger the form's onsubmit action; works just like its pure-HTML equivalent. By default, this attribute is "text".
tabIndex	Integer	Attribute	Used to provide an explicit tab index for keyboard navigation; works just like its HTML equivalent. By default, this attribute is "0".
disabled	Boolean	Attribute	Disables a control so that it cannot receive focus and is skipped in tabbing navigation; do not attempt to use this attribute on an element that does not support it, which per the HTML 4.01 spec include button, input, optgroup, option, select, and textarea. Controls that are disabled are not included in form submissions. This attribute is false by default.

Table 13-1. Supported attributes, methods, and extension points for form dijits via
_FormWidget (continued)

Name	Data type	Category	Comment
readOnly	Boolean	Attribute	Disables a control so that its value cannot be changed; however, it can still receive focus, is included in tabbing navigation, and is included in form submissions. Do not attempt to use this attribute on an element that does not support it, which per the HTML 4.01 spec include input and textarea. This attribute is false by default.
intermediateChanges	Boolean	Attribute	Whether to fire the onChange extension point for each value change. This attribute is false by default.
setAttribute (/* String */ attr, /* Any */ value)	Function	Method	The proper way to set an attribute value for a dijit. For example, setting a dijit's value attribute to "foo" would be accomplished via `<dijit name>.setAttribute ("value", "foo")`.
focus( )	Function	Method	Sets the focus on the control.
isFocusable( )	Function	Method	Returns information about whether the control can receive focus.
forWaiValuenow( )	Function	Extension point	By default, returns the current state of the widget to be used for the WAI-ARIA valuenow state, which may be set via dijit.removeState and dijit.setWaiState.
onChange(/* Any */ val)	Function	Extension point	Override to provide a custom callback function that fires each time the value changes.

For great online documentation on HTML 4.01 forms, see *http://www. w3.org/TR/html401/interact/forms.html.*

TextBox Variations

Ordinary text input via the HTML input element is by far the most commonly used form field. Countless hours have been spent formatting and validating what are generally small snippets of text, and the auxiliary scripts that have supported input boxes may single-handedly account for the most collective boilerplate that's even been written to support web pages. If any one of those comments resonates deep within your soul, the Dijit TextBox family will seem like a godsend.

Let's take a look at each member of the TextBox family and improve our example form from earlier in this chapter. The most basic member is the ordinary TextBox itself, which comes packed with several custom formatting operations as well as the ability to create your own using the format and parse extension points. The following listing summarizes TextBox's attributes and extension points. A TextBox is technically a kind of input element, so remember that the standard HTML attributes, if not listed here, still apply.

 TextBox's attributes and extension points are inherited by all other dijits in this family; they are especially important to be aware of because they are widely used.

TextBox

Table 13-2 provides a listing of pertinent features to the most basic TextBox dijit.

Table 13-2. TextBox attributes and extension points

Name	Category	Comment
trim	Attribute	Removes leading and trailing whitespace. This attribute is false by default.
uppercase	Attribute	Converts all characters to uppercase. This attribute is false by default.
lowercase	Attribute	Converts all characters to lowercase. This attribute is false by default.
propercase	Attribute	Converts the first character of each word to uppercase. This attribute is false by default.
maxLength	Attribute	Used for passing through the standard HTML input tag's maxlength attribute. This attribute is "" by default.

Table 13-2. TextBox attributes and extension points (continued)

Name	Category	Comment
`format(/* String */ value, /*Object*/constraints)`	Extension point	A replaceable function to convert a value to a properly formatted `String` value. The default implementation returns the result of a value's `toString` method if it has one; otherwise, it returns the raw value as a last resort. Returns an empty string for `null` or `undefined` values.
`parse(/* String */ value)`	Extension point	May be used to provide a custom parsing function to convert a formatted `String` to a value, a function that is common to all form dijits, before returning the value. The default implementation returns the raw `String` value.
`setValue(/*String*/value)`	Method	Used to set the `String` value for a `TextBox` and any subclass of `TextBox`. Do not use the `_FormWidget`'s `setAttribute('value', /*…*/)` function for this subclass hierarchy.
`getValue()`	Method	Used to fetch the `String` value for a `TextBox` and any subclass of `TextBox`. Do not access the value property directly and sidestep this method.

As of version 1.1, _FormWidget's setValue and getValue methods were deprecated in favor of using the setAttribute('value', /*...*/) function for setting values and getting values via the .value property where appropriate. TextBox, its subclasses, and a few other dijits, however, override the setValue and getValue methods for legitimate use. The rule of thumb is that setValue and getValue are used for *widget values*. For example, a TextBox has an obvious value (hence, the use of setValue and getValue), whereas you would use the setAttribute method for something like a Button because it does not have a widget value even though a value is submitted with the form.

To illustrate the most basic usage possible, Example 13-3 plugs some text boxes into our earlier form example, and switches on the propercase and trim attributes for the first and last fields in the form.

Example 13-3. Updated form with TextBox and theming

```
<html>
    <head>
        <title>Register for Spam</title>

        <link rel="stylesheet" type="text/css"
          href="http://o.aolcdn.com/dojo/1.1/dojo/resources/dojo.css" />
        <link rel="stylesheet" type="text/css"
          href="http://o.aolcdn.com/dojo/1.1/dijit/themes/tundra/tundra.css" />

        <script
            djConfig="parseOnLoad:true",
            type="text/javascript"
```

Example 13-3. Updated form with TextBox and theming (continued)

```
        src="http://o.aolcdn.com/dojo/1.1/dojo/dojo.xd.js">
    </script>

    <script type="text/javascript">
        dojo.require("dojo.parser");
        dojo.require("dijit.form.TextBox");

        function help() {
            var msg="Basically, we want to sell your info to a 3rd party.";
            alert(msg);
            return false;
        }

        //simple validation
        function validate() {
            var f = document.getElementById("registration_form");

            if (f.first.value == "" ||
                f.last.value == "" ||
                f.email.value == "") {
                    alert("All fields are required.");
                    return false;
            }

            return true;
        }
    </script>
<head>
<body class="tundra">
    <p>Just Use the form below to sign-up for our great offers:</p>
    <form id="registration_form"
        method="POST"
        onsubmit="javascript:return validate()"
        action="http://localhost:8080/register/">

        First Name:
          <input dojoType="dijit.form.TextBox" propercase=true
           trim=true name="first"><br>
        Last Name:
          <input dojoType="dijit.form.TextBox" propercase=true
           trim=true name="last"><br>
        Your Email:
        <input dojoType="dijit.form.TextBox" length=25 name="email"><br>
        <button type="submit">Sign Up!</button>
        <button type="reset">Reset</button>
        <button type="button" onclick="javascript:help()">Help</button>
    </form>
</body>
</html>
```

If you try to use dijits without properly including the *dojo.css* file and the relevant theme, your dijits may still be accessible—but they'll also look horrible. A common frustration with beginners to Dijit is either forgetting to load the CSS or forgetting to set the appropriate class attribute in the BODY tag.

In addition to the TextBox dijit improving the appearance of the control, it also saves you the work of implementing a dozen or so lines of custom scripting. Of course, you could override the format extension point to implement your own custom formatting by simply defining a JavaScript function and passing it into format. For example, the following formatting function would take a string and turn it into *MiXeD CaPiTaLiZaTiOn* like so:

```
function mixedCapitalization(value) {
    var newValue = "";
    var upper = true;

    dojo.forEach(value.toLowerCase(), function(x) {
        if (upper)
            newValue += x.toUpperCase();
        else
            newValue += x;

        upper = !upper;
    });

    return newValue;

}
```

Using the function in the TextBox dijit is just as easy as it should be:

```
<input dojoType="dijit.form.TextBox" format="mixedCapitalization"
    trim=true name="first">
```

If you interact with the form and cause a blur event by moving the cursor out of it, you'll see the conversion take place. The parse function may be overridden in the very same manner as format to standardize values when they are returned. Common operations include converting numeric types into Number values, or standardizing String values.

 The custom format and parse extension points are invoked every time a setValue or getValue operation is called—not just in response to explicit user interaction with the form.

ValidationTextBox

One thing that's probably on your mind is that pesky validation function that ensures the fields are not empty—and the fact that it wasn't all that great in the first place since it didn't validate an email address properly. ValidationTextBox to the rescue!

Table 13-3 includes a complete listing of additional functionality that ValidationTextBox offers.

Table 13-3. Attributes of ValidationTextBox

Name	Type	Comment
required	Boolean	Attribute that determines whether the field is required. If left empty when this attribute is set, the field cannot be valid. false by default.
promptMessage	String	Attribute used to define a hint for the field when the field has the cursor.
invalidMessage	String	Attribute that provides the message to display if the field is invalid.
constraints	Object	Attribute that provides a user-defined object that can be defined to (dynamically, if necessary) feed constraints to the regExpGen attribute. This object is used extensively for other dijits such as DateTextBox to provide custom formats for display.
regExp	String	Attribute that provides a regular expression to be used for validation. Do not define this attribute if regExpGen is defined. By default this attribute is ".*" (a regular expression that allows anything/everything).
regExpGen	Function	Attribute that denotes a user-replaceable function that may be used to generate a custom regular expression that is dependent upon the key/value pairs in the constraints attribute; useful for dynamic situations. Do not define this attribute if regExp is defined. By default, this attribute is a function that returns ".*" (a regular expression that allows anything/everything).
tooltipPosition	Array	Attribute used to define whether the tooltip should appear above, below, to the left, or to the right of the control. By default, this attribute returns the value of dijit.Tooltip.defaultPosition, which is defined internally to the dijit.Tooltip widget.
isValid()	Function	Method that calls the validator extension point to perform validation, returning a Boolean value.
validator(/* String */ value, /* Object */ constraints)	Function	Extension point that is called by onblur, oninit, and onkeypress DOM events.
displayMessage(/* String */ message)	Function	Extension point that may be overridden to customize the display of validation errors or hints. By default uses a dijit.Tooltip.

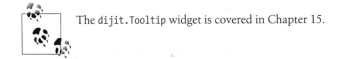 The dijit.Tooltip widget is covered in Chapter 15.

Drop-in usage for a ValiationTextBox in our example is as straightforward as adding required attributes to the various controls and tacking on an additional regex to validate the email address. The change in Example 13-4 incorporates a ValidationTextBox and eliminates the need for all of the JavaScript that was previously written; the Help button was also removed now that a tooltip more elegantly accomplishes that purpose.

Example 13-4. Updated form to use ValidationTextBox

```
<html>
    <head>
        <title>Register for Spam</title>

        <link rel="stylesheet" type="text/css"
          href="http://o.aolcdn.com/dojo/1.1/dojo/resources/dojo.css" />
        <link rel="stylesheet" type="text/css"
          href="http://o.aolcdn.com/dojo/1.1/dijit/themes/tundra/tundra.css" />

        <script
            djConfig="parseOnLoad:true",
            type="text/javascript"
            src="http://o.aolcdn.com/dojo/1.1/dojo/dojo.xd.js">
        </script>

        <script type="text/javascript">
            dojo.require("dojo.parser");
            dojo.require("dijit.form.ValidationTextBox");
        </script>

        <!-- lots of ugly JavaScript was removed -->

    <head>
    <body class="tundra">
        <p>Just Use the form below to sign-up for our great offers:</p>
        <form  id="registration_form"
            method="POST"
            action="http://localhost:8080/register/">

            First Name:
            <input dojoType="dijit.form.ValidationTextBox"
              properCase="true" trim=true required="true"
              invalidMessage="Required." name="first"><br>

            Last Name:
            <input dojoType="dijit.form.ValidationTextBox"
              properCase="true" trim=true required="true"
              invalidMessage="Required." name="last"><br>
```

Example 13-4. Updated form to use ValidationTextBox (continued)

```
        Your Email:
        <input dojoType="dijit.form.ValidationTextBox"
          promptMessage="Basically, we want to sell your info to a 3rd party."
          regExp="[a-z0-9._%+-]+@[a-z0-9-]+\.[a-z]{2,4}"  required
          name="email"><br>

        <button type="submit">Sign Up!</button>
        <button type="reset">Reset</button>
        <!-- tooltip message replaced need for help button -->

      </form>
    </body>
</html>
```

And with very little effort, you suddenly have richer, better-looking functionality, with less code to maintain.

We still need to do some work to those buttons in the next section, but first, let's work through the remaining members of the TextBox family.

MappedTextBox and RangeBoundTextBox

Two well-defined form dijit classes that are not covered in this chapter include MappedTextBox and RangeBoundTextBox. Basically, MappedTextBox provides some methods for serializing its data into a String value via a custom toString method, and RangeBoundTextBox facilitates ensuring that a value is within a specified range by allowing you to pass in max and min values to the constraints object. Although it might intuitively seem like the "validation" in ValidationTextBox should be handling tasks like range checking, keep in mind that ValidationCheckBox uses regular expressions to validate String values. RangeBoundTextBox explicitly deals with numeric types.

In short, these two classes provide some intermediate machinery that is used to enable the remaining form dijits in this chapter and are in place largely to facilitate the internal design. While you may want to be aware of these two classes if you plan on creating a highly custom form dijit, they are not really intended for general-purpose consumption.

TimeTextBox and DateTextBox

Custom validation routines for validating dates and times are another implementation detail that just about any web developer who has been around a while has had to produce at some point or another. Although dates and times have well-defined formats that are quite universal, the ultra-generic HTML INPUT element offers no support, and the load is pushed off to JavaScript for validation and custom formatting. Fortunately, Dijit makes picking dates and times just as easy as it should be. These dijits are also preconfigured to work with the most common locales, and extending them beyond the stock locale collection is straightforward.

The DateTextBox and TimeTextBox dijits use the Gregorian calendar, which is the default for the dojo.date facilities.

Let's suppose that instead of spamming you, an organization would instead like to bother you over the telephone once you get home from a long, hard day of work. Naturally, they would like to collect information from you ahead of time so as to avoid any unnecessary overhead of their own. Assuming they're smart enough to be using Dojo to minimize costs on the programming budget, they might produce some form fields like so:

```
<!-- Remember to dojo.require these dijits before using them! -->

Best Day to call:
<input dojoType="dijit.form.DateTextBox"><br>

Best Time to call:
<input dojoType="dijit.form.TimeTextBox"><br>
```

That's it! No additional effort is required. The DateTextBox in Figure 13-2 automatically pops up a beautiful little calendar for picking a date when the cursor enters the INPUT element, and a scrolling list containing times, broken into 15-minute increments, appears for the TimeTextBox in Figure 13-3.

Figure 13-2. The DateTextBox pop up that appears

As a reminder, programmatic creation is just as simple:

```
var t = new dijit.form.TimeTextBox();
var d = new dijit.form.DateTextBox();

/* now place them in the page via their domNode attribute*/
```

In addition to ease of use, these dijits allow for customized formatting of their displayed values—allowing you to do anything that you could do via dojo.date, which they use internally. Specifically, the formatLength, timePattern, and datePattern attributes may be specified within the constraints object to produce the corresponding effect.

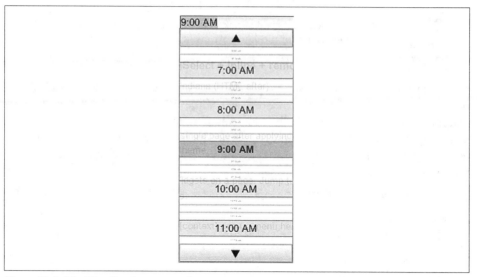

Figure 13-3. The TimeTextBox popup that appears

Zulu, Greenwich, Gregorian…What?!?

This chapter has been throwing around a lot of terms that you may have heard of but never quite got around to looking up. Here's the abbreviated version to partially satisfy your curiosity:

- Zulu time refers to the UTC (Coordinated Universal Time) time zone, which is local to parts of Western Europe and is said to originate from the Greenwich Observatory in London. This time zone has historically been denoted with the letter Z, and, as it turns out, the phonetic alphabet that the military and other organizations use maps the word Zulu in place of the letter Z when reading out alphanumeric codes (so as not to confuse letters that sound alike).

- Greenwich Mean Time is essentially the same thing as UTC, as far as time zones are concerned.

- The Gregorian calendar is named after Pope Gregory XIII, who decreed it in the late 1500s as a reform to the Julian calendar (as decreed by Julius Caesar as a reform to the Roman calendar in the first Century), which was slightly too long and was causing issues with the Christian holiday of Easter drifting forward in time with respect to the seasons.

Tables 13-4 and 13-5 summarize the various options available. In general, either the format length or one of the time or date patterns are specified, depending on the degree of granularity desired.

Table 13-4. Attributes for DateTextBox

Attribute	Comment

formatLength	Used to format a value for the default locale. Valid values are full, long, medium, or short. Custom values for specific locales are honored. Examples for the en-us locale include:
	
	full
	  Thursday, January 10, 2008
	
	long
	  January 10, 2008
	
	medium
	  Jan 10, 2008
	
	short *(default)*
	  1/16/2008

datePattern	Used to provide a custom format for all locales. Accepts a string formatted according to Java-like conventions. See *http://www.w3.org/TR/NOTE-datetime*. Common values with examples include:
	
	yyyy
	  2008
	
	yyyy-MM
	  2008-01
	
	MMM dd, yyyy
	  Jan 08, 2008

strict	When true, allows for slight relaxations of some abbreviations and whitespace. This attribute is false by default.
locale	Allows for overriding the default locale for this specific widget only. Be sure to configure the extra local via djConfig.extraLocale or you may receive an error or unexpected results.
selector	When submitting a form, the value of selector determines whether the date, the time, or both get passed with the submission, even though only a date or time is visible as a displayed value. By default, both are passed, specifying either date or time accordingly.

Table 13-5. Attributes for TimeTextBox

Attribute	Comment
clickableIncrement	A String representing the amount every clickable element in the time picker should increase. This value should be set in non-Zulu time without a time zone and divide visibleIncrement evenly. For example, the default value of "T00:15:00" would denote a 15-minute increment.
visibleIncrement	A String representing the increment that should visibly provide a text value indicating a time increment. The default value of "T01::00:00" creates text in one-hour increments. This value should be set in non-Zulu time without a time zone.
visibleRange	A String representing the time range to display. This default value is "T05:00:00", which is five hours of time. This value should be set in non-Zulu time without a time zone.

Table 13-5. Attributes for TimeTextBox (continued)

Attribute	Comment
formatLength	A String value used to format a value for the default locale. Valid values are long and short. Custom values for specific locales are honored. Examples for the en-us locale include: long 10:00:00PM CST short 10:00 PM
timePattern	Used to provide a custom format for all locales. Accepts a string formatted according to Java-like conventions. See *http://www.w3.org/TR/NOTE-datetime*. Common values with examples include: hh:mm 08:00 h:mm 8:00 h:mm a 8:00 PM HH:mm 22:00 hh:mm:ss 08:00:00 hh:mm:ss.SSS 08:00:00.000
strict	When true, allows for slight relaxations of some abbreviations (am versus a.m., etc.) and whitespace. This attribute is false by default.
locale	Allows for overriding the default locale for this specific widget only. Be sure to configure the extra local via djConfig.extraLocale or you may receive an error or unexpected results.
selector	When submitting a form, the value of selector determines whether the date, the time, or both get passed with the submission, even though only a date or time is visible as a displayed value. By default, both are passed, specifying either date or time accordingly.

In markup, the constraints object is provided like any other attribute:

```
<input constraints="{datePattern:'MMM dd, yyyy'}" dojoType="dijit.form.DateTextBox">
```

Just like always, the programmatic approach is a direct translation:

```
var d = new dijit.form.DateTextBox({datePattern:'MMM dd, yyyy'});
```

Commonalities between DateTextBox and TimeTextBox

Two additional methods that are available for TimeTextBox and DateTextBox are getDisplayedValue and setDisplayedValue. The difference between these methods and the ordinary getValue and setValue approaches involves the difference in what is actually displayed in the dijit versus what data type is used internally by the dijit. Both TimeTextBox and DateTextBox use JavaScript Date objects internally, and getting this Date object is just one method call away.

Recall that the machinery inherited from RangeBoundTextBox also allows for min and max values to be provided, which is highly useful for preventing a user from ever selecting an invalid value from the pop up. For example, to constrain a date from December 1, 2007 through June 30, 2008:

```
<input constraints="{min:'2007-12', max:'2008-06', datePattern:'MMM dd, yyyy'}"
dojoType="dijit.form.DateTextBox">
```

Additionally, MappedTextBox wires in facilities for serialization via the toString method; you can also get an ISO-8601 compliant string if you should need one, which can be quite useful for sending back to the server.

 It's important to understand the duality between datePattern, timePattern, and the ISO-8601 specification: basically, there isn't a connection. The datePattern and timePattern values are used for opaquely manipulating user-visible formatting for widgets, while the ISO-8601 formatting is what the parser accepts and sends to the server for processing.

Two additional methods provided by these two dijits include getDisplayedValue and setDisplayedValue. While setDisplayedValue produces the same results as setAttribute('value', /*...*/), getDisplayedValue returns the values you see in the dijit, while resolving the dijit's .value property to return a JavaScript Date object.

Table 13-6 provides a quick synopsis of these additional features that both DateTextBox and TimeTextBox provide.

Table 13-6. DateTextBox and TimeTextBox commonalities

Name	Comment
getDisplayedValue( )	Retrieves the formatted value that is actually displayed in the form element, whereas getValue retrieves an actual Date object.
setDisplayedValue(/*Date*/ date)	Sets both the displayed as well as the internal value for the dijit. (Calling setValue accomplishes exactly the same thing.)
toString( )	Returns an ISO-8601-compliant date or time value.
min and max values for the constraints object	Provided to constrain the values that are available via the pop ups.
serialize( )	An extension point that can be used to specify a custom implementation for the toString method. This extension point manipulates the value that is presented to the server when a form is submitted.

Serializing data to the server

As it turns out, the serialize extension point can be especially useful when transferring data to and from a server-side component that is expecting a date to be formatted in a special way. For example, you might use the code in Example 13-5 to extend the DateTextBox and provide a custom format when the toString method is used. Example 13-5 illustrates using a custom DateTextBox to submit a custom value that is different from what is displayed.

Example 13-5. Custom serialization of data to the server with a DateTextBox

```
<html>
    <head>
        <title>Custom DateTextBox</title>

        <link rel="stylesheet" type="text/css"
          href="http://o.aolcdn.com/dojo/1.1/dojo/resources/dojo.css" />
        <link rel="stylesheet" type="text/css"
          href="http://o.aolcdn.com/dojo/1.1/dijit/themes/tundra/tundra.css" />

        <script
            djConfig="parseOnLoad:false",
            type="text/javascript"
            src="http://o.aolcdn.com/dojo/1.1/dojo/dojo.xd.js">
        </script>
        <script type="text/javascript">
            dojo.require("dojo.parser");
            dojo.require("dijit.form.DateTextBox");

            dojo.addOnLoad(function( ) {
                dojo.declare("dtdg.CustomDateTextBox",[dijit.form.DateTextBox], {
                    serialize: function(d, options) {
                        return dojo.date.locale.format(d,
                        {
                            selector:'date',
                            datePattern:'dd-MMM-yyyy'}).toUpperCase( );
                    }
                });
                dojo.parser.parse(dojo.body( ));
            });
        </script>
    </head>
    <body class="tundra">
        <form action="http://localhost:8080" type="POST">
            <input dojoType="dtdg.CustomDateTextBox" name="customDate"/>
            <input type="submit" value="Submit"/>
        </form>
    </body>
</html>
```

A minimal CherryPy class can accept the form submission and display it for you:

```
import cherrypy

class Content:
    @cherrypy.expose
    def index(self, **kwargs):
        return str(kwargs)

cherrypy.quickstart(Content())
```

Don't forget about inherited properties

Although the inheritance hierarchy is getting a little bit deep by this point, recall that all of the methods inherited from TextBox and ValidationTextBox are also available to use and are essential for many common use cases. A review of dojo.date, as presented in Chapter 6, is also helpful for brushing up on some of the finer details associated with these dijits.

NumberTextBox

NumberTextBox inherits all of the great features you've grown to love from RangeBoundTextBox and its ancestors and expands upon them with customization for numeric types via the dojo.number facilities. In a nutshell, numeric value formatting defaults to the current locale and allows you to provide the constraints listed in Table 13-7.

Table 13-7. NumberTextBox constraints

Name	Comment
min and max constraints	Used to check the bounds of the input, just like any other RangeBoundTextBox descendant.
pattern	Used to provide the number of digits to require after the decimal, along with any additional formatting, such as a percent sign that follows.
type	Used to designate that the value should be a decimal or percentage.
places	Used to designate the number of places to require after the decimal (providing this value in addition to a custom pattern overrides the pattern).

For example, to require a value to have exactly two places after the decimal and a percent sign, the following does the trick:

```
<input constraints="{pattern: '#.##%'}" dojoType="dijit.form.NumberTextBox">
```

Although there is only a single hash before the decimal place, note that you can have multiple digits. Should you not want any dijits before the decimal, however, you can provide a pattern without a leading hash, such as {pattern:'.##%'}. Also note that when editing begins, the displayed values automatically convert to a pure numeric value; when editing ends, the value converts back to a formatted number.

Recall that dojo.number as presented in Chapter 6 is your one-stop shop for tons of custom facilities for number formatting and related operations. NumberTextBox directly builds upon these facilities.

NumberSpinner

The NumberSpinner was introduced in Chapter 11, and you can think of the NumberSpinner and a fancier NumberTextBox with small buttons on the edge that allow for incrementally increasing the value. The buttons are *typematic* in that you can hold them down and they will repeatedly affect the value. The NumberSpinner also has slightly different min and max constraints in that if min and max constraints are provided, the NumberSpinner's buttons will not allow you to move outside of those boundaries.

NumberSpinner offers the attributes listed in Table 13-8.

Table 13-8. NumberSpinner attributes

Name	Comment
defaultTimeout	The number of seconds a key or button is held down before it becomes typematic. This attribute is 500 by default.
timeoutChangeRate	The fraction of time that is used to change the typematic timer between events. A value of 1.0 means that each typematic event fires at defaultTimeout intervals. A value of less than 1.0 means that each typematic event fires an increasingly faster rate proportional to this value. This attribute is 0.90 by default.
smallDelta	The value to adjust the spinner by when using arrow keys or buttons. This attribute is 1 by default.
largeDelta	The value to adjust the spinner by when using the Page Up or Page Down keys. This attribute is 10 by default.

Creating a NumberSpinner is just like creating any other dijit:

```
<input dojoType="dijit.form.NumberSpinner" smallDelta="2" largeDelta="4"
constraints="{min:100,max:120}" value="100">
```

CurrencyTextBox

The CurrencyTextBox is the farthest dijit from the common ancestor, inheriting from NumberTextBox, and utilizes dojo.currency for much of its formatting handiwork.

This dijit, however, provides only one additional attribute, currency, which is formatted according to its specific locale. Values for currency must be one of the three letter sequences specified in the ISO4217 currency code standard, available from *http://en.wikipedia.org/wiki/ISO_4217*.

Anytime international characters such as currency symbols are used, you'll want to be especially aware of the encoding that your browser is using so that all symbols are rendered properly. There is always the possibility that the web server may not include this information in the header.

In HTML pages, the standard way of specifying an encoding is by placing a special META tag in the head of the page, and the Dijit project encourages this technique as a best practice. The following example is a META tag for the UTF-8 character set, which is almost always a safe bet:

```
<META http-equiv="Content-Type"
content="text/html; charset=UTF-8"/>
```

Note that as of version 1.1, you will need to use this tag if serving up Dojo from AOL's CDN because the server currently does not include encoding information in the headers, which is another means of achieving the same result. (Otherwise, currency and certain unicode symbols may not display properly.)

The following snippet illustrates a currency dijit for U.S. dollars that requires a value for the cents to be explicitly provided after the decimal point via the fractional constraint, which is the only additional constraint of interest that this dijit provides besides those that have already been inherited:

```
<input dojoType="dijit.form.CurrencyTextBox"
constraints="{min:1,max:100,fractional:true}" currency="USD"/>
```

Like NumberTextBox, the values for this dijit change to vanilla numeric values when editing begins, and format back to currency values once editing ends via a blur event.

ComboBox

ComboBox provides a drop-down list of values much like an HTML SELECT element; however, a ComboBox is based on an ordinary input element, so if an acceptable value is not identified by the list of possibilities, you may opt to type in any value you'd like. ComboBox inherits from ValidationTextBox, so you have the full gamut of features for validation available to you; some additional enhancements are that it also provides a filtered list of possible values based on the prefix you've entered. The list of values can be a static list that is established *a priori* or a dynamic list from a dojo.data store that may be fetched from a server.

In its simplest manifestation, you might use a ComboBox simply to provide a static list of common options, with the ability for the user to type in a custom option. The following code listing illustrates static data with the auto-complete feature enabled.

A Word On Encoding

The Universal Character Set (UCS) is an international standard defined by both the International Organization for Standardization (ISO) and the International Electrotechnical Commission (IEC) that specifies almost 100,000 symbols and assigns each of them a unique number called a "code point."

Unicode is an industry standard that was developed in tandem with UCS and may be thought of as either an implementation of UCS or the underlying idea behind it, although the exact relationship between the two is ambiguous and often the subject of philosophical debate. The key point to take away is that the two standards maintain synchronization with one another.

Encodings are important because information systems increasingly need to properly handle arbitrary characters for languages—even ancient languages that aren't commonly spoken anymore—and Unicode provides a means of key industry players standardizing on a common approach so as to maintain maximal compatibility. Clearly, there is tremendous value in arbitrary web servers and browsers being able to communicate, email servers and email clients being able to arbitrarily communicate, and so on.

While the 7-bit ASCII (American Standard Code for Information Interchange) fits the bill for the English alphabet quite nicely, it is grossly insufficient elsewhere. The UTF-8 (Unicode Transformation Format) encoding is able to represent any character in the Unicode standard and maintain complete backward compatibility with ASCII, so it has become very popular and has been largely adopted for web pages, email, and so on.

An interesting implementation detail about UTF-8 that allows it to maintain backward compatibility with ASCII is that it uses a variable length encoding in which one to four 8-bit bytes may be used for any given character. Thus, the web server identifying the specific encoding being used via response headers or the web page itself specifying the specific encoding via a META tag is especially important for symbols to be rendered properly. Without knowing the encoding, the browser is unable to properly translate the stream of bytes it receives into discrete symbols.

You can read more about Unicode at *http://www.unicode.org*.

```
<select name="coffee" dojoType="dijit.form.ComboBox" autoComplete="true">
  <option>Verona</option>
  <option>French Roast</option>
  <option>Breakfast Blend</option>
  <option selected>Sumatra</option>

  <script type="dojo/method" event="onChange" args="newValue">
    console.log("value changed to ", newValue);
  </script>
</select>
```

Hooking a `ComboBox` to an `ItemFileReadStore` is quite simple and involves little more than pointing the `ComboBox` to the data source. For example, consider a data source that contains coffee roasts and their descriptions in the following form:

```
{identifier : "name",
    items : [
        {name : "Light Cinnamon", description : "Very light brown, dry , tastes like
toasted grain with distinct sour tones, baked, bready"},
        {name : "Cinnamon", description : "Light brown and dry, still toasted grain
with distinct sour acidy tones"},

        ...lots more...
    ]
}
```

Assume that you'd like to populate the `ComboBox` with a `name` field, and when a change occurs, use the description in some other meaningful way. You might accomplish this task as shown in Example 13-6.

Example 13-6. ComboBox at work

```
<html>
    <head>
        <title>Pick a coffee roast, any coffee roast</title>

        <link rel="stylesheet" type="text/css"
          href="http://o.aolcdn.com/dojo/1.1/dojo/resources/dojo.css" />
        <link rel="stylesheet" type="text/css"
          href="http://o.aolcdn.com/dojo/1.1/dijit/themes/tundra/tundra.css" />

        <script
            djConfig="parseOnLoad:true",
            type="text/javascript"
            src="http://o.aolcdn.com/dojo/1.1/dojo/dojo.xd.js">
        </script>

        <script type="text/javascript">
            dojo.require("dojo.parser");
            dojo.require("dojo.data.ItemFileReadStore");
            dojo.require("dijit.form.ComboBox");
            dojo.require("dijit.form.Button");
            dojo.require("dijit.form.Form");
        </script>
    <head>
    <body class="tundra">

        <div dojoType="dojo.data.ItemFileReadStore"
            jsId="coffeeStore" url="./coffee.json"></div>

        <form action="localhost" dojoType="dijit.form.Form">
            <select name="coffee" dojoType="dijit.form.ComboBox"
                store="coffeeStore" searchAttr="name">
```

Example 13-6. ComboBox at work (continued)

```
            <script type="dojo/method" event="onChange" args="newValue">
                console.log("value changed to ", newValue);
                var f = function(item) {
                    console.log("new description is ",
                      coffeeStore.getValue(item, "description")
                    );
                };
                coffeeStore.fetchItemByIdentity(
                    {identity : newValue, onItem : f}
                );
            </script>
        </select>
      <button dojoTyype="dijit.form.Button">Submit</button>
   </form>
   </body>
</html>
```

To recap, all that takes place is that you hook up the `ComboBox` to the `ItemFileReadStore` via the store attribute, and tell the `ComboBox` which field to display via the `searchAttr` attribute. Then, when a change occurs, the `ComboBox`'s `onChange` method detects and uses the new value to look up the description from the store.

 Internally, the `ComboBox` only implements a specialized subset of the `dojo.data.Read/Notification` API that is necessary for it to work. Specifically, it implements the following methods:

- `getValue`
- `isItemLoaded`
- `fetch`
- `close`
- `getLabel`
- `getIdentity`
- `fetchItemByIdentity`
- `fetchSelectedItem`

For completeness, the specific attributes shown in Table 13-9 are also available for ComboBox.

Table 13-9. ComboBox attributes

Name	Type	Comment
item	Object	The currency selected item. `null` by default.
pageSize	Integer	Specifies the number of results per page (via the `count` key in an `ItemFileReadStore`'s fetch method). Useful when querying large stores. `Infinity` by default.
store	Object	A reference to the data provider such as an `ItemFileReadStore`. `null` by default.

Table 13-9. ComboBox attributes (continued)

Name	Type	Comment
query	Object	A query that can be passed to the store to initially filter the items before doing any further filtering based on searchAttr and the key that is currently typed in. { } by default.
autoComplete	Boolean	Whether to display a list of options for the key that is currently typed in (using the queryExpr as a search criteria). true by default.
searchDelay	Integer	How many milliseconds to wait between when a key is pressed and when to start search for that value. 100 by default.
searchAttr	String	The search pattern to match against for the values that should be displayed. name by default.
queryExpr	String	The dojo.data query expression pattern to use. (The default expression searches for any value that is a prefix of the current key that is typed in.) "${0}*" by default.
ignoreCase	Boolean	Whether queries should be case-sensitive. true by default.
hasDownArrow	Boolean	Whether to display the down arrow for the drop-down indicator. true by default.

FilteringSelect

A FilteringSelect is an enhanced version of the ordinary HTML select element in that provides a drop-down list of mandatory values and submits the hidden values and the displayed values. While FilteringSelect looks like and shares a lot of features with ComboBox, including the ability to filter a drop-down list as text is typed and the ability to fetch data from a serve via a store, it is built upon an HTML SELECT element.

Three particularly important distinctions between a FilteringSelect and a ComboBox are worth noting:

- ComboBox is built on an ordinary select element in which the value that is submitted to the server on a submit event is the control's hidden value, not the visible value in the control. This distinction is an important feature because FilteringSelect can be degradable and behave as much like an ordinary SELECT as possible.

- The FilteringSelect inherits from MappedTextBox (a serializable TextBox) instead of ValidationTextBox because validation is a nonissue because users cannot type free text into the control.

- FilteringSelect can display HTML as its label, not just text. Thus, you can include customizable markup such as images in labels.

In addition to common dijit.form operations such as getValue, setValue, getDisplayedValue, setDisplayedValue, and the various ComboBox options, FilteringSelect provides two additional attributes and one additional function, listed in Table 13-10.

Table 13-10. FilteringSelect additions

Name	Comment
labelAttr	The text to display in the control. If no value is specified, then searchAttr is used.
labelType	Whether to treat the text label as markup or ordinary text. Valid values include 'text' or 'html'.
labelFunc (/*Object*/ item, /*dojo.data.store*/ store)	The event handler that is called when the label changes; returns the label that should be displayed.

MultiSelect

MultiSelect is a simple wrapper (with the attributes listed in Table 13-11) around a native SELECT element (with the attribute multi=true) that inherits from _FormWidget. The primary reason that it is included in Dijit is because it facilitates interaction with the dijit.Form wrapper (coming up later in this chapter) and streamlines the task of otherwise having to style the SELECT element yourself.

Table 13-11. MultiSelect

Name	Comment
size	The number of elements to display on a page. 7 by default.
addSelected(/*dijit.form.MultiSelect*/ select)	Moves the selected nodes from another MultiSelect into this MultiSelect.
getSelected()	Returns the selected nodes in the widget.
setValue(/*Array*/values)	Sets the value of each node in the widget according to the sequential values provided in the values Array.
invertSelection(/*Boolean*/fireOnChange)	Inverts the selection. If fireOnChange is true, then an onChange event is fired.

Because MultiSelect is just a lightweight wrapper around the HTML equivalent, there is little to say about that is specific to Dojo. You can define a MultiSelect in markup, as shown in Example 13-7.

Example 13-7. Typical MultiSelect in markup

```
<select multiple="true" name="foo" dojoType="dijit.form.MultiSelect"
 style="height:100px; width:100px; border:3px solid black;">

    <option value="TN" selected="true">Tennessee</option>
    <option value="VA">Virginia</option>
    <option value="WV">West Virginia</option>
    <option value="OH">Ohio</option>

</select>
```

Textarea Variations

A bane of traditional web development has often been the dreaded TEXTAREA element that takes up a fixed amount of space on the screen, requiring somewhat of a black art to determine just how much space to allocate to it so as to maximize the amount of viewable area while minimizing wastage on valuable screen real estate.

Textarea

The Textarea dijit inherits from _FormWidget and gives the best of both worlds in that it supports the standard HTML attributes for an ordinary textarea, yet its appearance is a fixed width element that grows vertically as needed. The API for the Textarea dijit simple in that you'll normally only need to use the standard setValue and getValue methods. onChange is a valuable extension point that you can use as a callback when a change occurs:

```
<textarea dojoType="dijit.form.Textarea" style="width:300px">
    One fish, two fish...
</textarea>
```

SimpleTextarea

Although Textarea's ability to expand is convenient in a lot of cases, it doesn't lend itself well to situations in which an enclosing container (such as the layout dijits you'll learn about in Chapter 14) needs to dictate its overall size. For this reason, the SimpleTextarea dijit was introduced. For all practical purposes, the SimpleTextarea behaves just like an ordinary TEXTAREA element except that it can expand and contract in size. You populate it with the same attributes as an ordinary TEXTAREA element such as rows and cols and, like Textarea, you can use setValue and getValue to manipulate the text in it.

Button Variations

Dijit provides drop-in, degradable replacements for standard push buttons and checkboxes, yet it also gives you a lot of sophisticated options, such as the kinds of buttons that you normally find in toolbars. Let's start out with an ordinary Button and work our way up through more sophisticated options.

Button

Figure 13-4 shows a button, and Table 13-12 gives the rundown on the most basic kind of button dijit, a Button, which inherits _FormWidget.

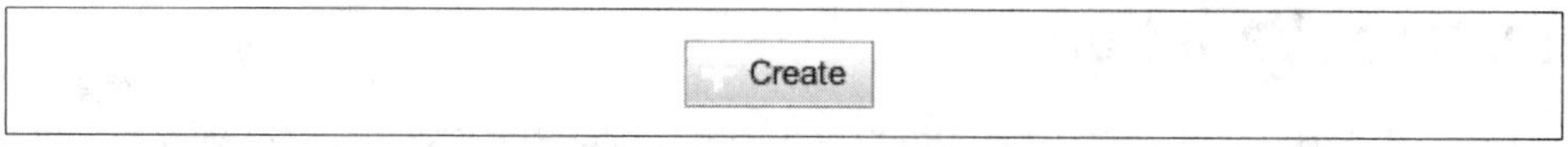

```
                    [ Create ]
```

Figure 13-4. A typical Button

Table 13-12. Button properties

Name	Comment
label	Used to provide the label for the button in markup or via programmatic creation.
showLabel	A Boolean value designating whether to display the text label in the Button. true by default.
iconClass	A class specifying an image that can make a button appear like an icon.
onClick(/* DOM Event*/ evt)	An extension point that is called in response to a click. This is a very common method to override.
setLabel(/* String */ label)	A method accepting an HTML string that can change a Button's label.

> Unlike TextBox and its descendants, the Button widgets require you to use the setAttribute('value', /*...*/) function, inherited from _FormWidget, to set value because Buttons don't have a *widget value* so much as they have a form value that is relayed to the server.

Let's dust off the code from Example 13-4 and provide some final polish by replacing those ugly buttons, as shown in Example 13-8. Remembering to add an obligatory dojo.require("dojo.form.Button") to the head of the page, the replacement is straightforward. Note how convenient providing the onClick handler in markup is for this situation.

Example 13-8. Typical Button usage

```
<button dojoTye="dijit.form.Button" type="submit">Sign Up!
    <script type="dojo/method" event="onClick" args="evt">
        alert("You just messed up...but it's too late now! Mwahahaha");
    </script>
</button>
<button dojoTye="dijit.form.Button" type="reset">Reset</button>
```

The Button's iconClass is especially snazzy in that it doesn't just replace the entire button with an icon. Instead, it embeds the icon into the button alongside an optional label if one is specified and showLabel is true. For example, if you had a small 20×20px thumbnail image of some spam that you wanted to embed into the "Sign Up!" button, you could do it by including iconClass="spamIcon" in the button tag and ensuring that the following class appeared in your page:

```
.spamIcon {
    background-image:url('spam.gif');
    background-repeat:no-repeat;
```

```
    height:20px;
    width:20px;
}
```

Of course, you can provide any customized styles you'd like for buttons to make them look any way that you'd like by applying an inline style or a custom class.

ToggleButton

Because form dijits leverage inheritance so heavily, they often have common ancestors that provide common functionality for descendant classes. `ToggleButton` is one such class; it inherits from `Button` and adds in functionality for a button that has an on/off state, like a `RadioButton` or a `CheckBox`. The only notable attribute it adds is checked, which can be toggled with `setAttribute`.

Although you would probably use a more conventional control like `CheckBox` to designate on/off states, you could choose to use `ToggleButton` directly, or subclass it and implement your own custom `ToggleButton`. The `onChange` extension point (common to all form dijits) is one particularly useful feature:

```
<button dojoType="dijit.form.ToggleButton">
  <script type="dojo/method" event="onChange" args="newValue">
    console.log(newValue);
  </script>
</button>
```

Most of the buttons that appear in a toolbar such formatting a text with italics, bold, underline, etc., use the `ToggleButton`. The `Menu` and `MenuItem` dijits are introduced in Chapter 15.

Several button dijits are not included in their own designated resource file. In particular, you should `dojo.require("dijit.form.Button")` for `Button`, `ToggleButton`, `DropDownButton`, and `ComboButton`. While it may seem odd to require one thing when you actually want another, the rationale is that the (inheritance-driven) implementations for the various buttons are so similar that they are included in the same physical file to minimize overhead in acquiring resources from the server. Additionally, recall that the mapping between classes simulated via `dojo.declare` and resource files is not designed to be a one-to-one mapping (although traditional object-oriented programming philosophy often deems it so).

This technique remains a source of consternation amongst Dojo circles, as the overhead from a synchronous request to the server would be a moot point in a production setting that uses the facilities from Util to optimize layers for each page of an application.

These kinds of nuances result from so many (well-intentioned) competing interests in the Dojo community.

CheckBox

CheckBox descends directly from ToggleButton and is a standard drop-in replacement for an ordinary `<input type="checkbox">` element. Using it is as simple as requiring it into the page and then using the dojoType tag. We might introduce it into Example 13-4 page by disabling the "Sign Up!" button until after user click the CheckBox to confirm that they're aware of our covert intentions to spam them:

```
<div name="confirmation" dojoType="dijit.form.CheckBox">
  <script type="dojo/method" event="onClick" args="evt">
    if (this.checked)
      dijit.byId("signup").setAttribute('disabled', false);
    else
      dijit.byId("signup").setAttribute('disabled', true);
  </script>
</div> I understand that you intend to spam me.<br>

<button id="signup" disabled dojoType="dijit.form.Button" type="submit">
  Sign Up!
</button>
```

Figure 13-5 shows a series of CheckBox dijits.

☑ Standard Dijit CheckBox
☐ Disabled Dijit
☑ Checked and Disabled Dijit

Figure 13-5. A series of CheckBox dijits

The reason that DIV tags are being used instead of INPUT tags is because you cannot embed SCRIPT tags inside of INPUT tags, and if you try, it is almost a certainty that the browser will strip them out. Thus, if you want to use SCRIPT markup inside of dijits, you should be especially cognizant that you can't use INPUT tags. If degradability is so important that this isn't acceptable for your application, simply write the methods in pure JavaScript instead of markup.

Thus, to programmatically check the CheckBox, you might use the setValue(true) method, which would check the box as well as set its checked attribute to true and its value attribute to true.

If it is really important to ensure every page is as degradable as possible, you can go the extra mile to explicitly include ordinary HTML attributes in tags. For example, instead of just specifying `<input dojoType="dijit.form.CheckBox"/>`, you could also include the extra type attribute, resulting in `<input dojoType="dijit.form.CheckBox" type="checkbox"/>`.

Like ordinary HTML checkbox elements, however, there is a difference in the *state* of the checkbox versus the *value* of the checkbox. The state of the checkbox is either that it is or is not checked, and you can detect the state via the standard checked attribute. The value attribute, however, may take on non-Boolean values to pass special values to the server if the box is checked when the form is submitted. For example, a tag like `<input name="pleaseSpamMe" value="yes"/>` would append pleaseSpamMe=yes to the query string if the form was submitted via GET. (The default for value is "on".)

The confusion comes in, however, when you find out that the getValue method and the value attribute do not always return the same thing. The way it works is that getValue returns whether the box is checked regardless of what the actual value attribute happens to be. The rationale for this design is that the most common use case for a getValue function would be to determine a visible on/off state—not getting the actual value, which may not reflect the on/off state.

Because it is possible to get yourself tangled up in the differences between some of the different possibilities, consider some of the common cases for a CheckBox dijit:

```
<input id="foo" dojoType="dijit.form.CheckBox"></input>
```

Example 13-9 shows a series of calls to manipulate the dijit along with extensive commenting to show the effects.

Example 13-9. Typical CheckBox usage

```
/* Check the initial state */
dijit.byId("foo").checked // false
dijit.byId("foo").getValue() // "on"

/* Use setValue with true */
dijit.byId("foo").setValue(true) // check the box and set the value to true
dijit.byId("foo").checked // true
dijit.byId("foo").getValue() // true

/* Use setValue with false */
dijit.byId("foo").setValue(false) //uncheck the box and set the value to false
dijit.byId("foo").checked // false
dijit.byId("foo").getValue() // false


/* Use setValue with a String */
dijit.byId("foo").setValue("bar") //check the box and set the value to "bar"
dijit.byId("foo").checked //true
dijit.byId("foo").getValue() // "bar"
```

These most common use cases for the CheckBox are using getValue and setValue with Boolean values as parameters, so the chances are reasonably good that you won't need to wade through the potentially esoteric effects that can arise when you start mixing state and values.

Here's one particularly unintuitive combination that accentuates some of the issues involved in mixing state and value that you should be especially aware of:

```
dijit.byId("foo").setAttribute("value", "foo")
// changes the value attribute but does not check the box

dijit.byId("foo").value // "foo"

dijit.byId("foo").getValue()
//false, because the box is not checked
```

The unintuitive part is that after setting a value you wouldn't expect a call to getValue( ) to return false because common idioms in JavaScript involve the ability to test a string value, and if it's not "", null, or undefined, then it evaluates as true. However, the thing to remember is that getValue( ) consistently returns whether the box is checked or not—regardless of what is actual value attribute is set to be. In this case, the box is not checked, so getValue( ) returns false.

Likewise, the dijit's onChange event will not fire for a dijit.byId("foo").setAttribute("value", "foo") method call since the checked state of the box did not visibly change.

RadioButton

A RadioButton is a drop-in replacement for the ordinary HTML equivalent descending from CheckBox, and like its HTML equivalent, is conceptually a group of checkboxes in which only one can be selected at any given time. Recall that each button in a radio group has the same value for name but distinct values for value. Figure 13-6 shows a RadioButton group.

Radio group #1: ◯ news ⦿ talk ◯ weather (disabled)

Figure 13-6. A RadioButton group

We might even further refine our working example (Example 13-4) by asking users how many times a day they'd like us to bother them. We could use radio buttons as shown in Example 13-10 to achieve this purpose quite easily, *having first required* dijit.form.CheckBox *in the page.*

Although you'd think that last sentence was a typo, it's not. Recalling that you dojo.require resources, not individual widgets, it turns out that the dijit.form.CheckBox resource provides dijit.formCheckBox and dijit.form.RadioButton.

This warning is along the same lines as the previous warning about how the dijit.form.Button resource provides multiple dijit implementations.

Example 13-10. Typical RadioButton usage

```
<input name="spamFrequency" value="1 per day" dojoType="dijit.form.RadioButton">
    1 per day<br>
<input name="spamFrequency" value="2 per day" dojoType="dijit.form.RadioButton">
    2 per day<br>
<input name="spamFrequency" value="3+ per day" dojoType="dijit.form.RadioButton">
    3+ per day<br>
```

DropDownButton

A `DropDownButton` is simply a descendant of `Button` that when clicked produces a drop-down menu with options you can select—just like you're used to seeing in a toolbar. `DropDownButton` and `dijit.Menu` are closely related, in that a `Menu` is one of the most common vehicles for supplying a drop-down list; `TooltipDialog` is another common option. Figure 13-7 shows the `DropDownButton` dijit.

Figure 13-7. A DropDownButton dijit

More complete coverage is given to `Menu` (and the individual `MenuItems` it contains) in Chapter 15. Example 13-11, however, demonstrates a `DropDownButton` in action and should get the point across. Note that the first child of the parent `DropDownButton` node is a label that appears on the button.

Example 13-11. Typical DropDownButton usage

```
<button dojoType="dijit.form.DropDownButton">
    <span>Save...</span>
    <div dojoType="dijit.Menu">
        <div dojoType="dijit.MenuItem" label="Save">
            <script type="dojo/method" event="onClick" args="evt">
                console.log("you clicked", this.label);
            </script>
        </div>
        <div dojoType="dijit.MenuItem" label="Save as...">
            <script type="dojo/method" event="onClick" args="evt">
                console.log("you clicked", this.label);
            </script>
        </div>
        <div dojoType="dijit.MenuItem" label="Save to FTP...">
            <script type="dojo/method" event="onClick" args="evt">
                console.log("you clicked", this.label);
            </script>
```

Example 13-11. Typical DropDownButton usage (continued)

```
        </div>
    </div>
</button>
```

If you want to use a `DropDownButton` as part of a form submission, you could do so by creating a hidden `INPUT` element and programmatically setting its value via the constituent `MenuItem`'s `onClick` method. The most common uses for `DropDownButton`, however, normally involve an application-level behavior, such as saving a document.

> In general, form fields that are submitted to a server via a form submission should be visible to the user at the time of submission. In that regard, `DropDownButton` may seem a bit misplaced with its inclusion into `dijit.form` because it isn't *that* kind of form control. The reason it appears in this section is that it is a descendant of `Button`, and it would make even less sense to try to have a `Button` ancestor living in another namespace.

ComboButton

A `ComboButton` inherits from `DropDownButton`, but with a twist: it provides a reserved area that produces a drop-down when it is clicked, whereas if you click on the "other" part of the button that is initially visible, it invokes a default action. For example, you might have a "Save" button that triggers an ordinary save action when clicked, while clicking the drop-down portion of the button produces a menu with options such as "Save", "Save as…", "Save to FTP site", and so on. Figure 13-8 shows a `ComboButton` before and after clicking on the expander.

Figure 13-8. Left: a ComboButton before clicking on the expander; right: the ComboButton after clicking on the expander

Example 13-12 illustrates using a `ComboButton`.

Example 13-12. Typical ComboButton usage

```
<button dojoType="dijit.form.ComboButton">
    <span>Save</span>

    <script type="dojo/method" event="onClick" args="evt">
        console.log("you clicked the button itself");
    </script>
```

Example 13-12. Typical ComboButton usage (continued)

```
    <div name="foo" dojoType="dijit.Menu">
        <div dojoType="dijit.MenuItem" label="Save">
            <script type="dojo/method" event="onClick" args="evt">
                console.log("you clicked", this.label);
            </script>
        </div>
        <div dojoType="dijit.MenuItem" label="Save As...">
            <script type="dojo/method" event="onClick" args="evt">
                console.log("you clicked", this.label);
            </script>
        </div>
        <div dojoType="dijit.MenuItem" label="Save to FTP...">
            <script type="dojo/method" event="onClick" args="evt">
                console.log("you clicked", this.label);
            </script>
        </div>
    </div>
</button>
```

Notice that the label for the ComboButton is still provided via the first child element, Save in this case, and the options that are provided via the drop-down are just the same as with a DropDownButton.

Slider

While a slider may not be a native HTML form control, there can be little dispute about how useful sliders can be for highly visual interfaces. Whether your goal is to adjust the transparency for an image, adjust the amount of a particular color in a custom color combination, or resize some other control on the screen, a slider can help you do it in a very intuitive manner. Dijit offers both horizontal and vertical sliders.

 The Slider dijit is an especially slick piece of engineering. Like some of the other dijits, it keeps track of the current value via a hidden form value so that when you submit a form, the value is passed over to the server just like any other form field.

To get all of the various Slider machinery into your page, simply do a dojo. require("dijit.form.Slider"). In addition to VerticalSlider and HorizontalSlider, you also get the supporting classes for rules and labels. Let's start with something simple and gradually add some complexity so that you get a better feel for exactly how customizable this fantastic little widget really is.

HorizontalSlider

Suppose that as a caffeine junkie, you want to create a horizontal slider that denotes caffeine levels for various beverages. Your first stab at getting a plain vanilla slider into the page might be something like the Example 13-13, remembering to first require dijit.form.Slider into the page.

Example 13-13. HorizontalSlider (Take 1)

```
<div dojoType="dijit.form.HorizontalSlider" name="caffeine"
    value="100"
    maximum="175"
    minimum="2"
    style="margin: 5px;width:300px; height: 20px;">

    <script type="dojo/method" event="onChange" args="newValue">
        console.log(newValue);
    </script>
</div>
```

To summarize, the code created a slider without any kinds of labels whatsoever; the slider displays values ranging from 2 through 175 with the dimensions provided by the inline style. The default value is 100, and whenever a change occurs, the onChange method picks it up and displays it to the console. Note that clicking on the slider causes its value to move to the click point. So far, so good.

To further refine the slider, let's remove the buttons that are on each end of it by adding showButtons="false" as an attribute and adding a HorizontalRule and some HorizontalRuleLabels to the top of the slider. Everything you need was already slurped into the page, so no additional resources are required; we pull in the dojo.number module, however, to facilitate formatting to the console.

Just add some more markup into the body of the existing slider, as shown in Example 13-14.

Example 13-14. HorizontalSlider (Take 2)

```
<div dojoType="dijit.form.HorizontalSlider" name="caffeine"
    value="100"
    maximum="175"
    minimum="2"
    showButtons="false"
    style="margin: 5px;width:300px; height: 20px;">

    <script type="dojo/method" event="onChange" args="newValue">
        console.log(dojo.number.format(newValue,{places:1,pattern:'#mg'}));
    </script>

    <ol dojoType="dijit.form.HorizontalRuleLabels" container="topDecoration"
        style="height:10px;font-size:75%;color:gray;" count="6">
    </ol>

    <div dojoType="dijit.form.HorizontalRule" container="topDecoration"
        count=6 style="height:5px;">
    </div>
</div>
```

Presto! The slider is already looking much sharper with the addition of some ticks to break up the space and some percentage labels. Note that it is not necessary to have a one-to-one correspondence between the rules and the rule labels, but in this case, it works out quite nicely. Additionally, the attribute container used an enumerated value, topDecoration, defined by the slider to place the rules and labels.

Although the slider contains a percentage rating, it would be nice to bring in some domain specific data for the bottom of the slider. The basic pattern is the same as before, except that we'll use the slider's bottomContainer instead of its topContainer. However, instead of relying on the dijit to produce some bland numeric values, we provide the contents of the list ourselves in Example 13-15, including explicit <br> tags in multiword beverages to keep the display looking sharp. Figure 13-9 shows the result.

Example 13-15. HorizontalSlider (Take 3)

```
<div dojoType="dijit.form.HorizontalSlider" name="caffeine"
    value="100"
    maximum="175"
    minimum="2"
    showButtons="false"
    style="margin: 5px;width:300px; height: 20px;">

    <script type="dojo/method" event="onChange" args="newValue">
        console.log(newValue);
    </script>
    <ol dojoType="dijit.form.HorizontalRuleLabels" container="topDecoration"
        style="height:10px;font-size:75%;color:gray;" count="6">
    </ol>

    <div dojoType="dijit.form.HorizontalRule" container="topDecoration"
        count=6 style="height:5px;">
    </div>

    <div dojoType="dijit.form.HorizontalRule" container="bottomDecoration"
        count=5 style="height:5px;">
    </div>

    <ol dojoType="dijit.form.HorizontalRuleLabels" container="bottomDecoration"
        style="height:10px;font-size:75%;color:gray;">
        <li>green<br>tea</li>
        <li>coffee</li>
        <li>red<br>bull</li>
    </ol>
</div>
```

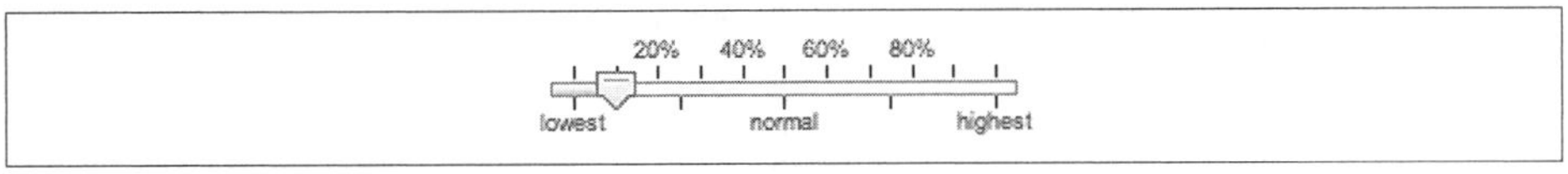

Figure 13-9. A HorizontalSlider

VerticalSlider

VerticalSlider works just like HorizontalSlider except that it renders along the y-axis, and you'll use leftDecoration and rightDecoration instead of topDecoration and bottomDecoration to specify container values for the rules and rule labels, as well as adjust your style to space elements out horizontally instead of vertically. Example 13-16 is the same slider, but adjusted for the vertical axis. Figure 13-10 depicts the result.

Example 13-16. VerticalSlider

```
<div dojoType="dijit.form.VerticalSlider" name="caffeine"
    value="100"
    maximum="175"
    minimum="2"
    showButtons="false"
    style="margin: 5px;width:75px; height: 300px;">

    <script type="dojo/method" event="onChange" args="newValue">
        console.log(newValue);
    </script>
    <ol dojoType="dijit.form.VerticalRuleLabels" container="leftDecoration"
        style="height:300px;width:25px;font-size:75%;color:gray;" count="6">
    </ol>

    <div dojoType="dijit.form.VerticalRule" container="leftDecoration"
        count=6 style="height:300px;width:5px;">
    </div>

    <div dojoType="dijit.form.VerticalRule" container="rightDecoration"
        count=5 style="height:300px;width:5px;">
    </div>

    <ol dojoType="dijit.form.VerticalRuleLabels" container="rightDecoration"
        style="height:300px;width:25px;font-size:75%;color:gray;">
        <li>green tea</li>
        <li>coffee</li>
        <li>red bull</li>
    </ol>
</div>
```

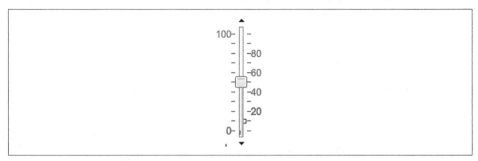

Figure 13-10. A VerticalSlider

Tables 13-13, 13-14, and 13-15 illustrate the important facets of the `dijit.form.Slider`; namely, the sliders themselves, the rules, and the labels. Remember that all of the ordinary form machinery, such as `setValue`, et al., is inherited and works as usual.

Table 13-13. Horizontal Slider and VerticalSlider

Name	Type	Comment
showButtons	Boolean	Whether to show increment/decrement buttons on each end of the slider. `true` by default.
minimum	Integer	The minimum value allowed. 0 by default.
maximum	Integer	The maximum value allowed. 100 by default.
discreteValues	Integer	The number of discrete value between the minimum and maximum (inclusive). `Infinity` is a continuous scale. Values greater than 1 produce a discrete effect. `Infinity` by default.
pageIncrement	Integer	The amount of adjustment to nudge the slider via the page up and page down keys. 2 by default.
clickSelect	Boolean	Whether clicking the progress bar causes the value to change to the clicked location. `true` by default.
slideDuration	Number	The time in milliseconds to take to slide the handle from 0% to 100%. Useful for programmatically changing slider values. 1000 by default.
increment( )	Function	Increments the slider by one unit.
decrement( )	Function	Decrements the slider by one unit.

Table 13-14. HorizontalRule and VerticalRule

Name	Type (default)	Comment
ruleStyle	String	The CSS class to apply to individual hash marks.
count	Integer	The number of hash marks to generate. 3 by default.
container	DOM Node	Where to apply the label in relation to the slider: `topDecoration` or `bottomDecoration` for `HorizontalSlider`. `leftDecoration` or `rightDecoration` for `VerticalSlider`.

HorizontalRuleLabel and VerticalRuleLabel inherit from HorizontalRule and VerticalRule, respectively.

Table 13-15. HorizontalRuleLabel and VerticalRuleLabel

Name	Type (default)	Comment
labelStyle	String	The CSS class to apply to text labels.
labels	Array	Array of text labels to render, evenly spaced from left-to-right or top-to-bottom. [ ] by default.
numericMargin	Integer	The number of numeric labels that should be omitted from display on each end of the slider. (Useful for omitting obvious start and end values such as 0, the default, and 100.)

Table 13-15. HorizontalRuleLabel and VerticalRuleLabel (continued)

Name	Type (default)	Comment
minimum	Integer	When the labels array is not specified, this value provides the leftmost label to include as a label. 0 by default.
maximum	Integer	When the labels array is not specified, this value provides the right-most label to include. 1 by default.
constraints	Object	The pattern to use (from dojo.number) to use for generated numeric labels when the labels array is not specified. {pattern:"#%"} by default.
getLabels	Function	Returns the labels array.

Form

Although form dijits can be wrapped in an HTML form tag, the dijit.form.Form dijit provides some additional conveniences that are quite useful. This section rounds off the chapter by reviewing ordinary HTML forms and then reviews the specific features provided by dijit.form.Form. A common source of confusion to many Dijit newcomers is that they expect Dijit to do something directly that already works just fine via ordinary HTML. Recall that a significant part of Dojo's design philosophy is to not reinvent aspects of web technologies that already work; rather, Dojo supplements and augments as needed where web technology is lacking or not standardized.

HTML Form Tag Synopsis

dijit.form.Form respects the standard form attributes as defined in the HTML 4.01 specification. All attribute values are assumed to be wrapped in quotes as string values, although DOM events such as onclick entail explicitly denoting that a script action is expected, like onclick="javascript:someScriptAction( )" or onclick="javascript: return someValidationAction( )". For mouse events, a "left-click" action is assumed.

Form

The Form dijit itself supplements the standard HTML form attribute by providing several methods that may be called to manipulate it directly, and one extension point that is called internally in response to a user action. Table 13-16 lists the key aspects of Form.

Table 13-16. Form methods and extension points

Name	Category	Comment
getValues( )	Method	Returns a JSON structure providing named key/value pairs for the form.
isValid( )	Method	Returns true if each enabled value in the form returns true for its isValid method.

Table 13-16. Form methods and extension points (continued)

Name	Category	Comment
setValues (/*Object*/ values)	Method	Provides a concise way of setting all values in the form at one time via a JSON structure where each key in the structure is a named form field.
submit()	Method	Used to programmatically submit the form.
reset()	Method	Systematically calls reset() on each contained dijit in the form to reset its value.
onSubmit()	Extension point	Called internally when the submit() method is executed. This extension point is intended to provide a way of canceling the form submission if it returns false. By default, it returns the value from isValid().
validate()	Method	Returns true if the form is valid, which is the same as isValid, but also highlights any form dijits that are valid and calls focus() on the first invalid dijit that is contained in the form.

Wrapping up the entire form into a dijit.form.Form is just like replacing any other element with the corresponding dijit, as shown in Example 13-17.

Example 13-17. Typical Form usage

```
<form id="registration_form" dojoType="dijit.form.Form">

  <!-- form elements go here -->

  <!-- override extension points as usual...-->

  <script type="dojo/method" event="onSubmit" args="evt">
    //return false if form should not be submitted. By default
    //onSubmit returns isValid() for the dijit.form.Form
  </script>
</form>
```

Summary

This chapter has covered some serious ground. After working through it, you should:

- Understand how ordinary HTML forms work
- Understand how to use drop-in form dijit replacements for standard form elements
- Be familiar with the general taxonomy of form dijits, understanding the broad strokes of the inheritance relationships
- Be able to create form dijits both programmatically and in markup
- Understand the difference between methods, attributes, and extension points
- Understand what is meant by a *degradable* form and be able to weigh the various factors involved in producing a degradable design

It's time to move on to layout widgets.

CHAPTER 14

Layout Widgets

Unfortunately, many web apps consume nontrivial amounts of time implementing and rediscovering CSS shenanigans to achieve layouts that have been realized many times already and that should be a lot easier than they often turn out to be. This chapter introduces the *layout dijits*, a number of useful containers for creating common layouts in markup. Layout containers allow you to automate incredibly common tasks such as producing a tabbed layout as well as producing arbitrary tiled layouts without resorting to custom CSS for floating content, calculating relative offsets, etc. Unlike the previous chapter on form widgets, this chapter is shorter, much simpler, and more predictable. There are only a handful of layout widgets; all of them have only a few configuration options and very few caveats.

Layout Dijit Commonalities

All layout dijits exist within the `dijit.layout` namespace and share a small set of baseline features that you should be aware of. In addition to inheriting from `_Widget`, `_Container`, and `_Contained`, they share a few extra commonalities. This section quickly reviews the commonalities, listed in Table 14-1, which are all pretty easy to get your head around.

Table 14-1. Layout dijit common methods

Name	Comment
isLayoutContainer	Returns whether the widget is a layout container.
layout()	Overridden by widgets to size and position their contents (child widgets). This is called after `startup`, when the widget's content box is guaranteed to be set, and anytime the widget's size has been changed via `resize`.
resize(/*Object*/ size)	Used to explicitly set the size of a layout widget; accepts an object specifying the upper left along with a width and a height of the form {w : Integer, h: Integer, l : Integer, t : Integer}. (Anytime you *override* resize, you will almost always call `layout` in the overridden method because `layout` is the canonical location for handling size and positioning for the contained child widgets.)

An especially important takeaway from Table 14-1 is the relationship between layout and resize. To be clear, resize is used to change the size of widget, and it is almost always the case that resize calls layout to adjust the size of its children in response to resizing. Normally speaking, child nodes do not lay themselves out. The parent node lays them out inside of layout. As a general pattern, the startup lifecycle method kicks off resize, which in turn calls layout.

The layout dijits leverage features of _Container and _Contained especially heavily, so they are worth a review as well, provided in Table 14-2.

Table 14-2. Layout dijit container machinery

Name	Comment
removeChild(/*Object*/ dijit)	Removes the child widget from the container. (Silently fails if the widget is not a child or if the container does not have any children.)
addChild(/*Object*/ dijit, /*Integer?*/ insertIndex)	Adds a child widget to the container, optionally using the insertIndex to place it.
getParent()	Commonly used by a child inside of a layout container to retrieve its parent. Returns a dijit instance.
getChildren()	Commonly used by a layout container to enumerate each of its children dijits. Returns an Array of dijit instances.
getPreviousSibling()	Used by descendants of StackContainer to reference the previous sibling, i.e., the one "to the left." Returns a dijit instance.
getNextSibling()	Used by descendants of StackContainer to reference the next sibling, i.e., the one "to the right." Returns a dijit instance.

Programmatic Creation

As we'll see in upcoming examples, the pattern for programmatically creating layout dijits follows the same dijit creation pattern that involves providing a first argument with a collection of properties and a second parameter that provides a source node reference for the layout dijit. Once the layout dijit is created, the source node reference becomes the dijit's domNode. This all takes place via _Widget's create method, which was introduced as part of the dijit lifecycle in Chapter 12. Unlike many dijits you've learned about so far, however, you'll almost always need to explicitly call a layout dijit's startup method if you programmatically create layout dijits because they generally contain child widgets, and startup signals that the container is finished adding children—at which point the layout can proceed. After all, it wouldn't be prudent at all for a widget to lay itself out only to have other sibling widgets repeatedly drop in and restart the layout process. Thus, the parent's startup method generally involves calling the startup method on each child widget, which is the green light to start rendering.

If you are implementing a parent container, startup is your last chance to manipulate children before they are displayed.

Keyboard Support

Like with other all other dijits, keyboard support is quite full featured. You'll find that in almost all circumstances, the "obvious" keys work. For example, to navigate through an AccordionPane, you can use the up and down arrows as well as the Page Down and Page Up keys. In addition to providing accessibility as part of Dijit's a11y goals, this extensive keyboard support also enhances the general user experience.

ContentPane

A ContentPane is the most basic layout tile and it inherits directly from _Widget; conceptually, it is like a super-duper variation of an iframe except that it fits right into the page with all sorts of bells and whistles, not the least of which are the ability to render arbitrary snippets of HTML (not just full documents), reload content via XHR on demand, render widgets, and respect the page's theme. More often than not, a ContentPane is contained within another widget such as a TabContainer, although a ContentPane has several interesting uses cases on its own.

In its most generic usage, a layout pane does nothing special at all, as shown in Example 14-1.

Example 14-1. Creating a ContentPane in markup

```
<html>
    <head><title>Fun with ContentPane!</title>

        <link rel="stylesheet" type="text/css"
          href="http://o.aolcdn.com/dojo/1.1/dojo/resources/dojo.css" />
        <link rel="stylesheet" type="text/css"
          href="http://o.aolcdn.com/dojo/1.1/dijit/themes/tundra/tundra.css" />

        <script
            djConfig="parseOnLoad:true",
            type="text/javascript"
            src="http://o.aolcdn.com/dojo/1.1/dojo/dojo.xd.js">
        </script>

        <script type="text/javascript">
            dojo.require("dijit.layout.ContentPane");
        </script>

    </head>
    <body class="tundra">
```

Example 14-1. Creating a ContentPane in markup (continued)

```
        <div dojoType="dijit.layout.ContentPane">
            Nothing special going on here.
        </div>
    </body>
</html>
```

 When browsing the source code or reading about Dojo online, you may notice that there is also a LinkPane dijit. Over the course of time, ContentPane evolved to absorb much of what LinkPane used to do, and it is likely that LinkPane will become deprecated because it offers a trivial amount of built-in functionality beyond that of ContentPane.

However, you can trivially fetch arbitrary content from a server and render it into the page by merely providing a reference to the server side URL. Suppose that a server-side URL called *foo* returns a snippet of text; you could use the ContentPane to display it like so:

```
    <div id="foo" preload="false"  dojoType="dijit.layout.ContentPane" href="foo">
```

In this particular case, the *foo* URL might have returned just a simple string value, although it could have returned a widget that would have been automatically parsed and rendered into the page. Just note that the widget must already have been dojo.require'd into the page. For example, let's suppose the foo URL returned <div dojoType="dijit.form.Textarea"></div>, then by default, the dijit would be parsed and rendered into the page.

Table 14-3 presents a summary of everything that a ContentPane supports.

Table 14-3. ContentPane API

Name	Type	Comment
href	String	Used to designate the external data the pane should load.
extractContent	Boolean	If true, the visible content between the BODY tags of the document the ContentPane retrieves is extracted from it and placed into the pane. false by default.
parseOnLoad	Boolean	If true, any dijits returned in the data are automatically parsed and rendered. true by default.
preventCache	Boolean	Acts just like the preventCache parameter for a dojo.xhrGet. If true, an additional parameter is passed that changes with each request to prevent caching from occurring. false by default.
preload	Boolean	Used to force the pane to load content, even if it is not initially visible. (If the node is styled with display:none then content may not load unless preload is set to true.) false by default.

Table 14-3. ContentPane API (continued)

Name	Type	Comment
refereshOnShow	Boolean	Used to indicate whether the pane should reload every time the pane goes from a hidden state to a visible state. false by default.
loadingMessage	String	Defined in dijit.nls.loading. Provides a default message to the user while a load is in process. "Loading..." by default.
errorMessage	String	Defined in dijit.nls.loading. Provides a default message to the user when a load fails. "Sorry, an error occurred" by default.
isLoaded	Boolean	Used to provide an explicit status for whether content is loaded. Useful for inquiries involving content that is often refreshed.
refresh()	Function	Used to force the content to refresh by downloading it again.
setHref(/*String*/ href)	Function	Used to change the location of the external content for the dijit. If preload is false, the content is not downloaded until the widget becomes visible again.
setContent(/*String | DOMNode | NodeList */data)	Function	Used to explicitly set local content for the pane.
cancel()	Function	Cancels the in-progress download of content.
onLoad(/*Event*/evt)	Function	Extension point that is called after the load (and optional parsing of widgets) takes place.
onUnload(/*Event*/evt)	Function	Extension point that is called before existing content is cleared by a refresh, setHref, or setContent.
onDownloadStart	Function	Extension point that is called just before the download begins. By default, returns the string that is displayed as the loading message.
onContentError(/*Error*/ e)	Function	Extension point that is called when DOM errors occur. The string that is returned is what is displayed to the user.
onDownloadError(/*Error*/ e)	Function	Extension point that is called if an error occurs during the download. By default, returns the string that is displayed as the error message.
onDownloadEnd()	Function	Extension point that is called when the download completes.

Given an existing node called foo, you could programmatically create a ContentPane like so:

```
var contentPane = new dijit.layout.ContentPane({ /* properties*/, "foo");
contentPane.startup(); //good practice to get in the habit of always calling startup
```

Because ContentPane is not a descendant of _Container, there are no built-in methods for adding children to a ContentPane. However, you can use a ContentPane's domNode reference to append another node inside of it using plain old JavaScript, which works just fine. For example, using the existing content pane from the previous example:

```
contentPane.domNode.appendChild(someOtherDijit.domNode);
```

Hacking ContentPane

One of the great things about a purely interpreted, highly dynamic language like JavaScript is that you can extend functionality as you need it on the fly. The discussion about fetching a dijit such as Textarea via a ContentPane cited that Textarea must first be required into the page. The natural tendency would be to dojo.require("dijit. form.Textarea") somewhere in the head of the page, and that probably covers most of the common cases. But what if you wanted to be able to have the server return to you *any* dijit to render in the ContentPane?

No problem—if the client is requesting a specific dijit, through the URL's query string perhaps, you could simply dojo.require it yourself, on the fly, before the request to update the ContentPane. If the server were returning you a dijit that you don't have knowledge of beforehand, then matters are a bit tricker, but not so tricky that you can't overcome. Simply set the ContentPane's parseOnLoad value to be false so that no automatic parsing occurs (resulting in an error since the corresponding dojo.require hasn't executed yet), and use the onLoad extension point to find the node, require it into the page, and parse it yourself.

Here's an example in markup:

```
<div dojoType="dijit.layout.ContentPane"
    href="bar" parseOnLoad="false">
    <script type="dojo/method" event="onLoad">
        dojo.query("[dojoType]", this.domNode)
        .forEach(function(x) {
          var _resource = dojo.attr(x, "dojoType");
          dojo.require(_resource);
            //don't parse till the module is loaded
            var _interval = setInterval(function() {
                if (eval(_resource)) { //does the object exist?
                    clearInterval(_interval);
                    dojo.parser.parse(x.parentNode);
                }
            }, 100);
        });
    </script>
</div>
```

 You may be wondering why ContentPane does not directly support the interface provided by _Container. The unofficial answer is that a ContentPane, in general, does not need to perform a specific action when a child is placed into it for a specific reason. The reasons for adding children to a ContentPane are wide and varied. If you really wanted to, however, you could mixin or extend _Container into ContentPane.

BorderContainer

BorderContainer is a new layout dijit introduced in version 1.1 that resulted in LayoutContainer and SplitContainer getting deprecated because BorderContainer is essentially a union of the two. Although you may see examples on the web using LayoutContainer and SplitContainer, it is not a good idea to start building an application with deprecated features. For this reason, these two deprecated widgets are not covered in this book.

A BorderContainer provides an easy way to define a layout that normally involves several layout tiles that occur on the top/bottom/left/right/center, top/bottom/center, or left/right/center of the page. These tiles may have resizable handles, so the BorderContainer is an especially notable value-added widget in that it simplifies what could have otherwise been a grueling workload into a really simple widgetized solution. As you might have guessed, it is called a "border" container because up to four tiles surround its border with the center filling in to whatever is leftover.

Table 14-4 shows the API.

Table 14-4. BorderContainer API

Name	Type	Comment
design	String	Valid values include "headline" (the default) or "sidebar" and determine whether the top and bottom tiles extend the width and height or the top and bottom of the container.
liveSplitters	Boolean	Whether to continuously resize while the mouse drags or to resize on the onmouseup event.
persist	Boolean	Whether to save splitter positions as a cookie.

When using a BorderContainer, the additional attributes shown in Table 14-5, which BorderContainer depends on, are available via ContentPane.

You might find it interesting to know that the means of making these additional attributes available via ContentPane is that the BorderContainer resource file extends _Widget's prototype to contain these values behind the scenes. This is a clever solution to the problem as it uses JavaScript's dynamism to provide these extras on demand, instead of requiring an *a priori* solution, which would really junk up and create unnecessary couplings on ContentPane's implementation.

Table 14-5. Attributes available to children of BorderContainer

Name	Type	Comment
minSize	Integer	If provided, the minimum size in pixels of the ContentPane is restricted to this value. By default, this value is 0.
maxSize	Integer	If provided, the maximum size in pixels of the ContentPane is restricted to this value. By default, this value is Infinity.
splitter	Boolean	If provided, a splitter appears on the edge of the ContentPane so that resizing can occur. By default, this value is false, which means that the content is not resizable.
region	String	The BorderContainer layout tiles are ContentPane widgets, each of which should have a region attribute to specify how to lay out the widget. Valid values include "top", "bottom", "left", "right", and "center". By default, this value is an empty String. Values of "leading" and "trailing" are also possible and differ from "left" and "right" in that they are relative to the bidirectional layout orientation.

A layout that involves a top and bottom that extends the width of the container is called a *headline* layout, and a layout that involves a left and right that extends the width of the container is called a *sidebar* layout. Either layout can optionally contain additional tiles that increase the number of layout areas from three to five. In any case, the remaining space that is leftover is the center area that gets filled in with the center tile.

Let's kick things off with a simple headline layout in markup, shown in Example 14-2. The top will be a blue pane, the bottom a red panel, and the middle will remain white. The top pane has minimum height of 10 pixels and a maximum height of 100 pixels (its default height).

Example 14-2. Creating a BorderContainer in markup

```
<html>
    <head><title>Fun with BorderContainer!</title>


        <link rel="stylesheet" type="text/css"
          href="http://o.aolcdn.com/dojo/1.1/dojo/resources/dojo.css" />
        <link rel="stylesheet" type="text/css"
          href="http://o.aolcdn.com/dojo/1.1/dijit/themes/tundra/tundra.css" />

        <script
            djConfig="parseOnLoad:true",
            type="text/javascript"
            src="http://o.aolcdn.com/dojo/1.1/dojo/dojo.xd.js">
        </script>

        <script type="text/javascript">
            dojo.require("dijit.layout.ContentPane");
            dojo.require("dijit.layout.BorderContainer");
```

Example 14-2. Creating a BorderContainer in markup (continued)

```
            dojo.require("dojo.parser");
        </script>
    </head>
    <body class="tundra">

        <div dojoType="dijit.layout.BorderContainer" design="headline"
            style="height:500px;width:500px;border:solid 3px;">

            <div dojoType="dijit.layout.ContentPane" region="top"
              style="background-color:blue;height:100px;" splitter="true"
                minSize=10 maxSize=100>top</div>

            <div dojoType="dijit.layout.ContentPane" region="center">center</div>

            <div dojoType="dijit.layout.ContentPane" region="bottom"
              style="background-color:red;height:100px;" splitter="true">bottom</div>

        </div>
    </body>
</html>
```

Adding tiles to fill in the left and right sides takes only two additional `ContentPane` dijits, as shown in Figure 14-1. Consider the following revision to the BODY tag:

```
    <body class="tundra">

        <div dojoType="dijit.layout.BorderContainer"
          design="headline" style="height:500px;width:500px;border:solid 3px;">

            <div dojoType="dijit.layout.ContentPane" region="top"
              style="background-color:blue;height:100px;" splitter="true"
                minSize=10 maxSize=100>top</div>

            <div dojoType="dijit.layout.ContentPane" region="center">center</div>

            <div dojoType="dijit.layout.ContentPane" region="bottom"
              style="background-color:red;height:100px;" splitter="true">bottom</div>

            <div dojoType="dijit.layout.ContentPane" region="left"
              style="background-color:yellow;width:100px;" splitter="true">left</div>

            <div dojoType="dijit.layout.ContentPane" region="right"
              style="background-color:green;width:100px;" splitter="true">right</div>

        </div>
    </body>
```

Like all other dijits, programmatically creating a `BorderContainer` entails the same basic constructor function that takes a collection of properties and a source node. Adding in the child `ContentPanes` involves systematically creating them one by one as well. Although more tedious than markup, it's the same basic pattern. Example 14-3 shows how you'd create Example 14-2 programmatically.

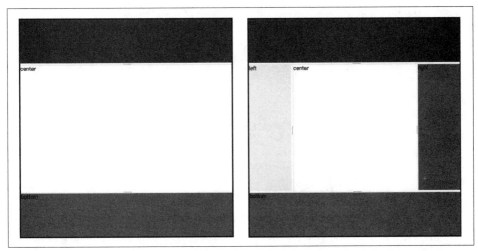

Figure 14-1. Left: the BorderContainer before adding in additional panels on the left and right; right: the BorderContainer after adding in left and right panels

Example 14-3. Programmatically creating a BorderContainer

```html
<html>
    <head><title>Fun with BorderContainer!</title>

        <link rel="stylesheet" type="text/css"
          href="http://o.aolcdn.com/dojo/1.1/dojo/resources/dojo.css" />
        <link rel="stylesheet" type="text/css"
          href="http://o.aolcdn.com/dojo/1.1/dijit/themes/tundra/tundra.css" />


        <script
            djConfig="parseOnLoad:true",
            type="text/javascript"
            src="http://o.aolcdn.com/dojo/1.1/dojo/dojo.xd.js">
        </script>

        <script type="text/javascript">
            dojo.require("dijit.layout.BorderContainer");
            dojo.require("dijit.layout.ContentPane");
            dojo.require("dojo.parser");
            dojo.addOnLoad(function() {
                //the BorderContainer
                var bc = new dijit.layout.BorderContainer(
                    {
                        design: "headline",
                        style: "height:500px;width:500px;border:solid 3px"
                    },
                    "bc"
                );

                var topContentPane = new dijit.layout.ContentPane(
```

Example 14-3. Programmatically creating a BorderContainer (continued)

```
            {
                region: "top",
                style: "background-color:blue;height:100px;",
                splitter: true,
                minSize : 10,
                maxSize : 100
            },
            document.createElement("div")
        );

        var centerContentPane = new dijit.layout.ContentPane(
            {
                region: "center"
            },
            document.createElement("div")
        );

        var bottomContentPane = new dijit.layout.ContentPane(
            {
                region: "bottom",
                style: "background-color:red;height:100px;",
                splitter: true
            },
            document.createElement("div")
        );

        bc.startup(); // do initial layout (even though there are no children)

        //now add the children.
        bc.addChild(topContentPane);
        bc.addChild(centerContentPane);
        bc.addChild(bottomContentPane);

    });
    </script>
    <head>
    <body class="tundra">
        <div id="bc"></div>
    </body>
</html>
```

The previous example called startup( ) to do initial layout and then
used the addChild method to add children. The following approach
would also have worked:

```
bc.domNode.appendChild(topContentPane.domNode);
bc.domNode.appendChild(centerContentPane.domNode);
bc.domNode.appendChild(bottomContentPane.domNode);
bc.startup( );
```

BorderContainer dijits are quite flexible and can be nested arbitrarily if the situation calls for it. They're also a great way to set up a headline style or sidebar style layout with virtually no effort, although you should generally consider plain old CSS for production situations in which widgets don't add any value.

StackContainer

A StackContainer is a layout dijit that displays a sequence of tiles one at a time. A StackContainer is conceptually just like a slideshow in which you can page backward and forward through a "stack" of tiles. Like LayoutContainer, you provide any number of child widgets to the StackContainer, and it takes care of the display. In its most basic usage, you simply page through the available tiles, as shown in Example 14-4.

Example 14-4. Creating a StackContainer in markup

```
<div id="stack" dojoType="dijit.layout.StackContainer"
  style="width:100px; height:100px; margin:5px; border:solid 1px;">

    <div dojoType="dijit.layout.ContentPane">
        One fish...
    </div>
    <div dojoType="dijit.layout.ContentPane">
        Two fish...
    </div>
    <div dojoType="dijit.layout.ContentPane">
        Red fish...
    </div>
    <div dojoType="dijit.layout.ContentPane">
        Blue fish...
    </div>

</div>

<button dojoType="dijit.form.Button">&lt;
    <script type="dojo/method" event="onClick" args="evt">
        dijit.byId("stack").back();
    </script>
</button>

<button dojoType="dijit.form.Button">&gt;
    <script type="dojo/method" event="onClick" args="evt">
        dijit.byId("stack").forward();
    </script>
</button>
```

The usual container and generic layout methods apply to StackContainer; additionally, you should also note the features in Table 14-6.

Table 14-6. StackContainer API

Name (default)	Type	Comment
doLayout	Boolean	Used to change the size of the currently displayed child to match the container's size. true by default.
selectedChildWidget	Object	References the currently selected child widget. null by default.
selectChild(/*Object*/ page)	Function	Used to select a specific child widget.
forward( )	Function	Used to page forward to the next child widget.
back( )	Function	Used to page backward to the previous child widget.

The StackContainer also supports several additional features:

- A closeChild(/*Object*/ child) method
- An onClose( ) extension point
- Children may exhibit the closeable, title, and selected attributes
- Topics that are published when children are added, removed, or selected, <id>-addChild, <id>-removeChild, and <id>-selectChild, respectively

Because these features are most commonly associated with the TabContainer (which inherits from StackContainer), however, their formal introduction will be delayed until the next section.

If you've followed along with the previous example of programmatically creating layout dijits, Example 14-5 should seem awfully familiar.

Example 14-5. Programmatically creating a StackContainer

```
var container = new dijit.layout.StackContainer({}, "foo");

var leftChild = new dijit.layout.ContentPane({});
leftChild.domNode.innerHTML="page 1";

var rightChild = new dijit.layout.ContentPane({});
rightChild.domNode.innerHTML="page 2";

container.addChild(leftChild);
container.addChild(rightChild);

container.startup( );

/* Skip from page 1 to page 2 with... */
dijit.byId("foo").forward( );
```

Procrastination (a.k.a. Lazy Loading) May Yield Better Performance

The previous example uses explicit buttons for paging, but it is not uncommon to use a StackContainer as an application container to control the flow of an application with multiple pages. For example, your application might initially display a page with a search bar; once a button is pressed to trigger a search, you might page forward to display a search results screen. Assuming that you've defined every page of the application as a child of a StackContainer, this approach has the advantage of never explicitly reloading a page—a little bit of snazzy flare for a Web 2.0 style interface.

Although loading the entire application at one time when the page loads *may* be the best option for some circumstances, you could also elect to lazy-load content by configuring a child ContentPane to lazy load via its href attribute. Recall that this behavior is controlled by a ContentPane's preload attribute, which when false (the default) does not fetch content until it becomes visible. You can watch the Firebug console to confirm this behavior. For example, if the URL referenced below, which is entitled *blueFish* contained the text "Blue fish..." from Example 14-4, then the following adjustment would lazy load the fourth page of the StackContainer:

```
<div dojoType="dijit.layout.ContentPane" href="blueFish"></div>
```

Lazy loading is ideal for situations in which there may be application features that are essential, but not often used. A preferences pane is a prime candidate for lazy loading that often involves gobs of controls that may not appear on any other page of the application.

TabContainer

As it turns out, a TabContainer is really just a fancier version of a StackContainer—the primary difference is that a TabContainer comes with a snazzy set of tabs that can be used to control which page is displayed at any given time. In fact, the TabContainer inherits from StackContainer and provides only a few additional features that pertain to the list of tabs itself. Example 14-6 illustrates basic usage of the TabContainer.

Example 14-6. Creating a TabContainer in markup

```
<div dojoType="dijit.layout.TabContainer"
  style="width:225px; height:100px; margin:5px; border:solid 1px;">

    <div dojoType="dijit.layout.ContentPane" title="one">
        One fish...
    </div>
```

Example 14-6. Creating a TabContainer in markup (continued)

```
<div dojoType="dijit.layout.ContentPane" title="two">
    Two fish...
</div>

<div dojoType="dijit.layout.ContentPane" title="red"
  closable=
"true">Red fish...
    <script type="dojo/method" event="onClose" args="evt">
        console.log("Closing", this.title);
        return true; //must return true for close to occur!
    </script>
</div>

<div dojoType="dijit.layout.ContentPane" title="blue">
    Blue fish...
</div>
```

```
</div>
```

Take special note that the tab controls take care of themselves; you simply provide a title attribute to each child of the TabContainer, and the rest is handled with internal automation that you don't have get be directly involved with (and that's the best kind). Additionally, notice that you may provide a closeable tab via the closable attribute, and an optional onClose extension point may perform a custom action when a close does occur. Be careful, though, because if true is not returned from onClose, the tab will not close.

Table 14-7 lists the features that pertain to TabContainer.

Table 14-7. TabContainer API

Name	Type	Comment
title	String	Mixed into _Widget from StackContainer. Used in a child to provide the title for its tab button.
closeable	Boolean	Mixed into _Widget from StackContainer. Used in a child to specify whether a tab should be closeable. When closeable, a small icon appears on the tab that provides a means of closing the tab. false by default.
onClose( )	Function	An extension point mixed into _Widget from StackContainer that provides a uniform way for children to provide an extension point that may be used to augment behavior when closed. Returns true by default.
tabPosition	String	Specifies where the list of tab buttons should appear. Possible values include "top" (the default), "button", "left-h", and "right-h".
<id>-addChild <id>-removeChild <id>-selectChild	dojo.publish topics	This functionality is inherited from StackContainer. The named topics are published when children are added, removed, or selected. <id> refers to the id value of the TabContainer.

The buttons you see on a tab container are honest to goodness dijit.form.Button buttons; do with them as you will.

Just like with StackContainer, you may lazy load content in a TabContainer via a ContentPane, as long as preload is set to be false.

And now, Example 14-7 shows how to use programmatic creation.

Example 14-7. Programmatically creating a TabContainer

```
var container = new dijit.layout.TabContainer({
    tabPosition: "left-h",
    style : "width:200px;height:200px;"
}, "foo");

var leftChild = new dijit.layout.ContentPane({title : "tab1"});
leftChild.domNode.innerHTML="tab 1";

var rightChild = new dijit.layout.ContentPane({title : "tab2", closable: true});
rightChild.domNode.innerHTML="tab 2";

container.addChild(leftChild);
container.addChild(rightChild);

container.startup( );
```

AccordionContainer

Like a TabContainer, AccordionContainer inherits from StackContainer and is a means of displaying one child at a time from a collection of widgets. The visual difference is that the container looks like a vertical accordion, and animates when each child is selected.

One important difference in how you use AccordionContainer, however, is that you must use a special child container called AccordionPane that provides an explicit wrapper for its child widgets. The actual reasoning for why this is the case is not very interesting and has to do with how the underlying implementation for AccordionContainer. In general, just treat an AccordionPane like a ContentPane and be on your merry way.

 As of version 1.1, AccordionPane does not support nested layout widgets such as SplitContainer; virtually all other types of content, however, should work just fine.

Example 14-8 shows a simple AccordionContainer in action.

Example 14-8. Creating an AccordionContainer in markup

```
<div id="foo" dojoType="dijit.layout.AccordionContainer"
  style="width:150px; height:150px; margin:5px">
    <div dojoType="dijit.layout.AccordionPane" title="one">
         <p>One fish...</p>
    </div>
    <div dojoType="dijit.layout.AccordionPane" title="two">
         <p>Two fish...</p>
    </div>
    <div dojoType="dijit.layout.AccordionPane" title="red">
         <p>Red fish...</p>
    </div>
    <div id="blue" dojoType="dijit.layout.AccordionPane" title="blue">
       <div dojoType="dijit.layout.ContentPane" href="blueFish"></div>
    </div>
</div>
```

With respect to API, AccordionContainer itself provides only one additional attribute beyond what StackContainer offers, shown in Table 14-8.

Table 14-8. AccordionContainer API

Name (default)	Type	Comment
duration (250)	Integer	An attribute of AccordionPane that provides the duration in milliseconds that it should take to slide the pane to select another one.

Although we could leave programmatic creation as an exercise for the interested reader, there is a slight difference to creation pattern because AccordionPane is a dijit on its own, as shown in Example 14-9.

Example 14-9. Programmatically creating an AccordionContainer

```
var container = new dijit.layout.AccordionContainer({}, "foo");

var child1 = dojo.doc.createElement("div");
child1.innerHTML="pane 1";

var content1 = dojo.doc.createElement("p");
content1.innerHTML = "content 1";

var ap1 = new dijit.layout.AccordionPane({title: "pane1", selected : true}, content1);
container.addChild(ap1);

var child2 = dojo.doc.createElement("div");
child2.innerHTML="pane 2";

var content2 = dojo.doc.createElement("p");
content2.innerHTML = "content 2";
```

Example 14-9. Programmatically creating an AccordionContainer (continued)

```
var ap2 = new dijit.layout.AccordionPane({title: "pane2"}, content2);
container.addChild(ap2);

container.startup();
```

Rendering and Visibility Considerations

You may have noticed while working through the examples in this chapter that you usually see the layout occur as the page loads; for example, you might see ordinary text HTML representing some of the layout content, and then all of a sudden it magically transforms into this great-looking layout. While not totally unacceptable, you will probably not want to see the rendering take place in many situations.

A common technique for working around the situation is to initially set the body of the page to be hidden, and then when the page finishes loading, make it visible all at one time. Accomplishing this technique is quite simple, and you merely have to provide a style (or class) indicating that the body of the page should be hidden, like so: `<body style="visibility:hidden;">` should do the trick. Just remember to add the corresponding call to make it visible at the desired time. Assuming you've made the entire body hidden, adding a `dojo.style(dojo.body( ), "visibility", "visible")` to a `dojo.addOnLoad` displays the page's content. Any callback could be used in place of page load if for some reason you wanted to delay showing the page until some arbitrary event occurred (like an asynchronous callback that provides data for a custom widget, perhaps).

Recall that the difference between the CSS styles of visibility and display has to do with taking up space on the screen. In general, nodes styled with `visibility:hidden` are hidden from display but still take up space; nodes styled with `display:none` would not be visible and would take up no space—resulting in a noticeable shift of content when the display is changed to `display:block`.

One caveat that should be noted, however, is that layout containers do not always respond well when they are initially created within a hidden container. If you find that your layout containers are not visible when they should be, you may need to manually call their `resize( )` method to force them to render properly. Historically, this issue has especially been the case when displaying a layout container within a `dijit.Dialog`.

Layout dijits do not always render properly if they are created in context that does not immediately make them visible. Almost all of the time, you can simply call the layout container's `resize( )` method to render it.

Summary

After reading this chapter, you should be able to:

- Appreciate the common design challenges (tabbed layouts, for example) that layout dijits alleviate
- Understand the basic features provided by the various layout dijits
- Create arbitrary layouts with the layout dijits both in markup and programmatically
- Use `BorderContainer` to create flexible, tiled layouts that can arbitrarily resize
- Use `ContentPane` to lazy load content either as a standalone or as part of another dijit
- Use `StackContainer` and `TabContainer` to display multiple pages of data in an application
- Understand some of the considerations with respect to initially displaying layout dijts as being hidden
- Understand the existing limitations of `AccordionPane` with respect to embedding layout dijits
- Understand the role that the base classes `_Container` and `_Contained` play with the layout dijits

Application widgets are coming up next.

## CHAPTER 15

Application Widgets

This chapter systematically works through all of the general-purpose application widgets provided in Dijit. In many ways, these are some of the most exciting dijits provided by the toolkit because they're not as familiar as form elements and, unlike the enabling layout dijits, they provide tremendous interactive functionality. `ProgressBar`, `Toolbar`, `Editor`, and `Tree` are just a few of the exciting dijits that are coming up. Chances are, you'll witness some of some highest quality DHTML hacking you've ever seen in this chapter—especially as we near the end of it.

Although not explicitly called out in all cases, the widgets in this chapter are fully accessible, as are all other widgets in Dijit.

Tooltip

Tooltips are a great means of providing user assistance for the context of a particular control on the page, and although the ordinary HTML `title` attribute is a good start for applications circa 1990, the current era of web applications calls for a richer variation of a tooltip. The `Tooltip` dijit does just that, providing the ability to display arbitrary HTML markup instead of a plain old snippet of text. Although you got a preview of `Tooltip` with `ValidationTextBox` and its descendants in a previous chapter, you'll be pleased to know that you can now use `Tooltip` as a standalone.

Consider Example 15-1, which captures some of the key features of a `Tooltip`, producing the results shown in Figure 15-1.

Example 15-1. Typical Tooltip usage

```
One <span id="one">fish</span>, two <span id="two">fish</span>.

<div dojoType="dijit.Tooltip" connectId="one,two">
    A limbless cold-blooded vertebrate...<img src='./fish.jpeg'/>
</div>
```

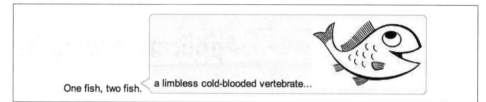

One fish, two fish. a limbless cold-blooded vertebrate...

Figure 15-1. The tooltip that appears when you mouseover either of the tags containing "fish"

Note that the syntax for passing in multiple values for connectId is inconsistent with normal JavaScript Array syntax: you provide multiple connectIds without brackets and without embedded quotes: connectId="id1,id2". It is likely that this syntax will normalize in a future release so that this isn't an exception to the rule.

As you can see from the example, you simply provide arbitrary HTML markup for Tooltip to render. Tooltip should be used for read-only content; TooltipDialog, coming up in the next section, is particularly suited for content such as input fields and buttons that requires interaction. Table 15-1 gives a complete listing of Tooltip's features.

Table 15-1. Tooltip API

Name	Type	Comment
connectId ("")	String	A comma-separated list of values that provides the node id values for which the Tooltip should be displayed.
label ("")	String	The text to display in the Tooltip. Although the label could include arbitrary HTML markup, it's generally better form to include HTML markup inside of the enclosing tag.
showDelay (400)	Integer	How many milliseconds to wait before displaying the Tooltip to a user.

Dialog Widgets

Dijit offers two related widgets that provide dialog functionality: Dialog, which is similar to the kind of interaction you normally have with something like an ordinary alert box (only a whole lot more aesthetically pleasing and flexible), and TooltipDialog, which is much like an ordinary tooltip except that it can render other widgets and provide for more interaction that an ordinary Tooltip.

Dialog

The Dialog dijit is conceptually like a pop up that sets up a translucent underlay below it. While it is visible, you cannot respond to anything below it, making it ideal for situations in which you need to temporarily prevent access to controls on a page or force the user to acknowledge or respond to an alert.

But in addition to the obvious uses, you might also use a `Dialog` for almost any situation in which the alternative would be to pop up a new window. From an implementation standpoint, using a `Dialog` is often easier than interacting with a separate window because everything that is contained in the `Dialog` is part of the current page's DOM.* You can query it and otherwise manipulate it like anything else on the page—even if it's currently not visible.

A `Dialog` may contain any DOM content you'd like to place in it, whether it is a simple HTML snippet, a complex layout dijit, or a custom widget of your own. Example 15-2 illustrates the most basic usage of a `Dialog`; in this case, it is automatically displayed on page load.

 As noted in the previous chapter, you may need to manually call a layout dijit's resize method to force it to redraw itself if you initially create it to be hidden—which it would be if you created it and then embedded it inside of a `Dialog`.

Example 15-2. Typical Dialog usage

```html
<html>
    <head>
        <title>Fun With Dialog!</title>

        <link rel="stylesheet" type="text/css"
          href="http://o.aolcdn.com/dojo/1.1/dojo/resources/dojo.css" />
        <link rel="stylesheet" type="text/css"
          href="http://o.aolcdn.com/dojo/1.1/dijit/themes/tundra/tundra.css" />

        <script
            type="text/javascript"
            src="http://o.aolcdn.com/dojo/1.1/dojo/dojo.xd.js"
            djConfig="parseOnLoad:true">
        </script>

        <script type="text/javascript">
            dojo.require("dojo.parser");
            dojo.require("dijit.Dialog");
            dojo.addOnLoad(function( ) {
                dijit.byId("dialog").show( );
            });
        </script>
    </head>
    <body class="tundra">
        <div id="dialog" dojoType="dijit.Dialog">
            So foul and fair a day I have not seen...
        </div>
    </body>
</html>
```

---

* In fact, some browsers will not even allow you to manipulate one window's DOM from another window—even if both windows are from the same origin.

Programmatically creating a Dialog is easily accomplished with Dialog's setContent method, which can accept a DOM node. Consider this example, which forces the user to click on a Button that is placed into a Dialog—even though you've expressly told them not to do it:

```
dojo.addOnLoad(function( ) {
    var d = new dijit.Dialog( );

    //hide the ordinary close button from the user...
    dojo.style(d.closeButtonNode, "visibility", "hidden");

    var b = new dijit.form.Button({label: "Do not press this button"});
    var handle = dojo.connect(b, "onClick", function( ) {
        d.hide( );
        dojo.disconnect(handle);
    });
    d.setContent(b.domNode);
    d.show( );
});
```

 Dialog's template contains a number of useful attach points, including the closeButtonNode attach point, which was used in the previous code example to hide the icon that normally closes a Dialog.

Like the other dijits, you'll often get by with just a few common methods and attributes, but Table 15-2 presents the rest of the story for when you need it.

 Dialog inherits from ContentPane, so all of ContentPane's attributes, methods, and extension points are also available if you need them. See Example 14-3 for that API.

Table 15-2. Dialog API that builds upon ContentPane's API

Name	Type	Comment
open	Boolean	The state of the Dialog. true if it is open, false (the default) otherwise.
duration	Integer	The duration in milliseconds it takes to fade in and fade out the Dialog. 400 by default.
duration( )	Function	Hides the Dialog.
layout( )	Function	Positions the Dialog and its underlay.
show()	Function	Display the Dialog.

TooltipDialog

TooltipDialog inherits from Dialog, but provides functionality that may sort of remind you of a menu out of a DropDownButton—except that you can interact with it. In fact, the current manifestation TooltipDialog must be housed in a DropDownButton or a ComboButton, although you could theoretically adjust the button's style to make it appear quite different. You may recall the concept of a `TooltipDialog` from interacting with a spreadsheet application.

 To get `TooltipDialog`, you must do a `dojo.require("dijit.Dialog")` because `TooltipDialog` is embedded into `Dialog`'s resource file.

Aside from the inability to programmatically create and display a `TooltipDialog` as a standalone, the rest of its functional API of a `TooltipDialog` is quite similar to `Dialog` with the caveat that it does not support a `show( )` method. Additionally, it offers a standard `title` attribute that you can fill in if you'd like to stay accessibility compliant.

A good use case for a `TooltipDialog` might be to provide an interactive means of tagging an image. For example, you might use a `DropDownButton` to provide an image via its `iconClass` attribute and then interactively supply the `TooltipDialog` when the user clicks on the image. The following snippet provides the basic outline for how you might get started with a custom image tagger, producing the results shown in Figure 15-2.

Figure 15-2. A custom image tagger built with DropDownButton and TooltipDialog

```
<!-- somewhere out there...
<style type="text/css">
.customImage {
                background-image : url('/static/path/to/apple.jpeg');
                backgrond-repeat : no-repeat;
                width : 120px;
                height : 120px;
            }
</style>
-->

<button dojoType="dijit.form.DropDownButton" iconClass="customImage"
  showLabel="false">
    <span>This label is hidden...</span>

    <div dojoType="dijit.TooltipDialog">
        <span>Tag this image...<span>
```

```
    <div dojoType="dijit.form.TextBox"></div>
    </div>
</button>
```

ProgressBar

The ProgressBar dijit behaves just like any other progress bar you've seen in an application, and it comes in both determinate and indeterminate variations. One of the greatest things about it is that there's just not that much to say. In fact, Example 15-3 should do a good job of speaking for itself.

Example 15-3. Typical indeterminate ProgressBar usage

```
<div dojoType="dijit.ProgressBar" indeterminate="true" style="width:300px"></div>
```

Of course, there will certainly be times when you'll want to fetch a real update from the server and display actual progress instead of an indeterminate indicator. Let's assume that you have a server-side routine that is returning some kind of progress indication. The following mockup simulates:

```
import cherrypy

config = {
    #serve up this static file...
    '/foo.html' :
    {
        'tools.staticfile.on' : True,
        'tools.staticfile.filename' : '/absolute/path/to/foo.html'
    }
}

class Content:
    def __init__(self):
        self.progress = 0

    @cherrypy.expose
    def getProgress(self):
        self.progress += 10
        return str(self.progress)

cherrypy.quickstart(Content(), '/', config=config)
```

The file *foo.html* that contains the ProgressBar might look like this:

```
<html>
    <head>
        <title>Fun with ProgressBar!</title>

        <link rel="stylesheet" type="text/css"
          href="http://o.aolcdn.com/dojo/1.1/dojo/resources/dojo.css" />
```

```
<link rel="stylesheet" type="text/css"
  href="http://o.aolcdn.com/dojo/1.1/dijit/themes/tundra/tundra.css" />

<script
    type="text/javascript"
    src="http://o.aolcdn.com/dojo/1.1/dojo/dojo.xd.js"
    djConfig="parseOnLoad:true">
</script>

<script type="text/javascript">
    dojo.require("dojo.parser");
    dojo.require("dijit.ProgressBar");

    dojo.addOnLoad(function( ) {
        var progressInterval = setInterval(function( ) {
            dojo.xhrGet({
                url : "http://localhost:8080/getProgress",
                load : function(response, ioArgs) {
                    console.log("load", response);
                    if (response <= 100) {
                        dijit.byId("pb").update({progress : response});
                    }
                    else {
                        clearInterval(progressInterval);
                    }
                }
            });
        }, 1000);
    });
</script>
</head>
<body style="padding:100px" class="tundra">
    <div>Loading...</div>
    <div id="pb" dojoType="dijit.ProgressBar" style="width:300px"></div>
    </div>
</body>
</html>
```

To summarize, every second the addOnLoad routine checks the /getProgress URL for an update and feeds it into ProgressBar via its update function. The use of JavaScript's setInterval function will be quite typical with a ProgressBar.

 Don't confuse setInterval with setTimeout. The former executes a function according to a set interval, while the latter executes a function *after* a specified amount of time.

The full range of ProgressBar options are shown in Table 15-3.

Table 15-3. ProgressBar API

Name	Type	Comment
indeterminate	Boolean	Whether to display an indeterminate indication (an animated image) or to actually render progress as provided via the update method.
maximum	Float	The maximum possible value. Although values of 0 through 100 (the default) are common, any range could be used.
places	Number	The number of decimal places to display for a determinate ProgressBar. 0 by default.
progress	String	The initial value for the ProgressBar. You may provide a percent sign, such as "50%", to indicate a relative amount versus an absolute amount.
update(/*Object*/ progress)	Function	Used to update the progress information. You may pass in progress, maximum, and determinate to configure the ProgressBar during any update.
onChange( )	Function	Extension point that is called after each call to update.

Finally, recall that if you need to display a ProgressBar as part of a blocking event, you can always stuff it inside of a Dialog to make the user wait while something happens in the background. Something along the lines of the following example would do the trick:

```
var pb = new dijit.ProgressBar;
var d = new dijit.Dialog;
d.setContent(pb.domNode);
d.show( );
```

ColorPalette

ColorPalette is another simple standalone widget that is helpful for providing a more visual and interactive way of allowing a user to select a color—perfect for situations in which you allow the user to customize the theme of an application, for example. By default, the palette comes in two canned sizes, 3×4 or 7×10, with pre-selected popular web colors.

 You may already be wondering why you can't configure your own set of colors for the palette. As it turns out, the palettes that appear are images, not panes of HTML markup, and they were designed this way for a11y reasons, even though it does not seem ideal. Thus, if you want to extend ColorPalette to display a custom selection, it is certainly doable—you'd just have to read the source and get your hands dirty by hacking on some of the private attributes.

Using a ColorPalette in markup is quite simple; the following listing illustrates:

```
<div dojoType="dijit.ColorPalette">
    <script type="dojo/method" event="onChange" args="selectedColor">
        /* hide the palette, perhaps? */
        console.log(selectedColor);
    </script>
</div>
```

Like `ProgressBar`, `ColorPalette` is a nice and simple standalone. Table 15-4 shows the full story.

Table 15-4. ColorPalette API

Name (default)	Type	Comment
defaultTimeout	Integer	The duration before a key that is held down becomes typematic. 500 by default.
timeoutChangeRate	Number	The amount of time that is used to change the typematic rate. A value of 1.0 means that typematic events are fired at regular intervals, while values less than 1.0 mean that the typematic rate accelerates accordingly. The default value is 0.9.
palette	String	The size of the palette, which must be either 7 × 10 (the default) or 3 × 4.
onChange(/*String*/ hexColor)	Function	Extension point triggered when a color is selected.

Programmatic creation is straightforward enough:

```
var cp = new dijit.ColorPalette({/*attributes go here */});
/* Now stick it somewhere on the page...*/
dojo.body().appendChild(cp.domNode);
```

Toolbar

The `Toolbar` is another familiar control that abbreviates the common task of providing a collection of common commands to the user. In short, the `Toolbar` does nothing more than house a collection of `Button` dijits, which when styled appropriately, can be very aesthetically pleasing. The various prepackaged themes that come with Dijit contain classes for many of the common operations such as cut/paste, bold/italic, etc., which you can provide through `Button`'s `iconClass` attribute.

The following listing illustrates placing a `Toolbar` on the page and then systematically wires up each of its buttons to a custom event handler.

 This particular example attempts to automate the methodology for hooking up buttons and custom handlers. Note that the peculiarity of connecting to `x.parentNode` inside of the `forEach` block instead of just connecting to `x` is related to the way that `Button` is implemented. As it turns out, the icon overlay is what contains an icon node that actually receives the click; you could have debugged this by inspecting with Firebug.

```
<html>
    <head>
        <title>Fun with Toolbar!</title>

        <link rel="stylesheet" type="text/css"
          href="http://o.aolcdn.com/dojo/1.1/dojo/resources/dojo.css" />
        <link rel="stylesheet" type="text/css"
          href="http://o.aolcdn.com/dojo/1.1/dijit/themes/tundra/tundra.css" />

        <script
            type="text/javascript"
            src="http://o.aolcdn.com/dojo/1.1/dojo/dojo.xd.js"
            djConfig="parseOnLoad:true,isDebug:true,>
        </script>

        <script type="text/javascript">
            dojo.require("dojo.parser");
            dojo.require("dijit.Toolbar");
            dojo.require("dijit.form.Button");

            dojo.addOnLoad(function() {
                var bold = function() {console.log("bold");}
                var italic= function() {console.log("italic");}
                var underline = function() {console.log("underline");}
                var superscript = function() {console.log("superscript");}
                var subscript = function() {console.log("subscript");}

                dojo.query(".dijitEditorIcon").forEach(function(x) {
                        if (dojo.hasClass(x, "dijitEditorIconBold"))
                            dojo.connect(x.parentNode, "onclick", bold);
                        else if (dojo.hasClass(x, "dijitEditorIconItalic"))
                            dojo.connect(x.parentNode, "onclick", italic);
                        else if (dojo.hasClass(x, "dijitEditorIconUnderline"))
                            dojo.connect(x.parentNode, "onclick", underline);
                        else if (dojo.hasClass(x, "dijitEditorIconSubscript"))
                            dojo.connect(x.parentNode, "onclick", superscript);
                        else if (dojo.hasClass(x, "dijitEditorIconSuperscript"))
                            dojo.connect(x.parentNode, "onclick", subscript);
                });
            });
        </script>
    </head>
    <body style="padding:100px" class="tundra">
        <div dojoType="dijit.Toolbar" style="width:175px">
            <button dojoType="dijit.form.Button"
                iconClass="dijitEditorIcon dijitEditorIconBold" ></button>
            <button dojoType="dijit.form.Button"
                iconClass="dijitEditorIcon dijitEditorIconItalic" ></button>
            <button dojoType="dijit.form.Button"
                iconClass="dijitEditorIcon dijitEditorIconUnderline" ></button>

            <span dojoType="dijit.ToolbarSeparator"></span>
```

```
            <button dojoType="dijit.form.Button"
                iconClass="dijitEditorIcon dijitEditorIconSubscript"></button>
            <button dojoType="dijit.form.Button"
                iconClass="dijitEditorIcon dijitEditorIconSuperscript"></button>
        </div>
    </body>
</html>
```

As a point of interest, Dijit themes currently define the following self-descriptive Editor-related icons (defined in the theme's stylesheet) that may be contained in Toolbar. (Editor is discussed at length in an upcoming section.)

Toolbar has a simple API, shown in Table 15-5, which is representative of a descendant of _Container.

Table 15-5. Toolbar API

Name	Type	Comment
addChild(/*Object*/ child, /*Integer?*/ insertIndex)	Function	Used to insert a dijit into the Toolbar.
getChildren( )	Function	Returns an array of the contained dijits in the Toolbar.
removeChild(/*Object*/ child)	Function	Used to remove a child from the Toolbar (removes its domNode, but does not destroy the dijit; you must call destroyRecursive( ) manually).

Menu

Menu models the kind of contextual menu that appears when you right-click on an application icon in a desktop environment. A Menu contains MenuItem widgets, which are bona fide menu items that may be selected, or PopupMenuItem widgets, which can provide another layer of menu items (similar to the Windows Start menu). The child of a PopupMenuItem is just another Menu. Although it would not be wise from a usability standpoint, you could theoretically embed an arbitrary number of PopupMenuItem and MenuItem dijits.

To start out, let's take a look at a simple Menu that contains only MenuItem children, as shown in Example 15-4.

By issuing a dojo.require("dijit.Menu") you also get MenuItem and PopupMenuItem.

Image Slicing to Minimize Latency

Instead of defining a ton of small images, resulting in a series of synchronous requests back and forth to the server that all incur HTTP overhead, Dijit themes use an approach in which all images are defined side-by-side on a single image. CSS styling is used to slice out the part of the image that should be displayed for any given icon like so:

```
.tundra .dijitEditorIcon
/* All built-in Editor icons have this class */
{
        background-image: url('images/editor.gif');
        background-repeat: no-repeat;
        width: 18px;
        height: 18px;
        text-align: center;
}

/* Individual icons are sliced out like so... */
.tundra .dijitEditorIconUnderline { background-position: -648px; }
```

The following list summarizes other Editor icons that are available:

- dijitEditorIconSep
- dijitEditorIconBackColor
- dijitEditorIconBold
- dijitEditorIconCancel
- dijitEditorIconCopy
- dijitEditorIconCreateLink
- dijitEditorIconCut
- dijitEditorIconDelete
- dijitEditorIconForeColor
- dijitEditorIconHiliteColor
- dijitEditorIconIndent
- dijitEditorIconInsertHorizontalRule
- dijitEditorIconInsertImage
- dijitEditorIconInsertOrderedList
- dijitEditorIconInsertTable
- dijitEditorIconInsertUnorderedList
- dijitEditorIconItalic
- dijitEditorIconJustifyCenter
- dijitEditorIconJustifyFull

—continued—

- dijitEditorIconJustifyLeft
- dijitEditorIconJustifyRight
- dijitEditorIconLeftToRight
- dijitEditorIconListBulletIndent
- dijitEditorIconListBulletOutdent
- dijitEditorIconListNumIndent
- dijitEditorIconListNumOutdent
- dijitEditorIconOutdent
- dijitEditorIconPaste
- dijitEditorIconRedo
- dijitEditorIconRemoveFormat
- dijitEditorIconRightToLeft
- dijitEditorIconSave
- dijitEditorIconSpace
- dijitEditorIconStrikethrough
- dijitEditorIconSubscript
- dijitEditorIconSuperscript
- dijitEditorIconUnderline
- dijitEditorIconUndo
- dijitEditorIconWikiword
- dijitEditorIconToggleDir

Example 15-4. Typical Menu usage

```
<body class="tundra">
    <!-- right click in here to get the contextual menu -->
    <div id="context" style="background:#eee; height:300px; width:300px;"></div>

    <div dojoType="dijit.Menu" targetNodeIds="context" style="display:none">
        <div dojoType="dijit.MenuItem">foo
            <script type="dojo/method" event="onClick" args="evt">
                console.log("foo");
            </script>
        </div>
        <div dojoType="dijit.MenuItem">bar
            <script type="dojo/method" event="onClick" args="evt">
                console.log("bar");
            </script>
        </div>
        <div dojoType="dijit.MenuItem">baz
            <script type="dojo/method" event="onClick" args="evt">
                console.log("baz");
            </script>
        </div>
```

Example 15-4. Typical Menu usage (continued)

```
    </div>
</body>
```

 Like Tooltip, the list of values passed in for Menu is a comma-separated string that does not include enclosing brackets that would be required of an ordinary JavaScript Array. A future release may very well standardize this anomaly.

As you can see, there's not much to it, and defining in markup makes matters even simpler. The one emphasized line of code that sets the display to be none is important because it may be the case that your Menu will initially be visible without this cue.

Now, suppose you wanted to make baz be a PopupMenuItem and you wanted the Menu to be contextual for the entire window. You could do it thusly:

```
<div dojoType="dijit.Menu" style="display:none"contextualMenuForWindow="true">
    <div dojoType="dijit.MenuItem">foo
        <script type="dojo/method" event="onClick" args="evt">
            console.log("foo");
        </script>
    </div>
    <div dojoType="dijit.MenuItem">bar
        <script type="dojo/method" event="onClick" args="evt">
            console.log("bar");
        </script>
    </div>
    <div dojoType="dijit.PopupMenuItem">
        <span>baz</span>
        <div dojoType="dijit.Menu">
          <!-- define onClick handlers as needed for each item -->
            <div dojoType="dijit.MenuItem">yabba</div>
            <div dojoType="dijit.MenuItem">dabba</div>
            <div dojoType="dijit.MenuItem">doo</div>
        </div>
    </div>
</div>
```

Hopefully, the only remotely tricky part about installing the PopupMenuItem was that there needed to be an explicit node set, its first child to be specific, which provides the title.

To round off this section on Menu, Table 15-6 provides a listing of the remaining API. Note that as a _Container descendant, Menu has token methods for adding, removing, and getting children, just like Toolbar and the others offer. The API for MenuItem and PopupMenuItem are shown in Table 15-7.

Table 15-6. Menu API

Name (default)	Type	Description
contextMenuForWindow	Boolean (false)	If true, right-clicking anywhere on the window opens the menu. If false, the targetNodeIds parameter should be provided that supplies one or more nodes that can trigger the menu.
popupDelay	Integer (500)	The number of milliseconds to wait before popping up the Menu after the click event occurs. (An interrupting click that occurs before this duration ends results in the time period resetting and starting over.)
targetNodeIds	Array ([])	A list of the node id values that support this Menu.
parentMenu	Object (null)	A pointer to the parent Menu, if any.
addChild(/*Object*/ child, /*Integer?*/ insertIndex)	Function	Used to insert a dijit into the Toolbar.
getChildren( )	Function	Returns an array of the contained dijits in the Toolbar.
removeChild(/*Object*/ child)	Function	Used to remove a child from the Toolbar (removes its domNode, but does not destroy the dijit; you must call destroyRecursive( ) manually).
bindDomNode(/*String|DOMNode*/node)	Function	Attaches a Menu to a particular node. (Useful for context menus, for example.)
unBindDomNode(/*String|DOMNode*/node)	Function	Detaches a Menu from a particular node.
onClick(/*Object*/item, /*Event*/evt)	Function	Extension point designed to handle clicks.
onItemHover(/*MenuItem*/item)	Function	Called when the cursor hovers over a MenuItem.
onItemUnhover(/*MenuItem*/item)	Function	Called when the cursor ends a hover over a MenuItem.
onCancel( )	Function	Extension point for handling when the user cancels the current Menu.
onExecute( )	Function	Extension point for handling when the user executes the current Menu.

Table 15-7. MenuItem and PopupMenuItem API

Name (default)	Type	Description
`label`	String	The text that should appear in the `MenuItem`.
`iconClass`	String	The class to apply to make the `MenuItem` appear as an icon (use background-image in CSS).
`disabled`	Boolean	Specifying whether the `MenuItem` is disabled. `false` by default.
`setDisabled(/*Boolean*/ value)`	Function	Programatically control whether the `MenuItem` is disabled.
`onClick(/*DomEvent*/ evt)`	Function	Used for attaching click handlers on the `MenuItem`.

TitlePane

A `TitlePane` is a widget that always displays a title, but whose body may be expanded or collapsed as needed; the actual resize is done with an animated wipe-in or wipe-out. As a descendant of `ContentPane`, `TitlePane` also has access to all of the inherited methods for loading content remotely, although they are not explicitly covered again in this section. (Refer to the previous chapter for complete coverage of `ContentPane`.) Example 15-5 shows the elementary usage.

Example 15-5. Typical TitlePane usage

```
<div dojoType="dijit.TitlePane" title="Grocery list:" style="width:300px">
    <ul>
        <li>Eggs</li>
        <li>Milk</li>
        <li>Bananas</li>
        <li>Coffee</li>
    </ul>
</div>
```

`TitlePane` supports the feature set shown in Table 15-8.

Table 15-8. TitlePane API

Name	Type	Comment
`title`	String	The title of the pane.
`open`	Boolean	Whether the pane is opened or closed. `true` by default.
`duration`	Integer	The number of milliseconds the animated wipe should last. 250 by default.
`setContent(/*DomNode|String*/)`	Function	Used to programmatically set the contents of the pane.

Table 15-8. TitlePane API (continued)

Name	Type	Comment
setTitle(/* String */ title)	Function	Sets the title.
toggle( )	Function	If the pane is opened, this closes it. If closed, then opens it.

Although you could use TitlePane as a static artifact on your page, you might soon find interesting uses for it as a more interactive kind of control. Consider, for example, how easy it would be to use it to mimic the kind of sticky note that you see in so many applications. Getting a simple widget working is as easy as inserting something like a Textarea into TitlePane, and retitling it whenever it closes, as shown in Example 15-6.

Example 15-6. Simulating a sticky note with a TitlePane

```
dojo.addOnLoad(function( ) {
    var ed = new dijit.form.Textarea({id : "titlePaneContent"});
    dijit.byId("tp").setContent(ed.domNode);
});

//And now for the ContentPane, which you might declare in markup:

<div id="tp" dojoType="dijit.TitlePane" style="width:300px">
    <script type="dojo/connect" event="toggle">
        if (!this.open) {
            var t = dijit.byId("titlePaneContent").getValue( );
            if (t.length > 15)
                t = t.slice(0,12)+"...";
            this.setTitle(t);
        }
    </script>
</div>
```

A little additional styling and some drag-and-drop action takes you just about the whole way towards having a small sticky-notes application.

InlineEditBox

The InlineEditBox is often described as a wrapper widget in that it provides a marked-up static display for what is really an editable control—then, when you're ready to edit it, you do so inline by simply selecting it. For example, instead of having a fixed size, editable TextBox always visible on the screen, you could wrap it in an InlineEdit box and it would appear as ordinary markup on the screen (like a label), but when you select it, it transforms back into a TextBox for editing. When editing completes as signaled by an event, such as the Enter key being pressed, it switches back to markup.

In its simplest usage, you might simply wrap a TextBox in an InlineEditable as part of a form letter application, like the following example. Note that what would have normally appeared as a TextBox and cluttered up the display is presented just like ordinary markup, while clicking on it transforms it into an editable control:

```
Dear <span dojoType="dijit.InlineEditBox" autoSave="false"
    editor="dijit.form.TextBox">Valued Customer</span>:

<div>We have received your request to be removed from our spam list. Not to worry,
we'll remove you when we're good and ready. In the meanwhile, please do not hesitate
to contact us with further complaints.</div>

<div>Sincerely,</div>
<span dojoType="dijit.InlineEditBox" autosave="false"
    editor="dijit.form.TextBox">Customer Service</span>
```

To recap, the autosave attribute being set to false results in the control presenting Save and Cancel buttons (the text would normally have been saved as it was typed with no controls displayed at all). That's the basic concept. Now, let's expand on these concepts by trying out a different Editor.

Here's a quick example of an InlineEditBox wrapping up a Textarea. Note that the renderAsHtml allows us to provide markup and have it automatically rendered on the spot:

```
Dear <span dojoType="dijit.InlineEditBox" autoSave="false"
    editor="dijit.form.TextBox">Valued Customer</span>:

<div dojoType="dijit.InlineEditBox" autoSave="false" editor="dijit.form.Textarea"
    renderAsHtml="true">
    Insert<br>
    Form<br>
    Letter<br>
    Here<br>
</div>

<div>Sincerely,</div>

<span dojoType="dijit.InlineEditBox"
    autoSave="false" editor="dijit.form.TextBox">Customer Service</span>
```

Like the previous dijits in this chapter, the basic usage is quite simple, but Table 15-9 shows a few extra configuration items to be aware of and keep on hand.

Table 15-9. InlineEditBox API

Name	Type	Comment
editing	Boolean	The edit state of the InlineEditBox. true when it is in editing mode.
autoSave	Boolean	Whether changing the value automatically should save it without requiring any kind of explicit action. true by default.

Table 15-9. InlineEditBox API (continued)

Name	Type	Comment
`buttonSave`	String	The text string to display on the Save button. Empty by default.
`buttonCancel`	String	The text string to display on the Cancel button. Empty by default.
`renderAsHtml`	Boolean	If `true`, renders the `InlineEditBox`'s editor contents as HTML. `false` by default.
`editor`	String	The class name for the dijit that should act as the editor. `dijit.form.TextBox` by default.
`editorParams`	Object	Any parameters that should be passed in when constructing the editor for the `InlineEditBox`.
`width`	String	The width of the editor. 100% by default.
`value`	String	The display value of the widget when in read-only mode.
`noValueIndicator`	String	The placeholder that should be displayed when there is no text value (so that the user has a place to click on and trigger an edit). A wingdings placeholder is there by default.
`setDisabled(/*Boolean*/ disabled)`	Function	Used to disable and enable the widget.
`setValue(/*String*/val)`	Function	Sets the value of the widget.
`save`	Function	Saves the contents of the editor and reverts to display mode.
`cancel`	Function	Discards any changes made in the editor and reverts to display mode.
`onChange`	Function	An extension point that can be used to be notified of changes to the value.
`enableSave`	Function	A user-replaceable function that can be used to enable and disable the Save button. (For example, you might disable the button because of invalid conditions in the editor.)

Tree

The Tree dijit is an amazing piece of engineering. Using completely native DHTML, it looks and acts just like you'd expect a hierarchical tree to look and act, it supports drag-and-drop operations, and it's flexible enough to bind to an arbitrary data source. Like any other complex piece of machinery, there are a few fundamentals to pick up before you get rolling with it, but they're all fairly intuitive once you've connected the dots that first time. This is one of the longer sections in the chapter because the Tree is quite powerful and offers an extensive set of features. Although we won't elaborate on a11y, you should also be cognizant that the Tree is quite accessible with the keyboard via arrow keys, the Enter key, and so on.

A good understanding of the dojo.data API is especially helpful for working with the Tree dijit. See Chapter 9 for more details.

Before reading through any code, it's helpful to be aware of at least a few things:

Trees and forests

A *tree* is a hierarchical data structure that contains a single root element. A *forest*, on the other hand, is a hierarchical structure just like a tree except that it does not have a single root node; instead, it has multiple root nodes. As we'll see, distinguishing between a tree and a forest is a common issue because many data views are conveniently expressed as a tree with a single root node even though the data that backs the view is a forest with an implied root node.

Nodes

A tree is a hierarchical organization of nodes and the linkages between them. The specific type of node that is used by dijit.Tree is dijit._TreeNode; the leading underscore in this case signals that you'd never be using a _TreeNode outside of a Tree. There are, however, several properties of _TreeNode that are useful to manipulate directly, as we'll see in upcoming examples.

Data agnosticism

The Tree dijit is completely agnostic to the data source that backs it. Prior to version 1.1, it read directly from an implementation of the dojo.data API, which is quite flexible and provides a uniform layer for data access, but as of the 1.1 release, the enhancement of an additional intermediating layer between the dojo.data model and the Tree was added. These intermediating layers are dijit.tree.TreeStoreModel and dijit.tree.ForestStoreModel, respectively. Much of the motivation for the change was to make the Tree much more robust and amenable to drag-and-drop operations.

 When you execute dojo.require("dijit.Tree") the ForestStoreModel and TreeStoreModel come along with the Tree itself.

Simple Tree

To ease in to what the Tree can do for you, assume that you have a really simple data source that serves up dojo.data.ItemFileReadStore JSON along the lines of the following:

```
{
    identifier : 'name',

    label : 'name',

    items : [
```

```
                {
                    name : 'Programming Languages',
                    children: [
                        {name : 'JavaScript'},
                        {name : 'Python'},
                        {name : 'C++'},
                        {name : 'Erlang'},
                        {name : 'Prolog'}
                    ]
                }
            ]
        }
```

So far, so good. Instead of parsing the data yourself on the client, you get to use `dojo.data` to abstract the data for you. Hooking up an actual `ItemFileReadStore` is as easy as pointing it to the URL that serves the data and then querying into it. The following tag, when instantiated by the parser, would do the trick if the file were served up from the working directory as *programmingLanguages.json*, and it would have a global identifier of `dataStore` that would be accessible:

```
<div dojoType="dojo.data.ItemFileReadStore"
    jsId="dataStore" url="./programmingLanguages.json"></div>
```

Before the data gets fed into the Tree, however, it will be mediated through a `TreeStoreModel`. (We'll work through the implications of using a `ForestStoreModel` in a moment.) The complete API listing for an intermediating `TreeStoreModel` will be presented momentarily, but for now, all that's pertinent is that we have to point the `TreeStoreModel` at the `ItemFileReadStore` and provide a query. The following `TreeStoreModel` would query the `dojo.data` store with global identifier `dataStore` for all name values:

```
<div dojoType="dijit.tree.TreeStoreModel" jsId="model" store="dataStore"
    query="{name:'*'}"></div>
```

Finally, the only thing left to do is point the Tree dijit at the `TreeStoreModel` like so:

```
<div dojoType="dijit.Tree" model="model"></div>
```

That's it. Example 15-7 puts it all together, and Figure 15-3 shows the result.

Example 15-7. Simple Tree with a root

```
<html>
    <head>
        <title>Tree Fun!</title>

        <link rel="stylesheet" type="text/css"
          href="http://o.aolcdn.com/dojo/1.1/dojo/resources/dojo.css" />
        <link rel="stylesheet" type="text/css"
          href="http://o.aolcdn.com/dojo/1.1/dijit/themes/tundra/tundra.css" />

        <script
            type="text/javascript"
            src="http://o.aolcdn.com/dojo/1.1/dojo/dojo.xd.js"
```

Example 15-7. Simple Tree with a root (continued)

```
                djConfig="parseOnLoad:true,isDebug:true">
        </script>

        <script type="text/javascript">
            dojo.require("dijit.Tree");
            dojo.require("dojo.data.ItemFileReadStore");
            dojo.require("dojo.parser");
        </script>
    </head>
    <body class="tundra">
        <div dojoType="dojo.data.ItemFileReadStore" jsId="dataStore"
         url="./programmingLanguages.json"></div>
        <div dojoType="dijit.tree.TreeStoreModel" jsId="model" store="dataStore"
            query="{name:'*'}"></div>
        <div dojoType="dijit.Tree" model="model"></div>
    </body>
</html>
```

Figure 15-3. The Tree that renders from the data store; clicking on the expando node closes it

Simple Forest

Many applications do not expressly represent a single root node, so let's adjust the previous example to work as a forest instead of a tree so that you can see the difference. First, a forest would have had a data source that didn't have a single root. Consider the following example, which lists programming languages as a forest because it does not include an explicit "programming languages" root:

```
{
    identifier : 'name',

    label : 'name',

    items : [
        {
            name : 'Object-Oriented',
            type : 'category',
            children: [
                {name : 'JavaScript', type : 'language'},
                {name : 'Java', type : 'language'},
                {name : 'Ruby', type : 'language'}
            ]
```

```
        },
        {
            name : 'Imperative',
            type : 'category',
            children: [
                {name : 'C', type : 'language'},
                {name : 'FORTRAN', type : 'language'},
                {name : 'BASIC', type : 'language'}
            ]
        },
        {
            name : 'Functional',
            type : 'category',
            children: [
                {name : 'Lisp', type : 'language'},
                {name : 'Erlang', type : 'language'},
                {name : 'Scheme', type : 'language'}
            ]
        }

    ]
}
```

With the updated JSON data, you see that there isn't a single root node, so the data is delivered such that it lends itself to a forest view. The only notable updates from Example 15-7 are that an additional parameter, showRoot, must be added to the Tree to expressly hide the root of it, the query needs to be updated to identify the top-level nodes for the tree, and the TreeStoreModel is changed to a ForestStoreModel. Example 15-8 shows the updated code with the updates emphasized.

Example 15-8. Updates to show a forest instead of a tree

```
<body class="tundra">
    <div dojoType="dojo.data.ItemFileReadStore" jsId="dataStore"
        url="./programmingLanguages.json"></div>
    <div dojoType="dijit.tree.ForestStoreModel" jsId="model" store="dataStore"
        query="{type:'category'}"></div>
     <div dojoType="dijit.Tree" model="model" showRoot=false></div>
</body>
```

Just because your data lends itself to being displayed as a forest, however, doesn't mean you can't update it to be rendered as a tree. As shown in Example 15-9, you can fabricate a root-level dojo.data item that backs a fabricated node via the rootId and rootLabel attributes on the ForestStoreModel.

Example 15-9. Updates to fabricate a root-level node so that a forest appears like a tree

```
<body class="tundra">
    <div dojoType="dojo.data.ItemFileReadStore" jsId="dataStore"
        url="./programmingLanguages.json"></div>
    <div dojoType="dijit.tree.ForestStoreModel" jsId="model" store="dataStore"
        query="{type:'category'}" rootId="root" rootLabel="Programming Languages"></div>
```

```
        <div dojoType="dijit.Tree" model="model" ></div>
</body>
```

For all practical purposes, the fabricated root node may now be treated uniformly with a dojo.data API such as getLabel or getValue. It may not seem like much, but having this façade behind the fabricated node is very convenient because you are freed from handling it as a special case. Figure 15-4 shows a simple forest.

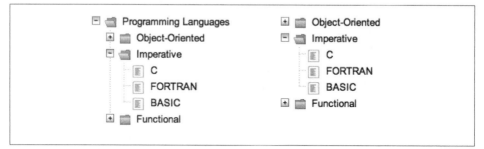

Figure 15-4. Left: the Tree (with a fabricated root node) that renders from the same data store; right: the Tree (without a root node) that displays as a forest

Responding to Click Events

Although displaying information in a tree is quite nice, wouldn't it be even better to respond to events such as mouse clicks? Let's implement the onClick extension point to demonstrate the feasibility of responding to clicks on different items. Both the actual _TreeNode that was clicked as well as the dojo.data item are passed into onClick and are available for processing. To implement click handling, you might update the example as shown in Example 15-10.

Example 15-10. Responding to clicks on a Tree

```
<body class="tundra">
        <div dojoType="dojo.data.ItemFileReadStore" jsId="dataStore"
          url="./programmingLanguages.json"></div>
        <div dojoType="dijit.tree.ForestStoreModel" jsId="model" store="dataStore"
          query="{type:'category'}" rootId="root" rootLabel="Programming Languages"></div>
        <div dojoType="dijit.Tree" model="model" >
            <script type="dojo/method" event="onClick" args="item,treeNode">
                //use the item or the node at will...
                console.log("onClick:",dataStore.getLabel(item); //display the label
            </script>
        </div>
</body>
```

Note that although an intervening model provides a layer of abstraction between the Tree and the dojo.data store, you still use the store directly to access the item; there's no need to have the intervening model that facilitates *display* provide unnecessary cruft between the dojo.data item and the usual means of accessing it.

Tree-Related APIs

If you've followed along with the examples and have a solid understanding of the dojo.data APIs, then you know a lot more about the Tree than you might think at this point. Still, Table 15-10's more formal API listing makes for a good reference and is helpful to skim over before we enter the next section, which covers drag-and-drop for the Tree. As you'll see, the Tree itself really just has a few simple attributes. Most of the heavy lifting is tucked away into the dijit.tree.model APIs or behind the scenes entirely.

 As of version 1.1, it is technically still possible to wire up a Tree directly to a dojo.data store; however, because it is quite likely that this pattern may be removed in version 2.0 and complicates the pattern for using a Tree, it is not presented in this chapter or included in the following API listing.

Table 15-10. Tree API

Name	Type	Comment
model	dijit.tree.model	Interface for uniformly accessing data.
query	Object	The data store query that returns the top-level item(s) for the tree. If the query returns exactly one item, use the TreeStoreModel as the intermediating layer; otherwise, use the ForestStoreModel.
showRoot	Boolean	Whether to display the root of the Tree; typically used to hide the root for a ForestStoreModel.
childrenAttr	Array	A collection of Strings that enumerate the attributes that hold children of a Tree. Default value is ["children"].
openOnClick	Boolean	If set to true, clicking on a node's label opens it (versus calling onClick, which handles opening it as well as other actions). false by default.
persist	Boolean	Uses cookies to save state of nodes being expanded or collapsed. true by default.
onClick(/*dojo.data.Item*/item, /*TreeNode*/node)	Function	An extension point for handling a click (as well as an Enter key press) on an item. Both the item and the node are passed in and are available for processing.

Next up is the `dijit.Tree.model` API, shown in Table 15-11. Anything that presents this interface is just a valid model as the `TreeStoreModel` used in the previous example. As would be the case with any other API, this means you can essentially create whatever abstraction you need to populate a Tree as long as it meets the spec—regardless of the underlying data source—whether it be a `dojo.data` API, some other open API, or a completely proprietary API.

Table 15-11. dijit.Tree.TreeStoreModel API

Name	Comment
getRoot(/*Function*/onItem, /*Function*/onError)	Used for traversing the Tree. Calls the onItem function with the root item for the tree, which may or may not be fabricated. Runs the onError function if an error occurs.
mayHaveChildren(/*dojo.data.Item*/item)	Used for traversing the Tree. Returns information about whether an item may have children, which is useful because it is not efficient to always check if an element actually has children before the expando is clicked.
getChildren(/*dojo.data.Item*/parentItem, /*Function*/onComplete)	Used for traversing the Tree. Calls the onComplete function with all of the child items for the parentItem.
getIdentity(/*dojo.data.Item*/item)	Used for inspecting items. Returns the identity for an item.
getLabel(/*dojo.data.Item*/item)	Used for inspecting items. Returns the label for an item.
newItem(/*Object?*/args, /*dojo.data.Item?*/parent)	Part of the Write interface. Creates a new dojo.data item in accordance with dojo.data.api.Write.
pasteItem(/*dojo.data.Item*/childItem, /*dojo.data.Item*/oldParentItem, /*dojo.data.Item*/newParentItem, /*Boolean*/copy)	Part of the Write interface. Moves or copies an item from one parent item to another, which is used in drag-and-drop operations. If oldParentItem is provided and copy is false, the child item is removed from oldParentItem; if newParentItem is provided, the childItem is attached to it.
onChange(/*dojo.data.Item*/item)	Callback used to update a label or icon. Changes to an item's children or parent(s) trigger onChildrenChange, so those changes should probably be ignored here in onChange.
onChildrenChange(/*dojo.data.Item*/ parent, /*Array*/ newChildren)	Callback used for responding to newly added, updated, or deleted items.
destroyRecursive()	Destroys the object and releases connections to the store so that garbage collection can occur.

On top of the `TreeStoreModel`, the `ForestStoreModel` (documented in Table 15-12) provides two additional functions that respond to events related to the fabricated root-level node; namely, adding and removing items from the top level. These functions are needed to adjust the query criteria so that the top level of the tree remains valid when changes occur. As a data agnostic view, the Tree itself has no responsibility for updating or manipulating items; the burden is on the application programmer to ensure that the query criteria remains satisfied. Hence, the reason these additional functions exist is to enable that to happen.

To update Example 15-9, adjusting an item to meet the top-level query criteria might be as simple as adjusting its type to be "category" instead of "language". For example, you might move "Java" to the top level, update its type to "category" and then provide an operation for adding specific Java implementations (having a type of "language") as children. As you'll see in the next section, the most common use case for needing to meet these stipulations probably involves drag-and-drop.

Table 15-12. dijit.tree.ForestStoreModel API additions

Name	Comment
onAddToRoot(/*dojo.data.Item*/item)	Called when an item is added to the top level of the tree; override to modify the item so that it matches the query for top-level tree items.
onLeaveRoot(/*dojo.data.Item*/item)	Called when an item is removed from the top level of the tree; override to modify the item so that it no longer matches the query for top-level tree items.

Drag-and-Drop with the Tree

The enhancements discussed in the previous section regarding the dijit.tree.model API were in no small part implemented to make drag-and-drop operations with the Tree a lot simpler and more consistent. In general, though, drag-and-drop is not a one-size-fits-all type of operation, so expect to get your hands dirty if you want a customized implementation of any sophisticated widget that responds to drag-and-drop. It's especially important to spend sufficient time answering these common questions:

- What happens when a drag is initiated?
- What happens when a drop is attempted?
- What happens when a drop is cancelled?

The current architecture for implementing drag-and-drop with the tree entails implementing much of the API as defined in the dojo.dnd module (introduced in Chapter 7) and passing it into the Tree via its dndController attribute. Because starting all of that work from scratch is a hard job, the version 1.1 release includes a dijit._tree module that contains an implementation providing a lot of the boilerplate that you can use as you see fit; you might use subclass and override parts of it, you might mix stuff into it, or you might just use it as set of guidelines that provide some inspiration for your own from-scratch implementation. So long as the ultimate artifact from the effort is a class that resembles a dojo.dnd.Source and interacts appropriately to update the dijit.tree.model implementation that backs the Tree, you should be in good shape. In particular, the Source you implement should give special consideration to and implement at least the following key methods that the Tree's dndController expects, listed in Table 15-13.

Table 15-13. Tree dndController interface

Name	Comment
onDndDrop(/*Object*/source, /*Array*/nodes, /*Boolean*/copy)	A topic event processor for /dnd/drop that is called to finish the drop operation, which entails updating the data store items according to source and destination of the operation so that three can update itself.
onDndCancel( )	A topic event processor for /dnd/cancel that handles a cancellation of a drop.
checkAcceptance(/*Object*/source, /*Array*/nodes)	Used to check if the target can accept nodes from the source. This is often used to disallow dropping based on some properties of the nodes.
checkItemAcceptance(/*DOMNode*/target, /*Object*/source)	Used to check if the target can accept nodes from the source. This is often used to disallow dropping based on some properties of the target.
itemCreator(/*Array*/nodes)	When completing a drop onto a destination that is backed by different a data source than the one where the drag started, a new item must be created for each element in nodes for the data source receiving the drop. This method provides the means of creating those items if the source and destination are backed by different data sources.

 A subtle point about the dndController functions is that if they are referenced in markup, they must be defined as global variables when the parser parses the Tree in the page; thus, they cannot be declared in the dojo.addOnLoad block because it runs after the parser finishes. You can, however, decide not to reference the dndController function at all in markup and defer wiring them up until the dojo.addOnLoad block. This is the approach that the upcoming example takes.

An incredibly important realization to make is that drag-and-drop involves DOM nodes—not _TreeNodes; however, you'll usually need a _TreeNode because it's the underlying data it provides that you're interested in, and the DOM node does not provide that information. Whenever this need occurs, such will be the case for any of the methods in Table 15-13. Use the dijit.getEnclosingWidget function, which converts the DOM node into a _TreeNode for you.

Drag-and-droppable Tree example

Because these methods are so incredibly common, they may be passed into the Tree on construction, which is especially nice because it allows you to maximize the use of the boilerplate in dijit._tree. Speaking of which, it's about time for another example.

Let's update the existing working example from Example 15-9 to be drag-and-droppable. We'll build upon the dijit._tree boilerplate to minimize the effort required. Also, note that we'll have to switch our store from an ItemFileReadStore to an ItemFileWriteStore as the very nature of drag-and-drop is not a read-only operation.

Although it might look like the Tree updates itself when you interact with it in such as way that it changes display via a drag-and-drop operation, it's important to remember that the Tree is only a view. Any updates that occur are the result of updating the data source and the data source triggering a view update.

To maintain a certain level of sanity with the example, we'll need to prevent the user from dropping items on top of other items, as items are inherently different from categories of items based upon the category of the item from our dojo.data store. Example 15-11 shows the goods, and Figure 15-5 illustrates.

Example 15-11. Simple drag-and-droppable Tree

```
<html>
    <head>
        <title>Drag and Droppable Tree Fun!</title>

        <link rel="stylesheet" type="text/css"
          href="http://o.aolcdn.com/dojo/1.1/dojo/resources/dojo.css" />
        <link rel="stylesheet" type="text/css"
          href="http://o.aolcdn.com/dojo/1.1/dijit/themes/tundra/tundra.css" />

        <script
            type="text/javascript"
            src="http://o.aolcdn.com/dojo/1.1/dojo/dojo.xd.js"
            djConfig="parseOnLoad:true,isDebug:true">
        </script>

        <script type="text/javascript">
            dojo.require("dijit.Tree");
            dojo.require("dojo.data.ItemFileWriteStore");
            dojo.require("dijit._tree.dndSource");
            dojo.require("dojo.parser");


            dojo.addOnLoad(function() {
                //wire up the checkItemAcceptance handler...
                dijit.byId("tree").checkItemAcceptance = function(target, source) {
                    //convert the target (DOM node) to a tree node and
                    //then get the  item out of it
                    var item = dijit.getEnclosingWidget(target).item;

                    //do not allow dropping onto the top (fabricated) level and
                    //do not allow dropping onto items, only categories
                    return (item.id != "root" && item.type == "category");
                }

            });
        </script>
    </head>
<body class="tundra">
```

Example 15-11. Simple drag-and-droppable Tree (continued)

```
        <div dojoType="dojo.data.ItemFileWriteStore" jsId="dataStore"
          url="./programmingLanguages.json"></div>
        <div dojoType="dijit.tree.ForestStoreModel" jsId="model" store="dataStore"
          query="{type:'category'}" rootId="root" rootLabel="Programming Languages"></div>
        <div id="tree" dojoType="dijit.Tree" model="model"
          dndController="dijit._tree.dndSource"></div>
    </body>
</html>
```

Figure 15-5. Moving a programming language item to a different category

When you find that you need a drag-and-droppable Tree implementation, it's well worth the time to carefully study the boilerplate code provided in dijit._tree. Each situation with drag-and-drop is usually specialized, so finding an out-of-the-box solution that requires virtually no custom implementation is somewhat unlikely.

Editor

At the time of this writing, the Editor and its plug-in architecture were undergoing some significant enhancements. Thus, you may find that this section is slightly more general with respect to technical details than many other sections of the book.

An increasing number applications are utilizing rich text editing capability; in fact, it's probably fair to say that if you have a slick RIA interface and then hand it to the user with an ordinary textarea element (even a Textarea dijit), it'll probably stick out like a sore thumb. Fortunately, the Editor dijit contains all of the common rich text editing functionality, with absolutely minimal overhead on your part.

You may find this reference interesting as you read the rest of this section: *http://developer.mozilla.org/en/docs/Rich-Text_Editing_in_Mozilla*.

Dojo builds upon native browser controls that enable content to be editable. As a little history lesson, Internet Explorer 4.0 introduced the concept of *design mode*, in which it became possible to edit text in a manner consistent with simple rich text editors, and Mozilla 1.3 followed suit to implement what's essentially the same API that eventually became formalized as the Midas Specification (*http://www.mozilla. org/editor/midas-spec.html*). Other browsers have generally followed in the same direction—with their own minor nuances. In any event, most of the heavy lifting occurs by first explicitly making a document editable and then using the JavaScript execCommand function to do the actual markup. Following the Midas Specification, something along the lines of the following would do the trick:

```
// Make a node editable...perhaps a div with a set height and width
document.getElementById("foo").contentDocument.designMode="on";

/* Select some text... */

// Set the selection to italic. No additional arguments are needed.
editableDocument.execCommand("Italic", false, null);
```

As you might imagine, you can use an arsenal of commands for manipulating content via execCommand, standardize the differences amongst browser implementation, assemble a handy toolbar, provide some nice styling, and wrap it up as a portable widget. In fact, that's exactly what Dijit's Editor does for you. Although Editor provides a slew of features that seem overwhelming at a first glance, the basic usage is quite simple. Example 15-12 illustrates an out of the box Editor from markup along with some light styling and a couple of buttons that interact with it.

Without any styling at all, the Editor has no border, spans the width of its container, and comes at a default height of 300px. The light styling here simply provides a background and adjusts the Editor's height to slightly smaller than its container so that the content won't run out of the visible background and into the buttons.

Example 15-12. Typical Editor usage

```
<div style="margin:5px;background:#eee; height: 400px; width:525px">
    <div id="editor" height="375px" dojoType="dijit.Editor">
        When shall we three meet again?<br>
        In thunder, lightning, or in rain?
    </div>
</div>
<button dojoType="dijit.form.Button">Save
    <script type="dojo/method" event="onClick" args="evt">
        /* Save the value any old way you'd like */
```

Example 15-12. Typical Editor usage (continued)

```
        console.log(dijit.byId("editor").getValue( ));
    </script>
</button>
<button dojoType="dijit.form.Button">Clear
    <script type="dojo/method" event="onClick" args="evt">
        dijit.byId("editor").replaceValue("");
    </script>
</button>
```

It's well worth a moment of your time to interact with the Editor and see for yourself that getting all of that functionality with such minimal effort really isn't too good to be true. Note that the Editor renders plain HTML, so saving and restoring content should not involve any unnecessary translation. Then, when you're ready to take a look at some of the many things that the Editor can do for you, skim over the feature list in Table 15-14.

The Editor API is by far the most complex in Dijit, and at the time of this writing, refactoring efforts to tame it were being seriously entertained. Thus, the following table contains a small subset of the most useful parts of the API. See the source file documentation for the complete listing if you *really* want to hack on the Editor.

Table 15-14. Small subset of the Editor API

Name	Type	Comment
focusOnLoad	Boolean	Whether to focus into the Editor when the page loads.
height	String	The initial height of the Editor. 300px by default.
inheritWidth	Boolean	If true, inherits the parent node's width; otherwise, spans the entire width. false by default.
minHeight	String	The minimum allowable height for the Editor. 1em by default.
name	String	If provided, the content is saved and restored when the user leaves the page and returns.
plugins	Array	The plugins that should be be loaded as a baseline for the editor. By default, common values like bold, italic, underline, and so on are included.
extraPlugins	Array	Additional plugins that should be loaded on top of the baseline defined by plugins.
getValue ( )	Function	Returns the value from the Editor.
setValue(/*String*/val)	Function	Sets the value of the Editor.
undo( )	Function	Undoes the previous action.
onDisplayChanged(/*Event*/evt)	Function	Connects to this event to perform a custom action each time the display changes.

Table 15-14. Small subset of the Editor API (continued)

Name	Type	Comment
close()	Function	Closes the Editor and serialize back out the content to it node of origin.
contentPreFilters	Array	Functions that may be optionally applied to text content as it is deserialized before it is transformed into a DOM tree.
contentDomPreFilters	Array	Functions that may optionally be applied to the DOM tree as it is deserialized before it is loaded for editing.
contentDomPostFilters	Array	Functions that may optionally be applied to the DOM tree before it is serialized.
contentDomFilters	Array	Functions that may be optionally applied to the text content before it is serialized.
execCommand	Function	Executes a command in the rich text area. Behaves like the standard JavaScript execCommand but accounts for deviations amongst various browser implementations.

Editor Architecture

The Editor's lifecycle supports three basic phases, shown in Figure 15-6. The following list summarizes these phases and the work involved in each:

Deserializing content

The loading phase entails loading a text stream supplied by a DOM node, converting it into a DOM tree, and placing it into the display for user interaction. Sequences of JavaScript functions may be applied to both the text stream as well as the DOM tree in order, as needed, in order to filter and convert content. Common examples of filters might entail such tasks as converting linebreaks from a plain text document into <br> tags so that the content displays as proper HTML in the editor.

Interacting with content

The interaction phase is just like any other rich text editing experience. Common operations such as markup may occur, and an undo stack is stored based on either a time interval or on the basis of every time the display changes.

Serializing content

When editing ends by way of the Editor's close method, the contents are serialized from a DOM tree back into a text stream, which then gets written back into the node of origin. From there, an event handler might send it back to a server to persist it. Like the deserializing phase, sequences of JavaScript functions may optionally be applied to manipulate the content.

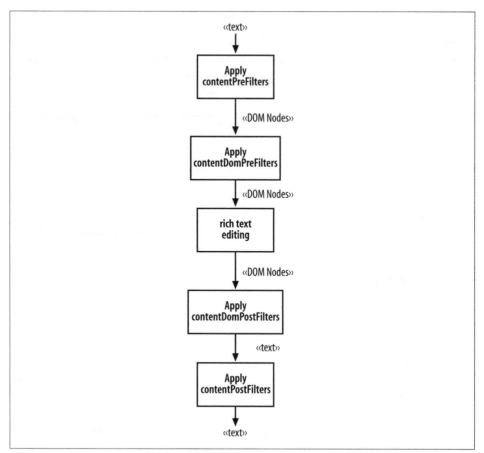

Figure 15-6. The basic phases that the Editor's architecture supports

Editor Plug-Ins

Although the Editor provides an onslaught of highly useful features of its own, sooner or later you'll be wishing that it were possible to tightly integrate some piece of custom functionality. Its plug-in architecture is your ticket to making that happen. A plug-in is just a way of encapsulating some additional functionality that, while useful, maybe shouldn't be a stock component; it could be anything from handling some special key combinations to providing a custom menu item with some canned commands that automate part of a workflow.

Snapping a plug-in into Editor is quite simple, and you may not have realized it, but everything in the toolbar you thought was built right in is technically a plug-in with one of the following self-descriptive values.

undo	justifyLeft
redo	justifyRight
cut	delete
copy	selectAll
paste	removeFormat
insertOrderedList	bold
insertUnorderedList	italic
indent	underline
outdent	strikethrough
justifyCenter	subscript
justifyFull	superscript

You can configure plug-ins by providing either the `plugins` or `extraPlugins` attribute and give it a list of valid plug-ins that you have first `dojo.required` into the page. By default, `plugins` contains all of the items in the toolbar that you see by default, and if you override it and provide something like `plugins="['bold','italic']"`, then all you'd see in the toolbar is the list of `plugins` you provided. However, the `extraPlugins` attribute adds extra `plugins` on top of what is already configured in `plugins` if you want to throw in a few extras.

Several packages of prefabricated plug-ins are available with the toolkit and are commonly used as values to `extraPlugins`; they are located in the *dijit/_editor/plugins* directory and include the following:

AlwaysShowToolbar

Shifts the contents of the toolbar, as needed, so that multiple rows of controls are displayed, and it always remains visible. (If you resize the window to be less than the width of the toolbar, the default action is to display a horizontal scrollbar and only display the portion of the toolbar that would normally be visible.) You must pass in `dijit._editor.plugins.AlwaysShowToolbar` to `plugins` or `extraPlugins` to enable this plug-in.

EnterKeyHandling

Provides a means of uniformly handling what happens when the Enter key is pressed amongst all browsers. For example, you can specify whether to insert a series of paragraph tags to surround the new text, a break tag, a set of DIVS tags, or not to disable the handling of the Enter key entirely. You must pass in `dijit._editor.plugins.EnterKeyHandling` to `plugins` or `extraPlugins` to enable this plug-in.

The Editor's plug-in architecture needs some work, and discussions are ongoing about how to improve it. Progress is already being made, and you can track it for yourself at *http://trac.dojotoolkit.org/ticket/5707*. In other words, if you want to create custom plug-ins, you'll likely have to hack on the *Editor.js* source code a bit until the plug-in architecture is smoothed out a bit more.

Also, don't forget that you have to manually `dojo.require` in the plug-in that you are using. The plug-in architecture does not perform any sort of autodetection at this time.

Currently, the default means of handling the Enter key is determined by the `EnterKeyHandling` attribute `blockNodeForEnter`, which has a default value of `'P'`. Currently, there isn't really a better way of changing it than by extending this plug-in's prototype and overriding it like so:

```
dojo.addOnLoad(function( ) {
    dojo.extend(dijit._editor.plugins.EnterKeyHandling, {
        blockNodeForEnter : "div" // or "br" or "empty"
    });
});
```

FontChoice

Provides a button with a dialog for picking a font name, font size, and format block. Arguments to `plugins` or `extraPlugins` may be `fontName`, `fontSize`, or `formatBlock`.

LinkDialog

Provides a button with a dialog for entering a hyperlink source and displayed value. Arguments to `plugins` or `extraPlugins` may be `createLink`.

TextColor

Provides options for specifying the foreground color or background color for a range of text. Arguments to `plugins` or `extraPlugins` may be `foreColor` or `hiliteColor`.

ToggleDir

Provides a means of involving the HTML `dir` attribute on the Editor (regardless of how the rest of the page is laid out) so that the Editor's contents could be left-to-right or right-to-left. Arguments to `plugins` or `extraPlugins` may be `toggleDir`.

To make matters a little less muddy, consider the differences in the snippets of markup shown in Table 15-15 when creating an editor.

Table 15-15. Different approaches to creating an editor

Code	Effect
`<div dojoType="dijit.Editor">`	Creates an Editor with the default toolbar.
`<div dojoType="dijit.Editor" plugins="['bold', 'italic']">`	Creates an Editor with a toolbar that has only the bold and italic buttons.

Table 15-15. Different approaches to creating an editor (continued)

Code	Effect
`<div dojoType="dijit.Editor" extraPlugins="['hiliteColor']">`	Creates an `Editor` with a default toolbar that has an additional button for highlighting text—assuming you've issued a `dojo.require("dijit._editor.plugins.TextColor")` statement.
`<div dojoType="dijit.Editor" plugins="['bold', 'italic']" extraPlugins="['fontName']">`	Creates an `Editor` with a toolbar consisting of a bold and italic button along with a control for selecting a custom font (assuming you've issued a `dojo.require("dijit._editor.plugins.FontChoice")` statement). Note that this has the exact same effect as including all three plugins inside the `plugin` attribute.

Summary

After reading this chapter, you should be able to:

- Understand where the general-purpose application dijits fit into the overall Dijit architecture and appreciate the special role that they play in designing a rich user experience
- Create application dijits in markup as well as JavaScript
- Understand the primary differences between when you should use `Tooltip` versus `TooltipDialog`
- Use the `Editor` to provide a control for entering and editing rich text
- Use `Toolbar` and `Menu` to provide a means of command and control for the user of your application
- Embed `TooltipDialog` into a `DropDownButton`
- Use a `ProgressBar` to display both determinate and indeterminate indications of progress to a user
- Use `Dialog` to provide a modal alert to the user or otherwise embed arbitrary content into the `Dialog` for the user to interact with
- Use `InlineEditables` to empower the user with the ability to edit what otherwise appears to be plain markup on the fly
- Use the `Tree` dijit to display hierarchical information via an interactive display

In the next chapter, we'll cover build tools, testing, and production considerations.

## CHAPTER 16

Build Tools, Testing, and Production Considerations

After all your hard work developing with Dojo, there comes a point when your application is ready for prime time. Util provides terrific build tools and a testing framework that can get you ready for production before you know it. The build tools provided by Util are the same ones that are used to produce each official Dojo release, and the Dojo Objective Harness (DOH) is a unit-testing framework that facilitates achieving some automated quality assurance before your app ever gets out the door.

Building

For any production setting, minimizing the overall footprint of your JavaScript files and the number of synchronous requests to the server is absolutely essential. The difference in downloading scores of individual resource files via synchronous requests incurred by dojo.require versus one or two calls back to the server makes all the difference in the world in terms of a snappy page load.

Dojo's build tools makes accomplishing what may initially seem like such an arduous task quite easy. In a nutshell, the build tools automate the following tasks:

- Consolidates multiple modules into a single JavaScript file called a layer
- Interns template strings into JavaScript files, including layers, so that a standalone template is no longer needed
- Applies ShrinkSafe, a JavaScript compressor based on Rhino, to *minify* the size of the layers by removing whitespace, linebreaks, comments, and shortening variable names
- Copies all of the "built" files into a standalone directory that can be copied and deployed to a web server

One reason you may not have been aware of the build tools is that they aren't included in the *util* directory of an official release. To get them, you have to download a source release (a source release will have the *-src* suffix on the file base part of the filename) or just grab the source from the Subversion trunk. Chapter 1 provides an overview of getting the Dojo from Subversion, but basically, all that is necessary is to point your client at the Dojo repository and wait for it to download everything, whether it is the trunk or a specific tag.

In either case, you'll find that the *util* directory now holds some additional directories; one of these directories is *buildscripts*, which contains the goods we're looking for.

 http://svnbook.red-bean.com/ contains the unofficial Subversion book, which is available in a variety of formats. Taking a moment to bookmark this valuable resource now will save you time later.

To run the build tools, you'll have to have Java 1.4.2 or later installed, available from *http://java.sun.com* (because ShrinkSafe is based on Rhino, which is written in Java). But don't worry about having to be a Java programmer to use ShrinkSafe; ShrinkSafe comes packaged as a single *jar* file (an executable Java archive), so you can treat it like any other executable.

A Word on Rhino

Rhino is a JavaScript engine written entirely in Java and is named after the rhinoceros on the cover of David Flanagan's well-known *JavaScript: The Definitive Guide* book (O'Reilly). Rhino originally started as a closed source project by Netscape in the late 1990s, but became an open source project when it was turned over to the Mozilla foundation. Rhino works by converting JavaScript scripts into Java classes and was developed with the intent of being embedded in applications

SpiderMonkey is another JavaScript engine, written in C, also developed by Netscape but later turned over Mozilla for maintenance. Like Rhino, SpiderMonkey is an embeddable technology. SpiderMonkey is used in a variety of popular applications including Firefox and Yahoo! Widgets (previously Konfabulator).

Running a Build

The primary entry point for kicking off a build is via the *buildscripts/build.sh* (or *build.bat* for Windows users), and is really just a call through to the custom Rhino *jar* that does all of the work based on a custom profile that is provided (more on that in just a moment). As an ordinary executable, however, build tools such as *Make* or *ant* can easily include the *jar* file as an ordinary part of the production build process.

This ability is especially convenient when server-side components are based on languages that must be compiled.

Executing the corresponding build script or executing the *jar* without any command-line options provides an impressive list of options. Table 16-1 is adapted directly from the standard option list that is displayed.

Table 16-1. Build script parameters

Option	Description
xdScopeArgs	If the `loader=xdomain` build option is used, then the value of this option will be used as the arguments to the function that defines the modules in the *.xd.js* files. This allows for more than one version of the same module to be in a page. See documentation on `djConfig.scopeMap` for more information.
cssOptimize	Specifies how to optimize CSS files. If `comments` is specified, then code comments and line returns are stripped. If `comments.keepLines` is specified, then code comments are stripped, but line returns are preserved. In either case, @import statements are inlined.
releaseName	The name of the release. A directory inside *releaseDir* will be created with this name. By default, this value is *dojo*.
localeList	The set of locales to use when flattening i18n bundles. By default this value is `cs,de-de,en-gb,en-us,es-es,fr-fr,hu,it-it,ja-jp,ko-kr,pl,pt-br,ru,zh-tw,zh-cn`.
releaseDir	The top-level release directory where builds end up. The *releaseName* directories will be placed inside this directory. By default, this value is *../../release/*.
copyTests	Turn on or off copying of test files. This value is `true` by default.
symbol	Inserts function symbols as global references so that anonymous functions will show up in all debuggers (especially in IE, which does not attempt to infer function names from the context of their definition). Valid values are `long` and `short`. If `short` is used, then a *symboltables.txt* file will be generated in each module prefix's release directory that maps the short symbol names to more descriptive names.
action	The build action(s) to run. Can be a comma-separated list, like `action=clean,release`. The possible build actions are: `clean` and `release`. This value is `help` by default.
internStrings	Turn on or off for widget template file interning. This value is `true` by default.

scopeMap	Change the default *dojo*, *dijit*, and *dojox* scope names to something else. Useful if you want to use Dojo as part of a JS library, but want to make a self-contained library with no external *dojo/dijit/dojox* references. Format is a string that contains no spaces, and is similar to the `djConfig.scopeMap` value (note that the backslashes below are required to avoid shell escaping):
	`scopeMap: [[\"dojo\",\"mydojo\"],[\"dijit\",\"mydijit\"],`
	`       [\"dojox\",\"mydojox\"]]`

optimize	Specifies how to optimize module files. If `comments` is specified, code comments are stripped. If `shrinksafe` is specified, the Dojo compressor is used on the files, and line returns is removed. If `shrinksafe.keepLines` is specified, the Dojo compressor is used on the files, and line returns are preserved. If `packer` is specified, Dean Edwards's Packer is used (see *http://dean.edwards.name/packer/*).
loader	The type of dojo loader to use. `default` (the default value) or `xdomain` are acceptable values.
log	Sets the logging verbosity. See *util/buildtools/jslib/logger.js* for possible integer values. The default value is 0.

Table 16-1. Build script parameters (continued)

Option	Description
profileFile	A file path to the profile file. Use this if your profile is outside of the profiles directory. Do not specify the profile build option if you use profileFile.
xdDojoPath	If the loader=xdomain build option is used, then the value of this option will be used to call dojo.registerModulePath( ) for *dojo, dijit.,* and *dojox.* The *xdDojoPath* should be the directory that contains the *dojo, dijit,* and *dojox* directories, and it should not end in a slash. For instance: *http://www.example.com/path/to/dojo.*
version	The build will be stamped with this version string. The default value is 0.0.0.dev.
profile	The name of the profile to use for the build. It must be the first part of the profile file name in the *profiles/* directory. For instance, to use *base.profile.js,* specify profile=base (the default).
layerOptimize	Specifies how to optimize the layer files. If comments is specified, code comments are stripped. If shrinksafe is specified, the Dojo compressor is used on the files, and line returns are removed. If shrinksafe.keepLines is specified, the Dojo compressor is used on the layer files, and line returns are preserved. If packer is specified, the Dean Edwards's Packer is used. shrinksafe is the default.
xdDojoScopeName	If the loader=xdomain build option is employed, the value of this option is used instead of dojo (the default) for the dojo._xdResourceLoaded( ) calls that are done in the *.xd.js* files. This allows for dojo to be under a different scope name, but still allows XDomain loading with that scope name.
cssImportIgnore	You can use cssOptimize=comments to force the @import inlining process to ignore a set of files. The value of this option should be a comma-separated list of CSS filenames to ignore. The filenames should match the string values that are used for the @import calls.
buildLayers	A comma-separated list of layer names to build. Using this option means that only those layers will be built. This helps if you are doing quick development and test cycles with layers. If you have problems with this option, try removing it and doing a full build with action=clean,release. This build option assumes you have done at least one full build first.
symbol	Inserts function symbols as global references so that anonymous functions will show up in all debuggers (especially IE, which does not attempt to infer function names from the context of their definition). Valid values are long and short. If short is used, then a *symboltables.txt* file will be generated in each module prefix's release directory, mapping the short symbol names to more descriptive names.

scopeDjConfig	Burns a djConfig object into the built *dojo.js* file, which is useful if you are making your own scoped build and you want a djConfig object local to your version that will not be affected by any globally declared djConfig object in the page. This value must be a string that will look like a JavaScript object literal once it is placed in the built source. Can also be useful for situations where you want to use Dojo as part of a JavaScript library that is self-contained and has no external *dojo, dijit,* or *dojox.* Example:
	
	 `scopeDjConfig={isDebug:true,scopeMap:[[\"dojo\",\"mydojo\"],`
	 `[\"dijit\",\"mydijit\"], [\"dojox\",\"mydojox\"]]}`
	
	 Note that the backslashes are required to avoid shell escaping if you type this on the command line.

While all of those options may seem like a lot to manage, the routine builds are really quite simple and involve only a handful of options. But first, we need a profile.

Build Profiles

A *profile* is the configuration for your build as provided via the profile or profileFile option. The most basic function of a profile is to specify the exact Dojo resources that should consolidated into a standalone JavaScript file, also known as a *layer*; a typical rule of thumb is that each page of your application should have its own layer. The beauty of a layer is that it is an ordinary JavaScript file, and can be included directly into the head of a page, loading everything you've crammed into it via a single synchronous request to the server—well, sort of. By convention, Base is so heavily used that it generally stays in its own individual *dojo.js* file, so you normally have two synchronous calls, one for Base, and one for your own layer.

Setting up a build profile

Assuming your application has three distinct pages, you might have three layer files and one copy of Base.

 If you really want to bundle up your own modules inside of the *dojo.js* file that normally only contains Base, you can name your layer *dojo.js*. However, it's often a good idea to keep Base separated because it would be used in every page of you application and is cacheable by your web browser.

Physically speaking, a profile is simply a file containing a JSON object. Example 16-1 shows a profile that consolidates several of the form dijits that are explicitly dojo.required into a page. All internal dependencies are tracked down automatically. Just like with dojo.require, you state what you need to use directly, and dependency tracking is automated behind the scenes for you.

Example 16-1. A simple build profile

```
dependencies ={
    layers: [
        {
            name: "form.js",
            dependencies: [
                "dijit.form.Button",
                "dijit.form.Form",
                "dijit.form.ValidationTextBox"
            ]
        }
    ],
    prefixes: [
        [ "dijit", "../dijit" ]
    ]
};
```

Assuming the previous profile is located at *util/buildscripts/profiles/form.profile.js* and you're working in a Bash shell, the following command from within the *util/buildscripts* directory would kick off a build. Note that the profile option expects profiles to be of the form *<profile name>.profile.js* and only expects the *<profile name>* as an option:

```
bash build.sh profile=form action=release
```

 If you don't want to save the file in *util/buildscripts/profiles/form.profile.js*, you can use the profileFile option instead of the profile option.

After executing the command, you should see a bunch of output indicating that the build is taking place and that of strings are being interned from template files into JavaScript files. The artifact of the build is a release directory containing *dojo*, *dijit*, and *util*. Inside of the *dojo* directory, you'll find the usual suspects, but there are four especially important artifacts to note:

- The compressed and uncompressed version of Base, *dojo.js* and *dojo.js.uncompressed.js*
- The compressed and uncompressed version of your form layer in *form.js* and *form.js.uncompressed.js* (go ahead and take a peek inside to see for yourself)

But what if you need resources that are not included in your custom layer file? No problem—if resources aren't included in a profile, they are fetched from the server whenever the dojo.require statement that specifies them is encountered. Assuming you take the entire release directory and drop it somewhere out on your server, the dojo.require statements requesting nonlayered resources will behave normally, though you will incur a small roundtrip cost for the request to the server.

Requests for Base functions and resources in your layer do not incur server-side requests when they are encountered in a dojo.require statement because they're already available locally. Resources not in your layer, however, incur the routine overhead of synchronous HTTP requests (Figure 16-1).

While you may generally want to include every possible resource that is needed in a build, there may be some situations where you want to lazy load. The tradeoff is always between a "small enough" initial payload size over the wire versus the cost of synchronous loading via dojo.require later.

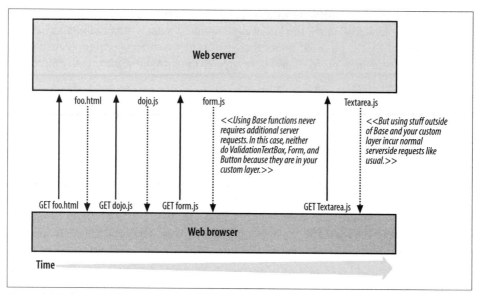

Figure 16-1. Conceptual server request illustrating various JavaScript files loading

 If you accidentally misspell or otherwise provide a dependency that does not exist, ShrinkSafe may still complete your build even though it could not find all of the dependencies. For example, if you accidentally specify `dijit.Button` (instead of `dijit.form.Button`), you'll most likely still get a successful build, and you may not ever notice that `dijit.form.Button` wasn't bundled because a call to `dojo.require("dijit.form.Button")` would fetch it from the server and your application would behave as normal.

It's always a good idea to double-check your build by taking a look at the Net tab in Firebug to ensure that everything you expect to be bundled up is indeed bundled up.

Setting up a (more clever) build profile

A slightly more clever way to set up the build profile just discussed is to create a custom module that does nothing more than require in all of the resources that were previously placed in the layer via the profile file. Then, in the profile file, simply include the custom module as your sole dependency for the layer.

First, Example 16-2 shows how your custom module would look. Let's assume the module is *dtdg.page1* and is located at called *dtdg/page1.js*.

Example 16-2. A custom module for a more clever build profile

```
dojo.provide("dtdg.page1");

dojo.require("dijit.form.Form");
```

Example 16-2. A custom module for a more clever build profile (continued)

```
dojo.require("dijit.form.Button");
dojo.require("dijit.form.ValidationTextBox");
```

Now, your profile need only point to the custom module, as the other dependencies are specified inside of it and will be tracked down automatically. Example 16-3 demonstrates an updated profile, which assumes your custom module directory is a sibling directory of *util*.

Example 16-3. Updated build profile

```
dependencies ={
    layers:  [
        {
            name: "form.js",
            dependencies: [
                "custom.page1"
            ]
        }
    ],
    prefixes: [
        [ "custom", "../custom" ]
    ]
};
```

Finally, your page might contain the following SCRIPT tag to pull in the module along with Base:

```
<script type="text/javascript"
djConfig="baseUrl: './',modulePaths: {custom:'path/to/custom/page1.js'},
    require: ['custom.page1']"
src="scripts/dojo.js"></script>
```

Standard build profile

Notice that the *util/buildscripts/profiles* directory contains a number of example build profiles as well as the *standard.profile.js* file that contains the layers for a standard build of Dojo. The standard profile builds Base as well as a baseline Dijit layer that contains common machinery that is used in virtually any circumstance involving dijits, as well as a couple of other useful layers. Note that any profile in the *standard.profile.js* file should be available over AOL's CDN. For example, to retrieve the baseline Dijit profile, you could simply execute the following statement:

```
dojo.require("dijit.dijit");
```

Remember, however, that the first SCRIPT tag should always be the one for Base (*dojo.xd.js*), so you'd include any additional SCRIPT tags for layers after the one for Base.

ShrinkSafe optimization and other common options

In virtually any production setting, you'll want to apply ShrinkSafe to minify all of your code. While the previous build example build did optimize the build in the sense that it minified *dojo.js* and *form.js* as well as interned template strings, ShrinkSafe can minify every file in the release.

Recall that the size "over the wire" is what really matters when you're talking about performance from a payload perspective. While files may be a set size as they exist on the server, most servers are able to apply *gzip* compression to them if the web browser is capable of handling it. While ShrinkSafe minifies JavaScript files by removing artifacts like whitespace, comments, and so on, the further compression is possible because the repetitive use of public symbols such as dojo, dijit, and your own custom tokens allows for actual compression to occur.

> *Minification* is the reduction of a file's size by removing artifacts such as commas, whitespace, linebreaks, etc. Compression is an algorithmic manipulation that reduces a file's size by using by finding multiple instances of the same tokens and encoding an equivalent file by using shorter placeholders for the repetitive tokens. To learn more, see *http://en.wikipedia.org/wiki/Gzip* for an overview of *gzip* compression.

An especially notable feature of ShrinkSafe is that it never mangles a public API; this is a direct contrast to some JavaScript tools that attempt to encrypt JavaScript by applying regular expressions or convoluted logic to "protect" the script. In general, attempting to protect your JavaScript is mostly pointless. As an interpreted language that runs in the browser, the user of your application will almost certainly have access to your source code, and it's not terribly difficult to use a debugger to unroll the protected script into something that's fairly intelligible.

> ShrinkSafe itself is not a Dojo-specific tool; you can apply it to any JavaScript file to gain the benefits of compression using the online demonstration at *http://shrinksafe.dojotoolkit.org/*. OS X users can download a version at *http://dojotoolkit.org/downloads*, and users of other platforms can grab the standalone custom Rhino jar from *http://svn.dojotoolkit.org/dojo/trunk/buildscripts/lib/custom_rhino.jar*.

In other words, ShrinkSafe shrinks your files without changing public symbol names. In fact, if you look at the *form.js* file that is an artifact of the previous build examples, you can see for yourself that ShrinkSafe strips comments, collapses and/or eliminates frivolous whitespace, including newline characters, and replaces nonpublic symbols with shorter names. Note that replacing all symbols with shorter, meaningless names qualifies as a lame attempt at encryption—not particularly useful for debugging purposes either.

Let's update our existing profile:

- Minify all files in the release with the `optimize="shrinksafe"` option
- Designate a custom notice that should appear at the top of every minified JavaScript file in an additional (mythical) foo module provided by *CUSTOM_ FILE_NOTICE.txt*
- Designate a custom notice that should appear at the top of the final *form.js* provided by the same *CUSTOM_LAYER_NOTICE.txt*
- Provide a custom name for the release directory via the `releaseName="form"` option
- Provide a custom version number for the build via the `version="0.1.0."` option

Here's the modified *form.profile.js* file from Example 16-1. Note that the information in the custom notices must be wrapped in JavaScript comments; the path for the custom notices should be relative to the *util/buildscripts* directory or an absolute path:

```
dependencies ={
    layers: [
        {
            copyrightFile : "CUSTOM_LAYER_NOTICE.txt",
            name: "form.js",
            dependencies: [
                "dijit.form.Button",
                "dijit.form.Form",
                "dijit.form.ValidationTextBox"
            ]
        }
    ],
    prefixes: [
        [ "dijit", "../dijit" ],
        [ "foo", "../foo", "CUSTOM_FILE_NOTICE.txt" ]

    ]
};
```

The augmented command to kick off this build is straightforward enough, and creates the artifacts in the *release/form* directory that exist alongside the *dojo* source directories:

```
bash build.sh profile=form action=release optimize=shrinksafe releaseName=form
version=0.1.0
```

To actually use your custom release, simply include the paths to the compressed *dojo.js* and *form.js* files in script tags in the head of your page, like so. The *dojo.js* layer must be included first, because *form.js* depends on it:

```
<html>
  <head><title>Fun With Forms!</title>
    <!-- include stylesheets, etc. -->
```

```
    <script type="text/javascript" path="relative/path/to/form/dojo.js"></script>
    <script type="text/javascript" path="relative/path/to/form/form.js"></script>
</head>
<!-- rest of your page -->
```

And that's it. It takes only two synchronous requests to load the JavaScript (which now have interned templates) into the page; other resources included in your build via the prefixes list are at your disposal via the standard dojo.require statements.

If you are completely sure you'll never need any additional JavaScript resources beyond *dojo.js* and your layer files, it is possible to pluck out just the individual resources you need from the release directory structure. However, you'll have to go through a little extra work to track down dependencies with built-in CSS themes such as *tundra* because some of the stylesheets may use relative paths and relative URLs in import statements.

 Inspecting the Net tab of Firebug is very useful in tracking down the dependencies you need to pluck out of the release directory, but be advised that Firebug may not display 404 (Not Found) errors for import statements that are used in stylesheets.

Custom Builds for Rhino

While the official platform for Dojo builds is the browser, you may also use the build system to produce a custom build of Dojo that can be used within Rhino itself. This may be useful if you use JavaScript to call through to Java classes, or if you use a tool like Helma (*http://dev.helma.org*) that employs JavaScript for server-side scripting.

In your build profile, you need only to include hostenvType= "rhino"; that's it. If you'd like to run the DOH unit tests from within the release directory for a Rhino build, you must also include an additional *shrinksafe* prefix. Here's an example profile for a custom Rhino build:

```
hostenvType = "rhino";

dependencies = {
  layers : [];
  prefixes : [
    ["dojox", "../dojox"],
    ["shrinksafe", "../util/shrinksafe"]
  ]
};
```

Dojo Objective Harness (DOH)

Automated testing practices for web applications are becoming increasingly common because of the sheer amount of coding and complexity involved in many of today's rich Internet applications. DOH uses Dojo internally but is not a Dojo-specific tool; like ShrinkSafe, you could use it to create unit tests for any JavaScript scripts, although no DOM manipulation or browser-specific functions will be available.

DOH provides three simple assertion constructs that go a long way toward automating your tests. Each of these assertions is provided via the global object, doh, exposed by the framework:

- doh.assertEqual(expected, actual)
- doh.assertTrue(condition)
- doh.assertFalse(condition)

Before diving into some of the more complex things that you can do with DOH, take a look at trivial test harness that you can run from the command line via Rhino to get a better idea of exactly the kinds of things you could be doing with DOH. The harness below demonstrates the ability for DOH to run standalone tests via regular Function objects as well as via test fixtures. *Test fixtures* are little more than a way of surrounding a test with initialization and clean up.

Rhino Test Harness Without Dojo

Without further ado, here's that test harness. Note that the harness doesn't involve any Dojo specifics; it merely uses the doh object. In particular, the doh.register function is used in this example, where the first parameter specifies a module name (a JavaScript file located as a sibling of the *util* directory), and the second parameter provides a list of test functions and fixtures:

```
doh.register("testMe", [

    //test fixture that passes
    {
        name : "fooTest",
        setUp : function() {},
        runTest : function(t) { t.assertTrue(1); },
        tearDown : function() {}
    },

    //test fixture that fails
    {
        name : "barTest",
        setUp : function() { this.bar="bar"},
        runTest : function(t) { t.assertEqual(this.bar, "b"+"a"+"rr"); },
        tearDown : function() {delete this.bar;}
    },
```

```
//standalone function that passes
function baz( ) {doh.assertFalse(0)}

]);
```

Assuming this test harness were saved in a *testMe.js* file and placed alongside the *util* directory, you could run it by executing the following command from within *util/ doh*. (Note that although the custom Rhino *jar* included with the build tools is used, any recent Rhino jar should work just fine):

```
java -jar ../shrinksafe/custom_rhino.jar runner.js dojoUrl="../../dojo/dojo.js"
testModule=testMe
```

The command simply tells the Rhino *jar* to run the testMe module via the *runner.js* JavaScript file (the substance of DOH) using the copy of Base specified. Although no Dojo was involved in the test harness itself, DOH does use Base internally, so you do have to provide a path to it.

Now that you've seen DOH in action, you're ready for Table 16-2, which summarizes the additional functions exposed by the doh object.

Table 16-2. doh module functions

Function	Comment
registerTest(/*String*/group, /* Function || Object */ test)	Adds the test or fixture object to the specified test group.
registerTests(/*String*/group, /*Array*/ tests)	Automates registering a group of tests provided in the tests Array.
registerTestNs(/*String*/group, /*Object*/ns)	Adds the functions included in the ns object to the collection that should be test group. Functions beginning with an underscore are not included since the underscore normally denotes the notion of private.
register(/* ...*/)	Applies the proper register function by inspecting the arguments and determining which one to use.
assertEqual(expected, actual)	Used to assert that two values should be equal.
assertTrue(/*Boolean*/condition)	Used to assert that a value should evaluate to true.
assertFalse(/*Boolean*/ condition)	Used to assert that a value should evaluate to false.
is(expected, actual)	Shorthand for assertEqual.
t(/*Boolean*/condition)	Shorthand for assertTrue.
f(/*Boolean*/condition)	Shorthand for assertFalse.
registerGroup(/*String*/ group, /*Array||Function||Object*/tests, /*Function*/ setUp, /*Function*/tearDown)	Adds an entire group of tests provided in tests to the group at one time. Uses a custom setUp and tearDown function, if provided.
run( )	Used to programmatically run tests.
runGroup(/*String*/groupName)	Used to programmatically run a group of tests.
pause	Can be used to programmatically pause tests that are running; they may be resumed with run( ).
togglePaused	May be applied sequentially to pause and run the tests.

Additionally, note that the *runner.js* file accepts any of the options shown in Table 16-3.

Table 16-3. Options for runner.js

Function	Comment
dojoUrl	The path to *dojo.js*.
testUrl	The path to a test file.
testModule	A comma-separated list of test modules that should be executed, such as foo.bar, foo.baz.

Rhino Test Harness with Dojo

Although it is possible to use DOH without Dojo, chances are that you will want to use Dojo with Rhino. Core contains some great examples that you can run by executing *runner.js* without any additional arguments. The default values will point to the tests located in *dojo/tests* and use the version of Base located at *dojo/dojo.js*.

If you peek inside any of Core's test files, you'll see the usage is straightforward enough. Each file begins with a dojo.provide that specifies the name of the test module, requires the resources that are being tested, and then uses a series of register functions to create fixtures for the tests.

Assume you have a custom foo.bar module located at */tmp/foo/bar.js* and that you have a *testBar.js* test harness located at */tmp/testBar.js*. The contents of each JavaScript file follows.

First, there's *testBar.js*:

```
/* dojo.provide the test module just like any other module */
dojo.provide("testBar");

/* You may need to register your module paths when using
   custom modules outside of the dojo root directory */
dojo.registerModulePath("foo.bar", "/tmp/foo/bar");

/* dojo.require anything you might need */
dojo.require("foo.bar");

/* register the module */
doh.register("testBar", [

    function() { doh.t(alwaysReturnsTrue()); },
    function() { doh.f(alwaysReturnsFalse()); },
    function() { doh.is(alwaysReturnsOdd()%2, 1); },
    function() { doh.is(alwaysReturnsOdd()%2, 1); },
    function() { doh.is(alwaysReturnsOdd()%2, 1); },
    {
        name : "BazFixture",
        setUp : function() {this.baz = new Baz;},
        runTest : function() {doh.is(this.baz.talk(), "hello");},
```

```
        tearDown : function( ) {delete this.baz;}
    }
]);
```

And now, for your foo.bar module residing in *foo/bar.js*:

```
/* A collection of not-so-useful functions */
dojo.provide("foo.bar");

function alwaysReturnsTrue( ) {
    return true;
}

function alwaysReturnsFalse( ) {
    return false;
}

function alwaysReturnsOdd( ) {
    return Math.floor(Math.random( )*10)*2-1;
}

// Look, there's even a "class"
dojo.declare("Baz", null, {
    talk : function( ) {
        return "hello";
    }
});
```

The following command from within *util/buildscripts* kicks off the tests:

```
java -jar ../shrinksafe/custom_rhino.jar runner.js dojoUrl=../../dojo/dojo.js
testUrl=/tmp/testBar.js
```

 Especially note that the test harness explicitly registered the module path for foo.bar before requiring it. For resources outside of the dojo root directory, this extra step is necessary for locating your custom module.

If all goes as planned, you'd see a test summary message indicating that all tests passed or failed. Registering a group of tests sharing some common setup and tear down criteria entails the very same approach, except you would use the doh.registerGroup function instead of the doh.register function (or a more specific variation thereof).

If you want more finely grained control over the execution of your tests so you can pause and restart them programmatically, you apply the following updates to *testBar.js*:

```
/* load up dojo.js and runner.js */
load("/usr/local/dojo/dojo.js");
load("/usr/local/dojo/util/doh/runner.js");

/* dojo.provide the test module just like any other module */
dojo.provide("testBar");
```

```
/* You may need to register your module paths when using
   custom modules outside of the dojo root directory */
dojo.registerModulePath("foo.bar", "/tmp/foo/bar");

/* dojo.require anything you might need */
dojo.require("foo.bar");

/* register the module */
doh.register("testBar", [

    function() { doh.t(alwaysReturnsTrue()); },
    function() { doh.f(alwaysReturnsFalse()); },
    function() { doh.is(alwaysReturnsOdd()%2, 1); },
    function() { doh.is(alwaysReturnsOdd()%2, 1); },
    function() { doh.is(alwaysReturnsOdd()%2, 1); },
    {
        name : "BazFixture",
        setUp : function() {this.baz = new Baz;},
        runTest : function() {doh.is(this.baz.talk(), "hello");},
        tearDown : function() {delete this.baz;}
    }
]);

doh.run();

/* pause and restart at will... */
```

Although we didn't make use of the fact that testBar is a module that dojo.provides itself, you can very easily aggregate collections of tests together via dojo.require, just like you would for any module that provides itself.

Although you could run asynchronous tests using Rhino as well, the next section introduces asynchronous tests because they are particularly useful for browser-based tests involving network input/output and events such as animations.

Browser-Based Test Harness

Although running tests from Rhino is tremendously useful, DOH also provides a harness that allows you to automate running tests from within a browser window. Basically, you just define a test as an ordinary HTML page and then load the test page into the DOH test runner using query string parameters in the test runner's URL; internally, JavaScript in the test runner examines the query string, pulls out configuration values such as testUrl and uses them to inject your test page into a frame.

Of course, you can still run your browser-based test without the DOH test runner, but you won't get a nice visual display with optional Homer Simpson sound effects if you're willing to read the test results as console output.

Browser Test Example

The following is an example test defined as an ordinary HTML page. Notice that the example uses a local installation of Dojo because as of version 1.1, DOH is not delivered via AOL's CDN:

```html
<html>
    <head><title>Fun with DOH!</title>

        <script
        type="text/javascript"
        src="local/path/to/dojo/dojo.js">
        </script>

        <script type="text/javascript">
            dojo.require("doh.runner");

            dojo.addOnLoad(function( ) {
                doh.register("fooTest", [
                    function foo( ) {
                        var bar = [];
                        bar.push(1);
                        bar.push(2);
                        bar.push(3);

                        doh.is(bar.indexOf(1), 0); //not portable!
                    }
                ]);

                doh.run( );
            });
        </script>

    </head>
    <body></body>
</html>
```

Asynchronous Browser Test Example

Almost any web application test suite worth its salt is going to involve a significant number of tests that depend upon asynchronous conditions such as waiting for an animation to happen, a server side callback to occur, and so on. Example 16-4 introduces how you can create asynchronous test with DOH. The key concept is that a doh.Deferred (pretty much an ordinary dojo.Deferred with some tweaks) except that it is internal to DOH and, as such, doesn't have external dependencies. Chapter 4 included an extensive discussion of Deferreds if you need a quick refresher.

Before the relevant code sample, here's the basic pattern at play for asynchronous testing with DOH:

- Create a doh.Deferred that will be used to verify the results from asynchronous function (that returns back a dojo.Deferred)
- Call whatever asynchronous function returns back the dojo.Deferred and save a reference to it
- Add callbacks and errbacks to the dojo.Deferred that will simply pass the asynchronous function's results through to the doh.Deferred's own callbacks and errbacks

Example 16-4. Skeleton for an asynchronous test

```
doh.register("foo", [

    function( ) {
        var dohDfd = new doh.Deferred();
        var expectedResult = "baz";

        var  dojoDfd = asynchronousBarFunction();
        dojoDfd.addBoth(function(response, io) {

            //reference the dohDfd as needed...
            if (response == expectedResult) {
                dohDfd.callback(true);
            }
            else {
                dohDfd.errback(new Error( /* ... */));
            }
        });

        //...and return back the dohDfd
        return dohDfd;
    }
]);
```

Depending on your specific test constraints, you might provide explicit timeout values to ensure that the asynchronous operations involved timeout according to your specific testing criteria. At any rate, the key takeaway is that asynchronous testing doesn't need to be terribly complicated; the Deferred abstraction simplifies most of that complexity, so you're left to focus on the task at hand.

Performance Considerations

This section touches on some of the low-hanging fruit that you can strive to achieve in your frontend engineering. For a fabulous reference on ways to improve performance, be sure to check out *High Performance Web Sites: Essential Knowledge for Front-End Engineers* by Steve Souders (O'Reilly). It's a quick read and really does live up to the "essential" part of the title. Much of the content is available at *http://developer.yahoo.com/performance/rules.html*.

While writing good JavaScript goes a long way toward having a snappy web application, there are a few considerations to be particularly cognizant of when it comes time for production. The topic of optimizing a web application's performance could be the subject of an entire book on its own, but the following list captures some of the most obvious low-hanging fruit that you can go after:

Dojo's build tools

The build tools accomplish a number of essential tasks for you and the effort required on your behalf is trivial. The build process minifies your source, reducing the overall size of the payload, and significantly reduces the HTTP latency by consolidating multiple JavaScript files into layers and interning template strings where applicable.

Lazy loading

While much has been said in this chapter on the virtues of using the build tools to create a minimal number of layer files for your application, there will certainly be times when it just makes more sense to do some lazy loading. For example, if you determine that users very infrequently make use of a particular feature that adds a nontrivial amount of script to your layer, you may just opt to dojo.require it on the fly instead of packaging it up.

Another consideration with respect to lazy loading is to intelligently use the layout widgets to load content on the fly. For example, you may choose to only initially load the visible tab of a TabContainer, and either load the other content when it is requested, or wait long enough that you are certain the rest of the page has been loaded before fetching the other tabs. The ContentPane dijit is a common vehicle for lazy-loading content.

Web server configuration

Explore options to have web browsers aggressively cache JavaScript files and other static content by configuring your server to issue a far future Expires header; configure your server to take full advantage of common configuration options such as *gzip* compression.

Maximize static content

Because static content can be served so quickly, the more of it you can serve, the less time your web server will spend per request. Maximize the use of static HTML files that are nearly identical by filling in the user-specific portions via cookies or XHR requests where possible. For example, if the only difference on a login page is a few hundred bytes of text containing some user-specific information, serve the page statically, and use script to asynchronously fetch the small bits that need to get filled in instead of dynamically generating the entire page.

Profiling

If a page seems particularly slow or performance is choppy once it has loaded, use the built-in Firebug profiler to get a better idea of where time is being spent in your JavaScript logic and consider optimizing the execution of the culprit functions.

Benefits of XDomain builds

Although it may not be initially obvious, if you opt to create and use an XDomain build for your application, you potentially gain a number of benefits:

- You'll be able to host Dojo on a dedicated machine and share it amongst various applications—whether or not they are on the same domain in your network.
- The dojo.require statements that happen when the page loads are satisfied asynchronously instead of synchronously (the case for a default build), which can improve page load times since the requests are nonblocking.
- Some browsers, such as IE, limit you to two open connections per subdomain by default, so using an XDomain build essentially doubles the number of potential connections for your application—two for Dojo and two for everything else in the local domain.
- If you serve multiple applications that all use the XDomain build, the overall HTTP latency your clients endure is likely decreased, as the overall amount of content that their browsers can cache locally is increased.

Don't optimize prematurely

As a final word of caution, don't prematurely optimize your application; when you do optimize it, never do so blindly based on guessing games. Always use demonstrable information such as profiling information or server logs to your advantage. Particularly with respect to optimization, our instincts can often be deceived. And remember: Firebug is your friend.

Summary

After reading this chapter, you should:

- Be able to use Dojo's build tools to create consolidated, compressed layers for your web application
- Be familiar with some of the most common options for creating a custom build
- Be aware that *dojo.js* generally remains in its own separate JavaScript file; it is not rolled up into a custom layer
- Be able to use DOH to write unit tests for JavaScript functions
- Be more familiar with Rhino and understand the role it plays in the build tools and with DOH
- Be aware that while ShrinkSafe and DOH are important parts of the toolkit, they aren't Dojo-specific, and you may be able to use them in other venues
- Be aware of some of the low-hanging fruit you can go after when it comes time to maximize performance for your web application

A Firebug Primer

If you're a web developer, the Firebug extension (*http://www.getfirebug.com*) for Mozilla's Firefox browser (*http://www.getfirefox.com*) is one tool that you'd be remiss to leave unnoticed, and this is especially the case when you're working with a high-powered JavaScript toolkit, because Firebug is absolutely essential for streamlining your debugging efforts. This appendix systematically glosses many of Firebug's key features in hopes of familiarizing you with possibly the best way to debug a web application (or deconstruct a page just for the fun of it).

 This appendix is more of a primer for motivating Firebug novices than a comprehensive tutorial.

Installation

Like any other Firefox extension, installing Firebug is a piece of cake. Head out to *http://www.getfirebug.com* and click on the installation button. Take note that a yellow warning bar may appear at the top of your screen and prevent the installation from taking place, so you may need to click on the "Edit Options..." button to authorize the installation. Once Firefox restarts, you should have a Firebug item in your Tools menu and a Firebug icon in the bottom-right corner of your browser window, as shown in Figure A-1.

To Allow or Not to Allow?

Before delving into all of Firebug's cool features involving DOM manipulation and JavaScript dissection, let's take a moment to review some helpful ways that you can customize Firebug to automatically switch on and off for particular web sites. This feature is often overlooked, yet very convenient to use because you can customize Firebug for development purposes. For example, you may choose to leave Firebug disabled by default because it noticeably bogs down JavaScript-heavy web apps like Gmail. However, you can still specify that Firebug should always turn itself on for a

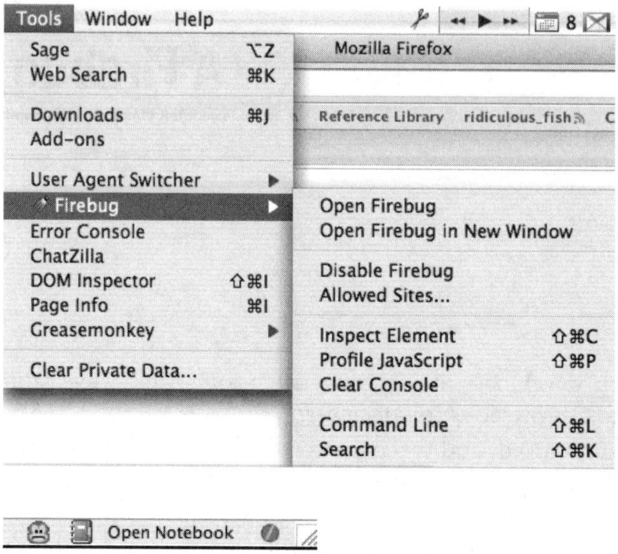

Figure A-1. Left: once Firebug is installed, an item appears in the Tools menu and presents you with a few standard options; right: in addition to the Tools menu item, an icon appears in the bottom-right corner of the browser window

custom list of URLs corresponding to web apps you're developing so that you don't have to manually switch it on and off as you multitask between various browser tabs. As you find a need to use Firebug with more sites, simply add them to the to the list of allowed sites.

Right-clicking on the Firebug icon in the bottom right corner of your browser brings up a contextual menu with options for configuring your Firebug settings for allowed sites. In particular, you have the following options, shown in Figure A-2:

Disable Firebug
> Turns off Firebug until you either uncheck it or navigate to a site that you've already specified should use Firebug through the "Allowed Sites…" menu item.

Disable Firebug for…
> Prevents Firebug from being enabled for the current site and adds it to the list of blocked sites—handy if you want to enable Firebug by default but want to disable it for a custom list of sites.

Allowed Sites…
> Brings up the "Firebug Allowed Sites" window, which allows you to specify a custom list of allowed and blocked sites.

Open Firebug in New Window opens Firebug in a separate standalone window—handy if you feel cramped in the default panel that opens in the bottom of the browser window.

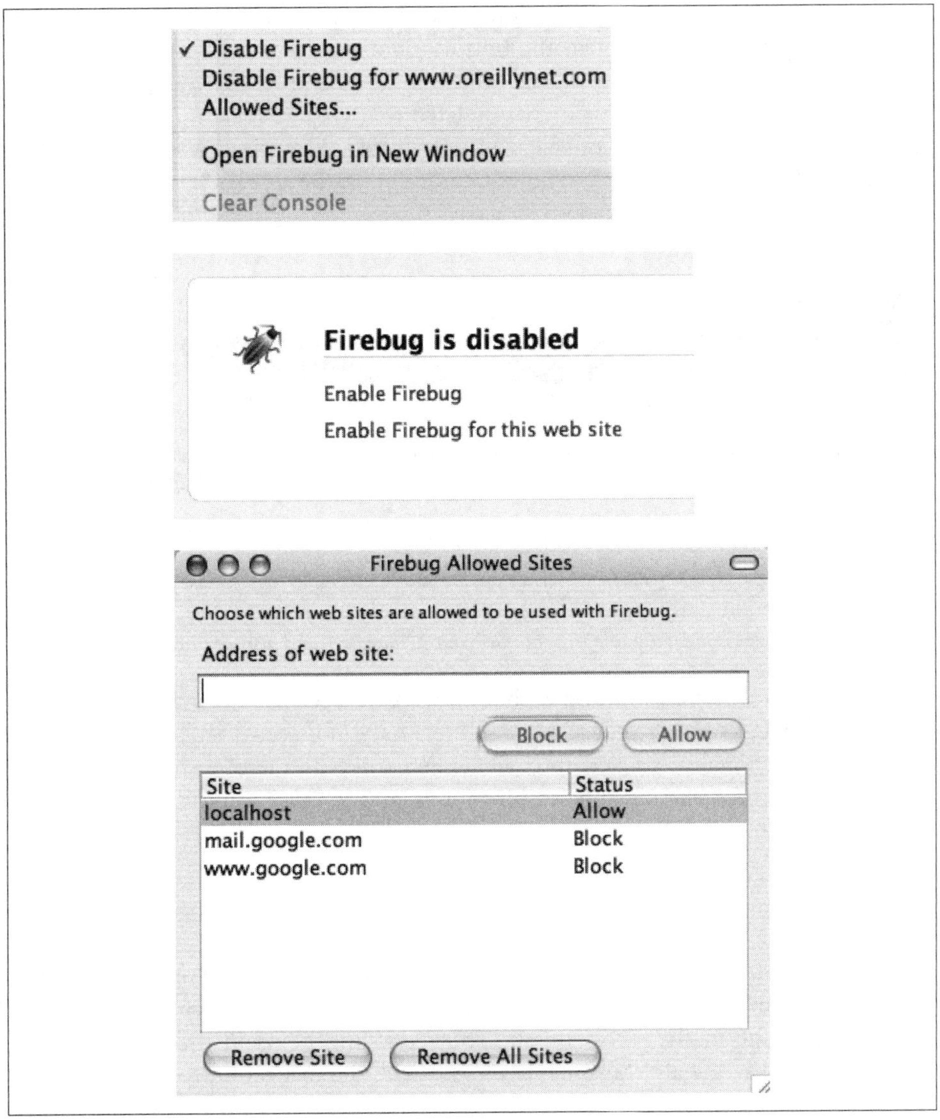

Figure A-2. Various configuration facets of Firebug

Now for the Fun Stuff

Now that you've equipped Firebug for use with particular sites, let's take a look at some of the coolness that has been spinning up so much Firebug buzz. The front page of the O'Reilly Network at *http://www.oreillynet.com* is as good a starting place as any.

Once you've navigated to *http://www.oreillynet.com,* enable Firebug, and notice that the previously grayed-out icon in the bottom-right portion of the browser window switches to a green circle with a check mark in it, as shown in Figure A-3. Shortly thereafter, you may notice some activity related to a GET request in the pane below the row of tabs while the "Console" tab is selected. Hovering over the hyperlink reveals a tooltip specifying the location of the script on the server.

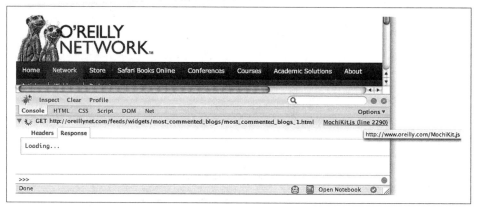

Figure A-3. Firebug delivers valuable insight into your debugging (and dismantling) activities

We'll systematically work through each of the tabs you see in the Firebug interface—Console, HTML, CSS, Script, DOM, and Net. As you'll see, there's a phenomenal amount of functionality packed into what seems like a "mere" extension. Thankfully, Firebug's interface is highly usable and organized fairly intuitively once you've spent some time with it.

Inspect

Notice the colorful Firebug icon in the upper-left corner of the Firebug pane. In addition to being a nice decoration, it also doubles as a button that reveals a menu fairly similar to the one in the Tools menu. The remaining items in the row—Inspect, Clear, and Profile—are also buttons. Let's start with the Inspect button.

The Inspect button allows you to instantly locate any element in the DOM tree by hovering over it in the browser window, which is really helpful when you're trying to troubleshoot a particular part of a complex layout or search for a needle in a haystack. Click on the Inspect button, shown in Figure A-4, so that it becomes depressed. The main menu provides all of the representative main menu items and is always located in the upper-left corner. The Inspect button, always beside it regardless of the selected tab, is incredibly handy and one of the most common features you'll probably find yourself using. Watch as Firebug switches to the HTML tab and displays the corresponding HTML and CSS as you hover over various elements on the page.

The corresponding HTML pertinent to the currently hovered-on item is highlighted in the HTML tab so that you can easily inspect the entire element and its context.

Clicking the hovered element in the page causes the corresponding content in the HTML tab to become highlighted and the scrolling ceases so that you can take control of your mouse again without losing your place. Once you've located the particular DOM element you're looking for, you can do just about anything from within the HTML tab: dynamically edit the node's content, add an attribute, remove an attribute, reveal the corresponding CSS that styles a particular node, etc.

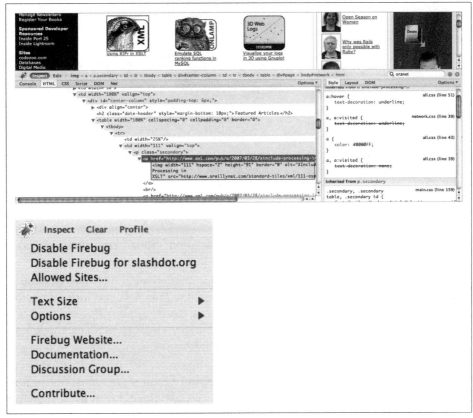

Figure A-4. The Inspect button at work

Take a few moments to get better acquainted with the inspection feature by exploring other aspects of the O'Reilly Network's main page. A particularly interesting activity includes modifying elements in the DOM tree and seeing the effects immediately take place in the browser. For example, Figure A-5 shows one of the graphics on the front page resized to be a little too wide. Again, just click on the HTML to modify the attributes of the various tags to see the changes take effect. You might also try adding a valid attribute to an element by selecting the DOM element and then clicking on the Edit button that appears whenever inspection is occurring.

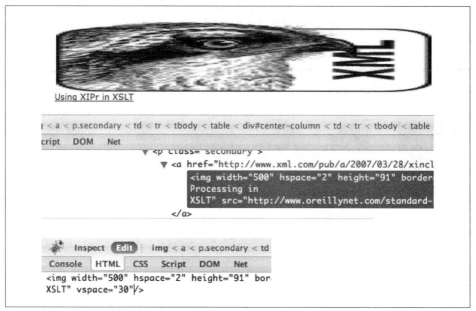

Figure A-5. You can use Firebug to hack on the HTML in the page and see live results

Console

By now, you must have noticed that there's a nice little command prompt in Firebug that appears whenever the Console tab is selected. In a nutshell, this little command prompt, shown in Figure A-6, will execute whatever JavaScript you throw at it. Use it to test out JavaScript concepts, or reach in and grab references to nodes for instant quick manipulation. In particular, you can grab references to any content in the page through JavaScript's document.getElementById function. So what if an element doesn't have an id value—give it one yourself and be on your merry way. From there, you might choose to use the console's built-in console.dir (just like in Python) to reveal methods available to it. Now would be a good time to divert to Firebug's documentation (*http://getfirebug.com/docs.html*), where you'll find details about console, incredibly useful built-in functions like dir, and more.

Another contextual button that's visible while the Console tab is selected is Profile, and it does exactly what you'd think: profiles the execution of JavaScript in the page, as shown in Figure A-7. You simply click on it once to start profiling and click on it again to stop profiling and display a summary of the statistics collected. Can it get any easier than that? The snapshot below is from *http://jobs.oreilly.com*, and displays some JavaScript stats related to clicking on the navigation bar that appears on the left side of that page.

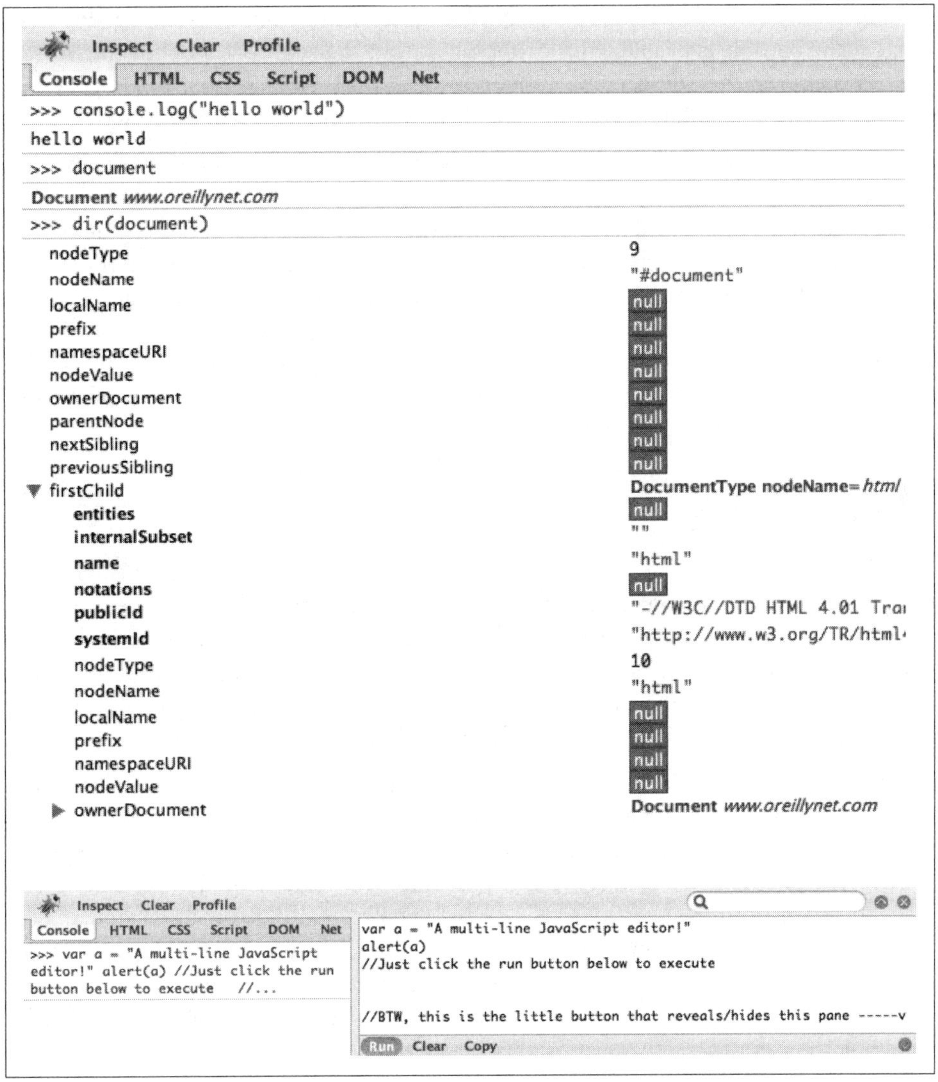

Figure A-6. Left: the console is your scripting interface into any web page; right: clicking the subtle button that looks like a ^ on the far right of the console prompt reveals a multiline JavaScript editor

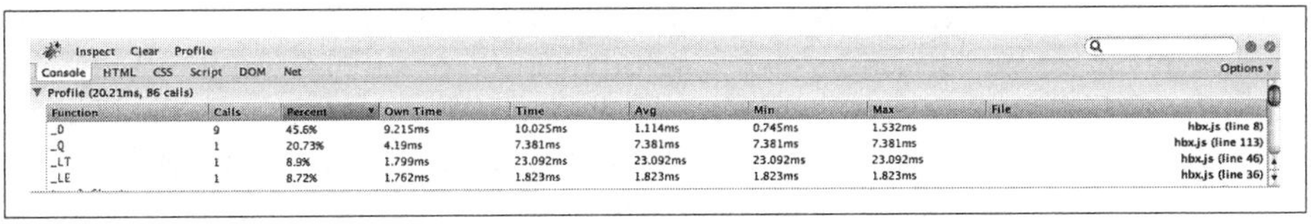

Figure A-7. Firebug comes with an incredible profiler that gives you all sorts of handy stats about the performance of JavaScript in web pages

It's especially noteworthy that Dojo binds tightly with Firebug. When it loads in Firefox, the console is available for dropping output that's great for debugging or status messages via the console.log function, and on other browsers, Firebug Lite (a minimalist console) still logs output and allows you to interact with the DOM.

Because console.log is by far the most commonly used function for debugging, it's helpful to know that you should separate items you'd like to log instead of other approaches such as concatenating them together. The reason is that Firebug allows you to inspect items by clicking on them, and if you implicitly convert them to a String you lose this benefit. For example, you might log a status message about a variable called foo as console.log("the value of foo is", foo) in order to be able to introspect foo. If you were to instead use console.log("the value of foo is "+foo), you'd be stuck with a String. It may not matter for primitives, but if foo were a complex Object, you want the benefit of introspection.

HTML and CSS

You should be fairly comfortable investigating the HTML and CSS tabs because you encountered the same content during your earlier escapade with the Inspect button. Still, a somewhat subtle feature worth pointing out is that you can right-click on items in either of these tabs to reveal a contextual menu with several useful options in it. Among these options are the ability to scroll the page to the element of interest, log events related to the element, directly modify the element, and so on.

A superset of the same content that appears under the CSS tab also appears in the HTML tab if you select the underlying Style tab, included in a pane on the right. Note that you can directly change the style of elements through the CSS tab, as shown in Figure A-8, or through the HTML tab. You can also click on a style element to disable it in the page depending what is most helpful for your particular situation. And wait, there's more: the Layout tab that's adjacent to the Style tab displays the active properties for the currently selected element's padding, borders, margins, and offset. As might be expected, you can preview changes to these properties by changing the values directly in the diagram.

Script and DOM

Firebug's Script tab reveals a powerful JavaScript debugger that allows you to set breakpoints in particular scripts and watch the values of variables in the code as it executes. Unlike some debuggers you may have previously encountered, the Firebug JavaScript debugger is intuitive and easy to learn. To set a breakpoint, just load the script of interest by using the contextual menu just above the Script tab and click on the line number where you want the breakpoint. A small red circle should appear, confirming the breakpoint. You can click on the red circle to remove the breakpoint,

```
#page {
  background-color: #FFFFFF;
  border-bottom: 1px solid #D4D4D4;
  border-left: 1px solid #D4D4D4;
```

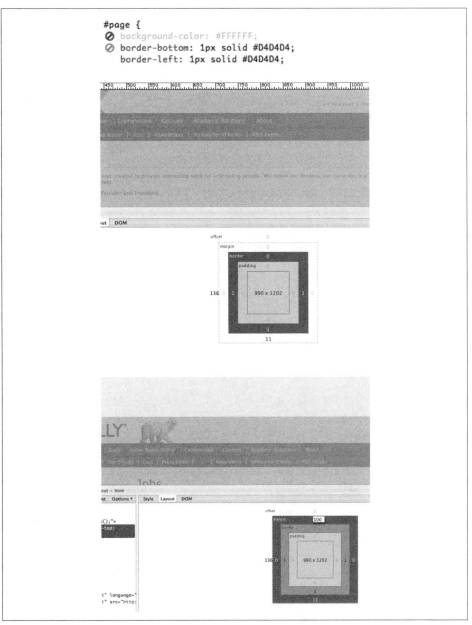

Figure A-8. Top: disabling elements; middle: Firebug's Layout ruler; bottom: manipulate the layout of a DOM element's margin, or anything else for that matter (this example shows the upper margin being changed to 100px)

or click on additional lines of code to add additional breakpoints. Likewise, you can type in the name of a variable or a derived expression into the accompanying Watch tab to keep an eye on how values are changing from breakpoint to breakpoint. Is debugging JavaScript getting easier, anyone?

The DOM tab, shown in Figure A-9, is fairly self-explanatory and essentially provides the same information you can already view in the HTML tab, but in a tree view it might be easier to inspect and manipulate, depending on the situation.

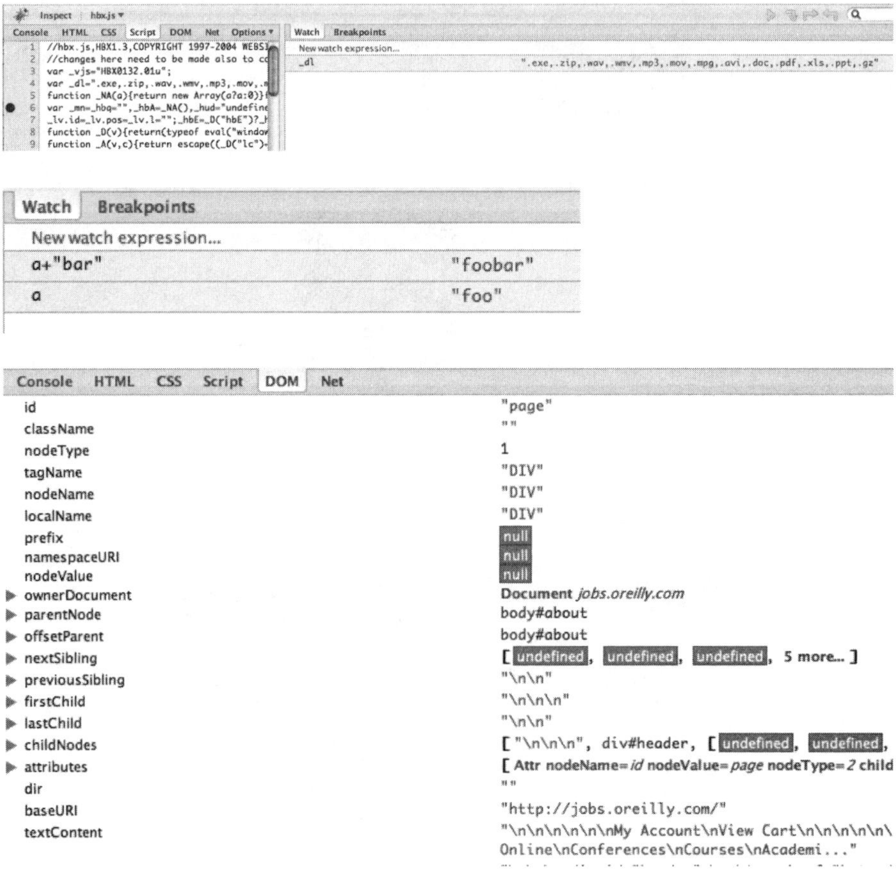

Figure A-9. Top: using Firebug's JavaScript debugger to set breakpoints; middle: watch expressions, even ones that you derive yourself; bottom: the DOM tab allows you to inspect and manipulate the DOM through a traditional tree view

Net

By now, you've seen most of Firebug's cool and useful features; however, the Net tab, shown in Figure A-10, is a "saved the best for last" type of thing. Basically, the Net tab gives you all of the info you'd ever typically need for performance analysis as it relates to pieces of the page loading, and conveniently, media types are logically categorized into groups such as CSS, JavaScript, images, and so on. As a special treat, there's even a category for viewing network statistics related to XHR (a.k.a. AJAX) requests. Overall, the Net tab provides valuable insight into potential performance bottlenecks and load times associated with content. For projects with a lot of dynamism, it's almost like having a crude network profiler at your fingertips.

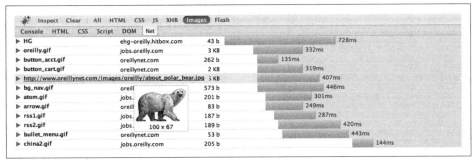

Figure A-10. Firebug's Net tab itemizes the media associated with a page by category and provides the associated load time

Go Forth and Dismantle

We've taken a look at the highlights of Firebug, but the best way to get comfortable with it is to spend some time dismantling the design of a few web pages. Head out to any site with a semi-complex layout and take a few minutes to learn more about how the designers put it together. In addition to having some fun doing detective work, you'll learn a lot along the way. Then—the next time you need to quickly debug some of your own work—you can just whip out your Firebug skills and remedy the situation without even breaking a sweat. (And again, the point of this appendix isn't to provide an exhaustive tutorial for Firebug—it is to give you a jumpstart and increase your awareness of just how much time Firebug can save you if you learn to use it well.)

APPENDIX B

A Brief Survey of DojoX

DojoX is the toolkit's canonical location for experimental and specialized extensions. Unlike the rest of this book, which covers Base, Core, Dijit, and Util in depth, this short appendix on DojoX provides survey-style coverage of what could really be another entire book on its own—a book that might even be about twice as long as this one. The hope is that once you've made the trek across the rest of the toolkit, picking up something from DojoX and running with it should be fairly straightforward.

 The author's semi-regular "Dojo Goodness" column available at *http://pipes.yahoo.com/ptwobrussell/dojo_goodness* includes topics on DojoX subprojects, so consider adding it to your RSS reader so that you can stay current.

DojoX is managed on a per-subproject basis, and the condition of any given project can vary widely. While some subprojects such as *cometd* and *charting* are quite stable, others are very much in their infancy, and DojoX acts as a proving ground for them. One commonality for all DojoX subprojects, however, is that they should all have a *README* file that contains the basic status and version information for the subproject as well as contact information for the authors. DojoX subprojects may have dependencies on Base, Core, or Dijit; however, they may also be completely standalone projects. Unlike Dijit, DojoX makes no official guarantees about accessibility or internationalization, and the overall style of implementation varies more so than what you would find in slightly more unified project like Dijit.

One thing you must have noticed about the rest of the toolkit by now is that it provides serious breadth and depth; well, DojoX is not different. In fact, a crude analysis of the number of functions (including anonymous inline functions) and statements across Core, Base, and Dijit works out to be roughly as shown in Table B-1, as calculated via:

```
grep -rc 'function' * | grep -v \.svn | cut -d : -f 2 | awk '{for (i=1; i<=NF; i++)
s=s+$i}; END{print s}'
```

And:

```
grep -rc '\;' * | grep -v \.svn | cut -d : -f 2 |  awk '{for (i=1; i<=NF; i++)
s=s+$i}; END{print s}'
```

Table B-1. Rough estimate for the number of functions and statements (in thousands) in the toolkit as of version 1.1

Base		Core		Dijit		DojoX	
Functions	Statements	Functions	Statements	Functions	Statements	Functions	Statements
0.7	2.2	1.9	9.5	1.6	15.1	7.1	54

At the very least, you can see that there is a tremendous amount of source code in DojoX. In any event, the additional breadth and depth that DojoX provides is astounding, and in may ways, there are lot more interesting things going on in DojoX than Dijit because DojoX is really is about the bleeding edge and specialized interests. Just because this book cannot cover DojoX doesn't mean that you won't find a lot of useful features that are likely to save you a lot of time.

The synopsis in Table B-2 is a helpful guide for determining exactly what's in DojoX as of version 1.1. Since DojoX is so fluid, however, your best bet for the most up-to-date coverage of DojoX is to download a nightly build from *http://archive.dojotoolkit. org/nightly/* and inspect the *README* file directly.

Table B-2. DojoX projects

Subproject	Description
analytics	An analytics and client monitoring system that can be used to log various events back to the server such as mouse clicks, idle activity, console.* messages, etc.
av	An audio/video project supporting Flash and QuickTime movies.
charting	An advanced charting engine based on *dojox.gfx* and *dojox.gfx3d*.
collections	A number of functions that provide support for data structures such as stacks, sets, queues, additional functionality for hashes, arrays, and so on.
color	Additional support for colorspaces such as CMYK and HSL as well as HSV.
cometd	An implementation of the Bayeaux protocol, which is a low-latency data transfer technique from servers to clients.
data	Support for custom data stores such as a FlickrRestStore, XmlStore, CsvStore, etc. that implement the dojo.data API as well as additional utility functions for dojo.data.
date	A placeholder for date operations such as formatters that are common to other programming languages or server technologies such as PHP.
embed	A means of easily embedding external objects that would normally require the use of OBJECT or EMBED tags.
dtl	A project that aims to fully implement the Django Template Language.
encoding	A set of routines for common encoding algorithms such as cryptography, digests, and compression.
flash	A project that aims to make it easy to extend Flash's capabilities into a DHTML environment.

Subproject	Description
form	A collection of useful form widgets including functionality such as a password validator, multiselects that use check boxes instead of Ctrl-clicks, etc.
fx	A set of animation effects that extend and enhance the effects provided in Base and Core.
gfx	A portable 2D graphics library that leverages technologies like VML, SVG, etc., to provide advanced graphics that may be static or animated.
gfx3d	A portable 3D graphics library. Builds upon features offered in *gfx*.
grid	A powerful data grid capable of rendering arbitrary amounts of data from a data store.
highlight	A syntax highlighting engine that provides client-side syntax highlighting of <CODE> blocks for various programming languages.
image	Provides support for common image operations such as playing slideshows, magnification, picking thumbnails, light box, and so on.
io	Support for XHR multipart functions and an XHR IFRAME proxy for accomplishing cross-domain `XmlHttpRequests`.
jsonPath	Similar to Xpath, but for querying JavaScript objects; very handy for querying complex JSON structures.
lang	Language utilities for additional operations on arrays, hashes, and extensions from functional programming (lambda).
layout	Additional layout widgets.
math	A set of advanced math functions such as abstract curve definitions, point calculations, and so on.
off	A wrapper around Google Gears that offers offline functionality for a web application.
presentation	A mechanism for various display-oriented tasks, such as presentations.
rpc	Extras on top of `dojo.rpc` for performing remote procedure calls.
sketch	A cross-browser drawing editor based on the `dojox.gfx` module.
storage	A JavaScript abstraction that provides limited support for persistent storage of data via a native browser extension, such as Flash or Google Gears.
string	Miscellaneous string utility functions.
timing	Support for advanced timing constructs.
uuid	An implementation of the Universally Unique Identifier, as described in RFC4122.
validate	A set of functions for common validation tasks such as email addressees, social security numbers, and so on.
widget	A set of widgets, similar to those found in Dijit, including an advanced color picker, a fish eye list, a toaster, a wizard, a magnifier, advanced scroll panes, and more.
wire	An API for providing simplified MVC patterns in clients by suppling a generic data binding and service invocation library.
xml	Utilities for XML processing.

Index

Symbols

" (quotation marks), 263
\# symbolic operator, 116
$= symbolic operator, 116
* symbolic operator, 116
*= symbolic operator, 116
, (comma)
    CSS expressions, 118
    as symbolic operator, 116
    trailing commas, 233
> operator, 118
^= symbolic operator, 116
{ } (curly braces), 263
~= symbolic operator, 116

A

a11y (see accessibility)
Academic Free License (AFL), xvii
accessibility
    Dijit support, 248–251, 300
    Tree dijit, 377
Accessible Rich Internet Applications
      (ARIA), 5, 246, 250
AccordionContainer dijit, 268, 355–356
AFL (Academic Free License), xvii
AJAX (Asynchronous JavaScript and XML)
    form support, 298
    hitch function and, 87–89
    OpenAjax Alliance, 41, 112
    overview, 80–82
    parameter property values, 82–85

WAI-ARIA support, 250
XHR examples, 85–87
    (see also server communication)
animation
    arbitrary CSS properties, 169–173
    chaining and combining, 181–184
    computing colors, 186–194
    controlling programmatically, 174–178
    dojo.fx support, 165
    drag-and-drop support, 185–186
    NodeList support, 129
    simple fades, 165–169
    sliding nodes, 176
    toggling nodes, 184, 185
    wipe effects, 179–181
_Animation class
    animateProperty method, 129
    chaining/combining animations, 181–184
    controlling animations, 174–178
    functionality, 165, 177, 178
    gotoPercent method, 174
    pause method, 174
    play method, 168, 174
    simple fades, 165–169
    status method, 174
    stop method, 174
anonymous functions, xxvii, 14, 75
ant build tool, 397
AOL, 7, 9, 319, 403
application dijits
    ColorPalette dijit, 269, 366–367
    Dialog dijit, 269, 357, 360–362
    Editor dijit, 269, 388–395
    InlineEditBox dijit, 269, 375–377

We'd like to hear your suggestions for improving our indexes. Send email to *index@oreilly.com.*

NumberTextBox dijit *(continued)*
   overview, 317
   pattern constraint, 317
   places constraint, 317
   type constraint, 317

O

Object type
   inheritance, 14, 234
   prototype property, 237
objects
   cloning, 51
   defined, 14
   first-class, 14
   manipulating context, 52–55
onAnimate event, 175
onBegin event, 174
onblur event, 128
onChange event, 330
onclick event
   dijit support, 255
   dojo.connect function, 67
   form considerations, 338
   NodeList support, 128
onDndCancel event, 161
onDndDrop event, 161
onDndSourceOver event, 160
onDndStart event, 160
onEnd event, 175, 181
onFirstMove event, 151
onfocus event, 128
onkeydown event, 68, 128
onkeypress event, 68, 128
onkeyup event, 68, 128
onmousedown event, 67, 128, 163
onmouseenter event, 68, 128
onmouseleave event, 68, 128
onmousemove event, 67, 128, 163
onmouseout event, 67, 128, 292
onmouseover event, 67, 128, 292
onmouseup event, 67, 128, 163
onMove event, 151
onMoved event, 151
onMoveStart event, 151
onMoveStop event, 151
onMoving event, 151
onPause event, 175
onPlay event, 175
onStop event, 175
onsubmit event, 300

opacity, 189
OpenAjax Alliance, 41, 112
OpenAjax Hub, 76, 112

P

packaging systems, 13
parameters
   build script, 398–399
   HelloWorld example, 288–290
   partially applying, 53
parseOnLoad:true directive, 145
parsers
   dojoType tag and, 145, 157
   overview, 145, 257–260
performance considerations, 404, 414–415
plug-ins (Editor)
   AlwaysShowToolbar, 393
   architectural overview, 392–395
   defined, 392
   EnterKeyHandling, 393, 394
   FontChoice, 394
   LinkDialog, 394
   TextColor, 394
   ToggleDir, 394
PopupMenuItem dijit
   disabled attribute, 374
   iconClass attribute, 374
   label attribute, 374
   onClick function, 374
   overview, 369–374
   setDisabled function, 374
portlets, 76
ProgressBar dijit
   depicted, 249
   indeterminate attribute, 366
   maximum attribute, 366
   onChange function, 366
   overview, 269, 364–366
   places attribute, 366
   progress attribute, 366
   update function, 366
properties
   adding to objects, 48
   animating CSS, 169–173
   defined, 14
   DOM events support, 68, 69
   extending object prototypes, 49
   simplified syntax, 173
prototype chain, 55, 237–239
pseudorandom number generators, 42

publish/subscribe communication, 76–79, 352
Python language, 11, 233

Q

querying child items, 210, 211
quirks mode, 60, 62
quotation marks ("), 263

R

race conditions, 17
RadioButton dijit, 330
RangeBoundTextBox dijit, 310, 315
Read API
    close function, 201
    ComboBox dijit and, 322
    containsValue function, 199
    fetch function, 200, 201
    getAttributes function, 199
    getFeatures function, 201
    getLabel function, 201
    getLabelAttributes function, 201
    getValue function, 199, 210, 216
    getValues function, 199, 216
    hasAttribute function, 199
    isItem function, 199
    isItemLoaded function, 199
    ItemFileReadStore support, 204–212
    ItemFileWriteStore support, 204, 212–219
    loadItem function, 199
    overview, 198
readings.js files, 138, 140
README files
    CherryPy support, 11
    DojoX requirements, 6, 428
Rehabilitation Act (1973), 248
Remote Procedure Call (RPC), 110–112
Representational State Transfer (REST), 82
resources
    clustering, 41–43
    defined, 13, 40
    importing, 40
REST (Representational State Transfer), 82
RFC 3066, 136
RGB color model, 187–188
RGBA color model, 187–188
Rhino JavaScript engine (Mozilla)
    background, 397
    ShrinkSafe and, 6
    testing support, 407–411

rollbacks, 213
Roman calendar, 312
RPC (Remote Procedure Call), 110–112
RpcService constructor, 110
Ruby, Sam, 82
runner.js file, 409

S

screen readers, 250, 300
script tag (HTML)
    build profiles, 403
    cross-site scripting, 99–101
    defining methods in, 264
    dijit considerations, 265
    djConfig support, 18
    dojo.connect function, 75
    input tag and, 328
    JSONP support, 100, 101
    parsing widgets, 260
    XDomain build, 9
scripting
    cross-site, 92, 99–101
    droppables, 163, 164
    server-side, 11, 62
    (see also build scripts)
Section 508, 248
security
    browser settings, 11
    cross-site scripting, 92
    JavaScript hijacking, 86
SELECT element (HTML), 319
select element (HTML), 323
Selector API
    deleteSelectedNodes method, 163
    destroy method, 163
    getSelectedNodes method, 163
    insertNodes method, 163
    onMouseDown method, 163
    onMouseMove method, 163
    onMouseUp method, 163
    onOutEvent method, 164
    onOverEvent method, 164
    selectAll method, 163
    selectNone method, 163
Selectors API, 114
serializing
    content, 391
    data types, 219–221
server communication
    asynchronous requests, 89–91
    Core IO support, 101–109

About the Author

Matthew Russell is a tenacious technologist with entrepreneurial zeal. He has completed more than 40 publications on technology, including work that has appeared or is upcoming in scientific conferences, *Linux Journal*, Apple Developer Connection, and *Make:* Magazine.

Matthew developed his passion for writing during undergraduate studies at the Air Force Academy, where he earned the prestigious Dean W. Gonzalez Award as the top cadet in the computer science major.

Matthew's most recent efforts include architecting and leading a team to build a classified end-to-end web application for the intelligence community, and serving the Defense Intelligence Agency, where he researches and assesses the next generation of technologies to build government intelligence systems.

He currently works for Digital Reasoning Systems as the director of advanced technology, where he pushes the limits of user interfaces in the web browser and researches bleeding-edge topics in unstructured text processing.

You can subscribe to Matthew's semi-regular "Dojo Goodness" column at *http://pipes.yahoo.com/ptwobrussell/dojo_goodness* to stay up to date with his latest online writing about Dojo.

Colophon

The animal on the cover of *Dojo: The Definitive Guide* is a lion-tailed monkey (*Macaca silenus*). This rare monkey lives primarily in the rain forests of southern India, where it spends its days avoiding humans, foraging, and exploring.

Easily recognizable for its silvery-white mane, the monkey (also known as the lion-tailed macaque or wanderloo) is also distinguished by the tuft of hair on its tail. Like other macaques, it lives in groups of 10 to 20 monkeys in a hierarchical order involving a few males and many females. The male is a territorial creature and will defend his home by screaming at monkeys or other invaders not native to his habitat.

According to the International Union for Conservation of Nature, the lion-tailed monkey is one of the most threatened primates in the world, due largely to the destruction of its habitat by humans. Many zoos now participate in breeding programs to help sustain the survival of the monkey.

The cover image is from *Lydekker's Royal History*. The cover font is Adobe ITC Garamond. The text font is Linotype Birka; the heading font is Adobe Myriad Condensed; and the code font is LucasFont's TheSans Mono Condensed.

Related Titles from O'Reilly

Web Authoring and Design

ActionScript 3.0 Cookbook

Ajax Hacks

Ambient Findability

Creating Web Sites: The Missing Manual

CSS Cookbook, *2nd Edition*

CSS Pocket Reference, *2nd Edition*

CSS: The Definitive Guide, *3rd Edition*

CSS: The Missing Manual

Dreamweaver 8: Design and Construction

Dreamweaver 8: The Missing Manual

Dynamic HTML: The Definitive Reference, *3rd Edition*

Essential ActionScript 3.0

Flex 8 Cookbook

Flash 8: Projects for Learning Animation and Interactivity

Flash 8: The Missing manual

Flash 9 Design: Motion Graphics for Animation & User Interfaces

Flash Hacks

Head First HTML with CSS & XHTML

Head Rush Ajax

Head First Web Design

High Performance Web Sites

HTML & XHTML: The Definitive Guide, *6th Edition*

HTML & XHTML Pocket Reference, *3rd Edition*

Information Architecture for the World Wide Web, *3rd Edition*

Information Dashboard Design

JavaScript: The Definitive Guide, *5th Edition*

JavaScript & DHTML Cookbook, *2nd Edition*

Learning ActionScript 3.0

Learning JavaScript

Learning Web Design, *3rd Edition*

PHP Hacks

Programming Collective Intelligence

Programming Flex 2

Web Design in a Nutshell, *3rd Edition*

Web Site Measurement Hacks

Our books are available at most retail and online bookstores.

To order direct: 1-800-998-9938 • *order@oreilly.com* • *www.oreilly.com*

Online editions of most O'Reilly titles are available by subscription at *safari.oreilly.com*